The Routledge Dictionary of English Language Studies

From abbreviation to zero-article, via fricative and slang, this dictionary contains over 600 wide-ranging and informative entries covering:

- the core areas of language description and analysis – phonetics and phonology, grammar, lexis, semantics, pragmatics and discourse
- sociolinguistics, including entries on social and regional variation, stylistic variation, and language and gender
- the history of the English language from Old English to the present day
- the main varieties of English spoken around the world, including North America, Africa, Asia, and Australasia
- stylistics, literary language and English usage.

Packed with real examples of the way people use English in different contexts, *The Routledge Dictionary of English Language Studies* is an indispensable guide to the richness and variety of the English language for both students and the general reader.

Dr Michael Pearce is Senior Lecturer in English Language at the University of Sunderland.

D0873496

Also available from Routledge

The Routledge Dictionary of English Language Studies

Michael Pearce

Routledge
Taylor & Francis Group

LONDON AND NEW YORK

For Clare, Matthew and Adam

First published 2007
by Routledge
2 Park Square, Milton Park, Abingdon, Oxon OX14 4RN

Simultaneously published in the USA and Canada
by Routledge
270 Madison Ave, New York NY 10016

Routledge is an imprint of the Taylor & Francis Group, an informa business

© 2007 Michael Pearce

Typeset in Times New Roman by
RefineCatch Limited, Bungay, Suffolk
Printed and bound in Great Britain by
TJ International Ltd, Padstow, Cornwall

British Library Cataloguing in Publication Data
A catalogue record for this book is available from the British Library

Library of Congress Cataloging in Publication Data
Pearce, Michael.
  The Routledge dictionary of English language studies /
    Michael Pearce.
       p.   cm.
  Includes bibliographical references.
  ISBN-10: 0–415–35187–1 (alk. paper)
  ISBN-10: 0–415–35172–1 (pbk. : alk. paper)
  ISBN-10: 0–203–69841–X (e-book)
  ISBN-13: 978–0–415–35187–4 (alk. paper)
  [etc.]
  1. English language – History – Dictionaries. 2. English
language – Glossaries, vocabularies, etc. 3. Philology – Dictionaries.
I. Title.
  PE1075.P36 2006
  420.3 – dc22

                                          2006012397

ISBN10: 0–415–35187–1 (hbk)   ISBN13: 978–0–415–35187–4 (hbk)
ISBN10: 0–415–35172–3 (pbk)   ISBN13: 978–0–415–35172–0 (pbk)
ISBN10: 0–203–69841–X (ebk)   ISBN13: 978–0–203–69841–9 (ebk)

Contents

Preface

This dictionary defines and illustrates over 600 terms from the field of English language and linguistics. Readers will find entries associated with the main branches of language study: phonetics and phonology, grammar, lexis, semantics and pragmatics, and discourse. Sociolinguistics, varieties of English, style, usage, and the history of the language are also covered. Many of the entries contain real world examples of English in use, taken mainly from the *The British National Corpus* (BNC). Additional material is drawn from *The Collins WordbanksOnline English Corpus* (CWEC), the *International Corpus of English* (ICE), *The Michigan Corpus of Academic Spoken English* (MICASE), *The Corpus of Spoken Professional American English* (CSPAE) and the World Wide Web. Readers should assume that the BNC is the source of the examples, unless otherwise indicated. Material from the other corpora is marked with the following symbols: CWEC •; ICE ±; MICASE ‡; CSPAE ◊; World Wide Web †.

The entries vary in length: some are discursive and exploratory; others are brief and factual. Cross-referencing is extensive, so that a reader can move between entries, building up a picture of related terms in a particular domain. SMALL CAPITALS refer readers to a related entry; **bold** is used to signal where further clarification for a particular term can be found.

The bibliography is supplemented by a list of useful websites. Two major works of scholarship have been particularly important in the compilation of this dictionary: *The Longman Grammar of Spoken and Written English* (Longman 1999) and *A Handbook of Varieties of English* (Mouton de Gruyter 2004).

Key to abbreviations, transcription conventions and symbols

Abbreviations and symbols

LGSWE	*Longman Grammar of Spoken and Written English*
LSGSWE	*Longman Student Grammar of Spoken and Written English*
BNC	*British National Corpus*
•	*Collins Wordbanks*Online *English Corpus* (CWEC)
±	*International Corpus of English* (ICE)
‡	*Michigan Corpus of Academic Spoken English* (MICASE)
◊	*Corpus of Spoken Professional American English* (CSPAE)
†	World Wide Web
/ /	enclose phonemic and broad phonetic transcriptions
[ ]	enclose narrower phonetic transcriptions
< >	enclose spellings
*	indicates a sentence that it is ungrammatical and/or unacceptable in the variety of English in question
?	indicates a sentence with questionable acceptability or grammaticality
'	indicates that the following syllable receives primary stress, as in '*eighty*
ˌ	indicates that the following syllable receives secondary stress, as in '*poly,syllable*
Ø	zero, loss of word
→	'becomes'

Consonant phonemes of English

p	pat	b	bat	t	tin	d	din
k	cot	g	got				
m	met	n	net	ŋ	fang		
tʃ	chump	dʒ	jump				
f	fat	v	vat	θ	thin	ð	this
s	sip	z	zip	ʃ	ship	ʒ	beige
h	hag	w	wag	l	lag	j	yak
r	rack						

Other consonant symbols used in this book

t̪	dentalized [t]
d̪	dentalized [d]
ʔ	glottal stop
ɾ	alveolar flap
ɽ	retroflex flap
β	voiced bilabial fricative
ç	voiceless palatal fricative
x	voiceless velar fricative
ɣ	voiced velar fricative
ɬ	voiceless lateral fricative
ʋ	labiodental approximant
ɹ	alveolar approximant
ʍ	voiceless labial-velar fricative

British and American English vowels

British English vowels (Received Pronunciation) *monophthongs*		American English vowels *monophthongs*	
i	city	i	city
iː	bead	i	bead
ɪ	bid	ɪ	bid
ɛ	bed	ɛ	bed
ɛː	bared	ɛ (r)	bared
a	bad	æ	bad
ə	banana	ə	banana
əː	bird	ə (r)	bird
ʌ	bud	ə	bud
uː	booed	u	booed
ʊ	Bud(dha)	ʊ	Bud(dha)
ɔː	bored	ɔ	bored
ɔː	bought	ɔ, ɑ	bought
ɑː	bard	ɑ	bard
ɒ	bod(y)	ɑ	bod(y)
diphthongs		*diphthongs*	
eɪ	bade	eɪ	bade
ʌɪ	bide	aɪ	bide
ɔɪ	Boyd	ɔɪ	Boyd
aʊ	bowed, bout	aʊ	bowed, bout
əʊ	bode	oʊ	bode
ɪə	beard		

Other vowel symbols used in this book

y	high front rounded vowel
ʉ	high central rounded vowel
e	high-mid front unrounded vowel
o	high-mid back rounded vowel
œ	low-mid front rounded vowel
ɐ	near-low central vowel
ɜ	open-mid central unrounded vowel

A

Abbreviation A shortened form of a word or phrase. Phrases can be abbreviated in two main ways. 1) The first letter(s) of each word in the phrase stands in for the whole word: *MBA, CSI, USAF* and so on. This is sometimes known as an *initialism*. In some cases, the abbreviation is pronounced as a sequence of letters (/em bɪː eɪ/); in others, the word that each initial letter stands for is usually spoken ('United States Airforce'). 2) The first letter(s) of each word in a phrase stands in for the whole word, but the abbreviation is spoken as a word: *FIFA, aids, SETI.* These are known as **acronyms**. Individual words can also be abbreviated by retaining parts of the word (usually, but not always, the start) and discarding others: *Mon., geog., Staffs.* Initialisms and shortenings can also be combined: *DPhil, MSc.* Other forms of abbreviation involve the use of special symbols: *&, %, $.* Abbreviations are also used in text messaging and internet chat room interaction: *LOL* ('laugh out loud'), *BFN* ('bye for now') *OMG* ('oh my God'), *GR8* ('great'). The last of these employs the **rebus** principle.

Initialisms and acronyms usually start life by being written in upper case (e.g. *FIFA*). When an acronym becomes fully lexicalized it is usually written in lower case (e.g. *aids*). Sometimes stops separate the letters, but there is a growing tendency not to use these. Where shortening takes place, lower case is generally used. However, there is considerable variation in the **orthography** of abbreviations. See ALPHABET, BLENDING, CLIPPING, ELLIPSIS.

Aboriginal English English spoken by Aboriginal people in Australia. Dialects of Aboriginal English exist on a continuum, with **basilect**al varieties close to **Kriol** at one end (usually spoken in remote areas), and varieties close to Standard **Australian English** at the other. Some of the features of Aboriginal English are shared with other non-standard varieties of English around the world, while others show the influence of Aboriginal languages. The following example features of Aboriginal English can be found across the continuum.

A characteristic lexical feature is the use of words derived from Aboriginal languages. These words either maintain their original meanings (e.g. *kulunga, yarga*), or undergo a meaning shift (e.g. *manach* originally meant 'black cockatoo', but is now used to refer to police officers). The meanings of some English words have also changed to reflect Aboriginal cultural practices (e.g. *mother* means biological female parent and her sisters, and *father* means biological male parent and his brothers).

Some of the most well-known grammatical features of Aboriginal English are listed below (examples are from Malcolm (2004) and Honeybone (1996)). 1) Use of the base form of the verb with third **person** subjects, where Standard English has the -*s* ending: *This go on top.* 2) Past tense marking is often optional (particularly with regular verbs): *You went right through, we all pull out*; and perfect **aspect** is rare. 3) The progressive aspect is normally marked with the use of the participle only: *They jumping around everywhere.* 4) The copula *be* is often absent, and in existential clauses, *got* is used instead of be: *They all over the place; E got some sand there* ('There is some sand').

5) Aboriginal English uses articles differently from Standard English, sometimes omitting them (*We was playing game*), or inserting them (*Bloke with the long hair*). 6) Nouns are not consistently marked for the plural (*That's probably one of the cane toad*), nor is the - *'s* suffix used to mark possession (*Look at John boat*). 7) Questions are often formed by adding rising intonation to a statement, as in *You like banana?* The question **tag** *eh?* is also common.

Some of the most characteristic pronunciation features of Aboriginal English concern consonant 'substitutions' (see Malcolm 2004): /f/ and /v/ → /p/ (as in /pɔl/ 'fall'; /faɪp/ 'five'); /θ/ and /ð/ → /t/ and /d/ (see *TH-STOPPING*). /s/, /z/, /ʃ/ and /ʒ/ are not always clearly distinguished and are sometimes substituted for one another; /h/ is sometimes dropped initially, but it is also added initially where it does not occur generally in Australian English (see *H-DROPPING*).

Abstract noun   A noun whose referent is *not* a person or thing. Abstract nouns typically refer to qualities, states, events, occasions, and so on: *ugliness, madness, fight, birthday*. See CONCRETE NOUN, NOMINALIZATION, NOUN.

Academy   A body set up to monitor language and prescribe certain usages (see PRESCRIPTIVISM). The first European academy was established in Florence in 1582 by a group of intellectuals wishing to 'purify' the Italian language. The French soon followed with the establishment of the *Académie Française* in 1634. This institution still functions as a source of linguistic authority for French speakers around the world, by publishing dictionaries and commenting on what it often sees as regrettable foreign influences, particularly that of English (although it is arguable whether the academy has altered the rate or direction of language change to a significant extent). There is no equivalent body for English, but from time to time people have called for one. One of the earliest and most well-known advocates was Jonathan Swift (author of *Gulliver's Travels*), who famously complained about the 'imperfections' of English, claiming that its 'daily Improvements are by no means in proportion to its daily Corruptions', and that in many instances, 'it offends against every Part of Grammar' ('Proposal for Correcting, Improving and Ascertaining the English Tongue', 1712). See AUTHORITY.

Accent   No two people sound exactly alike. All speakers have accents – a set of pronunciation features which can reveal information about their regional and social identity. Linguists generally distinguish between accent (which is concerned with how speakers sound) and **dialect** (which includes accent, together with a speaker's regionally and socially distinctive vocabulary and grammar).

People are capable of making very fine distinctions when it comes to accent. When we meet someone for the first time we might note their 'American' accent. If we are a little more familiar with the varieties of English in the USA, we might say they have an 'East Coast' accent; perhaps we could narrow it down to a particular city, identifying it as a 'Boston' accent. Finally, on the basis of the sounds a person makes when they speak, we might even hazard a guess at the social background of a speaker ('a middle-class Boston accent').

Accents can have a profound effect on people's lives, because they carry particular connotations. In the UK, for example, some accents attract extraordinary levels of hostility. It is quite common to hear, even from people who regard themselves as socially liberal and tolerant, utterances such as 'I hate the Birmingham accent' (see BRUMMIE, WEST MIDLANDS). They are not responding to the linguistic features of the accent as such but to the accretion of social stereotypes and cultural myths that have built up around the people of the particular region in which the accent is used. The serious investigation of attitudes to accent began in the 1970s, when the British social psychologist Howard Giles carried out research which revealed that people generally rated speakers of **Received Pronunciation** (RP) highly for such character traits as confidence, intelligence, competence, reliability and education. On the other hand, RP speakers rated lower for friendliness, sociability and companionability. Regional accents were more strongly associated with these traits. Since Giles carried out his research, RP has become less highly regarded, and is no longer seen as a prerequisite for certain careers (although it is still unusual to come across non-RP speakers in the higher ranks of the armed forces or the law). See ACCOMMODATION, APPROPRIATENESS, DIALECT, FOLKLINGUISTICS, INTONATION, PRESTIGE, RECEIVED PRONUNCIATION, RHOTIC ACCENT, SOLIDARITY, STANDARD ENGLISH.

Acceptability Any usage which a fluent speaker of a language regards as possible or usual in his or her variety is 'acceptable'. Unacceptable utterances are usually marked with an asterisk: *I am liking mayonnaise* is unacceptable in Standard English. 'Marginal' cases are marked with a question mark: *?His wife changed the topic at the sudden drop of a hat.*

Accommodation A sociolinguistic term to describe what can happen when people from different social and/or regional backgrounds talk to each other. Sometimes their speech patterns grow more alike; this is known as *convergence*. Alternatively, their speech can become less alike; this is known as *divergence*. These processes are related to the degree of social or personal 'distance' between speakers. Convergence might be triggered by the conscious or unconscious desire to convey **solidarity** and equality; divergence has the opposite motivation. Accommodation can have powerful strategic uses in public domains. Professionals whose concern is to change the behaviour and beliefs of others, such as salespeople, teachers and politicians, often alter their speech style depending on their audience and goals (SEE STYLE SHIFTING). Accommodation can also lead to **language change** (see DIFFUSION).

Accusative case An alternative term for the objective **case**.

Acrolect A term coined by the sociolinguist Derek Bickerton (along with **basilect** and **mesolect**) to describe the most prestigious variety of a **creole** (i.e. the variety closest to a standard language). It is sometimes used more broadly to refer to the most prestigious varieties of any language. See CREOLE CONTINUUM.

Acronym A word formed from an *initialism* (see ABBREVIATION). An initialism is pronounced as a sequence of letters: *BBC, CNN, WWF.* An acronym is pronounced as a word: *NATO, aids, radar.* Some acronyms loosen their connections with the phrases from which they are derived, as in *aids* and *radar*, becoming fully fledged **lexical word**s.

Active voice See VOICE [1].

Activity verb   A verb which describes an action performed intentionally by an **agent**. Activity verbs can be **transitive** (*I threw the water over the English boy*) or **intransitive** (*Gazzer coughed*). See also DYNAMIC VERB, SEMANTIC ROLE, TRANSITIVITY.

Actor   See TRANSITIVITY.

Address, terms of   Forms used to refer to or name people. These include names (*Anthony, Tony, Tony Blair*), titles (*Mr, Dr, Professor*), endearments and insults (*mate, darling, love*). The choice of address form is dependent on a variety of factors, and is particularly closely related to issues of status and **solidarity**. **Asymmetry** in address forms is a marker of power differentials. In educational contexts, for example, teachers generally address pupils by their given names, yet expect to be addressed with a title and surname.

Addressee   A term used in **discourse analysis** for the person who is being spoken to, or otherwise addressed. **Second person** pronouns are associated with addressees: *Are you listening to me Fiona?*•

Adjacency pair   A sequence in **conversation** consisting of two parts which are adjacent, and produced by different speakers. Questions and answers, offers and acceptances (or rejections), greetings and greetings, requests and compliances, summons and acknowledgements are examples of adjacency pairs. The parts are ordered, in that the first part must precede the second part, and be of a specific type, so that a particular first part requires a particular second part: A. *What time is it?* B. *Seven o'clock* (question-answer); A. *Would you like a baked potato?* B. *Yes please*• (offer-acceptance); A. *Good morning.* B. *Morning Mattie*• (greeting-greeting); A.

Can I have a jam sandwich then please dad? B. *Yes sunshine* (request-compliance); A. *Mum, mum, mum, mum, mum?* B. *Yes?* (summons-acknowledgement). See SPEECH AND WRITING.

Adjective (Adj)   One of the four **lexical word** classes. Adjectives are most commonly used to modify nouns (see MODIFIER). In particular, they describe and classify objects, entities and ideas. 1) Descriptive adjectives are used to denote a wide range of qualities: *The acacia trees were **heavy** with **red** and **purple** blossoms; It's **beautiful**, it's **efficient**, it's **terrifying**, it's **funny**.* 2) Classifying adjectives typically limit the reference of a noun in some way. In *We have traces of **interstellar** dust in meteorites*, the classifier *interstellar* indicates that the dust belongs to a specific category of cosmic material; in *I sent you the **initial** report*, the classifier *initial* is singling out the report from a real (or potential) sequence of reports, rather than describing an intrinsic quality of the report itself.

Adjectives can be placed on a continuum with prototypical adjectives at one end and non-prototypical adjectives at the other. Prototypical adjectives, which tend to have a descriptive meaning, are gradable, meaning that the quality conveyed by the adjective can vary along a scale: *large/small; old/young; heavy/light*. Gradable adjectives can have **comparative** and **superlative** forms: -*er* and -*est* can be added to many one- and two-syllable adjectives, as in *He was **colder** now;* and *It was the **coldest** week imaginable.* The degree adverbs *more* and *most* are used with other adjectives, including all those with three or more syllables: *Everyone is **more intelligent** than them; Porpoises were the **most intelligent**.* Some two-syllable adjectives can take both inflectional and phrasal comparison: *I'm cleverer than you;*• *Paddy is much more clever than me.*• Other degree adverbs, such as *very, really, completely,* can also be used to modify gradable adjectives: *We have to carry a very heavy suitcase; He looks really silly.* Non-prototypical adjectives are not usually gradable: **The most initial report.* (See GRADABILITY.)

Prototypical adjectives can also have both an *attributive* and a *predicative* role. **Attributive adjectives** premodify the head of the noun phrase: *The rough surface of brickwork was exposed.* **Predicative adjectives** can be subject **complements** of **copular verbs** (*The fabric of his jerkin was rough*), and also object complements (*His terrible fear had made him ill*). Less prototypical adjectives do not usually occur predicatively: **The parents are lone.*

There are three main ways in which new adjectives can be formed: by adding derivational **suffixes**, by the use of **participle** forms and by **compounding**. 1) Derivational suffixes can be added to a noun or a verb to form adjectives: *comical, prevalent, combative, ridiculous, foolish, harmful, fearless.* 2) Participle adjectives are formed from the *ing*- and *ed*-participles: *the collapsing star's mass; the snapped cruciate ligament;* and so on. 3) Adjectival compounds are formed by combining two words: *wordly-wise* (adjective+adjective); *small-scale* (adjective+noun); *ice-cold* (noun+adjective); *well-known* (adverb+participle); *blindingly-obvious* (adverb+adjective); *thought-provoking* (noun+participle).

Adjective phrase (AdjP) One of the five major **phrase** types. The **head** is an **adjective**, and this is sometimes accompanied by one or more **modifiers**. In the following examples, the head is underlined and modifiers are in bold. Premodifiers are always adverbs: *He was too*

tentative; I'm very tired. Postmodifiers are usually prepositional phrases: *You'll be late for breakfast.* Only the adverb *enough* postmodifies the head: *We could not buy the material we wanted at a cheap enough price.*

At phrase level, adjective phrases function as pre- and (much more rarely) post-modifiers in noun phrases. In the following examples, the adjective phrase is in bold and the head is underlined: *a large saucepan; a very beautiful place; the people concerned.* At clause level, adjective phrases function as subject and object **complements**: *The weather is cold; Mary was rather quiet.*

Adjunct See ADVERBIAL.

Adverb (Adv) One of the four **lexical word** classes. Adverbs are mainly used to modify verbs (*I quickly capture what I can on film*), adjectives (*They seemed a really happy family*), and other adverbs (*It's going to be light pretty soon*). There are seven major meaning categories into which most adverbs fall: time, place, manner, degree, stance, linking and additive. 1) Time adverbs express temporal position, duration and frequency: *If you want to give me more input now, fine;*◊ *His face looked continuously hungover; He likes to print gossip occasionally.* 2) Place adverbs express location, direction and distance: *It's great to be here; He stumbled sideways; You could go far in this business.* 3) Manner adverbs provide information about the way in which an action is performed or an event occurs: *This group worked diligently;*◊ *They can do well;*• *The fighting went badly.* 4) Degree adverbs indicate the extent to which a particular characteristic holds: *These diagrams are partially complete; An extremely conceited, very lecherous, nearly alcoholic bore; It is a quite complex problem.* Degree adverbs such as *completely,* *extremely, totally* and *very* are known as amplifiers or **intensifiers**, because they increase intensity; on the other hand, adverbs such as *less, slightly, rather* and *quite* are called **downtoners** or diminishers, because they lessen it. 5) **Stance** adverbs provide information about the speaker's attitude towards or feelings about the propositional content of a clause. They can signal levels of certainty or doubt (***Possibly**, but I doubt it*); or the speaker's evaluation of the clause content (***Luckily**, I've got a job to go to*); they can also comment on the style or form of an utterance (*I've **honestly** no idea*). 6) Linking adverbs connect parts of a discourse together: *We're supposed to start with the discussion of the draft specification document. **However**, some people have only had a chance to glance at it.◊* 7) Additive adverbs add one idea to a previous one, indicating that both should be regarded equally: *I think we have to be clear to say that there are some things that you can understand from this assessment, but there are **also** going to be some things that we don't get now.◊* Restrictive adverbs direct attention towards what follows them, emphasizing a particular part of a proposition and excluding others: *He often relived the war years and still remembered his many comrades, **especially** those who did not return.*

As these examples show, adverbs are frequently formed by adding the *-ly* suffix to an adjective such as *quick* + *-ly, real* + *-ly, continuous* + *-ly*. However, many of the most common adverbs are not formed in this way, such as *now, near, well, also*. The use of the adjective form as an adverb is common in **non-standard** and **colloquial** English: *She's grown up very quick;• You have to go slow towards him.*

Like adjectives, many adverbs are gradable; that is, they can be modified with degree adverbs such as *very* or *extremely*: *Then she spoke, very **loudly** but*

very **calmly**; *I think I behaved extremely **badly*** (see GRADABILITY). Also like adjectives, some adverbs have comparative and superlative forms: *One person can travel **faster** than two; It hits **hardest** those who are poorest.* However, adverbs usually form the comparative and superlative using *more* and *most*: *An adequate sociology of culture must work **more** rigorously; This is also the place to enjoy the **most** ridiculously tame bird of prey you have ever seen.* See ADVERBIAL, COHESION.

Adverbial (A)   One of the five **clause elements**. There are three main types: circumstance adverbials, stance adverbials and linking adverbials. The term *adjunct* is sometimes used as a synonym for adverbial.

Circumstance adverbials add information to the clause about time, place, process, dependency, degree; they can also be used to mark addition. 1) Circumstance adverbials of time are used to express four meanings: point in time (*Everybody seemed so well **yesterday***); duration (*Magistrates banned the couple from keeping dogs **for five years***); frequency (*That butcher gets ruder **every week***); time relationships (***Before that** we were fellow medics at Barts*). 2) Circumstance adverbials of place express position/place (*Serve with the frankfurters **on the side***); distance (*I walked **twenty miles***); direction (*She rushed **from the room***). 3) Circumstance adverbials of process express four main meanings. Manner (*She breathed out **noisily***); means (*I enjoy travelling **by train***); instrument (*Dry **with a hairdryer***); agent (*I have been chased **by wolves***). 4) Circumstance adverbials of dependency show how one event or state is dependent on another, expressing meaning relations of cause/reason (*He is labelled a criminal **because of his extra-marital affair***); purpose (*Reporters and* *police rushed for cover*); concession (*In spite of everything she felt regret*); condition (*These eels appear to feel insecure unless they are wedged into an impossibly small hole*); result (*Or had she perhaps been pecked to death?*). 5) Circumstance adverbials of degree provide answers to questions about quantity ('how much/ many?') or give information about the extent to which a particular condition holds; they can also be used to intensify or diminish meaning: *Her heart jerked and accelerated to a steady two hundred beats a minute; The poll tax failed completely; You'll just have to hang on a bit.* As these examples show, extent and quantity can be conveyed either through the use of exact figures or by more general terms. 6) Circumstance adverbials of addition show that one idea is being added to another one: *She must also become more efficient herself in the use of the time available.*

Stance adverbials can be divided into three main categories: epistemic, attitude and style. 1) Epistemic stance adverbials express meanings such as certainty and doubt (*She certainly looked and acted odd beforehand*); actuality and reality (*Actually, I'm quite looking forward to it*); source of knowledge (*A sequel apparently has an even higher body count*); limitation (*On the whole I'm glad it's not*); viewpoint (*He was just better than anyone else in my view*); imprecision (*The babies, so to speak, are helplessly powerful*). 2) Attitude stance adverbials typically express some kind of evaluation of the propositional content of the clause: *Predictably, they ordered lager; Even worse, the curves into the new depot were too tight; More significantly, the organization was now free to manage itself.* 3) Style stance adverbials comment on the content or manner of an utterance: *Generally speaking, you're expected to be a self-starter at college;*

They'd be a blot on the landscape, to put it mildly.

Linking adverbials clarify the relationship between parts of a discourse, and are therefore important for text **cohesion**. The main uses of linking adverbials are to show contrast (*We keep animals in pens to fatten them. Homo sedentarius, in contrast, does not need to be kept in pens*); result (*Any blow to the head can be potentially dangerous, so if there is nausea or blurred vision I must be called immediately*); enumeration (*This raises two issues. Firstly, who cares for the carers?*); addition (*Problems in one area are likely to lead to difficulties in another. Similarly, solutions to problems in one area will help resolve difficulties in others*); summation (*In conclusion, there is a wide variety of social and physical contexts of soil erosion*); clarification (*This can occur when, for example, you no longer need to get up early for work*).

As this overview of the semantics of adverbials shows, the clause element is syntactically varied. There are five main syntactic forms in which adverbials occur. 1) Prepositional phrase: *on the side*. 2) Single adverb or adverb phrase: *also, more significantly*. 3) Noun phrase: *every week*. 4) Finite clause: *unless they are wedged into an impossibly small hole*. 5) Non-finite clause: *generally speaking*. See ADVERBIAL CLAUSE, CIRCUMSTANCE, CLAUSE ELEMENT.

Adverbial clause A subordinate clause with an **adverbial** function. Both finite and non-finite clauses can function as an adverbial. The main semantic categories to which adverbial clauses belong are position/place (*The main spars were burnt where the control cables had been melted away*); time (*When the cloth was taken from the loom, it was loose and open in texture*); duration (*She'd been into biking *since she went out with a Hell's Angel*); frequency (*Dana did not shave as often as I did*); manner (*Just behave as if we were back at home*); means (*He startled them by driving the car into the space in front of McCabe's*); reason/purpose (*They are visiting Thailand because they were denied visas by Rangoon*); result (*I didn't think it was helping, so I left*); condition (*If she hurried she would catch him*); concession (*Although waste disposal sites are well controlled, there is an ever present risk of pollution*). See ADVERBIAL, CONDITIONAL CLAUSE.

Adverbial particle   See MULTI-WORD VERB, PREPOSITION.

Adverb phrase (AdvP)   One of the five major **phrase** types. The **head** is an **adverb**, and this is sometimes accompanied by one or more **modifiers**. In the following examples, the phrase is in bold and the head is underlined. Premodifiers are usually degree adverbs (*The women had behaved very stupidly*). Postmodifiers can be adverbs (*Writing screenplays is something the British do very badly indeed*) or prepositional phrases (*They understood each other too well for comfort*).

At phrase level, adverb phrases function as modifiers in adjective and adverb phrases (*That sounded intriguingly glamorous; Timman started the game very aggressively*); pre- and post-modifiers in noun phrases (*That's quite a frightening thought; I'll be fine on the trip back*); modifiers of prepositions (*From there they sailed to America*), and premodifiers in prepositional phrases (*It's sort of on one side*). At clause level, adverb phrases function as **adverbial**s (*Everybody responded tremendously well*).

Affix   A bound **morpheme** (i.e. a morpheme which cannot stand alone as a word) which in English is usually fixed to

the start (**prefix**) or the end (**suffix**) of a **base form**. Affixes can have a derivational or inflectional function. 1) Derivational affixes are used to form (derive) new words. For example, the prefix *un-* can be added to adjectives such as *happy, willing, able, welcome* to form adjectives with the 'opposite' meaning: *unhappy, unwilling, unable, unwelcome*. Affixes can also be used to form words in a different **word class** from the original, as in these examples, where the suffixes *-ness* and *-tion* are used to derive nouns from adjectives and verbs: *sadness, greatness, communication, production*. 2) Inflectional affixes are bound morphemes which convey certain kinds of grammatical information. For example, in English the **plural** is normally marked by adding *-s* to the base form of the noun (*trees*), and the past **tense** of a regular verb is marked by adding *-ed* to the base form of the verb (*walked*).

Africa   See EAST AFRICAN ENGLISH, SOUTH AFRICAN ENGLISH, WEST AFRICA.

African American Vernacular English (AAVE)   The non-standard varieties of English associated with people of African descent in North America, also known as African American English (AAE) and Black English Vernacular (BEV). No definitive answer has yet been arrived at concerning the origins of AAVE. As Wolfram and Schilling-Estes point out, 'Given the limitations of data, the different local circumstances under which African Americans lived, and the historical time-depth involved' there will probably always be speculation about its origins and early development (2006: 224). However, several hypotheses have been proposed, the most influential of these being the 'creolist hypothesis' and the 'Anglicist hypothesis'. 1) *Creolists* argue that AAVE has its origins in an

English-based **creole** which arose as people speaking many different African languages came into contact under conditions of slavery on the west coast of Africa, the Caribbean, and the plantations of the southern USA. Subsequently, it has gone through a process of **decreolization**. Many of the features of AAVE, the creolists claim, can be traced back to this early contact variety (see SUB-STRATE EFFECT). 2) *Anglicists*, on the other hand, maintain that when black slaves were transported to North America, they learned the non-standard varieties of British English spoken by the white settlers and slave-owners around them (just as any other group of non-English speaking immigrants to the USA would have learned English), hence the many similarities between AAVE and 'white' English vernacular varieties. An extension of the Anglicist position, known as the 'divergence hypothesis', maintains that, until the late nineteenth century, the speech of blacks and whites in the southern USA was very similar, but during the period of Reconstruction, when the states of the southern Confederacy which had seceded from the United States in the Civil War were reintegrated into the Union, speech patterns began diverging, and have continued to diverge. According to proponents of the divergence hypothesis, therefore, the distinctive features of AAVE have arisen relatively recently.

What are some of these distinguishing linguistic features? Many of the features found in AAVE, such as **multiple negation** and the **regularization** of irregular grammatical patterns, are shared with other non-standard varieties of English. The list below (based on Wolfram and Schilling-Estes (2006) and Edwards (2004)) contains a sample of features which *differentiate* AAVE from 'white' vernacular varieties of North American

English (either because they occur only in AAVE or because they are particularly common in the variety). For a full discussion of AAVE phonology, grammar and lexis see, for example, Lippi-Green (1997) and Rickford (1999).

1) *Be* for habitual activity (compare AAVE *She be good* with its Standard English equivalent *She is usually good*). 2) Zero-copula (see COPULA DELETION) for contracted forms of *is* and *are* (compare AAVE *She Ø good* with SE *She's good*). 3) Absence of *-s* in third-person forms of present tense verbs (compare AAVE *She Ø talk* with SE *She talks*). 4) Absence of **genitive** *-s* (compare AAVE *Sarah car* with SE *Sarah's car*). 5) General absence of plural *-s* (compare AAVE *two boy* with AAVE *two boys*). 6) Stressed *been* to mark a state or action that began in the past and is still relevant (compare AAVE *She been sick* with its SE equivalent *She has been sick for a long time*). 7) *Ain't* for *didn't* (compare AAVE *She ain't do it* with SE *She didn't do it*). 8) Reduction of final consonant clusters preceding a word beginning with a vowel (*lif' up* for *lift up; bus' up* for *bust up*). 9) Use of /d/ for /ð/ at the start of words such as *the, this, these, those* and *that* (see TH-STOPPING). 10) Use of /f/ and /v/ for word- and syllable-final /θ/ and /ð/ (see TH-FRONTING), so that *mother* is sometimes pronounced [mʌvə]. 11) /r/ is often deleted after a vowel in certain environments, so that *record* is pronounced [ɹekəd] and *floor* [floə]. 12) /l/ is often deleted in certain environments, resulting in pronunciations such as [hɛp] for *help* and [ɹo] for *roll*. See AMERICAN ENGLISH.

Affricate A **consonant** produced by a manner of **articulation** in which the **airstream** is obstructed at some point in the **vocal tract**, then released gradually. In English, only two consonants are produced in this manner: the voiceless **post-alveolar** affricate /tʃ/ as in *chip*, and the voiced post-alveolar affricate /dʒ/ as in *jam*. These sounds are made by combining the **plosives** /t/ and /d/ with the **fricatives** /ʃ/ and /ʒ/.

Age An important **social variable** in sociolinguistics. Patterns of pronunciation and grammar differ between age groups. For example, adolescents tend to use the highest frequency of **vernacular** forms in their speech. During adulthood, the frequency declines, but then increases when their working lives are over. The explanation for this general pattern is that young people often face considerable peer-pressure to rebel against society's norms, and use vernacular forms to mark group membership and **solidarity**. But when they start work, people tend to reduce vernacular forms in favour of more prestigious ones (see LINGUISTIC MARKETPLACE). During old age, people often re-introduce vernacular features into their speech, because the social pressures to conform have lessened.

Agency The human capacity to act or to exert power. Agency is not distributed evenly. Some human beings experience all sorts of constraints on their ability to act, while others are comparatively free. Where language is implicated in constraining human agency, **critical linguistics** can intervene.

Agent The **semantic role** of the being or entity which performs the action described by an **activity verb**. Prototypical agents are conscious and purposeful. The agent is very often (but not always) the grammatical **subject**, as in the following clause: *The man leans against the gate.* But sometimes, the agent may not be the subject, as in *One of the frogs was eaten by a lizard.* Here, *a lizard* is the agent (it is

performing the action of the verb), and *one of the frogs* is the subject. This is an example of the **passive voice**, a construction which allows the agent to be omitted all together, as in *One of the frogs was eaten.* Sentences in which the grammatical subject is not the agent are common. For instance, in the following examples the subjects are not agents because the verbs do not describe an action: *My son has a very good memory for songs; This lecture was a bit special; It belongs to her mum and dad.* See SEMANTIC ROLE, VERB.

Agentless passive A passive construction with no *by*-phrase containing the agent: *The station house and the fire truck were destroyed.*• This is sometimes known as the 'short passive'. See VOICE [1].

Agreement See CONCORD.

Airstream A term used in **phonetics** to describe the movement of air through the vocal tract and out of the mouth. Most speech sounds are 'pulmonic' (because the airstream originates in the lungs) and 'egressive' (because they involve the expulsion of air from the body).

Alliteration The **repetition** of the same **consonant**s in close proximity: *Carrie caught a crab in a copper kettle.* Alliteration can be more or less prominent depending on where it occurs. The most prominent type of alliteration is the repetition of the same consonant at the start of a stressed **syllable**, particularly when the syllable occurs word-initially. Alliteration is common in popular idioms (*beat about the bush; green around the gills*), advertising and political slogans (*Frank's factory flooring; compassionate conservatism*), newspaper headlines ('*Corrupt' Copper Arrested; Mad Monkeys Attack Kids*) and tongue-twisters (*Round and round the rugged rock the ragged rascal ran*). These examples show the way alliteration can be used for emphasis, and to forge links between elements.

Alliteration is often associated with literary language, particularly poetry. Indeed, it is the main organizing principle of most **Old English** verse, where the first stressed syllable of the second half-line alliterates with one or both of the stressed syllables of the first half-line:

hige sceal þe heardra   heorte þe cenre
mod sceal þe mare   þe ure mægen
lytlað
(*The Battle of Maldon*, tenth century)

('Courage must be the harder, heart the keener, spirit the greater, the more our strength lessens.')

Although alliteration is no longer a central structuring device of English poetry, it is often used by writers to produce a range of effects: *I caught this morning morning's minion, king-/dom of daylight's dauphin, dapple-dawn-drawn Falcon* (Gerard Manley Hopkins, 'The Windhover' 1877); *He clasps the crag with crooked hands* (Tennyson, 'The Eagle' 1851). Verse for children often exploits alliteration for comic effect, as in these lines from Judith Nicholls' 'Sounds Good!' (1990): *Baked beans bubble, / Gravy grumbles; / popcorn pops, / and stomach rumbles.*

Allomorph A variant phonological form of a **morpheme** (coined by analogy with **allophone**). For example, the pronunciation of the English plural morpheme (represented in spelling as <s> or <es>) varies according to context. Compare the pronunciation of the -*s* in *cats*, *dogs* and *horses* for example. After an unvoiced sound (e.g. /t/), it is /s/; after a voiced sound (e.g. /g/ or /ɪ/) it is /z/ (see VOICE [2]).

Allophone Predictable and environmentally dependent variants of a phoneme which do not affect meaning. For example, in some (but not all) accents of English, the phoneme /l/ is realized differently depending on its position. For most speakers of **Received Pronunciation**, for example, when /l/ occurs before a vowel, as in *love, live, lake, fling, slow*, and so on, it is phonetically different from when it occurs after a vowel, in words such as *coal, fail, foal, hail, heel*, and so on. In the first case, it is said to be 'clear'; in the second case it is 'dark' (in phonetic terms, the back of the tongue is drawn towards the **soft palate**). An RP speaker who replaces a dark /l/ with a clear one at the end of a word (perhaps for emphasis) does not change the meaning of the word: these sounds are not contrastive in English, which makes them allophones of the phoneme /l/ (see MINIMAL PAIR).

Allusion A literary device in which a writer makes an explicit or implicit reference to another text. For example, in his poem 'Deceptions', Philip Larkin writes 'Your mind lay open like a draw of knives', an allusion to a line from George Herbert's poem 'Affliction' (1633): 'My thoughts are all a case of knives'. Compare INTERTEXTUALITY. See also PARODY, PASTICHE.

Alphabet A type of writing system in which symbols ('letters') stand for the **phoneme**s of a language. For example, in English the letter <t> symbolizes the phoneme /t/. English, like most other languages with origins in Europe, uses a version of the **Latin** alphabet. This was based on the Greek alphabet (the word itself comes from the names of its first two letters: *alpha* and *beta*), which in turn is derived from the North Semitic alphabet, which was developed in Palestine and Syria c.1700 BC. The alphabet used to write present-day English has 26 letters, each with a *capital, majuscule* or *upper case* form (e.g. A, B, C), and a *minuscule* or *lower case* form (e.g. a, b, c). Originally, the Latin alphabet consisted entirely of majuscule forms. 'Small' letters were gradually introduced from the fourth century onwards, as scribes developed new techniques for writing rapidly on parchment. Modern lower-case letters are based on Carolingian Miniscule, a script developed in the eighth and ninth centuries during the reign of the Emperor Charlemagne.

Different languages vary in the regularity with which letters are matched to phonemes. Spanish, for example, has quite a close correspondence. In English, however, the same phoneme is sometimes represented by different letters (e.g. the /k/ sound is symbolized by <c> in 'cat' and <k> in 'kitten'), and some phonemes are symbolized by a letter combination (e.g. /ʃ/ is usually represented by the **digraph** <sh>). See ENGLISH SPELLING, RUNE.

Alveolar   A term used in the description of **consonants**. A sound is *alveolar* when it is produced with the tip of the tongue touching or almost touching the roof of the mouth at the *alveolar ridge* – the point where the back of the upper teeth meet the **hard palate**. Most accents of English have the following alveolar consonant phonemes: /t/, /d/, /n/, /s/, /z/, /l/, /r/. See APPROXIMANT, FRICATIVE, NASAL, PLOSIVE.

Alveolar ridge   See ALVEOLAR.

Ambiguity   A state which arises when two or more meanings can be derived from a single utterance. Ambiguity is often divided into two types. 1) Lexical (or semantic) ambiguity occurs when a word or phrase displays **polysemy** (that is, it has more than one meaning). For example, the sentence *The sailors loved the*

port is interpretable in two ways, depending on the meaning of *port* (a harbour, or a kind of wine). As this example shows, lexical ambiguity is often a result of **homonymy**. 2) Grammatical (or syntactical) ambiguity occurs when a grammatical structure is interpretable in more than one way. For example, the meaning of *Helen saw the man with a telescope* depends on whether the **prepositional phrase** *with a telescope* is postmodifying *the man* (suggesting that the man is carrying a telescope) or acting as an **adverbial** at clause level (suggesting that Helen used a telescope to look at the man).

Disambiguation is, of course, usually possible when a listener or reader has access to the wider situational or textual context. As a disembodied utterance 'Mind moving joint', is ambiguous; on a sign for the benefit of passengers boarding a ferry from a floating pontoon it is not. See PUN.

Amelioration   A process of **semantic change** in which the **connotation**s of a word 'improve' over time. For example, in Old English, *prættig* ('pretty') meant 'sly' or 'crafty' and *cniht* ('knight') meant 'boy' or 'servant'. Samuel Johnson in his *Dictionary* (1755) defined *amaze* as 'to confuse with terrour'. Amelioration is sometimes called 'elevation'. Compare PEJORATION.

American English   A general term for the English language used in the United States of America. The first permanent settlement of English speakers on territory which would later become part of the USA was in Jamestown, Virginia (established 1607). This was followed by several others along the Atlantic seaboard, the most well-known of which was established by the Pilgrim Fathers at Plymouth, Massachusetts in 1620.

Throughout the seventeenth and eighteenth centuries, more people from Britain and Ireland arrived, and the early patterns of settlement had important effects on the subsequent development of English in America. Eastern New England and Virginia were mainly settled by people from the south-east of England; the New Jersey and Delaware area attracted emigrants from the north and west of England; people of Scots-Irish descent from the north of Ireland established themselves in Western New England, upper New York and parts of Appalachia (Wolfram and Schilling-Estes 2006). The dialect of each area reflected, to a certain extent, the language background of the original settlers. For example, most accents of American English are **rhotic** (the /r/ is pronounced in words such as *your*, *car* and *farm*). However, some speakers in the South and in parts of the north-east do not pronounce /r/ in these contexts. This is because some of those who first set up residence in these areas came from parts of the south-east of England where /r/ was being lost after vowels.

By the time the USA won independence from Britain in 1776, three main dialect areas had emerged along the Atlantic coast: Northern (extending from northeast New England to Metropolitan New York), Midland (centred on Philadelphia and Pittsburgh) and Southern (extending from Maryland to South Carolina). In the nineteenth century, as the interior of the continent was opened up, Europeans and their descendants tended to move directly westwards from the coast. This meant that the northern interior states were initially settled by people from New England and New York, while the middle and southern states were settled by people from the Midland and Southern part of the Atlantic seaboard (for a full account

of these patterns of settlement and migration, see Wolfram and Schilling-Estes 2006: 118–124).

Although the details are much disputed, the general consensus of dialectologists working in the USA is that at present there are three (or possibly four) broad dialect areas. *Northern* is found in the north and north-east, historically focused on New England and New York and extending westwards to include the northern parts of Pennsylvania, the Midwestern states of Ohio, Indiana and Illinois, and north-west into the Dakotas and the Pacific north-west, where it mixes with Western. *Southern* extends from Virginia, down through the Carolinas into Georgia, Florida, Alabama, Mississippi, Louisiana, the Gulf coast of Texas and Arkansas, where it mixes with Midland. The *Midland* area is often divided into two, with a *Western* area consisting of most of the Pacific coast, the Rockies, the Great Plains and the western Mississippi Valley, and an eastern central area from Pennsylvania to the eastern Mississippi region (Crystal 2004: 431). Such general statements are convenient, but it should be stressed that there is, of course, considerable regional and social variation *within* these areas, as well as between them.

Some illustrative differences between the present-day dialect of these three areas are outlined below. Since these differences are particularly marked at the level of phonology, it is the accents which are compared, rather than grammar and lexis (see Trudgill and Hannah 2002: 40–47).

Western pronunciation. 1) The accent is **rhotic**, meaning that /r/ is pronounced when it occurs after a vowel in words such as *car* and *yard*. 2) The *cot-caught* merger is currently in progress. This means that the vowel /ɔ/ in *caught* is disappearing, to be replaced with the vowel /ɑ/ of *cot* (a feature more prevalent in the speech of younger speakers rather than older ones). 3) The vowels /æ/ and /ɛ/, /iː/ and /ɪ/, /ɛ/ and /ei/, and /ʌ/ and /ə/ are merging before /r/ when it comes between two syllables. This means that *marry* and *merry* are **homophones**; *nearer* and *mirror* rhyme; *merry* and *Mary* are homophones; *hurry* and *furry* rhyme. 4) /ɑ/ may be replaced by /ɔ/ or /ou/ before /r/, so that *horrid* has the same initial syllable as *hoary* and *horrible* rhymes with *deplorable*.

Midland pronunciation is essentially the same as Western pronunciation with the following exceptions. 1) The vowels in *cot-caught* have merged, so that both words are pronounced /kɑt/. 2) The vowels /ɪ, ɛ, æ, ʊ, ʌ/ preceding the fricative consonants /ʃ/ and /ʒ/ are sometimes realized as [i, ei, æɪ, u, ɔɪ]. This results in pairs such as *fish/fiche* and *special/spatial* becoming **homophones**, and pairs such as *push/douche* becoming rhymes. Words such as *mash* and *hush* are pronounced with the vowels [æɪ] and [ɔɪ].

Northern pronunciation is essentially the same as Western pronunciation with the following exceptions. 1) It is essentially **rhotic**, but the Boston area is well-known as a place where many speakers do not pronounce /r/ when it occurs after a vowel, a feature jokily captured in respellings such as 'Pahk the cah in Hahvud Yahd' for 'Park the car in Harvard Yard' ('r-lessness' is also a feature of the accent of some people from Metropolitan New York). 2) The Northern dialect lags behind the Midland and Western varieties in the *cot-caught* vowel merger. 3) Some parts of this area are undergoing the **northern cities vowel shift**.

Southern pronunciation has a number of characteristic features. 1) Generally, the accents of the South are non-rhotic.

2) The vowels /ɪ/, /ɛ/ and /æ/ are sometimes realized as [ɪə], [ɛə] and [æə], resulting in pronunciations such as [bɪət], [bɛət] and [bæət] for *bit, bet* and *bat*. 3) The vowel /ai/ is often [aː], resulting in pronunciations such as [maː] for *my* and [haː] for *hi*. 4) /ɪ/ and /ɛ/ are not distinct before nasal consonants, so that *pin/pen* and *since/cents* are homophones.

See also AFRICAN AMERICAN VERNACULAR ENGLISH, BRITISH AND AMERICAN ENGLISH, CAJUN ENGLISH, CANADIAN ENGLISH, CHICANO ENGLISH, DIALECT ATLAS, ENGLISH SPELLING, FLAP, GENERAL AMERICAN, LATINO ENGLISH, NORTHERN CITIES VOWEL SHIFT, RHOTIC ACCENT, STANDARD ENGLISH, WORLD ENGLISH.

Amplifier See INTENSIFIER.

Analepsis A **narrative** technique sometimes known as 'flashback'. Analepsis is a kind of 'anachrony', which is a discrepancy between the order in which the events recounted in a story take place, and the order in which these events are presented in the text. In analepsis, the narration 'returns' to an earlier point in the story, after later events have already been told. For example, the 1946 film *The Killers* begins with the murder alluded to in the title, and the rest of the film recounts the events leading up to that event.

Analogy [1] A comparison between two things on the basis of a shared characteristic or characteristics. Analogies are often made for purposes of explanation, as this example from a politics textbook demonstrates: *Reduced to its simplest form, political realism has been characterized as the 'billiard ball' model. This analogy represents the global political system as a vast billiard-table on which the actors, the nation-states, are the billiard-balls: self-contained sealed units whose interaction is limited to superficial clashes.*

Because analogies invite us to compare (and sometimes contrast) objects and concepts, they often take the form of **metaphors** and **similes**.

[2] The concept of analogy is central to some processes of **word formation**. For example, in the early 1990s, the term *greenwash* was coined by analogy with *whitewash* to describe measures taken by certain large corporations to give the impression that their activities are 'environmentally friendly', when in fact they are not. Other examples of word-formation by analogy are *software* (from *hardware*); *inner-space* (from *outer-space*); *house-sit* (from *baby-sit*).

[3] A linguistic process which reduces irregularities. For example, in English some verbs which once had irregular forms have been regularized by analogy: at one time, *clomb, low, shove* and *yold* were past-tense forms of *climb, laugh, shave* and *yield*. See REGULARIZATION.

Analytic language See LINGUISTIC TYPOLOGY.

Anaphora (Greek: 'carrying back') [1] In **rhetoric**, a **figure of speech** in which the first word or group of words in successive phrases, clauses or sentences is repeated: *To raise a happy, healthy, and hopeful child, **it takes** a family; **it takes** teachers; **it takes** clergy; **it takes** business people; **it takes** community leaders; **it takes** those who protect our health and safety. **It takes** all of us.* (Hillary Clinton 1996)

[2] In **discourse**, the meaning of some linguistic forms can only be arrived at with reference to another linguistic form somewhere in the surrounding text (or **co-text**), since they have no fixed meaning of their own. For example in the sentence *She quickly pulled it in and shoved it through the slot*, we have no idea who and what the pronouns *she* and *it* refer to without access to the co-text. If the rele-

vant co-text precedes these 'empty' forms, this is an example of *anaphoric* reference. If it follows these forms, it is known as *cataphoric* reference. See COHESION, REFERENCE.

Angles An ethnic label for a group of Germanic people who settled in Britain about 1500 years ago. The name is probably derived from *Angul* (now 'Angeln'), a stretch of land on the Baltic sea in Schleswig (northern Germany). However, it cannot be said with any certainty if this is the place of origin of these people. The Angles settled along the east coast of England in Northumbria and East Anglia, and also inland in Mercia. They were also the first English-speaking inhabitants of Scotland (settling in the south of the country). See ANGLO-SAXON, JUTES, SAXONS.

Anglophone English speaking. Both individual people and communities of speakers can be described as 'anglophone'.

Anglo-Saxon A conflation of 'Angle' and 'Saxon' which is used as a cover term for all the Germanic peoples who began their settlement of **Britain** about 1500 years ago. It is also used as a synonym for **Old English**. The phrase 'Anglo-Saxon heptarchy' is used by historians to describe the seven Anglo-Saxon kingdoms of Northumberland, Mercia, East Anglia, Wessex, Sussex, Essex and Kent, which were united under Alfred the Great (c.849–899), the first king of England.

Antilanguage A term coined by the British linguist Michael Halliday (1925–) to describe the distinctive language of an 'antisociety': a social group which has an antagonistic or oppositional relationship to the mainstream. Antilanguages are particularly associated with groups whose activities place them outside the law (e.g. Elizabethan criminals, computer hackers, drug-dealers and users, sexual minorities in certain historical and cultural contexts). Antilanguages serve to maintain solidarity and social identity amongst members of the antisociety, and embody an alternative social hierarchy and system of values. See ARGOT, POLARI, SLANG.

Antonymy A type of **semantic relation** involving opposition. Antonyms fall into two main categories. 1) Binary antonyms express an 'either/or' relationship. For example, in the following pairs of words the meanings are mutually exclusive: *dead-alive, true-false, continue-stop*. Something cannot be simultaneously dead *and* alive; true *and* false. Furthermore, the assertion of one element in the binary entails the denial of the other (*He is alive* entails *he is not dead*); and conversely, the denial of one element entails the assertion of the other (*He is not alive* entails *He is dead*). 2) Gradable antonyms (sometimes known as 'polar' antonyms) typically occur at opposite ends of a scale: *hot-cold, large-small, strong-weak* and so on. This makes it possible to express gradations of meaning with degree **adverbial**s (*very/slightly/rather/quite/too* and so on). The assertion of one element entails the denial of the other (*She is hot* entails *she is not cold*); but, unlike binary antonyms, the denial of one element does not entail the assertion of the other (*She is not hot* does not entail *She is cold*). A further property of gradable antonyms is that one of the pair has an unmarked sense: in other words it is used to represent the entire scale. For example, when we want to find out someone's weight we ask 'How heavy are you?' not 'How light are you?' (unless we are making a particular point about a person's slimness). See LEXICAL COHESION.

Aphesis A type of **elision** in which unstressed **syllable**s at the start of a word are lost. In connected speech, this is common (e.g. *about→'bout; because →'cause*). Sometimes, this process can lead to the formation of new words (e.g. *opossum→possum; esquire→squire; espy→spy*). See SOUND CHANGE.

Apocope (Greek: 'cutting off') The removal of the final element of a word, as in the deletion of the second syllable from *kitten* to form *kit* or the reduction of the word *of* to /ə/ in phrases such as 'a lot of people' ('a lotta people') and 'cup of tea' ('a cuppa tea'). The motivation for such a process is usually economy of expression and/or ease of articulation. Apocope contributed to the loss of unstressed final sounds in words during the **Middle English** period (compare Old English *singan* and Middle English *sing*). See CLIPPING, ELISION.

Apostrophe The **punctuation** mark <'>. It has two main uses in present-day English: to mark omission and **elision** (e.g. *didn't* for *did not*; *she's* for *she is* or *she has*); and to signify possession (e.g. *the girl's hat, the girls' hats*). In the past, the apostrophe has also been used to signal plurality, as in this example: *O me! the very **boy's** will laugh at me* (Peter Hausted, 1632).

There are several problems of usage associated with the apostrophe. In standard orthography, a singular common noun or proper noun is marked with -'s to signal possession: *the university's governing body, Tom's best friend*. A plural common noun ending in -s is marked with -': *the universities' representatives*. A proper noun ending in -s can be marked *either* with -'s or with -' (*James's address, James' mum*). The association between words ending in -s and the apostrophe sometimes leads to confusion, with writers using it to signal plurality, and also the third person ending on present tense verbs: *My two cat's are driving me crazy;*† *He run's fast.*† See CONTRACTION, GENITIVE CASE.

Appositive A **noun phrase** which post-modifies a noun phrase preceding it. In *His mother was there, hurrying round the stalls with her sister the dressmaker,* the noun phrases *the dressmaker* and *her sister* are in apposition.

Appropriateness People profession-ally involved in language, such as teachers, linguists, editors and so on, often suggest that speakers and writers should be encouraged to use language which is 'appropriate' for a particular purpose or **context**. So someone who says *I were working* in a formal context, such as a job interview, is deemed to be using language inappropriately. Here, non-standard subject–verb **concord** is 'inappropriate', whereas in a less formal context (a conversation with friends), such an utterance might be deemed 'appropriate'. Although the wording makes it possible to avoid prescriptive comments such as 'It's wrong to say *I were*', it is perhaps worth asking whether there really is much difference between claiming something is 'wrong' and some-thing is 'inappropriate'. Both statements involve the denigration of **vernacular** forms and the elevation of the standard (since it is only standard forms which are 'appropriate' in high status, public domains).

Approximant A **consonant** produced by a manner of **articulation** in which the **articulator**s come close enough together to form a constriction in the **vocal tract**, but not close enough to produce audible friction. Most accents of English have the

following four approximant consonant phonemes. 1) A voiced labio-velar approximant /w/ as in wig. 2) A voiced alveolar lateral approximant /l/ as in leg. 3) A voiced alveolar approximant /r/ as in red. 4) A voiced palatal approximant /j/ as in yellow.

Arbitrariness The relationship between *signifier* (the form taken by a **sign**) and the *signified* (the concept which the sign represents) is almost always an *arbitrary* one: it is not motivated by similarity. The sequence of sounds /lɛg/ bears no resem-blance to the limb it signifies in English; nor does the written form of the word look like its referent. In **semiotic** terms, a word is therefore a **symbol**. Compare ICONICITY.

Archaism An old word, phrase or grammatical structure which has fallen out of general use, but which is delib-erately employed by contemporary speakers or writers to produce a particu-lar stylistic effect. Archaism can range in seriousness from the banality of *Ye Olde Tea Shoppe* to the painstaking recreation of English from an earlier period in his-torical novels, such as William Golding's *Rites of Passage* (1980): *I returned to my cabin, called Wheeler and bade him get off my boots.* See also OBSOLESCENCE, PASTICHE.

Argot A term sometimes used to describe the **slang** or **antilanguage** of a particular group: *The argot of the under-world;*† *The argot of nineteenth-century market and street traders.*†

Article The **determiner**s *a/an* and *the. A/ an* is often referred to as the 'indefinite' article. It is used to introduce an entity (in the form of a singular countable noun phrase) which has not been mentioned before in the discourse. For example, if a speaker or writer produces the sentence

*We have **a** new cat*, the assumption is that this is the first time the cat has been mentioned in this particular stretch of discourse. Subsequently, the cat may be referred to by pronouns (*he, she, it*) or definite noun phrases (*the cat*) (see GIVEN AND NEW). The indefinite article is also used when the noun phrase does not refer to a specific entity, as in *I wish we had **a** cat*. Here the addressee will assume that the speaker does not have a specific cat in mind; presumably any feline will do. *A/an* also has a classifying function, as in *My cat is **a** large tabby tom*.

The definite article *the* occurs with both countable and uncountable nouns. In most, but not all circumstances, *the* is not used unless the noun phrase it introduces has already been mentioned in the discourse: *Behind his horse **a** dog loped obediently. **The** dog suited the man*. This is a case of **anaphora**, where the article refers back to a previous part of the discourse. In some circumstances, *the* can be used when the entity referred to has not already been mentioned – this is possible when the referent of the noun phrase is generally known by all participants in the discourse: *Close **the** door* (there is only one door in the immediate vicinity). See DEFINITE/INDEFINITE, REFERENCE, ZERO-ARTICLE.

Articulation, manner of Consonants are classified according to three main parameters: manner of articulation, place of articulation and voice. 'Manner of articulation' refers to the type of constriction produced in the **airstream**. This is *how* the sound is produced. See AFFRICATE, APPROXIMANT, ARTICULATION (PLACE OF), FRICATIVE, NASAL, PLOSIVE, VOICE [2].

Articulation, place of Consonants are classified according to three main parameters: place of articulation, manner of articulation and voice. 'Place of articula-

tion' refers to the point in the **vocal tract** where a constriction in the airstream occurs. This is *where* the sound is produced. See ALVEOLAR, ARTICULATION (MANNER OF), BILABIAL, DENTAL, LABIO-DENTAL, PALATAL, POST-ALVEOLAR, VELAR, VOICE [2].

Articulator A part of the **oral cavity** used in the production of speech sounds. The articulators are the lips, teeth, tongue, **alveolar** ridge, **hard palate**, **soft palate**.

Aspect A **grammatical category** concerned with the relationship between the action, state or process denoted by a verb, and various temporal meanings, such as duration and level of completion. There are two aspects in English: the **progressive** and the **perfect**.

1) The progressive is formed from the **auxiliary** verb *be* and the ***ing*-participle**. Typically, it occurs with a **dynamic verb** and describes an event currently in progress: *Candice **is** eating a dish of beans*. It is less common in constructions with a **stative verb**, because states, almost by definition, are ongoing (compare *She is owning her own home* with *She owns her own home*). However, some **mental verb**s can be used with a dynamic meaning, as well as a stative one, and can therefore occur in the progressive aspect. For example, the verb *think* can be used statively to express an opinion or belief: *I think you are very attractive*. In **Standard English** it would not be possible to say **I am thinking you are very attractive*, except in some limited contexts (for example, if someone asked 'What are you thinking *now*?'). In this case, *think* is being used to express an ongoing activity, and is therefore being used dynamically, as in *I'm thinking about you*.

To indicate that the event *was* ongoing

at a point in the past, speakers can use the past tense of auxiliary *be* + the *ing*-participle: *She **was** teaching in a private school before she came to us.* The progressive aspect is also used to refer to a future event that is quite certain: *I'm leaving tomorrow.* There is considerable variation in the use made of the progressive form. For example, some speakers of **Indian English**, **Scottish English** and **Irish English** will use the progressive with stative verbs: *They were knowing the names* (Indian English); *I'm wanting one in the kitchen* (Scottish English).

2) The perfect aspect, which is formed from the auxiliary verb *have* and the **ed-participle**, usually indicates that a past situation has some relevance for, or effect on, the present: *I **have eaten** nothing for five days* (suggesting that I still have not eaten yet). The past tense of auxiliary *have* can be used to indicate that the entire event described occurred in the past and had some relevance · for, or effect on, another more recent time in the past: *A few crumbs from the biscuits they **had eaten** the night before pricked her skin.* The progressive and perfect aspect can be combined in sentences such as *She **has been** eating a seagull.*

There is variation in the perfect aspect in non-standard English. Meanings which are usually expressed using the perfect in English can be conveyed in a number of different ways. For example, some speakers of Irish English use the *be after doing* construction to convey the sense of Standard English *have just*, as in this example from James Joyce's *Finnegans Wake* (1939): *I'm after eating a few natives.* Some speakers of **African American Vernacular English** use *done*, as in *He done walked*, to indicate that an event is complete and in its resultant state.

Aspiration The puff of air accompanying some voiceless **plosives**. In English, these sounds are aspirated when they occur at the start of a stressed syllable. The symbol for aspiration in the **International Phonetic Alphabet** is [ʰ]. See ALLOPHONE, PHONEME.

Assimilation A process in connected speech in which adjacent sounds are 'influenced' by their neighbours and come to resemble each other. Assimilation can be anticipatory, progressive or coalescent. 1) If a sound is influenced by one which occurs later in an utterance, it is *anticipatory* (or *regressive*). For example, most speakers of English, when asked to say the word *rainbow* slowly and carefully, will produce something like [ˈɹeɪnˌbəʊ]. But in rapid connected speech, [ˈɹeɪmˌbəʊ] is a more likely pronunciation. This is because at the end of the first syllable the organs of speech are anticipating the position they need to be in to produce the [b] at the start of the second syllable. In phonetic terms, the alveolar nasal [n] moves closer to the bilabial plosive [b] by turning into a bilabial nasal [m]. 2) If a sound is influenced by one which occurs earlier, it is *progressive*. For example, in fast connected speech, *hedge school* is realized as [hɛdʒˈʃkuːl]. The palatal element in the voiced post-alveolar affricate [dʒ] at the end of *hedge* has been carried over into the initial consonant in *school*, which has become a voiceless post-alveolar fricative [ʃ]. 3) If two sounds merge to produce a different sound, this is an example of *coalescence*. For example, this often happens in English when the alveolar plosives [t] and [d] are followed by the voiced palatal approximant [j], resulting in a post-alveolar affricate [tʃ] or [dʒ]: many speakers of British English varieties pronounce *tune* as [tʃuːn] and *dune* as [dʒuːn]. Coalescence can also occur across word boundaries, as in *let you* [lɛtʃuː] and *could you* [kʊdʒuː].

Assimilation plays an important role in **language change**. Particular kinds of assimilation in connected speech become conventionalized, and the pronunciation of a word, or a whole set of words, changes. For example, in words such as *treasure, measure, pleasure*, and so on, the sound at the start of the second syllable was once /sj/. Today, most speakers of English pronounce these words with a /ʒ/, because the original /j/ conditioned a change in the preceding /s/. See SOUND CHANGE, SPEECH AND WRITING.

Assonance A stylistic device involving the repetition of the same or similar **vowel** sounds. In the following poetic description of falling snow, the vowels /ɛ/ and /iː/ are particularly prominent: 'Stealthily and perpetually settling and loosely lying' (Robert Bridges 1953). Compare ALLITERATION.

Association See CONNOTATION.

Asymmetry Very few (if any) human interactions are 'symmetrical'. Usually, speakers' rights are distributed unevenly. This is particularly obvious in institutional settings, such as a law court, a medical consultation or a classroom. In such contexts, not only are there constraints about when a person can speak, but also about the form and content of a speaker's contributions. But asymmetry is also prevalent in non-institutional settings, and even 'casual conversation' between friends is influenced by the unequal distribution of power, experience, knowledge and expertise. In contexts where there is a power differential between participants in a discourse, certain constraints are in operation concerning the choice of particular expressions. For example, in some languages relative status, power and authority can be marked through choices in the pronoun system. Particularly well known is the choice, in the second person pronouns, between T forms (familiar, informal, from the French *tu*) and V forms (polite, formal, from the French *vous*). Where asymmetrical use occurs, the person using the familiar form is generally of a higher status than the person using the polite form. (This, however, is not *invariably* the case; speakers usually maintain some degree of **agency** in most contexts.) **Address** forms are also used asymmetrically to indicate differences of status. For example, it is usual in some English-speaking contexts for higher status individuals to address those of a lower status using their given names, while expecting to be addressed in return with a title and surname. Friends usually use given names with each other, whereas strangers use titles and surnames. However, there is a growing tendency in Western Anglophone cultures for given names to be used between strangers who have equal status. This form of 'instant' intimacy is an aspect of **informalization**.

Atlantic slave trade The capture and enslavement of black Africans and their transportation to the Caribbean and North, Central and South America, mainly by white Europeans and Americans. The large-scale importation of African slave labour to the Caribbean began in the mid-seventeenth century. By the time the trade came to an end in the nineteenth century, a total of 12 million people had been forcibly removed from Africa. This vast system of exploitation has played an important part in the history of English. See AFRICAN AMERICAN VERNACULAR ENGLISH, CARIBBEAN, CREOLE, JAMAICAN CREOLE, LANGUAGE CONTACT, PIDGIN.

Attributive adjective Adjectives which precede the noun they modify: *You've got big muscles.* Compare PREDICATIVE ADJECTIVE.

Audience design See STYLE SHIFTING.

Australian English A general term used to describe the English spoken in Australia. The starting date for the history of the English language in Australia is usually given as 1788: the year in which a penal colony was established at a place the British called Sydney Cove. Although the earliest permanent European inhabitants were prisoners, prison officers and their families, free settlers arrived soon after the first settlement, spreading disease amongst the indigenous people (known collectively as Aborigines) and appropriating their land and water. Incomers came from all over the British Isles, and as speakers of different dialects of English came into contact, a process of **dialect levelling** took place, resulting in what are widely recognized as the characteristic features of Australian English. This, at least, seems to be the majority view of linguists, although some maintain that the English spoken in London and the south-east of England (where so many of the earliest immigrants were from) formed the basis of Australian English, with only a minimum input from other dialects. Until the abandonment of the 'white Australia' policy in the mid-twentieth century, most of the people allowed to migrate to Australia were of white, northern European descent. But the ethnic make-up of the country is changing, with people from Italy, the Federal Republic of Yugoslavia, Vietnam, China, Greece, the Philippines and India now making up a considerable proportion of the people born overseas.

Although English in Australia does not display as much regional variation as

English in the British Isles or even the United States, it is far from homogeneous (see, for example, ABORIGINAL ENGLISH). There is general agreement among linguists that a **sociolect**al continuum of Australian English exists, particularly in relation to accent, with broad, vernacular Australian at one end and 'cultivated' Australian at the other. In the middle is 'mild' or 'general' Australian. Broad Australian is generally the most stigmatized and has the lowest **prestige**. Cultivated Australian once had the highest prestige, perhaps because it is closest to **Received Pronunciation**, but is now less favoured than it once was (probably because of its associations with Britain). Some of the characteristics of the accent of English speakers in Australia are outlined below (based on Trudgill and Hannah 2002).

1) It tends to have /ə/ in unstressed syllables, where some other accents of English (including RP) have /ɪ/. For example, the vowel in the final syllable of words such as *foxes, sharpest, chances, velvet, placid, naked, honest, village* is /ə/ (see SCHWA). When /ə/ occurs word-finally it is often realized as [ɐ]. 2) Like RP and varieties of English in southern England, it has the trap-bath vowel split (so that words in the TRAP **lexical set** have a different vowel from those in the BATH set). However, in words in which orthographic <a> is followed by a **nasal** cluster (such as *dance, sample, plant, branch*) the vowel is /æ/. 3) Like RP and most varieties of English in England (with the exception of south-west England, and parts of the north-west), it is *non-rhotic*, so that *spa* and *spar* are **homophone**s (see RHOTIC ACCENT). 4) Intervocalic /t/ (as in *pity, better*) sometimes becomes the alveolar **flap** [ɾ]. 5) Australian speakers of English tend to use what non-Australians might perceive as a narrower range of pitch, and

the use of **high rising tone** in statements is common (but by no means universal) among younger speakers.

As far as grammar is concerned, there is little that might be described as 'Australian', in the sense that it is unique to Australian English. Non-standard constructions do occur, of course, but these are of the general kind found in English used in other parts of the world. However, some of these constructions do perhaps occur more frequently in Australian English than in other varieties, such as assigning gender to inanimate referents, as in this farmer's comment on a storm: *She made a mess of that crop* (Pawley 2004). The vocabulary, on the other hand, reflects the country's geographical and ecological distinctiveness, its colonial history, and interaction between Anglophone settlers and the indigenous people: *billabong, koala, kookaburra, outback*. Colloquial English in Australia also has some distinctive patterns of usage, including a high frequency of **abbreviation**s (sometimes with the addition of -/iː/, -/oʊ/ and -/zə/): *beaut* (beauty), *roo* (kangaroo), *barbie* (barbecue), *tinny*

(can of beer), *arvo* (afternoon), *garbo* (garbage collector), *reffo* (refugee), *Bazza* (Barry).

Authority People often appeal to an authority over issues of language usage. Dictionaries, grammars, style guides and so on, are invoked when there is a disagreement over what is 'correct' grammar, spelling, or word meaning. Some linguists are often suspicious of appeals to authority, and are at pains to point out that many of the 'rules' which writers (and less often, speakers) are required to adhere to, are the product of social prejudice. See DICTIONARY, GRAMMAR, PRESCRIPTIVISM.

Auxiliary, Auxiliary verb (Aux) A closed set of verbs which have an auxiliary or 'helping' role, marking **voice**, **aspect** and **modality**. The primary verbs *be, have* and *do* have both a lexical and an auxiliary function: compare *Chris **has** everything* with *Chris **has** worked for the company for four years*. The **modal verb**s have an entirely auxiliary role. See LEXICAL VERB, OPERATOR, PRIMARY VERB.

B

Backchannel device A word (*okay, yeah, sure*) or 'minimal response' (*mmm, uh-huh*) which addressees in a conversation use to signal to the speaker that they are listening to what is being said. See SPEECH AND WRITING.

Backformation A new word which is created when the morphology of an existing word is incorrectly analysed. For example, the final *-er/-or* in *peddler, swindler, stoker* and *editor* was wrongly analysed as an agentive suffix (by **analogy** with the *-er* and *-or* in words such as *runner, rider, driver* and so on) and removed to form the verbs *peddle, swindle, stoke* and *edit.* More recent backformations include *self-destruct* from *self-destruction, enthuse* from *enthusiasm,* and *liaise* from *liaison.* See WORD FORMATION.

Back vowel A vowel produced with the body of the tongue positioned towards the back of the **oral cavity**, as in the vowel /ɒ/ in an RP pronunciation of *lot.* See VOWEL.

Base form The form of a word to which inflectional and/or derivational **affix**es can be added (*walk + er = walker; walk + ing = walking*). Any **root** or **stem** can be called a base. Most verbs and nouns have such a base form.

Basilect A term coined by the sociolinguist Derek Bickerton (along with **acrolect** and **mesolect**) to describe the least prestigious variety of a **creole** (i.e. the variety furthest from a Standard language). It is sometimes used more broadly to refer to the least prestigious varieties of any language. See CREOLE CONTINUUM.

Bathos [Greek: 'depth'] A **figure of speech** involving a sudden 'fall' from an 'elevated' style: *I came, I saw, I blogged.*† Bathos is often used for humorous or satirical purposes.

BBC English See RECEIVED PRONUNCIATION.

Behavioural process See TRANSITIVITY.

Beneficiary The **semantic role** of the noun phrase referring to the being or entity which benefits from the process described in the **verb element**. There are two types of beneficiary. The *recipient* receives something (*She gave you some tablets•*); the *client* has something done for them (*I'll find you a pencil*). Grammatically, beneficiaries are often **direct objects**, but they can be subjects in a **passive** construction: *Mr Assad will be given a formal farewell ceremony.•*

Beowulf The longest of the known poems in **Old English**. Its 3182 lines make up about 10 per cent of the entire corpus of Old English verse. It was probably composed in the eighth century, but the only surviving manuscript was produced in the tenth century. The story is in two parts. The first part tells of the adventures of the warrior Beowulf, after he is hired by Hrothgar, King of the Danes, to kill the marauding monster Grendel (and his mother). The second part tells of Beowulf's struggle with a fire dragon, which eventually kills him.

Bible, the The scriptures of the Old and New Testaments have played an important role in the history of the English language. In the **Old English** period, translations of parts of the Bible were made, but the first full English version did not appear until the late fourteenth century, when John Wyclif translated the Latin Vulgate. During the **Reformation**, a series of **vernacular** translations of the Bible from the original Hebrew and Greek were produced across Europe. In England, the sixteenth and early seventeenth centuries saw the production of seven great Bibles: Tyndale's New Testament (1525, revised 1534); Coverdale's Bible (1535); Matthew's Bible (1537); The Great Bible (1539); The Geneva Bible (1560); The Bishops' Bible (1568); The King James Bible, or 'Authorized Version' (1611). Tyndale's New Testament and Coverdale's complete Bible were the basis for much of the text of subsequent versions, including the most important and influential Bible ever published in English, the King James Bible (some scholars maintain that up to 80 per cent of its text draws on Tyndale's work).

The Authorized Version (AV) came about when King James I approved a plan proposed by a group of reformers in the Church of England for a new translation, which was to be used in all the churches throughout the country. Fifty-four scholars were appointed to carry out the task, which they completed in eight years. Their work was linguistically conservative, preserving much of the language of earlier versions and choosing vocabulary and grammatical constructions which were falling out of use more generally. For example, the third-person present tense ending -*eth* is used, as in *When he bringeth in the firstbegotten into the world, he saith, And let all the angels of God worship him.* Even in the early seventeenth century this had a somewhat archaic flavour (the spread of the northern -*s* ending through the language was well under way by this time).

The direct and simple style of the King James Bible is eminently suited for the main purpose for which it was designed: to be read from the pulpit to people of all social backgrounds. This directness can be seen by comparing the opening of the book of *Genesis* in the King James Bible with an eighteenth-century translation: *In the beginning was the Word, and the Word was with God, and the Word was God* (AV 1611); *Before the origin of this world existed the LOGOS – who was then with the Supreme God – and was himself a divine person* (Harwood 1768). The later version is both more verbose and more grammatically complex.

The King James Bible has had a profound influence on English literature. It is a source of images and stories in the works of writers such as John Bunyan, John Milton and John Dryden; and its rhythms and cadences have been incorporated into the styles of writers as varied as Walt Whitman, Emily Dickinson and Dylan Thomas. It has also been a rich source of **idioms** and sayings: *my brother's keeper, the apple of his eye, the root of the matter, the skin of my teeth, go from strength to strength, at their wit's end, eat sour grapes, the salt of the earth, in sheep's clothing, all things to all men, in the twinkling of an eye.*

Later versions of the Bible have been motivated either by a desire to get closer to the original Hebrew and Greek of the scriptures (for example, the *Revised Version* of 1884); or to provide a translation into more 'contemporary' language (for example, *The New English Bible* of 1961 and the *Good News Bible* of 1976).

Bidialectalism   The ability to speak more than one dialect of a language (usually the standard dialect and one or more non-standard varieties). In educational contexts, the term is used to describe a position on language and literacy teaching which sees Standard English as an 'additive' dialect, to be incorporated into a pupil's linguistic repertoire alongside any **vernacular** varieties he or she might speak. Both the standard and the vernacular are valued for the different functions they can perform (the vernacular serving a broadly 'personal' and 'social' function; the standard serving a broadly 'public' and 'instrumental' function). See APPROPRIATENESS, PRESTIGE, STIGMATIZATION.

Bilabial   A term used in the description of **consonant**s referring to a place of **articulation** (the point in the **vocal tract** where a constriction of the **airstream** occurs). The production of bilabial consonants involves bringing both lips together. Most accents of English have the following bilabial consonants: /p/, /b/, /m/, /w/.

Bilingualism   Displaying communicative competence in two languages. In everyday usage, the term is often limited to people who are equally proficient in both languages. However, so-called 'balanced' bilingualism is quite a rare phenomenon. Most bilinguals use different languages in different domains (e.g. home and school) and for different purposes (e.g. speaking with family members, writing essays). This results in different skills being acquired and developed in each language. See CODE-SWITCHING, MONOLINGUALISM, MULTI-LINGUALISM, POLYGLOSSIA.

Blending   A process of **word formation** in which elements from two or more words are combined to produce a new one. Often, the beginning of one word is joined to the end of another: *Oxbridge* (**Ox**ford+Cam**bridge**), *Singlish* (**Sing**a-pore+En**glish**), *chugger* (**ch**arity+m**ugger**),

Paralympics (**para**llel+**Olympics**). Sometimes, a whole word is combined with part of another word: *docudrama* (**docu**mentary+**drama**), *podcast* (**pod**+broad**cast**). See COMPOUNDING.

Borrowing   English speakers have borrowed widely from foreign sources to enrich the vocabulary of the language. Lexical borrowing often takes place when people from different language communities are in contact (see LANGUAGE CONTACT). For example, in the early Middle Ages, **Viking**s raided and then settled in parts of northern and eastern England and Scotland. Later, in 1066, the Norman French arrived in southern England. As a consequence of these events, **Norse** and **French** words were borrowed by English speakers and eventually became nativized. Examples of Norse borrowings include *anger, awkward, cake, crooked, dirt, egg, fog, freckle, kid, leg, neck, skill, skirt, window.* French loanwords from this period include *beef, bacon, dinner, barber, grocer, parliament, county, judge, prince, fortress, tower.* Occasionally, structural borrowing takes place (e.g. English has borrowed bound **morpheme**s from French and combined them with native lexical items to form new English words, such as *lovable* and *oddity*).

Norse and French borrowing has been augmented by contributions from widely dispersed languages, often when there is a **lexical gap** to be filled. These borrowings have entered the language through a variety of channels: some were introduced when English-speakers and speakers of other languages came into direct contact as a result of trade or colonialism; others arrived as part of the process of **elaboration** of English during the **Renaissance**, when words were extensively borrowed from Greek and **Latin**. The following list, based on Cannon, McArthur and

Gachelin (1992), illustrates the geographical diversity of such borrowings. Some of these words arrived directly into English, others through one or more 'intermediary' languages, such as Spanish or French. 1) The Americas: *caucus, chipmunk, moose, skunk* (Algonquian language family); *cannibal, canoe, hurricane* (Carib); *avocado, chocolate, tomato* (Nahuatl); *condor, guano, puma* (Quechua). 2) Western Asia: *admiral, alcohol, lemon, sofa* (Arabic); *alphabet, camel, sodomy* (Hebrew); *check, paradise, spinach* (Persian); *coffee, mammoth, yoghurt* (Turkish). 3) Southern and South-east Asia: *bungalow, dinghy, shampoo* (Hindi/Urdu); *bamboo, gong, paddy* (Malay); *catamaran, curry, pariah* (Tamil). 4) Central and Eastern Asia: *chopsticks, ketchup, tea* (Chinese); *futon, judo, tycoon* (Japanese). 5) Africa: *chimpanzee, mamba, zombie* (Bantu language family); *mumbo-jumbo, voodoo, yam* (West African languages); *aardvark, commando, trek* (Afrikaans). 6) Oceania: *boomerang, kangaroo, wombat* (Australian Aboriginal languages); *ukulele, taboo, tattoo* (Polynesian languages). 7) Europe: *bog, shamrock, Tory* (Celtic languages); *cookie, hunk, skipper* (Dutch); *frankfurter, hamster, kindergarten* (German); *avant-garde, bidet, petite* (modern French); *broccoli, grotto, soprano* (Italian); *alligator, sherry, negro* (Spanish); *howitzer, pistol, robot* (Czech). See also LOAN TRANSLATION.

Bound morpheme   See MORPHEME.

Brackets   The **punctuation** marks ( ), which can be used as an alternative to **comma**s to enclose parts of a text which are parenthetical or distinct. As the following examples show, removing the material within brackets does not affect the grammaticality of the sentence: *Alan McLeod (age 21) of Edinburgh College of Art; In this poem we see their shared Jewishness, and the 'irreverence' (as some would see it) they each had for the Tradition; Nothing about Niki is particularly reverent: the coldness of his family (their 'twenty-room garret' in Vienna), the autocratic 'old' Lauda, his grandfather, his school-and-garage days (hopeless), the various 'borrowings' by which he wangled his cars, all that passes in a breeze.* The examples also illustrate some of the main functions of brackets: to enclose extra information, asides, afterthoughts, and so on.

Britain   The largest island in the **British Isles**, an archipelago off the north-west coast of Europe. Britain (sometimes known as 'Great Britain') is divided into three countries: England (the largest), Scotland and Wales. Together with Northern Ireland, these are the constituent countries of the United Kingdom of Great Britain and Northern Ireland.

British and American English   As with all national varieties of a language, there is great variation within **British English** and **American English**. Therefore, for the purposes of illustrating the main points of difference between the English of Britain and the USA, the standard varieties of British and American English are compared. In the discussion of pronunciation, which is based on Trudgill and Hannah (2002), **Received Pronunciation** (RP) and so-called **General American** (GA) are contrasted.

The most obvious and well-known differences between American and British English are in the area of pronunciation. These differences can be categorized according to whether they are concerned with the phoneme inventory of the two varieties, the phonetic quality of certain phonemes, or differences in the distribution and combination of sounds.

1) Phoneme inventory. Some of the

phonological differences between GA and RP derive from the fact that GA is a **rhotic accent**, meaning that the orthographic <r> occurring after the vowel in words like *here* and *there* is pronounced. One consequence of this is that GA does not have the centring diphthongs /ɪə/ (as in *pier*), /ɛə/ (as in *pair*) and /ʊə/ (as in *poor*) of 'traditional' RP. A GA speaker pronounces these words /pɪr/, /pɛr/ and /pʊr/. Furthermore, the RP phonemes /ɒ/ and /ɑː/ have merged into /ɑ/ in GA, so that *got* and *father* are pronounced /ɡɑt/ and /faðər/. Before voiceless fricatives, where RP has /ɑː/, GA usually has /æ/, so that *path* is pronounced /pæθ/ in GA and /pɑːθ/ in RP. The same difference is found before consonant clusters consisting of a nasal+voiceless consonant, such as GA /kænt/ versus RP /kɑːnt/ (*can't*).

2) Differences in the realization of phonemes. In GA, /t/ and /d/ are usually pronounced alike (as the alveolar **flap** [ɾ]) when they occur between vowels after a stressed syllable, so that pairs such as *bitter/bidder* and *latter/ladder* are **homophone**s. The main difference in the realization of the vowel phonemes is in the pronunciation of words such as *pot* and *paw*. The vowel in *pot* is unrounded /ɑ/ in GA and rounded /ɒ/ in RP; the vowel in *paw* is /ɔ/, which is shorter and less rounded than the equivalent vowel /ɔː/ in RP.

3) Non-systematic differences. Sometimes, differences between the two varieties involve the pronunciation of individual or small groups of words (see Trudgill and Hannah 2002: 50–53). Some of these are very well known: *tomato* (with /eɪ/ in GA and /ɑː/ in RP); *leisure* (with /i/ in GA and /ɛ/ in RP); *vitamin* (with /aɪ/ in GA and /ɪ/ in RP); *schedule* (with /sk/ in GA and /ʃ/ in RP).

4) Differences in stress patterns. A number of words are often stressed on the first syllable in GA, but the stress falls elsewhere in RP. These include 'a,ddress (GA) and a'ddress (RP); 'ciga,rette (GA) and ,ciga'rette (RP); 'maga,zine (GA) and ,maga'zine (RP). Also, many polysyllabic words ending in -*ory* or -*ary* have stress on the first or second syllable and reduction of the penultimate syllable in RP, whereas in GA there is secondary stress on the penultimate syllable: 'commen,tary (GA) and 'comm(ə)nt(ə)ry (RP); 'li,brary (GA) and 'libr(ə)ry (RP).

Vocabulary differences between the two national varieties are a common source of amusement and interest for speakers on both sides of the Atlantic. Some of these, exemplified in the following word pairs, involve different words for the same referent (the American term comes first). Food and cooking: *jello/jelly*; *jelly/jam*; *zucchini/courgette*; *pitcher/jug*. Clothing and accessories: *garter/suspender*; *suspenders/braces*; *undershirt/vest*; *vest/waistcoat*; *purse/handbag*; *diaper/nappy*. Transportation: *station wagon/estate car*; *truck/lorry*; *trailer/caravan*. Other vocabulary differences involve the same word having different meanings. Examples include *pavement* (US English 'road surface'; British English 'area for pedestrians by the side of the road'); *pants* (US English 'trousers'; British English 'underpants'). Finally, some words may have a shared central meaning, but also have additional meanings in one or other of the varieties. Examples include *dumb* (shared meaning 'mute'; additional meaning in US English 'stupid'); *school* (shared meaning 'institution of elementary education'; additional meaning in US English 'all educational institutions, including universities'); *leader* (shared meaning 'one who leads, guides or directs'; additional meaning in British English 'editorial piece in newspaper'); *surgery* (shared meaning 'medical operation or operating room'; additional meaning in British English 'office of any doctor').

Spelling differences are also highly visible manifestations of difference between the two varieties. American English favours -*ize* over -*ise* (*generalize, subsidize*), although -*ise* is losing out to -*ize* in British spelling. It also prefers -*er* to -*re* in words like *theatre, center* and *meager*, and -*se* over -*ce* in words such as *offense* and *defense*. American English also prefers double consonants in words such as *installment, fulfillment* and *skillful* and single consonants in *canceled, dialed, traveled, traveler*.

Finally, there are some grammatical differences between standard British and American English (see Finegan 2004). 1) Agreement rules between verbs and subjects which are collective nouns, the names of sports teams, companies and organizations. The following clauses are allowable in British English, but unlikely in American English: *Kenny Dalglish's team have lost three of their last four games; IBM have refrained from making this public*. In American English, the subject–verb agreement pattern is determined by the form of the noun, rather than by its sense, as it often is in British English. 2) Auxilaries in question forms and replies. British English shows a preference for question forms with *have* + *got* while American English prefers *have* + *do*: *Do you have any wire cutters?*• (American English); *Have you got any wrapping paper?*• (British English). 3) **Relative clauses** and **relative pronouns**. American English prefers to introduce restricted relative clauses with *that* rather than *which: A refugee ship that ran out of food and water*• (American English); *The Indian ship which docked in southern Iraq* (British English). 4) American English has *gotten* as a past participle of *get*,

whereas British English only has *got: The minimalists have gotten all the press*• (American English). 5) Prepositions are sometimes used contrastingly in British and American English. For example, in American English prepositions are often omitted from references to days of the week (compare American English *We all went Monday* with British English *I went on Monday*). In telling time, British English uses the prepositions *to* and *past*, while American English can also use *of, till* and *after*, so that *twenty to four* can be expressed as *twenty of four* or *twenty till four*, and *twenty past four* can be expressed as *twenty after four* in American English. Occasionally, the form of prepositions differ: *Railroad tracks ran in back of the house*• (American English); *The lane behind the house* (British English).

British Black English (BBE) A general term for the English associated with people of Caribbean descent in Britain. BBE is the product of dialect contact between the language varieties of migrants from the **Caribbean** (particularly those from Jamaica) and vernacular varieties of urban English in England (Patrick 2004). Some older speakers retain the full West Indian speech continuum (from Creole to Standard English), while younger British-born speakers use local British varieties alongside, and sometimes mixed with, Caribbean usages (McArthur 2002: 61). This hybrid variety (which is often referred to by its speakers as *Jamaican* or *Patwa*) is an important means by which young people assert aspects of their identity and symbolize group membership. In recent years, it has become more widely known as a means of cultural expression in the work of writers, poets and performers such as Benjamin Zephania and John Agard. See also CREOLE, JAMAICAN CREOLE.

British English (BrE)   A term used to describe the English language used in Britain (especially when it is contrasted with other national varieties of English, such as **American English** or **Australian English**). The term is most commonly employed as a synonym for Standard (British) English, but it is also used as a cover term for all varieties of English in England, Wales and Scotland. See separate entries on ACCENT, ANGLES, ANGLO-SAXON, BBC ENGLISH, BRITISH BLACK ENGLISH, BRUMMIE, COCKNEY, DANELAW, DIALECT, EAST ANGLIA, ESTUARY ENGLISH, GEORDIE, JUTES, KENTISH, MERCIAN, NORTHERN ENGLAND, NORTH-UMBRIAN, OLD ENGLISH, RECEIVED PRONUNCIATION, SAXONS, SCOTS, SCOTTISH ENGLISH, SCOUSE, SOUTH-EAST ENGLAND, SOUTH-WEST ENGLAND, WELSH ENGLISH, WESSEX, WEST MIDLANDS.

British Isles   An archipelago off the north-west coast of Europe. The two main islands are Britain and Ireland (although many people in Ireland dislike the term because of its associations with Britain).

Broadening (of meaning)   A process of **semantic change** (also known as 'extension' or 'generalization') in which the denotational meaning of a word becomes broader and more inclusive. For example, *aunt* once meant 'father's sister', but has broadened to include either parent's sister, and the wife of either parent's brother. *Novice* once meant an initiate in a religious order, now it can be used to refer to a beginner in any field or discipline.

Brummie   A colloquial term for the people, and by extension the dialect, of Birmingham, a city in the English midlands. See WEST MIDLANDS.

C

Cajun English The Cajuns are an ethnic group living in southern Louisiana in the USA. They are descended from French-speaking Canadians from Nova Scotia, who left for Louisiana in the 1760s. Cajun English is the label given to the French-influenced variety of English spoken in the area.

Calque See LOAN TRANSLATION.

Canadian English The English language as used in Canada. Many people from outside North America have problems distinguishing between English speakers from Canada and those from the USA. This is a source of annoyance to most Canadians, although it is perhaps not surprising, since Canadian English has a great deal in common with northern varieties of **American English**. The origin of these similarities lies in patterns of settlement in the eighteenth and nineteenth centuries. During the eighteenth century, the French and British colonial powers were struggling for ascendancy. As the British gained control of French-held areas, many French settlers were deported or fled (see CAJUN ENGLISH), to be replaced with settlers from New England. After the US Declaration of Independence in 1776, further waves of migrants came from New England, this time as political refugees who were loyal to the British crown and did not want to stay in the United States. Some linguists have argued that the similarities between Canadian English and American English can be traced back to the influence of these 'United Empire Loyalists', who were well-established in Newfoundland, Nova Scotia, Quebec and Prince Edward Island before mass immigration from Europe began in the nineteenth century. When English speakers from Britain and Ireland began arriving in Canada, it was this established variety which they accommodated towards. Nevertheless, English in Canada does show the influence of British English in some areas, particularly in writing, where British spelling is sometimes preferred over American spelling.

Canadian English shows remarkably little regional variation. There are, however, a few exceptions to the general homogeneity. For example, in Newfoundland, relative isolation and a pattern of settlement involving immigrants drawn mainly from counties in the south-west of England and the south-east of Ireland has led to the development of a distinctive dialect. Other notable regional varieties include the English of Quebec, which shows the effects of language contact with French, and the English of the far north, whose vocabulary contains many borrowings from the Inuit language.

There are few phonological or grammatical features which can be described as 'uniquely' Canadian. However, there is one well-known **shibboleth** of Canadian English: the vowel in words from the MOUTH **lexical set** is often [ʌʊ] or even [oʊ], so that to many English speakers outside Canada, a Canadian pronunciation of *about* resembles *a boat* or *a boot*.

Caribbean An archipelago of approximately 7000 islands in the Caribbean Sea forming an arc between the coast of Venezuela in South America and the southern tip of Florida in North

America. The islands were originally home to Amerindian peoples such as the Arawaks and Caribs (from which the region gets its name). The Caribbean is culturally and linguistically mixed, as a result of European colonialism and the **Atlantic Slave Trade**. The English language arrived in the Caribbean (along with Spanish, French, and Dutch) in the sixteenth century, and 19 political units now have English as an official language. See CARIBBEAN ENGLISH.

Caribbean English   English exists in the Caribbean on a continuum, with Standard English (the **acrolect**al variety) at one end and English-based **creoles** (the **basilect**al varieties) at the other. In between are numerous **mesolect**al varieties. Standard English, which is used by only a small proportion of people, is spoken in a variety of local accents. It is generally acquired through the education system, and is used in formal contexts. The majority of people use localized mesolectal and basilectal varieties (see separate entries on CREOLE CONTINUUM, JAMAICAN CREOLE, PATOIS).

To outsiders, one of the most distinctive aspects of English in the Caribbean is the accent. A number of features have wide geographical and social distribution. One of the most prominent unifying features is the tendency for syllables to receive equal stress (see RHYTHM), resulting in pronunciations such as /ˈkan-ˈsɪˈkwɛns/ for *consequence*, rather than /ˈkansəkwəns/ (the likely pronunciation in North America). The following consonants and vowel features are also widespread: the realization of /θ/ and /ð/ as [t] and [d] (see TH-STOPPING); the realization of /v/ as [b] or [β]; the simplification of final consonant clusters; the merger of /a/ and /ɒ/ to /a/, so words such as *hat* and *hot* are pronounced the same (/hat/); the

merger of the diphthongs /ɪə/ and /ɛə/, so that *hear* and *hare* are **homophones** (Crystal 2003: 344–345).

Case   A grammatical category associated in English mainly with **pronouns** and, to a lesser extent, **nouns**. Members of these word classes have different forms which vary according to the word's grammatical role in a clause. In many languages, the case system is complex, with nouns being inflected to show a number of cases (German, for instance, has nominative, accusative, dative and genitive). In comparison with **Old English**, the noun case system of modern English is relatively impoverished: only the **genitive** or 'possessive' case survives (as in *the dog's tail*), with the 'common' case being used elsewhere. The **personal pronouns**, however, have three cases.

Subjective (nominative)	Objective (accusative)	Genitive
I	me	mine
we	us	ours
he	him	his
she	her	hers
it	it	its
they	them	theirs

Subjective personal pronouns are used for the **subject** of the clause (*She thumped the pillow*); objective personal pronouns are used for **direct object** (*She thumped them*) and **indirect object** (*She bought me a mug*). When a pronoun occurs in a **prepositional phrase** it is always in the objective case (*Nicaraguan women are an example to us*). Genitive personal pronouns mark possession (*The horse is mine*).

Cataphora, Cataphoric reference   See ANAPHORA.

Causative verb   A verb which indicates that someone or something is helping to bring about a new state of affairs: *Unemployment* **causes** *crime; Intonation* **enables** *us to express emotions.* See AGENT, SEMANTIC ROLE, VERB.

Causer   The **semantic role** of the being or entity which causes an event to happen, or instigates it: *Vandals smashed the glass front door.* See SUBJECT.

Celtic languages   The term is used to describe a group of **Indo-European** languages which, in the first millennium BC were spoken across Europe by a number of related ethnic groups, but which are now limited to parts of the **British Isles**, Ireland and Brittany. The Celtic languages are often divided into two main branches. 1) *Continental Celtic* is a term used for the now extinct languages spoken between about 500 BC to AD 500 from Asia Minor to the Iberian peninsula. 2) *Insular Celtic* consists of two subgroups: Brythonic Celtic includes Welsh, Breton and Cornish; Goidelic Celtic includes Scots Gaelic, Irish Gaelic and Manx. Estimates vary for the number of speakers of these languages. Welsh has about 600,000 speakers (20 per cent of the population of Wales) who are bilingual in Welsh and English, and Breton has about 500,000 speakers who are bilingual in Breton and French. The last native speaker of Cornish died in 1777, although there have been various attempts to revive the language since the nineteenth century. In the highlands and islands of Scotland there are about 60,000 Scots Gaelic speakers; and in Ireland about 75,000 people are native speakers of Irish Gaelic (although both groups also speak English). Manx is a dialect of Scots Gaelic that was once spoken on the Isle of Man.

The geographical distribution of the Celtic languages in the British Isles is a result of the original Celtic-speaking population coming into contact first with the Romans, then, after the decline of Roman power, with the **Anglo-Saxons**. The Romans killed many Celts, and drove others to the extreme west and north of Britain (although many did remain in areas of Roman control). When the Germanic tribes started to arrive in the fifth century, they either imposed the Anglo-Saxon way of life on the indigenous people, or forced them, like the Romans had done before, to the farthest reaches of Britain. As a consequence of this, only a small number of words were borrowed into Old English. Some survive today, particularly words associated with the landscape: *ben, cairn, corrie, crag, glen, loch, tor.* Some place names also have Celtic origins: *Belfast, Cardiff, Dublin, Glasgow, London, York, Avon, Clyde, Dee, Forth, Severn, Thames, Cumbria, Devon, Kent.* Celtic influence is also evident in modern varieties of English spoken in Ireland, Wales and Scotland (see SUBSTRATE EFFECT).

Central vowel   A vowel produced with the body of the tongue positioned towards the centre of the **oral cavity**, as in the vowel /ɜː/ in an RP pronunciation of *bird*. See VOWEL.

Chain shift   A process whereby a change in the pronunciation of one sound leads to a change in the pronunciation of another, then another, and so on, producing a 'chain' of change. This process is usually associated with **vowels**, since it only takes a very slight alteration of the position of the tongue in the mouth to change the sound of a vowel. The chain reaction develops when the sound that changes first comes to resemble very closely another sound, so the second sound must change in order to preserve a **phonemic** distinction. See GREAT VOWEL SHIFT, NORTHERN CITIES VOWEL SHIFT.

Chancery English   A term for the written English of the London Chancery scribes in the fifteenth century, who produced documents for the king. It is often claimed that Chancery English exerted a standardizing influence, as scribes in other public domains adopted its norms of usage. See STANDARD ENGLISH.

Change from above   A term associated with **Labovian sociolinguistics**. 'Above' means that a particular language change in a community occurs 'above the level of consciousness'. In other words, speakers are aware of the change they are making in speech. Change from above often comes about when speakers of a stigmatized, non-standard variety alter an aspect of their speech so that it more closely resembles an external **prestige** variety. For example, the vernacular accent of New York City is 'r-less'. That is, /r/ is not pronounced in words where there is an <r> in the spelling after a vowel (so *store* is pronounced /stɔə/). However, some speakers from New York City insert /r/ in this context, in a conscious attempt to sound like speakers of more 'prestigious' accents, so that *store* is pronounced /stɔr/. Although members of higher social classes are often the instigators of change from above, it should be stressed that 'above' does not refer to social class or status. Compare CHANGE FROM BELOW. See LANGUAGE CHANGE, STIGMATIZATION.

Change from below   A term associated with **Labovian sociolinguistics**. 'Below' means 'below the level of consciousness'. In other words, speakers are unaware of the changes they are making in speech.

Most language change is from 'below'. Although lower social classes are often the instigators of change from below, it should be stressed that 'below' does not refer to social class or status. Compare CHANGE FROM ABOVE. See LANGUAGE CHANGE.

Channel   See REGISTER.

Chicano English   A variety of **Latino English**, Chicano English is a dialect associated with people of Mexican ancestry in California and the South-west USA (particularly Texas, Arizona and New Mexico). Although Chicano English is often spoken by people who are bilingual in English and Spanish, many speakers of the variety are monolingual English speakers. Chicano English, therefore, cannot be regarded simply as a 'learner variety' of English, since it exists independently of bilingualism.

Some of the features of Chicano English derive from the dialect's historical origins as an English–Spanish **contact variety**; it is also shaped by contemporary influences from Spanish. The imprint of Spanish is particularly evident in pronunciation. The **rhythm** of Chicano English, like Spanish, is syllable-timed, which means that unstressed syllables are given their full value, and not reduced to [ə] as they are in most varieties of American English. For example, speakers of Chicano English would tend to have [i] and [u] in the initial syllables of *because* and *today*, rather than [ə]. Further evidence for the influence of Spanish on Chicano English prosody is the stress placement in words of four or five syllables, which is sometimes closer to the Spanish, rather than the general English pattern. Phonological influences from Spanish (in addition to the lack of vowel reduction already mentioned) are evident in some of the vowels, such as the merger of the vowels in the **lexical set**s KIT and FLEECE so that pairs of words such as *hit*, *heat* and *bit*, *beat* sound the same (the vowel being somewhere between [ɪ] and [i]). One consonant clearly shows the influence of Spanish: /v/ is frequently realized as [b] or [β]. However, it should be stressed that Chicano English also shares many phonological features with other vernacular dialects in the USA, including the simplification of syllable-final consonant clusters and the realization of /θ/ and /ð/ as [t] and [d] (see *TH*-STOPPING).

The grammar of Chicano English also combines features derived from Spanish and features shared by other vernacular US dialects (see Bayley and Santa Ana 2004, from where the examples are drawn). Examples from the first category probably include some usages of prepositions (e.g. *We start on July*), and the omission of subject pronouns (although this is quite rare). Some grammatical features shared with other vernacular dialects in the USA which occur frequently in Chicano English include the regularization of irregular verbs (*when she striked me with that*), absence of the *-s* ending in the **third person**, **auxiliary** deletion (as in *I been doing dancing for a long time*), and **multiple negation**.

Circumstance See TRANSITIVITY.

Clause A grammatical unit which usually contains at least a **subject** and a **verb**, and often other **clause element**s such as **object**, **complement**, **adverbial**. Clauses can be classified in various ways. There is an important distinction between **main clause**s and **subordinate clause**s. Main clauses are capable of standing alone as a simple **sentence** (*I'll go downstairs*). Clauses which are part of a larger structure are called **subordinate** or 'dependent' clauses: *I thought **that it was just brilliant**.*

Clauses may also be categorized according to whether the verb is **finite** (marked for tense) or **non-finite** (not marked for tense). Main clauses almost always contain a finite verb phrase (*He lives in Singapore*), whereas dependent clauses are often non-finite (***Knowing what lay ahead** made him excited and nervous*). Main clauses may also be classified according to **mood**. They are either **declarative** (*Carra went downstairs*•), **imperative** (*Go downstairs*) or **interrogative** (*Can we go downstairs?*). See ADVERBIAL CLAUSE, CLAUSE ELEMENT, COMPLEMENT CLAUSE, CONDITIONAL CLAUSE, *ED*-CLAUSE, FINITE CLAUSE, INFINITIVE CLAUSE, *ING*-CLAUSE, MAIN CLAUSE, NON-FINITE CLAUSE, RELATIVE CLAUSE, SUBORDINATE CLAUSE, *THAT*-CLAUSE, *TO*-CLAUSE, VERBLESS CLAUSE, *WH*-CLAUSE.

Clause element Phrases with a particular role in the clause. The main clause elements are **subject (S)**, **verb element (V)**, **direct object (DO)**, **indirect object (IO)**, **complement (C)**, **adverbial (A)**. See CONSTITUENT.

Clefting A process in which a simple clause is split (or 'cleft') into two clauses (a **main clause** and a **subordinate clause**). Compare *I need money* with *It's money that I need* / *What I need is money*. The purpose of clefting is to put extra focus on a particular clause element. In these cases *money* is emphasized.

There are two types of cleft sentence: *it*-clefts and *wh*-clefts. 1) The first half of an *it*-cleft (e.g. *It's money*) consists of the pronoun *it* + a form of the verb *be* + the focused clause element (which can be a noun phrase, prepositional phrase, adverb phrase or adverbial clause); the second half consists of a structure resembling a restrictive relative clause (e.g. *that I need*). The following examples illustrate some of the structural possibilities for *it*-clefts: *It* was Billy who threw the punch;† It was for you that Jesus came;† It is here that the story begins;† It was because she loved him that she shared his grief.† 2) The first half of a wh-cleft contains a wh-clause, usually introduced by what (e.g. What I need); the second half consists of a form of the verb be followed by the focused clause element, usually a noun phrase or a complement clause (e.g. is money). Wh-clefts can also be reversed, producing sentences such as Money is what I need. The following examples show some of the structural possibilities for wh-clefts: What we really want is a soulmate;† What you can do is change your attitude;† Stability is what they need.† See INVER-SION, WORD ORDER.

Cleft sentence See CLEFTING.

Clipping A process of word formation in which part of a longer word (usually the end or the beginning) is removed to produce a shorter one. The new word usually has the same denotational mean-ing as the word from which it is derived, but it does have a more informal quality: telephone/phone, gymnasium/gym, influ-enza/flu, champion/champ. See APOCOPE, BLENDING, ELISION.

Closed class A term sometimes used to refer to **grammatical words**. These words belong to a 'closed' class because it is only very rarely added to. Compare OPEN CLASS.

Cockney A person (usually working class) from the East End of London. By extension, the term is used for the working-class speech of the city. Well-known features of the Cockney accent (most of which are present in other accents of British English) include **H-dropping**; the reduction of [ɪŋ] to [ɪn] in words such as running and smoking; **TH-fronting**; the dropping or coalescence

of /j/ after an alveolar consonant (so that tune is pronounced [tuːn] or [tʃuːn]); /l/ vocalization (so that fill is pronounced [fɪo]). Grammatical features of Cockney include **multiple negation**, use of them as a **demonstrative** determiner and pronoun (You know when **them** girls walked past and they were laughing?), generalization of the past participle to the past tense (Do you know what he **done**?), negative contraction ain't (I **ain't** got a diary). See SOUTH-EAST ENGLAND.

Coda See SYLLABLE.

Code-switching A phenomenon (sometimes known as 'code-mixing') in which speakers who share more than one language or variety ('code') in a situation of **language contact**, alternate between codes in the course of a conversation. Several kinds of code-switching have been identified, and they are often categorized according to their formal properties (see Poplack 1980 for an influential typology). They are illustrated here with extracts from ICE. 1) Tag-switching involves insert-ing a **tag** (or other kind of set phrase, such as an **idiom** or saying) from one language into an utterance in another language: Me I don't know, **lakini** I was suspicious (East Africa). 2) Inter-sentential switching involves switching languages at sentence or clause boundaries: Sa kabilang panig **naman** and uh we'll see this point being played (Philippines). 3) Intra-sentential switching involves alternating between languages within the clause or sentence boundary: Ich bin sehr **happy** (Germany).

A variety of motivations for code-switching have been proposed. Some have to do with broad contextual factors; others are related to local requirements in the ongoing interaction. In some situ-ations, particular codes are associated with particular contexts: as the context changes, so does the code. For example, a business meeting might begin with pleasantries and **phatic** talk in one language or variety, before switching to another language or variety. Language choice is also related to social **identity**: multilingual speakers shift between languages according to which aspect of their identity they wish to emphasize (or de-emphasize). Factors in the ongoing interaction which might trigger code-switching include the filling of a linguistic need (one of the interactants' shared languages or varieties might have a 'better' word for something than another); the exclusion or inclusion of someone; the specification of a particular addressee, the communication of emotion or **stance**, etc. See also STYLE SHIFTING.

Codification   Part of the process of language **standardization**. Norms for usage of vocabulary, spelling, grammar and sometimes pronunciation are established and set down in dictionaries and grammar books, in an attempt to reduce variability within the standard variety. In English, the most important period of codification was probably the eighteenth century, which saw the publication of hundreds of dictionaries and grammars, including Samuel Johnson's monumental *Dictionary of the English Language* (1755) in England, and Noah Webster's *The American Spelling Book* (1783) in the United States. See ELABORATION, LATER MODERN ENGLISH.

Cognate   Words in different languages which have a common ancestor in a 'parent' language. For example, English *three*, German *drei*, French *trois*, Spanish *tres* and Norwegian *tre* (amongst others) originate in the (reconstructed) **Indo-European** word *treyes*. As these examples show, cognates have a formal resemblance, though they may have different meanings (compare English *compromise*

with Spanish *compromiso* – they are cognates deriving from the Latin *compromittere*, but the Spanish word means 'commitment, promise').

Coherence   A **text** is coherent when readers or listeners perceive it to be a unified entity which makes sense. Sometimes a distinction is made between 'surface' coherence and 'underlying' coherence. Surface coherence is a product of grammatical and lexical linkages between units of discourse (see **cohesion**). However, some texts which lack these links are still perceived as coherent as long as the intended audience has access to the relevant situational and cultural **context** in which the text is embedded. 'The fish are dead. There was a powercut', might still be considered coherent, if the addressee knows (or is able to infer) that the fish were tropical and lived in an electrically heated tank.

Cohesion   A **text** displays cohesion when its sentences are linked together by grammatical and lexical devices known as 'cohesive ties'. See separate entries on GRAMMATICAL COHESION and LEXICAL COHESION. Compare COHERENCE.

Coining   The invention of new words. See NEOLOGISM, ROOT CREATION.

Collective noun   A type of noun that refers to a group: *team, flock, gang*. See CONCORD, NOUN.

Colligation   The tendency for some word forms (**lexemes**) to show distinct patterns of grammatical 'preference'. That is, to co-occur with items from a particular grammatical category or to prefer certain syntactic positions. As these examples from the CWEC demonstrate, the verbs *think, say* and *know* commonly occur with **that-clause**s (*I think that you are no slouch*), while *want, try* and *seem* favour **to-clause**s (*I want to see mummy*).

These lexico-grammatical patterns can vary across **genres**. For example, the structure Subject + copula *be* + *right* (e.g. *Nancy is right°*) is about ten times more common in conversation than it is in academic prose (*LGSWE*: 440). Advances in **corpus linguistics** have made such patterns much easier to identify. See COLLOCATION, LEXICOGRAMMAR.

Collocation A term associated with **corpus linguistics**. When two or more words in a text show a tendency to occur in close proximity to each other more frequently than might be expected by chance, they are said to be collocates. 'Close proximity' is generally taken to mean within a 'span' of four words to the left and right of the 'node' word (the word whose collocates a researcher might be interested in). For example, a frequent collocate of *gamut* is *whole* (in phrases such as *run the whole gamut*) and the word *spick* is almost always found near *span* (in the phrase *spick and span*). This phrase illustrates the fact that collocations are not always symmetrical: although *spick* 'predicts' the occurrence of *span* it does not work the other way round: *span* does not predict the occurrence of *spick*. A special kind of collocational phenomenon is known as **semantic prosody**. See COLLIGATION, CONCORDANCE.

Colloquial A descriptive term for language at the informal end of the stylistic continuum. Colloquial usage is generally not socially exclusive (as is **slang**); nor is it associated with a particular place (as is regional **dialect**) – although different national varieties of English tend to have their own distinctive colloquial forms. In the following examples, colloquial words and structures are in bold: *Put the kettle on for a **cuppa**; This is a **right one** (British English). Nothing worth the effort down here **this arvo**†* (Australian English). *Thirty reasons why baseball is **way better** than football†* (US English). See FORMALITY, STYLE.

Colon The punctuation mark <:>, first used in fifteenth-century manuscripts to show a major pause or separation of senses. It is now mainly used for the following purposes. 1) To signal the start of a list, as in *Six different tipsheets match the fruits found on the billboards: apples, pears, bananas, peaches, kiwifruits, and oranges/orange juice.†* 2) To introduce an amplification, explanation, example or summary of what has just been said, in which case it has a similar function to words and phrases such as *namely, that is, for example, because*, as in *The film is available in two formats: DVD and VHS;†* *Hong Kong people have only one thought: money, money, money.* ± 3) To introduce a long quotation, as in *Nietzsche wrote: 'But how could we do this? How could we drink up the sea? Who gave us the sponge to wipe away the entire horizon? What were we doing when we unchained this earth from its sun?'†*

Comma The **punctuation** mark <,>, first used in early manuscripts to show a minor pause or change of sense. Commas are now mainly used for the following purposes. 1) To separate independent clauses when they are joined by coordinating conjunctions: *The weather is getting seriously cold here, but I'm still glad to be back.†* 2) To separate off material which is not *essential* to meaning, but which provides extra information: *Travelling with my dad, who is crazy, is a pain in the arse;†* *My son, the lawyer-to-be, didn't miss a beat;†* *To tell people they have no right to revolt is, I think, ridiculous.†* (see RELATIVE CLAUSE, APPOSITION). 3) To separate

adverbial elements from the main clause which they precede: *However, we never promised you a rose garden.*† 4) To separate items in a list: *Sonic Youth, Pearl Jam, Jesus and Mary Chain, St Etienne, The Pixies.* 5) To introduce and end direct quotation: *She said, 'You're doing great';* *'You're doing great,' she said.*†

Common noun See NOUN.

Communication verb A type of **activity verb** which refers to a way of communicating: *ask, claim, describe, say, speak, write.* Sometimes they are referred to as 'reporting' verbs. See SEMANTIC ROLE, SPEECH ACT THEORY, SPEECH PRESENTATION, VERB, VERBAL PROCESS.

Comparative One of the 'degrees' (together with **superlative**) of **adjective** and **adverb** comparison. It is marked by the suffix *-er* (*French prospects grew* **bleaker**; *I want it to happen* **sooner**), or by the adverb *more* (*Nietzsche was* **more** **enthusiastic** *about Wagner*; *Why are you not eating it* **more enthusiastically?**). A common **non-standard** way of marking comparison is to combine the *-er* suffix with the adverb *more* (the so-called 'double comparative'): *It's getting more easier.* See SUPERLATIVE.

Complement [1] One of the five **clause elements** (often abbreviated to C). Its role is to complete the meaning of the subject or the object in the clause. In some grammatical systems this is called the 'predicative'. Subject complements characterize or specify the referent of the subject. For example, in *The car was* **clean**, the **adjective phrase** *clean* is the subject complement, giving information about what the car was like. Subject complements can be adjective phrases (*He became* **very nervous**), noun phrases (*He is* **the boss**), and sometimes prepositional phrases (*She must remain* **in control**).

Finite and non-finite **complement clauses** can also act as subject complements: *Zero inflation is* **what the Prime Minister wanted**; *Their prime responsibility is* **to attend to the political affairs of the nation**. Syntactically, subject complements immediately follow the verb phrase, which must contain a **copular verb**, such as *be, seem, become, remain, appear*.

Object complements characterize or specify the referent of the **direct object**. Only a few verbs in English (known as complex transitive verbs) can take a direct object and an object complement. In the following examples, the direct object is underlined and the object complements are in bold: *I've painted* the picture **black**; *She called* me **a liar**. Object complements are typically adjective phrases and noun phrases. Occasionally, *wh*-clauses function as object complements: *Our childhood experiences have made* us **what we are**. See COPULAR VERB.

[2] A phrase **constituent** which completes the meaning of the **head** of the phrase. Unlike **modifiers**, complements cannot be omitted without affecting the grammaticality of a sentence. The heads of all the five major phrase types can take complements (in the following examples the heads are underlined and the complements are in bold). 1) Verb phrase complements can be noun phrases (*Mitchell's header* hit **the crossbar**), prepositional phrases (*The taxi driver* looked **at the money**) and clauses (*He* thought **that I was still a little mad**). 2) Prepositional phrases typically require noun phrase complements (*I'm just back* from **India**). They may also take a clause as a complement (*I called in to see dad* before **coming here**), an adverb (*It isn't safe to come* in **here**), or another prepositional phrase (*From* **inside the arcade** *came the murmur of children's voices*). 3) The typical complements of a noun phrase head

are prepositional phrases (*A basic knowledge of German would be helpful*), and **finite** and **non-finite** clauses (*It is always the teenagers who get picked on; He hadn't the strength to close the doors*). 4) Complements of adjective phrase heads are generally prepositional phrases (*He was guilty of carelessness*) and clauses (*Good referees are quick to pick up on this; I'm amazed that a club as big as Manchester United can react in this way*). 5) Complements of adverb phrase heads are prepositional phrases (*Unfortunately for a bustard, its flesh tastes good*).

Complement clause A type of **subordinate clause** which can perform many of the roles of a **noun phrase**, and is therefore sometimes called a noun or nominal clause. They function as **subject, direct object,** or **subject complement** in the main clause, and are controlled by a preceding verb, adjective or noun. Their structure varies according to the type of **subordinator** linking them to the main clause. There are four types of complement clause: *that*-**clause**, *to*-**clause**, *ing*-**clause** and *wh*-**clause**.

The following examples have been annotated to show the structure and function of the complement clause (in bold). 1) Complement clauses as subjects: *That it also truly addresses its audiences as Filipinos is quite clear from the formal shapes and conceptual approaches*± (*that*-clause functioning as subject); *What they wanted was romance*± (*wh*-clause functioning as subject); *Eating good food can be fun* (*ing*-clause functioning as subject); *To have flags is not important*± (*to*-clause functioning as subject). 2) Complement clauses as direct objects: *He thought that she was someone else* (*that*-clause functioning as direct object); *He had seen what had happened* (*wh*-clause functioning as direct object); *I enjoy being*

a woman± (*ing*-clause functioning as direct object); *I want to eat other things*± (*to*-clause functioning as direct object). 3) Complement clauses as subject complements: *Their hope is that someone will rescue them* (*that*-clause functioning as subject complement); *The question is why didn't you listen to them* (*wh*-clause functioning as subject complement); *The main concern is getting a good routine with the baby* (*ing*-clause functioning as subject complement); *The main aim was to prevent excessive smoke emission* (*to*-clause functioning as subject complement).

Complex sentence A sentence containing a **main clause** and one or more **subordinate clause**s: *I am sure that he is right; I don't know what to say*. Compare COMPOUND SENTENCE.

Compounding A highly productive process of **word formation**, in which two words are combined to make a new one (*skin + head = skinhead*). Compounds can be written as a single word (*blackbird*), two separate words (*Moog synthesizer*), or conjoined with a hyphen (*body-blow*). Compounds are often categorized according to the **word class** of their constituents and the class of the resulting compounds themselves (it should be pointed out that most compounds are nouns). The following examples show the most commonly occurring patterns for nouns, verbs and adjectives (compound adverbs are rare). 1) Compound nouns: noun+noun (*teapot, handbag*); verb+noun (*pickpocket, cut-throat*); noun+verb (*nosebleed, sunshine*); verb+verb (*make-believe*); adjective+noun (*fast food, software*); particle+noun (*overtime, off-piste*); verb+particle (*drop-out, put-down*). 2) Compound verbs: noun+verb (*speed date, sky-dive*); adjective+verb (*double-book, fine-tune*); particle+verb (*underperform, outclass*); adjective+noun (*bad-*

mouth). 3) Compound adjectives: noun-+adjective (*foolproof*, *fat-free*); adjective+adjective (*big-boned*, *supersized*); adjective+noun (*red-brick*, *white-collar*); particle+noun (*on-line*, *in-house*); verb-+verb (*go-go*, *pass-fail*); adjective+verb (*low-rent*, *high-rise*); verb+particle (*see-through*, *wrap-around*). See BLENDING.

Compound sentence A sentence consisting of two or more main clauses linked by **coordinating conjunctions**: *I hate him, and I hate you, and I won't listen!*

Conceptual metaphor A term associated particularly with the work of Lakoff and Johnson (1980) to describe routine and everyday metaphorical conceptualizations of ideas and experiences. In conceptual metaphor, one domain (the source) is 'mapped' onto another (the target), and such mappings can give rise to a huge variety of linguistic expressions. For example, in English the creation of an object or an idea is often represented as reproduction and giving birth: *This book was born out of the Channel 4 television series of the same name; The decade that spawned Slade, Kojak and Abba; Born and bred a Land Rover, but crossed with the might and muscle of a Range Rover; I loathe the plots hatched by the Spanish government.*

Lakoff and Johnson categorize conceptual metaphors according to whether they are *orientational, ontological* or *structural*. 1) Orientational metaphors organize concepts spatially, such as up-down, in-out, front-back, centre-periphery. For example, 'positive' concepts and states (such as happiness, health, life and goodness) are frequently associated with 'up', while 'negative' ones (such as unhappiness, illness, death and badness) are associated with 'down': *Make sure that the appraisal interview ends on a positive note, with the other per-*

*son feeling **up**, not **down**; Reading them **lifts** my spirits so much; She **fell** into a post-natal **depression**; She arrived one day in the clinic in the **peak** of health; I came **down** with a very nasty bout of influenza; Things are looking **up**.* Orientational metaphors probably have a basis in physical reality. 'Up' is the positive pole of the up-down dimension, because when a person is alive, healthy and active they tend to be physically up and about, whereas death, illness and inactivity causes humans to be physically down. 2) Ontological metaphors represent abstractions, such as ideas and mental states, as concrete entities. The following examples conceptualize emotions as entities inside a person: *Laura could barely **contain** her fury; He **poured out** his hate in a bitter **torrent**; Sycorax was **filled** with rage at her condition.* Conceptualizing 'non-things' as objects, substances, containers, people and so on, allows them to be ordered, categorized, and quantified. 3) Structural metaphors involve mapping a richly structured source domain onto a target domain. In the following examples, people are being conceptualized as plants: *Jamie is a **budding** cricketer; The **rosy bloom** of her cheeks had faded; She looked middle-aged, over-dressed, a show-girl **gone to seed***. Structural metaphors provide ways of understanding multi-faceted, complex topics (in this case, human growth and development).

Conceptual metaphors are so fundamental to thought and language that they can often be difficult to spot. People use them automatically, to such an extent that they can become part of the 'natural', common-sense way of thinking and speaking about a particular topic. The consequences of this are especially worrying in the domain of politics and economics, where metaphors matter more 'because they constrain our lives' (Lakoff and Johnson 1980: 236). What happens, for example, when human beings moving from one nation state to another as a result of war, oppression or poverty are represented (as they routinely are) as a liquid, in expressions such as *a flood of refugees*? Metaphors like this highlight certain aspects of a situation or process, while obscuring others. See also META-PHOR, METONYMY.

Concord Correspondence between the **verb phrase** and **subject** in a **finite clause** in terms of **person** and **number**. For example, in Standard English, concord (sometimes called 'agreement') between a singular third-person subject (*she, the doctor, a car*) and a present-tense verb phrase is signalled by adding *-s* or *-es* to the **base** form of the (regular) verb: *I eat, she eats; I go, she goes.* There is sometimes doubt about concord when the subject is formally singular but semantically plural, as illustrated in the following paired examples: *The team is truly international / The team are doing well*; *The government is wrong / The government are confident*. In some non-standard varieties of English, different patterns of concord are in operation. For example, in the present tense, the *-s* form of the verb might be used with all persons: *I knows you get upset; You gets what you pay for.* Alternatively, the base form might be used invariantly: *She don't really like it.*

Concordance A term used in **corpus linguistics** to describe the output of a 'key word in context' program. Such software allows a researcher to identify all instances of a target word or phrase in the corpus, together with the surrounding **co-text**. A concordance is usually presented in a series of lines, as in this example from the Collins Wordbanks Corpus:

the faith and **feelings** of many
bring up the **feelings** of futility
these **feelings** of entitlement
hidden **feelings** of isolation
grandiose **feelings** of power
produces **feelings** of failure
foster **feelings** of resentment
ordinary **feelings** of sexuality
the **feelings** of nausea
pent up **feelings** of love
strong **feelings** of hate
strong **feelings** of anger
your **feelings** of respect
nasty **feelings** of panic
the **feelings** of others

See COLLOCATION.

Concrete noun A **noun** which refers to a tangible entity: *dog, tree, chair*. Compare ABSTRACT NOUN.

Conditional clause A type of **adverbial clause** which states a condition: *Promotion to the premier league will be assured if they win their remaining games*. Conditional clauses are usually introduced by *if* or *unless*, but not always: *Were you to continue on this path*, *it would take you to Corrour Station.*

Conjunction Linking words, such as *and, or, because, than, when*, and so on used to join phrases and clauses. They are divided into **coordinating** and **subordinating** conjunctions. See COHESION.

Connotation A word or expression's affective or emotional meaning, as opposed to its strictly **denotation**al meaning. For example, the word *sea* denotes 'a large expanse of water'. But it can connote adventure, danger, nature's power, freedom, instability, and so on. Connotations can be highly personal and idiosyncratic: *sea* might have negative connotations for someone who has narrowly escaped drowning in it recently; but they can also be socially and culturally conditioned (the connotations of *socialism*, for instance, are dependent on the political beliefs of the person who hears or reads the word). Also, different words may have very similar denotations, but markedly contrasting connotations. For example, *steed* and *nag* can both be used to refer to a horse, but the associations of the two words are very different. See AMELIORATION, PEJORATION.

Consonant A category of speech sound produced when the **airstream** is blocked by a total or partial closure of the **vocal tract** (in contrast to **vowel**s, which are produced with an open configuration of the vocal tract). They are generally categorized according to place and manner of **articulation**, and whether they are voiced or not. Consonants occur either at the start or finish of **syllable**s. See AFFRICATE, ALVEOLAR, APPROXIMANT, ARTICULATION (MANNER OF), ARTICULATION (PLACE OF), BILABIAL, CONSONANT CLUSTER, DENTAL, FRICATIVE, INTERVOCALIC, LABIODENTAL, LATERAL, NASAL, PALATAL, PLOSIVE, POST-ALVEOLAR, RETROFLEX, VELAR, VOICE [2].

Consonant cluster A sequence of two or more consonants in a single **syllable** with no intervening vowels. Consonant clusters can occur at the start and finish of syllables. In all languages, certain **phonotactic** 'rules' govern the ways in which consonant clusters are formed. Classical Arabic, for example, does not allow any syllable-initial consonant clusters. On the other hand, Georgian permits initial clusters of up to six items. English allows initial clusters of two or three items. There are from 33 to 46 permissible two-item initial consonant clusters in English, depending on the **variety** in question, such as /pleɪ/ *play*, /driːm/ *dream*, /θriː/ *three*. There are only nine three-item initial consonant clusters,

illustrated in the following words: /spl/ *split*, /spr/ *sprig*, /spj/ *spume*, /str/ *strip*, /stj/ *stew*, /skl/ *sclerotic*, /skr/ *screen*, /skw/ *squad*, /skj/ *skua*. Syllable-final consonant clusters of two, three and four items are allowable in English, such as /sk/ *risk*, /skt/ *risked*, /mpst/ *glimpsed*, but in connected speech long final clusters are often simplified (e.g. /glɪmpst/ becomes /glɪmst/).

Constituent A clause consists of groupings of elements, known as constituents. These units perform a single function, and can usually be replaced by a single word. For example, the sentence 'The yellow truck squashed the tiny rabbit' consists of three constituents: a noun phrase functioning as subject ('The yellow truck'), a verb phrase functioning as verb element ('squashed') and a noun phrase functioning as direct object ('the tiny rabbit'). See CLAUSE ELEMENT, WORD ORDER.

Contact variety A language or variety of a language which arises in a situation of **language contact**, and whose vocabulary and/or grammar is derived from more than one source language. The most well-known examples of contact languages are **pidgin**s and **creole**s. However, many contact varieties (such as **Chicano English** or **Singapore Colloquial English**) are neither pidgins nor creoles.

Content word See LEXICAL WORD.

Context The environment surrounding a particular word, phrase, sentence or larger linguistic unit. Context can refer to the immediate verbal environment (the term 'co-text' is sometimes used to describe this aspect of context); or it can describe the broader situational, social and cultural circumstances which influence language use and interpretation, such as audience and purpose. See DEIXIS,

GIVEN AND NEW, REGISTER, SPEECH AND
WRITING, STYLE SHIFTING.

Contraction   The process in which a
reduced form of an **auxiliary verb** or
negative particle is attached to an
adjacent word. Contraction is more
common in speech than it is in writing.
There are two main kinds of contraction
in English: verb contraction and negative
contraction. 1) In verb contraction,
certain forms of the verbs *be* and *have* are
reduced to their final consonants and
then attached to the subject. In **Standard
English,** *am, is, are, has, have,* and *had*
have the following contracted forms: *I'm
not going to set fire to it; The dog's sitting
with the cat; Malcolm's splashed out;
They've all denied manslaughter; I'd been
in prison* (contraction of auxiliary *had*).
Note also that when *be* functions as a
primary verb it can be contracted in the
present tense: *I'm a good swimmer; Kelly's
a little bitch.* Less commonly, primary
have is contracted: *We've the President
to thank for that* (this is more usual in
British English than **American English**).
Contractions of *will* and *would* are also
quite common: *They'll eat anything;*•
She'd eat her hat. Finally, auxiliary *have*
can be reduced and attached to the preceding modal verb when the perfect
aspect is being used to express past **modality**: *I should've tidied up a bit.* In rapid
connected speech, *have* is often reduced
further to an unstressed vowel [ə]. This is
sometimes represented in informal writing as *coulda, shoulda, woulda*: *I **coulda**
had class. I **coulda** been a contender. I
coulda been somebody.*† 2) Negative contraction involves reducing *not* to *n't* and
attaching it to a preceding modal verb or
primary verb functioning as auxiliary or
main verb (all examples are from
CWEC): *There isn't any time; Political
parties aren't giving much choice to the*
*people; Captain Largo wasn't in; The
women weren't voting; We haven't yet con-
summated our love; Cleveland hasn't won a
pennant since 1954; The boy hadn't given
Hall the rifle; I don't understand them;
Dora doesn't like it; Tony didn't eat many;
You can't stop it; You couldn't walk to the
soda shop; I mustn't think about it; You
shouldn't make fun of your body; You
won't believe it's low fat; You wouldn't
understand; I shan't be long.* (Note that
will not and *shall not* have the special
forms *won't* and *shan't*.) See SPEECH AND
WRITING.

Contrastive linguistics   The comparative study of languages or dialects in
order to discover points of similarity and
difference.

Convergence   See ACCOMMODATION.

Conversation   The most common and
pervasive form of linguistic interaction,
which is central to all human cultures.
See separate entries on ADJACENCY PAIR,
BACKCHANNEL DEVICE, CODE-SWITCHING,
CONVERSATION ANALYSIS, CO-OPERATIVE
PRINCIPLE, DIALOGUE, DIRECT SPEECH,
FLOOR, FORMALITY, INDIRECT SPEECH,
INFORMALIZATION, LEXICAL BUNDLE,
REPETITION, SPEECH AND WRITING, STYLE
SHIFTING, TRANSCRIPTION, TURN.

Conversational maxim   See CO-
OPERATIVE PRINCIPLE.

Conversation analysis (CA)   The
analysis of conversational interaction – a
discipline which has its origins in pio-
neering work by the American sociologist
Harvey Sacks in the 1960s. Its central
concern is to examine how people
engaged in conversation are able to produce sequentially organized talk. The
main data for research in CA is audio and
video recordings of naturally occurring
conversations, which are transcribed.

Conversion   A process of **word**

formation in which the **base form** of a word is converted to a different class *without* the addition of an **affix** (for this reason it is also known as *zero-derivation*). It is a common process in English because the base forms of many nouns and verbs are identical. The most common patterns of conversion are noun to verb, verb to noun, adjective to verb and adjective to noun. Noun to verb: *I like my **mushrooms** / The amount of freight on the tracks has **mushroomed***. Verb to noun: *They could have **called** me on Wednesday / Give me a **call** sometime*. Adjective to verb: *A mound of **dirty** crockery hid the draining board / I felt **dirtied** by the corruption of pimps*. Adjective to noun: *I failed because I was **dyslexic** / Only a small proportion of **dyslexics** receive adequate help*. See DERIV-ATION, NOMINALIZATION.

Co-operative principle A principle introduced by the English philosopher H.P. Grice (1975) which proposes that communication is essentially a co-operative activity and that people partici-pate in a conversation (or, indeed, any other act of communication) with the implicit assumption that those involved are co-operating in trying to keep the conversation going. This co-operation is arrived at because speakers generally adhere to a maximally efficient way of communicating which is captured in four 'maxims'. 1) The maxim of *quantity*: do not give too much or too little informa-tion. 2) The maxim of *quality*: do not lie or mislead. 3) The maxim of *relevance*: do not be irrelevant. 4) The maxim of *manner*: do not be unclear, disorderly, ambiguous or obscure. Grice claims that in a conversation, participants generally assume that the 'co-operative principle' is being followed, and if an utterance on the surface appears to be 'flouting' (violating) any of these maxims, participants will try

to discover the 'implicit' meaning of the utterance. For example, if A asks 'Are you going to the cinema tonight?' and B replies 'It's Tuesday', A will assume that B is co-operating and that, despite initial appearances, the response has some rele-vance, inferring perhaps that B knows that A knows that B always goes to yoga on a Tuesday, so he cannot go to the cinema tonight. It should be stressed, of course, that Grice does not claim that all conversations actually *are* co-operative; speakers often do 'flout' the maxims, either accidentally or deliberately, by lying, being irrelevant, saying too much, and so on. See POLITENESS, PRAGMATICS, PRESUPPOSITION.

Coordinating conjunction A type of conjunction used to link coordinate struc-tures. The main coordinating conjunc-tions (sometimes called 'coordinators') are *and, or* and *but*. Addition is signalled by *and*, alternativity by *or* (or in negative constructions *nor*), and contrast by *but*. Coordinating conjunctions can link phrases (*He was big **and** tough; He wanted to be a painter **or** a writer*), clauses (*Georgina is a chef **and** Rachel is a hair-dresser*), and sentences (*They plead, cajole, offer bribes. **But** it's too late*). See COHESION.

Coordination The linking together of **word**s, **phrase**s and **clause**s with the **coordinating conjunction**s *and, but* and *or*. The units linked in this way are of equal grammatical status (compare **subordination**). See PARATAXIS AND HYPOTAXIS.

Copula deletion In some varieties of English, the **copular** verb *be*, which links the **subject** with the **complement** (*He **is** sick*), can be deleted (*He sick•*). This feature is common in **African American Vernacular English** (AAVE) and **creole**s, and is sometimes known as *zero*-copula.

Copular verb   A verb which links the **subject** with its **complement**. Copular verbs have three main functions. They express an ongoing state (*He **is** mad;*• *The question **seemed** strange;*± *Tension **remains** high*±); a result (*Life **became** easier; Everyone **ends up** much happier; His cheeks **grew** puffy*); a sensory perception (*He **feels** that he is cured now; They don't **look** overworked; Her voice **sounded** mechanical*). The most frequently occurring copular verb is *be*, and it is sometimes referred to as *the copula*. Other verbs with a copula function include *appear, keep, stay, smell, taste, get, go, grow, prove, come, turn, turn out, end up*. See COPULA DELETION.

Cornish   See CELTIC LANGUAGES.

Corpus-based grammar   A **descriptive grammar** which bases its account of morphology and syntax on how people actually use language. Evidence for usage is gleaned from corpora: large, electronically stored repositories of spoken and written language. The most well-known corpus-based grammar of English is the *Longman Grammar of Spoken and Written English* (1999).

Corpus linguistics   The study of linguistic phenomena through the analysis of *corpora*. A *corpus* (from the Latin for 'body') is a large collection of electronically stored texts, which are analysed using specially developed software. Corpora vary according to the type of text which they contain. Some consist entirely of spoken language in the form of transcripts (e.g. *The Michigan Corpus of Academic Spoken English*); others contain only written texts (e.g. *The Brown Corpus*). Some corpora are **synchronic**, consisting of texts produced in approximately the same time-period (e.g. *The Corpus of Spoken, Professional American-*

English); others are **diachronic**, containing texts from different historical periods (e.g. *The Helsinki Corpus of English Texts*). 'General corpora' are made up of a wide variety of text types (e.g. *The British National Corpus*), whereas specialist corpora focus on particular **genre**s or **register**s (e.g. *The Air Traffic Control Corpus*). Many corpora are annotated. For example, in the British National Corpus words are 'tagged' to provide information about which **word class** they belong to; speakers are categorized according to their geographical location, gender and social class, and written texts are categorized according to the social domain with which they are associated (e.g. business, education). Most corpora are finite; others, however, are open-ended – these are known as 'monitor' corpora because they are continuosly being added to and can therefore be used to keep track of language change (the *Bank of English* is one such corpus).

Because corpora provide thousands of examples of how words and structures are actually used by speakers and writers, corpus linguistics has been used widely in the compilation of dictionaries and grammars, and also in the study of language variation and change. Additional applications include language teaching, translation, **stylistics** and **discourse analysis**. See also COLLIGATION, COLLOCATION, CONCORDANCE, CORPUS-BASED GRAMMAR, LEXICAL BUNDLE, LEXICO-GRAMMAR, SEMANTIC PROSODY, SURVEY OF ENGLISH USAGE.

Co-text   See CONTEXT.

Count noun   See NOUN.

Couplet   Two lines of verse which usually **rhyme**: *Humpty-Dumpty sat on a wall / Humpty-Dumpty had a great fall.*

Covert prestige   A term used in

Labovian sociolinguistics to label the kind of **prestige** associated with non-standard features of English. For example, some speakers identify with vernacular and non-standard forms because they can be used to show **solidarity** with other members of the same social group, and convey desirable qualities such as friendliness and loyalty. The prestige associated with these forms is 'covert' because it is 'hidden' and less publicly acknowledged than the **overt prestige** of the standard. See LANGUAGE CHANGE.

Creole   A language which develops in a context of **language contact**. Creoles arise when a **pidgin** (which is developed as a temporary means of communication between speakers of different languages) becomes a native language of a community. This usually happens when the pidgin is learned by children, and becomes their main language. In this process, the pidgin develops structurally and stylistically. Linguists have been struck by the similarities between widely separated creoles. These include such features as SVO word order, pre-verbal **negation**, lack of a formal **passive voice**, questions with the same form as statements, and **copula deletion**. Some linguists argue that such similarities are evidence of an innate language faculty or 'bioprogram' – that in conditions of impoverished linguistic input, children will nevertheless develop a fully fledged syntax based on 'universal grammar'.

Sociolinguists categorize creoles according to where they are spoken and the **lexifier language** (the language which provides the creole with most of its vocabulary): this leads to labels such as *Jamaican English Creole, Haitian French Creole*. The most well-studied creoles are those based on European languages such as English, French, Dutch and Portuguese. They are spoken mainly in the **Caribbean** and coastal **West Africa** and are therefore sometimes known as Atlantic creoles. See AFRICAN AMERICAN VERNACULAR ENGLISH, CARIBBEAN, CONTACT VARIETY, CREOLE CONTINUUM, JAMAICAN CREOLE, KRIOL, PATOIS.

Creole continuum   A term used in creole linguistics to describe the range of varieties that exist between the prestigious **acrolect** (the variety of a creole closest to the standard language) and the stigmatized **basilect** (the variety of a creole furthest from the standard language). Between the acrolect and the basilect are the 'intermediate' forms which can be described as **mesolect**al. Most speakers of a creole will have access to a span of the continuum, shifting between styles according to contextual factors. See CREOLE, DECREOLIZATION.

Critical discourse analysis   See CRITICAL LINGUISTICS, DISCOURSE ANALYSIS.

Critical linguistics   When the term 'critical' is applied to any approach in the social sciences, it means that the description and explanation of social phenomena it provides is combined with critique, and that this critique has an overt political aim: to identify injustice, discrimination and abuses of power. This 'unmasking' is seen as a first step towards the eventual creation of a just, rational society. There have been several influential critical approaches to language. The most well-known of these are: Critical Linguistics (CL), which emerged in the late 1970s, mainly in the UK and Australia; and Critical Discourse Analysis (CDA), its intellectual successor. Central concerns of researchers working in the critical field include the dialectal relationship between language and the social; the construction and maintenance of power relations through language; the role played by language in structuring human experience and world-view; language and forms of political, social, economic and environmental change. Key figures in critical linguistics include Roger Fowler, Teun A. van Dijk and Norman Fairclough. See also AGENCY, GRAMMATICAL METAPHOR, INCLUSIVE AND EXCLUSIVE *WE*, INFORMALIZATION.

Crossing   A term associated with the work of the English sociolinguist Ben Rampton (1995) which is used to describe the act of speaking a dialect which is not 'naturally' one's own. Rampton discovered this happening amongst school-children in a multi-racial community in south-east England, where adolescents from one ethnic group would regularly and systematically adopt aspects of the speech of those from another group. People engage in crossing for a variety of reasons. They might do it to mock; or out of admiration; they might do it to show social solidarity or to mark social distance. In contemporary **Anglophone** societies, one of the most widely remarked upon instances of crossing occurs when white adolescents, particularly males, affiliate with aspects of Black culture (especially the musical genre known as hip hop). See BRITISH BLACK ENGLISH, CODE-SWITCHING, COVERT PRESTIGE, STYLE SHIFTING.

Cultural difference approach   A term to describe an approach towards language and **gender** which regards women's language not as 'deficient' in comparison to men's (see **deficit approach**) but as culturally different. People who maintain this position argue that the segregation of males and females into different speech communities during the years of child-hood and adolescence (for example, in same-sex peer groups at school) has far-reaching effects on their language acquisition and development. Such differences are maintained into adulthood, resulting in the contrasting communicative preferences and styles of men and women. In recent years, the cultural difference approach has become particularly associated with the work of the American sociolinguist Deborah Tannen who, in a series of popular titles such as *You Just Don't Understand: Women and Men in Conversation* (1990), attempts to explain cross-sex communication 'problems' as a product of cultural difference: men are culturally conditioned to 'compete' in conversation; women are conditioned to 'co-operate'. The cultural difference approach has been criticized by some scholars who are concerned that it has little to say about the way men and women's conversational styles are influenced by asymmetries of political and economic power. See also DOMINANCE APPROACH.

D

Dane A term which is sometimes used interchangeably with **Viking** in discussions of the history of English. However, since not all Vikings were from Denmark (the traditional homeland of the Danes), the two terms are not equivalent. Although most of the Scandinavian people who went to the north and east of England between the eighth and eleventh centuries were indeed from Denmark, settlements were also established by Norwegians (particularly in north-west England) and Swedes (who arrived in small numbers towards the end of the period). See DANELAW, NORSE.

Danelaw, the The part of England which was ruled by the **Viking**s from 878 AD. It consisted of territory north and west of a line running roughly from London to Chester. The Danelaw came about as the result of a truce between King Alfred and the invaders, and it lasted until the **West Saxon** kings reconquered the north and east in the tenth century. By then, however, there had been massive Scandinavian settlement of the territory, with profound effects on English language and culture. The most visible legacy is in the distribution of place names with Scandinavian elements, most of which occur within the old Danelaw, such as *by* 'village, homestead' (*Grimsby*, *Whitby*); *thorp* 'secondary settlement, outlying farmstead' (*Towthorpe*, *Gawthorpe*). The Danelaw has also influenced dialect boundaries. For example, the differences in the **Middle English** period between East Anglian/East Midland dialects on the one hand, and West Midland dialects on the other are in part due to the fact that the East Midlands were in the Danelaw and the West Midlands were not. See also NORTHERN ENGLAND.

Dangling participle A potentially ambiguous use of a fronted ***ing*-clause** or ***ed*-clause** functioning as an **adverbial**. For example, in the following (invented) sentence there is a clear relationship between the subordinate *ing*-clause and the subject of the main clause: ***Boarding the bus with several heavy suitcases***, *Patricia gave a sigh of relief*. However, the relationship is ambiguous in the following sentence: ***Boarding the bus with several heavy suitcases***, *the driver sold Patricia a ticket*. Here, the reader is not at first sure whether it was the driver getting on with the cases or Patricia (although the context points towards the second interpretation). Here are some more potentially ambiguous examples (invented): ***Faced with a huge pile of exam scripts***, *the students pitied their tutor;* ***Galloping rapidly over the savannah***, *the tourists observed the zebras*. In most cases where participles are left dangling like this, a reader would have to willfully read against the author's intentions to be genuinely confused.

Declarative A term used in the classification of independent clauses according to **mood**. Declarative clauses are typically statements: *Elephants are very intelligent*. They generally have a subject–verb structure. See CLAUSE, INDICATIVE, INTERROGATIVE, SENTENCE, SPEECH ACT THEORY, SPEECH AND WRITING.

Decorative English A term sometimes used to describe the kind of English used on clothing, packaging, stationery, and so on, for ornamental purposes in contexts where English is not used widely for everyday communication. It is particularly associated with Japan, although it is widespread in East Asia: *A recent girl is easy and likes cute shape!!* (Japanese T-shirt); *We'll advise you about your 'stickiness' about your daily life* (Japanese pencil case).

Decreolization The loss of **creole** features in a creole language as a result of contact with its **lexifier language**. During decreolization, speakers who once used **basilect**al varieties of a creole gradually shift to more prestigious **acrolect**al varieties, which are closer to the standard variety of the lexifier language. See AFRICAN AMERICAN VERNACULAR ENGLISH, JAMAICAN CREOLE.

Deficit approach A term to describe an out-dated approach towards language and **gender** which regards women's language as a 'deficient' version of men's language: limited in vocabulary, simpler in structure, lacking in substance. This position can be dated at least as far back as the 1920s, when the linguist Otto Jespersen devoted a chapter to 'The Woman' (but not to 'The Man') in his famous book *Language: Its Nature, Development and Origin* (1922). Most of Jespersen's 'evidence' for his claims about women's language comes from art and literature, rather than systematic scientific study.

The origins of the modern study of language and gender are often traced to the work of Robin Lakoff. Her paper 'Language and woman's place' (1973), though ground-breaking and widely influential, also adopted a deficit approach, comparing women's speech unfavourably with men's and listing typical features which she regarded as less powerful than the male 'norm', such as

tag questions, questioning intonation in statements and 'weak' directives (requests rather than commands). Compare CULTURAL DIFFERENCE APPROACH, DOMINANCE APPROACH.

Definite and indefinite When a speaker uses a *definite* expression, he or she has a specific, particular concept or entity in mind: *She sat down at the table.* Definite reference can be made with the definite article (as in the previous example), possessives (*I've a stack of paperwork on my table*; *Jessica's parents were a miniature smooth-haired Dachshund and a whippet*), demonstrative determiners (*This kitten was a stray*), personal pronouns (*Give it to him*), proper nouns (*Mozambique, Augusto Sandino*). When a speaker uses an *indefinite* expression, he or she does not usually have a specific referent in mind: *Can I have a brochure please?*± Indefinite reference can be made with the indefinite **article** (as in the previous example), quantifiers (*I'll have some brochures going around*), **indefinite pronoun**s (*Someone's been playing jokes*), bare plural noun phrases (*Symbols are useful on charts, for example*), mass nouns (*I've got to get milk*). See GIVEN AND NEW, REFERENCE.

Deixis Reference by means of an expression whose meaning depends entirely on the **context** of situation. In other words, the referent of a deictic item will change according to the location in time and/or space of the participants in a speech event, and their role (whether they are speaker or addressee). There are five main kinds of deixis: place, time, person, social and discourse. 1) Place deixis encodes location in space relative to the participants in the speech event. It is manifest mainly in place (locative) **adverb**s such as *here* and *there*; **demonstrative**s such as *this, that, these* and *those*;

prepositional phrases such as *in front of*, *in back of*, *to the left*, *to the right*. The changing referents of deictic items relating to place can be seen in the following (invented) exchange: A: *Put that one there please.* B: *This one here?* A: *Yes.* We infer from this that both the object and the point in space A and B are talking about are the same, yet different words are used to refer to them. From A's (more distant) location it is ***that one there***; from B's (closer) position it is ***this one here***. Some verbs are also deictic (e.g. *come* and *go*, *bring* and *take*). Place deixis can also be extended into psychological 'space'. For example, 'distal' terms are sometimes used to express emotional distance, as in *I don't like **that** clown.* 2) Time deixis encodes location in time relative to the time of the speech event. It is usually marked by temporal adverbs such as *now* and *then* and *yesterday*, *today* and *tomorrow*: *She's leaving **now**; He left **yesterday***. **Tense** also has a deictic function. 3) Person deixis concerns the speaker (marked by **first person** pronouns e.g. *I*, *me*, *we*, *us*), the addressee (marked by **second person** pronouns e.g. *you*), and others who are not directly addressed but have a role in the discourse (marked by the **third person** pronouns e.g. *he*, *him*, *she*, *her*, *they*, *them*). In the course of a conversation, a single participant ('X') might be referred to as *I* (if X is the speaker), *you* (if X is the addressee) and *she* (if X is a participant being spoken about). 4) Social deixis is marked by terms which are sensitive to the social status of participants in discourse. For example, different terms of **address** might be used to refer to the same person: *Ricky, Rick, Richard, Mr Flood, My Right Honourable Friend.* Which term is chosen depends on both the context and the relationship between addresser and addressee: *Ricky* at home, *My Right Honourable Friend* in the British House of Commons. 5) Discourse deixis is deictic reference to part of an ongoing discourse which is temporally removed (in speech) or temporally and spatially removed (in writing) from the current 'position' of the addressee/reader. For example, when a speaker is about to tell a joke and prefaces it with an utterance such as 'you'll like this one', *this* is pointing 'forward' to an upcoming stretch of discourse and is therefore deictic. When the joke-teller's audience responds with 'That was terrible', *that* points 'back' to an earlier stretch of discourse. In written texts, 'signposts' which help to orientate the reader are deictic: ***In the next chapter** we shall extend this theological enquiry;*• *As explained **in the previous section**, any reasonable complete system is bound to be sometimes infinitary.* See COHESION, SPEECH AND WRITING.

Demonstrative   *This, that, these* and *those* can function as demonstrative **determiner**s, providing information about the **number** of the referent of a noun phrase (whether it is singular or plural), and the distance of the referent from the speaker: ***This** little map here shows a very small area of West Ham; Oh look at **that** bird; **These** chips are hot; They're in **those** trees up there; Look at **those** boxes.* They also function as demonstrative **pronoun**s, standing in for a noun phrase: *Anyone want **these**? Can I have **those**?* As these examples show, demonstratives are often used in the marking of **deixis**. In many **non-standard** varieties of English, *them* is used as a demonstrative determiner: *Shut **them** big doors.*

Denotation   A word or expression's direct, literal or referential meaning. The denotational meaning of a word is usually captured in its **dictionary** definition, and is often the first answer people give to the question 'What does X mean?' Compare CONNOTATION.

Dental A term used in the description of **consonants** referring to a place of **articulation** (the point in the **vocal tract** where a constriction of the **airstream** occurs). Dental consonants are produced when the tip of the tongue comes into contact with or comes near to the back of the upper teeth. Most varieties of English have the following dental consonant phonemes: /θ/ and /ð/. These consonants are sometimes described as 'interdental'. See FRICATIVE.

Dependent clause See SUBORDINATE CLAUSE.

Derivation The most productive method of **word formation** in English. It consists of 'deriving' new words by adding **affix**es to pre-existing **base forms**. Nouns, verbs, adjectives and adverbs can be created in this way. Derived nouns are formed by prefixation and suffixation. Prefixation usually maintains the word class of the base form (in other words, a new noun is derived from an existing noun): *biochemistry, disbelief, hypertext, monosyllable, subgroup, underclass*. Suffixation, on the other hand, usually turns a verb or adjective base into a noun: *assistant, boredom, childhood, socialism, happiness, kinship*. Derived verbs are also formed by prefixation and suffixation. As with nouns, prefixation maintains the word class of the derived form (deriving a new verb from an existing verb): *rebuild, disobey, overturn, undo, misspell, outperform*. Suffixation usually turns a noun or an adjective into a new verb: *computerize, moisten, activate, codify*. Adjectives are derived by adding a prefix to another adjective, as in *unhappy, inhospitable, non-standard*, or by adding a suffix to a noun or verb, as in *national, persistent,*

combative, woeful, talentless. Adverbs can also be derived by suffixation, usually by adding *-ly* to an adjective: *tightly, persistently*.

Descriptive grammar Descriptive grammarians are interested in providing a principled and systematic account of the grammar of a particular language. Their findings are compiled in reference grammars, such as *The Cambridge Grammar of the English Language* (2002) and *The Longman Grammar of Spoken and Written English* (1999). They are *not* concerned with devising rules about which grammatical structures can and cannot be used (compare **prescriptivism**). See GRAMMAR.

Determiner A grammatical word which signals the reference of a noun. Definiteness or indefiniteness can be indicated through the use of the definite or indefinite **article**: *We hired a truck and a driver; The driver wound down his window*. Possession can be signalled through **possessive determiner**s: *My husband and my children are Welsh; I saw you shaking your head; This is her first meeting.◊* Things can be pointed out in space and time using **demonstrative** determiners: *Look at this cat; Take that cat to your room; These cats look well cared for; They do smell, don't they – those dogs?* Quantifying determiners can be used to express quantity: *Both parents will be affected. Each ship carried seventy-five men.* Numerals can also act as determiners: *She had spent ninety minutes at the meeting.* Sometimes a noun phrase contains more than one determiner: *all the other teams.●* See DEFINITE AND INDEFINITE.

Deviation A term used in **stylistics** to describe a departure from some kind of linguistic norm. This might involve deviation from a norm which is external to the text, such as the 'rules' of a particular language: the 'usual' ways in which **morphemes** combine to produce words, words slot into syntactic structures to produce sentences, sentences are arranged to produce texts. Or the deviation might be from a norm established by the text itself – a sudden and striking change of metrical patterning in a poem, for example, or an unexpected choice of word (see example 1 below).

Deviation can take place at any 'level' of language. For example, at the **semantic** level, it occurs when meaning relations appear illogical or paradoxical. This is perhaps most obvious in the use of **metaphor**, which involves describing one entity or concept in terms of another, producing a fresh awareness of the thing being described (example 2). Deviation at the level of lexis might involve the coining of entirely new words (example 3), or taking a word which is usually a member of one word class, and using it as if it belonged to another (example 4).

Syntax and morphology can also be manipulated. For example, 'typical' word order (within phrases, and also at the level of clause constituents and clauses themselves) can be altered to produce particular effects (example 5). Morphological deviation involves adding affixes to words which they would not usually have, or indeed removing their 'usual' affixes; it can also involve breaking words up into their constituent morphemes, or running several words together so they appear as one long word (examples 6, 7).

Phonological and graphological deviation are often closely linked. This is because authors sometimes use respelling to provide information about how something sounds when spoken aloud, often to capture (and emphasize) regional or social variation (example 8).

The kinds of deviation considered so far occur at sentence level; but texts can also deviate at the level 'above' the sentence. For example, texts sometimes display 'genre' deviation: words, grammatical features, and so on, which we typically associate with one type of speech and/or writing are deployed in another genre. Such **intertextuality** is often related to the kinds of deviation outlined above. For example, in example 9 there is lexical deviation in the use of 'fake ink blot', 'joy buzzer' and 'great fun'. These phrases draw attention to themselves, largely because they clash with the surrounding text, the style of which resembles that of a serious historical study.

Although it is largely a linguistic phenomenon, deviation has the important psychological effect of making prominent, or **foregrounding**, certain aspects of a text.

Examples of deviation

1   *King of the perennial holly-groves, the riven sandstone: overlord of the M5* (Geoffrey Hill 1971).

2   *There is no frigate like a book / To take us lands away, / Nor any coursers like a page / Of prancing poetry* (Emily Dickinson 1924).

3   *When he awakened under the wire, he did not feel as though he had just cranched. Even though it was the second cranching within the week, he felt fit* (Cordwainer Smith 1950).

4   *But me no buts* (Henry Fielding 1730).

5   *What dire Offence from am'rous Causes springs* (Alexander Pope 1714).

6   *a billion brains may coax undeath / from fancied fact and spaceful time* (e.e. cummings 1960).

7   *coldtonguecoldhamcoldbeefpickled gherkinssaladfrenchrollscresssandwiche spottedmeatgingerbeerlemonadesoda water* (Kenneth Grahame 1908).

8 *'Man . . . dis life no easy'* (Zadie Smith 2000).

9 *There is no evidence of a fake ink blot appearing anywhere in the West before the year 1921, although Napoleon was known to have had great fun with the joy buzzer, a device concealed in the palm of the hand causing an electric- like vibration upon contact* (Woody Allen 1992).

Diachronic variation Linguistic vari- ation in time. Compare SYNCHRONIC VARIATION.

Dialect A particular **variety** of a **lan- guage** which is regionally or socially dis- tinctive. Languages are made up of a number of dialects, which tend to flourish when speakers are divided by geo- graphical barriers (such as mountain ranges, rivers and oceans) and social bar- riers (such as class, race or religion). Although the term is perhaps more fre- quently associated with geographical variation, as in phrases such as 'Yorkshire dialect', 'regional dialect', 'rural dialect', 'urban dialect', it is also used to cover other types of variation, such as 'social dialect', 'occupational dialect', 'class dialect', 'standard dialect'. Linguists generally distinguish between dialect (which refers to the distinctive **phonology**, **lexis** and **grammar** of a variety), and **accent** (which refers *only* to the pronunci- ation features of a particular variety).

From a purely linguistic perspective, all dialects are equal: no argument can be made for the *intrinsic* superiority of one over another. However, from a social perspective, there are major inequalities between different dialects. Some dialects are high status and routinely used in a wide range of public domains; other dialects lack **prestige** and are limited to a narrower range of private contexts. The most prestigious dialect of English is

Standard English. Its pre-eminence is so taken for granted that when people refer to the 'English language' it is often Standard English they mean. Take the following sentence from a US college's careers website: *'I ain't got no'* is *not proper English*. 'English' is being used here when it would in fact be more accurate to use the term *Standard* English, since *ain't got no* is a common construction in a wide variety of English dialects around the world, and from a linguistic perspective this utterance is therefore quite 'proper'. Although lin- guists use 'dialect' neutrally to describe a particular type of variation in language, the word in general use sometimes has negative connotations: dialect speakers are often wrongly regarded as elderly, rural, working class, poorly educated, and so on. For this reason, some linguists avoid it, preferring the more neutral term **variety**. See DIALECT LEVELLING, DIALECTOLOGY, EYE-DIALECT, SOCIOLECT, VARIETY.

Dialect atlas A book of maps showing the geographical distribution of linguistic features. Phonological, lexical and gram- matical features can be mapped, often using **isoglosses**. English is served by a number of important atlases, including *The Linguistic Atlas of England* (1978) (see **Survey of English Dialects**) and *The Atlas of North American English* (2005). Most atlases are **synchronic**, but some map historical varieties e.g. *A Linguistic Atlas of Late Mediaeval English* (1986). See DIALECTOLOGY.

Dialect levelling This is what fre- quently happens to language varieties when geographical and social mobility brings speakers of different dialects into close contact. As people come together in new contexts, they *accommodate* to one another's speech in order to ensure

mutual intelligibility and social acceptance (see ACCOMMODATION). This involves
the reduction of differences between
the varieties. A result of this may be the
formation of a new dialect. See KOINÉ,
LANGUAGE CONTACT.

Dialectology The academic discipline
concerned with the study of dialect and
dialects. Traditionally, dialectology
focused on regional variation. The
nineteenth-century dialectologists, such
as Georg Wenker in Germany and Jules
Gilliéron in France, used data collected
during fieldwork to find out about the
geographical distribution of linguistic
forms (phonological, lexical and grammatical), and these findings were presented in the form of **dialect atlas**es,
dictionaries and grammars. During the
second half of the twentieth century the
remit of dialectology, under the influence
of developments in **sociolinguistics**,
broadened to include other factors
involved in linguistic variation, including
age, gender and social class; and there
has also been growing interest in urban
dialects. See FOLKLINGUISTICS, ISOGLOSS,
PERCEPTUAL DIALECTOLOGY, SURVEY OF
ENGLISH DIALECTS, SURVEY OF REGIONAL
ENGLISH.

Dialogue [1] Speech or writing in
which two (or more) people are engaged
in the interaction. [2] The representation
of **conversation** in written texts (especially
novels and plays). See SPEECH
PRESENTATION.

Dictionary A book or electronic text
containing the words of a language or
languages. Monolingual dictionaries
contain **headword**s and their definitions,
alphabetically arranged. Bilingual dictionaries have headwords in one language
and their meanings in another language.
Dictionary definitions are usually accom-

panied by information about a word's
pronunciation and the part of speech it
belongs to. Larger dictionaries give a
word's history (**etymology**), its status
(e.g. *slang*, *formal*, *vulgar*), its variety (e.g.
Scots), variant spellings and so on. The
most comprehensive dictionaries (such as
the **Oxford English Dictionary**) contain
citations: extracts from texts illustrating
how the words are actually used. Other
kinds of dictionaries exist, including
etymological dictionaries, pronunciation
dictionaries, dialect dictionaries, technical
dictionaries (in fields such as law, medi-
cine, business, and so on) and dictionaries
for language learners. Computer technology now means that many dictionaries
are available electronically, making
searching and information retrieval
extremely rapid.

Diffusion The spread of features from
one dialect to another as a result of
sustained contact between people from
different speech communities. For this to
happen, individuals in one community
have to 'acquire' a particular feature from
individuals in another community as a
result of convergent **accommodation**, and
the accommodated form must become
a permanent feature of their speech.
Diffusion can be geographical or social.
Geographical diffusion is the spread of
features between regions; social diffusion
is the spread of features between social
classes.

Diglossia See POLYGLOSSIA.

Digraph In an alphabetic writing system, the representation of a single sound
using two letters, such as <sh> for /ʃ/ and
<ea> for /iː/. See ALPHABET, ENGLISH
SPELLING.

Diminutive The result of a process of
word formation in which a word is altered
in some way to convey 'smallness',

'youth', 'familiarity', 'affection' (in English usually by the addition of a **suffix**, such as *-ie*, *-ette*, *-let*, *-kin*, *-een*, and/or by **clipping**): *dog→doggy*, *Angela→Ang*. See GENDER, ICONICITY.

Diphthong A vowel forming a single syllable which changes quality as it is produced. For example, the vowel in *boy* is [ɔɪ] in most accents of English. It begins with a back mid-vowel, with something like the quality of the vowel in RP *pawn* and ends with a front, close, lax vowel, resembling the vowel in *pin*. The number of diphthongs in English varies according to variety. For example, RP speakers have between six and eight, depending on whether they are 'conservative' in their speech style or more 'mainstream' (see RECEIVED PRONUNCIATION). Other varieties have fewer diphthongs. Scottish English, for example, has three: [aɪ] as in *price*; [aʊ] as in *mouth*; [ɔɪ] as in *boy*. Diphthongs should be regarded as a phenomenon of the *sound* system of English. In spelling, diphthongs are often represented by a single letter (as in <try>). Conversely, monophthongs are sometimes represented by two letters (as in <meet>). A combination of three vowel sounds in one syllable, as in some RP pronunciations of *fire* and *hour*, is a *triphthong*. See MONOPHTHONG, VOWEL.

Directive An utterance in which the speaker tries to get someone else to act in a particular way, by ordering, commanding, requiring, advising, recommending, and so on. Directives take many different forms, as illustrated in the following examples: *Put that back in my pencil case; Don't just sit there; You should make some pies out of it; Gloves and goggles must be worn; We recommend you book early.* Although **imperative**s (as in the first two examples) are 'prototypical' directives,

not all directives use this **mood**. See SPEECH ACT THEORY.

Direct object (DO) Noun phrases (and sometimes **complement clause**s) which usually refer to a **patient**, the entity affected by the process or action of a **transitive verb**: *She hugged her sister.* In such typical instances, the subject is the 'doer' of the action and the direct object is acted on by the subject. However, some transitive verbs take less 'typical' direct objects, with a range of **semantic roles**. For example, certain verbs can cause an **experiencer** direct object (which is usually an animate entity capable of cognition) to achieve a new psychological state, as in the following examples: *Nicaraguan coffee annoys Reagan; The word 'object' amuses me.* Another important semantic role played by direct objects is as a **locative**, with verbs such as *climb, swim, sail*: *Columbus sailed the ocean blue.* Finally, 'created' or 'resultant' direct objects are brought into existence by a transitive verb: *His son built a stone wall.* See BENEFICIARY, OBJECT, SEMANTIC ROLE, VALENCY PATTERN.

Direct speech A type of **speech presentation** (often, but not exclusively associated with **narrative** fiction) in which the words of a speaker are quoted directly (usually in quotation marks) and are accompanied by a reporting clause containing a **communication verb** (such as *say* or *reply*). Sometimes these verbs – either alone or combined with other references to **paralinguistic** features such as intonation, pitch and stress – convey the style of an utterance: *'You're only an hour late,' she said with staccato coolness.* The equivalent of 'stage directions' can also be used to provide information about the non-verbal accompaniments of speech (gesture, facial expression, movement, and so on). The thoughts of characters can also be reported directly, by changing the verb in the reporting clause: *'My God,' she **thought**.*

A variant of direct speech, known as 'free' direct speech, involves removing overt signs of authorial intervention, such as the reporting clause and quotation marks. Sometimes, a passage may consist mainly of free direct speech, so that it resembles drama dialogue. Compare INDIRECT SPEECH.

In everyday conversation, speakers often quote the words of others. As the following examples show, in such circumstances speakers sometimes use different strategies from those outlined above:

1 *Ryan and Gran argue continuously, and **he was going** erm, and **he went**, 'Gran,' and **Gran went**, 'Yeah,' and **he went**, 'Do you know what you are?' and **Gran went** 'No,' and **he went**, 'Well, I can't remember what it's called.'*

2 ***She's all**, 'Why would I do that?' and **I'm like** 'Cuz you're crazy!'*†

In example 1, the verb *go* and in example 2, *be + all* and *be + like* are being used to introduce speech.

Direct speech is usually indicated in writing with either single or double inverted commas, known as *speech marks* (see PUNCTUATION).

Discourse   A term which is used widely, with different but related meanings, in many academic disciplines, including linguistics, critical theory, literary studies, sociology, anthropology, philosophy, social psychology, and so on. In language study, *discourse* has three main meanings. 1) Any naturally occurring stretch of speech or writing bigger than a sentence. 2) Language taken together with all aspects of **context**, including context of situation, and the wider social, cultural and political contexts. 3) The language

associated with a particular social domain or practice. This meaning is captured in phrases such as *the discourse of New Labour*, *the discourse of advertising*, *the discourse of cyberculture*. See DISCOURSE ANALYSIS.

Discourse analysis   The study of **discourse**. Because *discourse* itself is a complex and various phenomenon, the remit of discourse analysis is extremely broad. Approaches in discourse analysis include interactional **sociolinguistics**, **pragmatics**, **conversation analysis**, **critical discourse analysis**. See also ADDRESSEE, ANAPHORA, DEIXIS, DISCOURSE MARKER, FUNCTION [2], GENRE, GRAMMAR, GRAMMATICAL COHESION, INFORMALIZATION, LANGUAGE LEVEL, LEXICAL COHESION, REGISTER, SPEECH AND WRITING, TEXT.

Discourse marker   Short words or phrases which perform a wide variety of functions related mainly to structuring and organizing spoken language. Common discourse markers include *oh, well, now, right, like, I mean, you know, you see, okay, anyway*. Different linguists have different ideas about which items belong in this category, but a 'prototypical' discourse marker (such as *well, right* or *now*) will occur frequently at the start of utterances, and be only loosely attached to the clause (which means it can be removed without making the sentence ungrammatical). Discourse markers can be used to lessen the force of an utterance (***Well** I'm quite angry*); indicate that a decision has been made (***Right** I'm going to bed now*); 'launch' an utterance (***Now** I know that's easier said than done*); highlight the main point of an utterance (*I was **like** getting beaten and stuff*•); elaborate meaning (*I had the hardest time imagining that your brother could be involved in something like that. **I mean**, he seems like such a fine young man*•); change orientation towards information (*A. Jim dies as well. B. Does he? A. Yeah. B. Oh I heard that Jim and Helen were going to be the only two original cast left in* Neighbours); enhance the salience of information (*I thought before the tournament, but, you know, gradually I've just been, you know, saying OK, one match at a time•*).

As the examples above show, discourse markers have a range of functions. Single discourse markers can also be multifunctional. For example, *well* can qualify a previous utterance (*I've got a pain in my, well not a pain, it's just an ache*); lessen the force of an utterance (*Well put it somewhere a bit safer*); signal topic change (*Well on the issue of what's happening in the Health Authority here*); signal delay or deliberation (*Well I'm not sure*). Frequently, sequences of two or more discourse markers occur: *A. Because they're late they'll have to miss the video. B. Oh. Right well okay*.

Dislocation A disruption of 'typical' word order which occurs when an element in the clause is 'detached' and placed at the beginning ('left' dislocation) or the end ('right' dislocation) of the clause. Both kinds of dislocation are more common in speech than in writing.

The following sentence illustrates left dislocation (the non-dislocated version is in brackets): *My mum, she was in hospital•* ('My mum was in hospital'). Left dislocation involves detaching and **fronting** a full noun phrase (*My mum*), then following it by a clause starting with a pronoun which refers back to the initial noun phrase. Left dislocation announces the status of the fronted element as **theme**. In some grammars, the fronted noun phrase is known as a 'preface'.

The following sentence illustrates right dislocation (the non-dislocated version is in brackets): *He's brilliant, that guy•* ('That guy's brilliant'). Right dislocation involves detaching a full noun phrase (*That guy*) and moving it to the end of the clause; its 'place' being taken at the start of the clause by a pronoun (*he*). Right dislocation helps speakers to reinforce or clarify what they are saying.

Ditransitive A verb which is capable of taking both a **direct** and an **indirect** object: *He **gave** Michael an injection; She **loaned** them money; He **sent** John Peel a demo tape*. This **valency pattern** requires a transference of possession of the indirect object (*an injection, money, a demo tape*) to the direct object (*Michael, them, John Peel*). Compare MONOTRANSITIVE.

Divergence See ACCOMMODATION.

Dominance approach A term used to describe an approach to language and **gender** which argues that differences between male and female conversational styles, preferences and competencies should be placed in the context of the asymmetries of power between men and women in society. At its most general, the dominance approach maintains that men use language to construct and reinforce their dominance, while women enact their subordination through language. Compare CULTURAL DIFFERENCE APPROACH, DEFICIT APPROACH.

Doublet Two separate words in a language which either share the same historical source (in which case they are a *lexical* doublet), or have related meanings (in which case they are a *semantic* doublet). Such pairings originate in a situation of **language contact**. For example, English has a number of lexical doublets made up of **Old English** and Old **Norse** constituents: *shirt/skirt; shuttle/ skittle; ditch/dike; church/kirk*. Contact with **French** has also provided English with many semantic doublets: *house/ mansion*; *guts/entrails*; *sorrow/distress*; *wish/desire*. 'Triplets' (made up of English, French and **Latin** components) are also quite common: *ask/question/ interrogate*; *holy/sacred/consecrated*.

Downtoner A word or phrase which softens or diminishes meaning (for this reason they are sometimes known as 'diminishers'): *Moby became **mildly** excited*. See ADVERB, ADVERBIAL, HEDGE, INTENSIFIER.

Dummy-*it* Non-referential *it* functioning as **subject**: ***It's** raining; **It's** cold in here*. In such cases, the pronoun *it* does not refer to any entity (either in the physical context or in the preceding discourse). It is simply a 'dummy' pronoun, used to fill the subject position. See CLEFTING, EXTRAPOSITION, SUBJECT.

Dynamic verb Verbs with 'dynamic' meaning are those which can be used to describe events, actions and activities with an identifiable start and finish: *build, swim, walk, laugh*. They can occur with the progressive and the imperative: *His dogs **are running** well today; She **was cooking** a goose; And **stop** that noise!*• Dynamic verbs are often contrasted with **stative verbs**. See ASPECT.

Dysphemism A 'harsh' or 'offensive' word or expression which is used as a substitute for a more polite or inoffensive term: *Put a new bog roll in the shithouse.*† See EUPHEMISM, TABOO.

E

Early Modern English (EModE) The period in the history of the English language which follows **Middle English** and precedes **Later Modern English**. Boundaries between such periods are generally fuzzy (and somewhat arbitrary), but most scholars put the start of early modern English at c.1450 and the end at c.1700. The following texts, produced in 1484, 1567 and 1704, give a sense of the written English across the period.

Here foloweth the copye of a lettre whyche maistre Alayn Charetier wrote to hys brother / whyche desired to come dwelle in Court / in whyche he rerseth many / myseryes & wretchydnesses therin vsed / For taduyse hym not to entre in to it / leste he after repente / like as hier after folowe / and late translated out of frensshe in to englysshe / whyche Copye was delyuerid to me by a noble and vertuous Erle / At whos Instance & requeste I haue reduced it in to Englyssh.

(William Caxton 1484)

The Realme declares the nature of the people. So that some Countrey bringeth more honor with it, then an other doth. To be a French man, descending there of a noble house, is more honor then to be an Irish man: To bee an English man borne, is much more honor then to bee a Scot, because that by these men, worthie Prowesses haue beene done, and greater affaires by them attempted, then haue beene done by any other.

(Thomas Wilson 1567)

The *English* Nation has always carried a figure equal to their Neighbours, as to all sorts of Learning, and in some very much superior, and tho' without all those Encouragements, have not yet sunk their Character that way. But we cannot say that Learning is grown to such a height that it needs a Check, that it wants a Tyrant of the Press to govern it: Knowledge is much Improv'd, 'tis confess'd, but the World is not so over-run with Letters, that it should be Tax'd as a Vice, and Laws made to Suppress the little Degrees of it, that are attain'd to.

(Daniel Defoe 1704)

The spelling becomes recognizably more 'modern' over time. For example, compare Caxton's <frensshe>, <englysshe> and <Englyssh> with Wilson's <French> and <English>, and Defoe's <English> (notice also the internal variability in Caxton's text – *English* is spelled in two different ways). The **punctuation** is closer to current norms in the later texts. Caxton's unfamiliar *virgules* (the slanted lines) are replaced with commas, full stops and colons. An exception to this is the *increasing* use of capitalization: Defoe capitalizes much more frequently than Wilson, and Wilson more frequently than Caxton, who writes 'English' with and without an initial capital letter. The capitalization of any words other than proper nouns in the main body of a text is no longer practised. These texts also provide information about changing grammar. For example, Caxton uses the *-eth* ending for present tense verbs in the third-person (*foloweth, rerseth*); Wilson uses both the -*eth* and -*s* endings (*bringeth, declares*); and Defoe uses only the -*s* ending (*wants*).

The most significant events in this history of the language during this period were the **Great Vowel Shift**; the development of **Standard English** (which includes the **elaboration** of the language associated with the massive influx of Greek- and Latin-derived vocabulary during the sixteenth and seventeenth centuries); the proliferation of translations from the classical languages into English; the production of vernacular **Bible** translations; the growth of literature in English (e.g. Shakespeare); the spread of English beyond the British Isles to colonies in the **Caribbean** and the Americas; the arrival of English in Asia and Africa (as a consequence of trade expansion). Many of these developments originate in two great social and cultural movements that overlap with this period: the **Renaissance** and the **Reformation**.

East African English   A term used to describe the varieties of English spoken mainly in the East African countries of Kenya, Uganda and Tanzania. The establishment of British colonial power in the region in the late nineteenth century added the English language to an already complex cultural and linguistic situation. A number of African languages from the Bantu and Nilosaharan language families are spoken in the region, and Kiswahili is a common lingua franca. English is spoken mainly as a **second language**.

Some distinctive pronunciation features of East African English (some of which are present as a result of **transfer** from indigenous African languages) include the merger of /r/ and /l/ (so that *lorry* is pronounced something like /loli/ or /rori/); /tʃ/ and /ʃ/ may be merged with /s/ (so that *chip* and *ship* sound a bit like *sip*); /dʒ/, /ʒ/ and /z/ are often not distinguished, so that *jam* is pronounced /ʒam/ or /zam/. Most speakers of East African English have a five vowel system, which means that many words which are distinct in other varieties of English are **homophone**s: *hit/heat* are both pronounced [hit] and *hat/hurt/hut* are all pronounced [hat]. Patterns of word stress are also different. For example, speakers will often put stress on suffixes such as -*ate* and -*ize* in words such as *duplicate* and *rationalize*.

There seem to be no grammatical features which occur *uniquely* in East African English. Nevertheless, some features have been noted as occurring particularly frequently. These include the use of *be* + -*ing* in stative contexts (*Almost everybody is having a car*±); absence of third person singular -*s* ending (*He say that the list is only six*±); invariant tag questions (*So she threw them away, isn't it?*±). Many lexical items, however, are unique to the region. These include loanwords from African languages (some of which have entered the vocabulary of general English): *daktari, askari, baobab, bwana, safari, babu*. Extensions in the sense of general English words used to reflect aspects of local culture also occur. Examples include *mother* (which refers to the biological mother together with her sisters and co-wives) and *father* (which is often used to refer to any elderly man). See Schmied (2004).

East Anglia   The area of eastern England consisting of the modern-day counties of Norfolk and Suffolk together with parts of Cambridgeshire, Essex and Hertfordshire. There is considerable linguistic variation in the region, but it is possible to make some general statements about the phonology and grammar of East Anglian English. In particular, I focus on those features which are salient in distinguishing it from other varieties spoken in England. Material is drawn mainly from Trudgill (2004a, 2004b), and Hughes, Trudgill and Watt (2005).

The accent of East Anglia is generally southern, in the sense that /ʌ/ and /ʊ/ are both present and /a/ and /ɑ:/ are distributed as they are in **Received Pronunciation**. Features often cited as being 'typical' of an East Anglian accent include the following. 1) The vowel of certain words in the TRAP **lexical set** is realized as [ɛ], e.g. *catch, have, has, had*. 2) The vowel in the LOT lexical set is sometimes realized as [ɑ], so that *cot* sounds similar to an American pronunciation of *caught*. 3) Some words which belong to the GOAT lexical set in RP belong to the GOOSE set in East Anglian varieties, so that the vowel in *moan, soul* and *nose* is [u:] (making *moan* and *moon* **homophone**s). 4) For some speakers, the lexical sets NEAR and SQUARE have merged to [ɛ:], so that the following pairs are homophones: *beer/bear*; *fear/fair*; *cheer/chair*. 5) /j/ is lost before /u:/ after all consonants. This means that the following words rhyme with 'moo': *new, pew, few, view, cue, hew*. 6) East Anglian English has a distinctive rhythm, as a result of stressed syllables being longer than they are in RP and unstressed syllables being reduced to schwa [ə] or lost entirely.

The most well-known morphological characteristic of East Anglian English is the absence of the *-s* ending in third-person present-tense verb forms: *My daughter always laugh about that*. Other features include *wus* (pronounced /wʊz/) for all persons as a past-tense form of *be* (with *weren't* being used for all persons in the negative); /ɛnt/ or /ɪnt/ corresponding to the more widespread *ain't*.

Ebonics   A term sometimes used as a synonym for **African American Vernacular English**.

Ed-clause   *Ed*-clauses are **non-finite subordinate** clauses which function mainly as **adverbials** in the main clause: *Consumed with guilt, she looked questioningly at Bridget*. They can also function as noun postmodifiers: '*Women in Christian Publishing*' *is the theme chosen for the seminars*. Compare *ING*-CLAUSE and *TO*-CLAUSE.

Ed-participle   A **non-finite** form of the verb which, in regular verbs, is constructed from the base form plus *-ed*: *floated, walked, trapped*. Irregular verbs have a variety of *ed*-participle forms: *beaten, broken, put, rung, brought* and so on. It is used alongside **auxiliary** verb *have* to form the perfect **aspect**: *Roy Orbison has eaten pie and mash here*. *Ed*-participles also head one of the three main types of **non-finite clause**, the **ed-clause**. *Ed*-participle forms can also be used as **adjectives**: *A sparrow with a broken wing*.

In some non-standard varieties of English, there are special past participle forms: *I've also saw some in there for Danny; I've went to that doctor; She's gave it her best shot; I've took illegal drugs*.

Elaboration   A stage in the process of **standardization** in which the linguistic resources of a language are developed to fulfil any new functions which it is required to serve (mainly in writing or formal speech). In the history of English, the most important period of elaboration was the sixteenth and seventeenth centuries, when it is estimated that over 30,000 new words entered the language. Many of these terms were introduced to make English suitable for scholarly discourse, as English replaced **Latin** as the language of learning. The vocabularies of science, mathematics, law and the humanities were expanded, either by borrowing directly from Latin (and to a lesser extent Greek), or by combining elements from the classical languages to form new words. This list gives an idea of the sort of words introduced: *atmosphere, catastrophe, caveat, delirium, encyclopedia, epilepsy, idiosyncrasy, lexicon, momentum, monosyllable, pancreas, pneumonia, skeleton, species, temperature, vacuum.* Compare INKHORN TERM.

Elision   The omission of vowels, consonants or syllables in connected speech. Common processes of elision include the omission of unstressed vowels, as in [pliːs] for *police*; the simplification of consonant clusters, as in [kaɪn] for *kind*; the omission of whole syllables, as in [ˈlaɪbɹɪː] for *library.* See APHESIS, CLIPPING, CONSONANT CLUSTER, CONTRACTION, SPEECH AND WRITING, STRESS, SYNCOPE.

Ellipsis   (Greek: 'defect, omission') The omission of part of the structure of a sentence (words, phrases or clauses). There are two main types of ellipsis: textual and situational.

In textual ellipsis, ellipted elements (in square brackets in the following examples) can be recovered from the surrounding text: *They bobbed, and* [they] *wallowed, and* [they] *were gripped by something and* [they were] *thrust up; Most of us do this because we have to* [do this]. In these examples, the complete structure occurs before the ellipsis (see ANAPHORA [2]). Occasionally, the complete structure occurs after the ellipsis: *People who can* [start] *must start over Christmas.* Textual ellipsis occurs for reasons of economy and style, and is an important cohesive device (see GRAMMATICAL COHESION).

In situational ellipsis, ellipted elements can be recovered from the wider **context** in which an utterance is embedded.

For example, in *Saw James over by the accordion earlier* the subject can be supplied by the context: *I saw James, we saw James, she saw James,* and so on.

End-weight, principle of   The tendency for lengthier and more complex clause elements to appear at the end of a clause, in order to ease the burden of processing. For example, the **extraposition** of **complement clause**s, as in the following example, follows the principle of end-weight: *It is a pity* **that Diana and Charles did not think more of these poor little boys before they encouraged their friends to take part in this public squabble•** (extraposed *that*-clause). Placing the 'heavy' subject (in bold) before the verb would make the sentence much more difficult to process (compare **That Diana and Charles did not think more of these poor little boys before they encouraged their friends to take part in this public squabble** *is a pity*). A further example of the principle of end-weight concerns what happens when a sentence contains a **ditransitive** verb (a **valency** pattern which selects a direct and an indirect object). A speaker can use a noun phrase to express the indirect object (*She gave* **the runner-up** *the money†*) or replace the indirect object with a prepositional phrase beginning with *to* or *for* (*She gave the money* **to the runner-up**). This choice sometimes depends on the 'heaviness' of the clause elements. When the indirect object is lengthy, it tends to be expressed as a prepositional phrase: *The Jury awarded its prize* **to the Italian film 'Il Ladro di Bambini' (The Child Snatcher) by Gianni Amelio** (compare the much more unlikely *The Jury awarded* **the Italian film 'Il Ladro di Bambini' (The Child Snatcher) by Gianni Amelio** *its prize*).

English as a foreign language (EFL)   English in contexts where it has no special status, such as Brazil, Turkey, France, Indonesia, and so on. Compare ENGLISH AS A SECOND LANGUAGE. See WORLD ENGLISH.

English as a second language (ESL) English in contexts where it is not a widely used **first language**, but does have special status (e.g. India, Malawi, Bangladesh). Compare ENGLISH AS A FIRST LANGUAGE. See WORLD ENGLISH.

English language A member of the West **Germanic** branch of the **Indo-European** language family, which includes Dutch, German and Frisian. English has its origins in England about 1500 years ago, and until the sixteenth century was not spoken much beyond the British Isles. But now it has the widest geographical distribution of any language in history, due mainly to the political and economic influence of Britain in the seventeenth, eighteenth and nineteenth centuries, and the USA in the twentieth and twenty-first (see WORLD ENGLISH). It is estimated that between 320 and 380 million people have English as a **first language**, and between 300 and 500 million have it as a **second language**. Between 500 and 1000 million people are believed to speak it as a foreign language (Crystal 2003: 107).

English spelling The English spelling system uses an **alphabet**, consisting of 26 letters. These letters are used to create graphemes, units consisting of one or more letters which are used to represent the **phonemes** of the language. For example, the phoneme /p/ is represented by the grapheme <p>; and the phoneme /ʃ/ is represented by the grapheme <sh>. Graphemes made up of two letters (like <sh>, <ch>, <oa>, and so on) are called **digraphs**. English has never been a 'phonetic' language, since most varieties of the language have many more phonemes than there are letters in the alphabet.

The English spelling system is often characterized as being chaotic and inconsistent. However, it is much more regular than many people imagine. Crystal (2003: 272) suggests that 80 per cent of English words are spelled according to regular patterns, and only 3 per cent are so irregular that they have to be learned by heart. Nevertheless, because so many of the most common words in English are 'irregular' in their spellings, the system appears to be more chaotic than it actually is.

What follows is a brief overview of the factors which have led to some of the most well-known irregularities (see Crystal 2003: 274–275). 1) The origin of the problem was the attempt by Christian missionaries to represent the 35 or so phonemes of **Old English** with the 23 letters of their Latin **alphabet**. Some letters (e.g. <c> and <g>) were used to represent more than one sound, and some sounds were represented by a combination of letters (e.g. <sc> = /ʃ/). The mismatch between the number of phonemes in English and the number of letters in the alphabet means that this practice has continued throughout the history of English spelling. 2) The Norman Conquest resulted in the introduction of spelling conventions derived from French. Old English <cw> for /kw/ was replaced with <qu>; <h> was replaced by <gh> in words like *might*; <c> was replaced by <ch> in *church* and <u> by <ou> in *house*. <c> was used before <e> and <i> to spell /s/, such as *city, cell*. Because the letter <u> was written very similarly to present-day *v, i, n* and *m* it was sometimes replaced with an <o>, resulting in spellings such as <come>, <love>, <one>, <son>. See the entry on **French** for further examples. 3) The **Great Vowel Shift** had an important effect on spelling. Many spellings are based on the way a word was pronounced before the shift occurred. For example, *name* has an <a> and <e> in the spelling because prior to the shift it was pronounced /nɑːmə/. The tendency towards preservation of earlier forms can also be seen in words such as *night* and *right*, which displays evidence of Middle English /x/ in the spelling <gh>, even though it is no longer pronounced. In some words with <gh> in the spelling, /x/ became /f/, such as *laugh, cough, rough*. 4) During the Early Modern English period, scholars began to take an interest in English spelling, and some words which were thought to derive from Latin, French or Greek were re-spelled according to their presumed etymologies. In this way, *doute* became *doubt*, and *Temes* became *Thames*. Sometimes, a respelling has led to a change in pronunciation, including the <d> in *advance* and the <c> in *verdict*.

The effect of **standardization** on written English is very clear at the level of spelling. There are some minor differences between national varieties of English (e.g. American English *color* and British English *colour*), but on the whole spelling is uniform. Spelling can, of course, be manipulated for a variety of artistic and creative purposes. This can vary in seriousness from the attempt to capture vernacular speech in literature, to 'stunt' spellings of the kind found in shop and product names (*Kwik Save*). Respellings can also be used to make a political point: *Amerika, George Bu$h*.

Epenthesis   The introduction of additional sounds into words. The motivation for this is often ease of articulation. For example, consonant clusters are sometimes simplified by the introduction of vowels (e.g. *film* is pronounced ['fɪləm] by some speakers). See SOUND CHANGE.

Eponym   A word derived from the name of a real or fictitious person: *boycott, cardigan, sandwich*. A sub-category of eponyms consists of brand names which have lost most of their original associations with a particular company or product and have become general terms: *hoover, thermos, walkman, selotape* (UK), *scotch tape* (USA).

Ergative verb   A **lexical verb** which is capable of being used in such a way that the action it denotes affects the subject of the clause. Intransitive verbs are intrinsically ergative: *Emily* **sneezed**; *Charles had* **slept** *well*. Many transitive verbs can be used non-ergatively and ergatively. Compare *Maggie* **closed** *the door* with *The door* **closed**. In the first sentence, *Maggie* is the subject of the sentence, *closed* is a transitive verb, and *the door* is the direct object of the verb; in the second sentence the subject is *the door* and the verb *close* is being used intransitively, so that the action denoted by the verb affects the subject. See OCCURRENCE VERB, VOICE [1].

Estuary English   A controversial term used by some people to describe a variant of **Received Pronunciation** containing features which are deemed to have their origins in the working-class speech of London and the south-east (such as glottal stops and /l/ vocalization). The problem with the term 'Estuary English' is that there is little reliable linguistic evidence to support the existence and separate identity of such a variety (see Trudgill 2001). 'Estuary English' has become a convenient shorthand for media pundits wishing to comment on the fact that some RP speakers import features into their speech which are associated with traditionally stigmatized accents (such as **Cockney**), in an attempt to sound less aloof and snobbish. It tends to disguise the fact that there are other variants of RP which are influenced by local accents (e.g. 'northern' RP and 'midlands' RP).

Ethnicity A **social variable** used in sociolinguistics. An ethnic group is made up of people with a number of shared traits by which they may be distinguished from other groups, including race, culture, religion, history and language. See ETHNOLECT.

Ethnolect A language variety associated with a particular ethnic group. See AFRICAN AMERICAN VERNACULAR ENGLISH, CAJUN ENGLISH, CROSSING, LATINO ENGLISH, PATOIS.

Etymology The study of word origins and histories. See DICTIONARY, FOLK ETYMOLOGY.

Euphemism A 'mild' or 'inoffensive' word or expression which is used as a substitute for a harsher, more direct term. For example, some speakers of English feel uncomfortable talking about death, and will sometimes replace the verb *die* with the euphemism *pass away*. See DYSPHEMISM, TABOO.

Exclamation An utterance expressing a strong emotion. In speech the meaning is often augmented by prosodic features such as volume or intonation; in writing an exclamation is usually signalled with an exclamation mark. Some linguists reserve the term for a clause (which is often verbless) beginning with *what* or *how* followed by a noun phrase (*What an idiot!*) or an adjective phrase (*How lovely!*). See SENTENCE, SPEECH ACT THEORY, SPEECH AND WRITING.

Exclamation mark The **punctuation** mark <!>, which is sometimes placed at the end of an emphatic statement or

command: *I think that's absolutely crazy!*† *Sit down and shut up!*†

Existence verb Verbs which either report a state of existence (e.g. *exist, stay, live*) or the existence of a relationship between entities (e.g. *contain, include, involve, represent*). Some of the most common **copular verb**s are existence/relationship verbs (e.g. *be, seem* and *appear*).

Existential process See TRANSITIVITY.

Existential *there* A construction in which *there* is used as a 'dummy' subject at the start of an utterance, usually in order to state the existence of something (in a clause with positive **polarity**), or the non-existence of something (in a clause with negative polarity): *There's a phone in the kitchen;* *There's no alternative.* Because the structure is often used to state that something exists in a particular place, it is often accompanied by an **adverbial** (e.g. *in the kitchen*). However, existential *there* should not be confused with *there* as an adverbial.

Typically, in existential *there* constructions the verb phrase contains the **copular verb** *be* and the noun phrase following the verb is usually indefinite. The verb phrase may be simple, as in the examples above, or complex: *There would have been a hearth in the middle.* Occasionally, verbs other than copula *be* occur with existential *there*, particularly intransitive verbs of **existence** and **occurrence**. As these examples show, this usage often has a formal or literary flavour: *There exist many different types of cohesive tie; There arose a mighty famine in that land.*

The noun phrase is the logical subject of the clause; it is what the utterance is about. Consequently, it is this noun phrase which agrees with the verb in terms of number, even though *there* is the grammatical subject: *There's **a** cat stuck under the gate; There **are** cats all over the place*. However, a common **non-standard** usage is existential *there* with a singular form of the verb *be* when the logical subject is plural: *There's **loads** of jobs; There **was** hundreds of them*.

Expanding circle See WORLD ENGLISH.

Experiencer The **semantic role** of the being or entity experiencing, accepting or undergoing something. Experiencers also receive sensory impressions. In the clause they can be **subject** or **direct object**: *Adolf Hitler admired Wagner's bigotry;* • *Dawn astonished **doctors***.

Expository prose A term sometimes used to describe writing which is factual, informative and explanatory. Many **genre**s of writing fall into this category, including essays, academic papers, newspaper feature articles, reports, and so on. See SPEECH AND WRITING.

Extraposition A term most commonly used to describe the process of moving a linguistic clausal subject from its 'typical' position in the clause, to a less typical position (usually after the other obligatory clause elements). In the following example, the subject (in bold) has been extraposed: *It is likely **that you will also become interested in film making***. The subject of the sentence is the *that*-clause, but placing this element first (in order to maintain the canonical SVC order of

clause **element**s in a declarative) results in a sentence which is quite difficult to process: ***That you will also become interested in film making is likely***. Therefore, the lengthy clausal subject is placed after the complement (*likely*) and the empty subject position is filled with **dummy-*it*** (see PRINCIPLE OF).

Extraposed subjects are not always *that*-clauses; they can also be *to*-clauses (*It was necessary **to control noise***), ing-clauses (***It's** difficult **keeping a body-count***), and *wh*-clauses (***It's** pretty obvious **how this works***). Dummy-*it* can also be used to anticipate a following object clause: *My grandmother finds **it** difficult **to show her true feelings***. This happens when the sentence includes an object complement (in this case, *difficult*). See END-WEIGHT, FRONTING, INVERSION, WORD ORDER.

Eye-dialect A written representation of dialect which gives no information about pronunciation, but is designed to convey something about the level of education or literacy of the speaker. For example, in *The Mill on the Floss* (1860), George Eliot respells *pretty* as <pritty> when the word is spoken by a gypsy: '*That's pritty; come, then, Why, what a nice little lady you are, to be sure*'. However, when the heroine Maggie Tulliver utters the word, Eliot uses standard orthography: *O, Tom, isn't it pretty?* Both <pritty> and <pretty> are graphemic representations of the same sequence of sounds: /prɪti/.

F

Field See REGISTER.

Figurative language See FIGURE OF SPEECH.

Figure of speech A verbal expression which achieves a particular effect by deviating from what is generally accepted to be 'usual' or 'normal' language use (see DEVIATION). Figures of speech are generally divided into two main categories: 'schemes' and 'tropes'. Schemes involve the manipulation of sounds, words, phrases and clauses, particularly through **parallelism**, **repetition** and **inversion**: *When the going gets tough, the tough get going.* Tropes are figures which involve 'deviations' from literal meaning (such as **metaphor** and **simile**): *She's like a bit of laundry that's been left out to dry too long, till it gets bleached and stiff.* Tropes are sometimes described as 'figurative language': language which is being used in a non-literal way to produce a particular effect. See RHETORIC.

Filled pause While speaking, people often pause. Sometimes, these pauses are 'filled' with sounds which can be represented in writing in various ways: *It was* **erm er er**, *was it an old English sheepdog?;* **Um** *she looked for* **um** *she looked at* **er** *a survey of two thousand odd adults.* Filled pauses mark hesitation, at the same time as indicating that the speaker has not yet finished what they are saying. See SPEECH AND WRITING.

Finite Said of a verb phrase or clause where the verb is marked for tense or there is a modal verb. The following sentences illustrate the three finite verb forms. 1) Base form: *I stop the car* (first and second person present tense; third person plural present tense); *Stop it!* (imperative). 2) Third person singular present tense: *She stops about an hour.* 3) Past tense: *They stopped for a bite and a drink* (not to be confused with the past participle, which is **non-finite**). Finite verb phrases can consist of a finite verb only (as in the previous examples) or of a finite verb plus **non-finite** forms: *My heart has* (finite) *stopped* (non-finite); *Women and children were* (finite) *stopping* (non-finite) *traffic.* See FINITE CLAUSE, NON-FINITE, TENSE.

Finite clause A clause which is marked for tense or contains a modal verb (compare NON-FINITE CLAUSE). If a finite verb phrase consists only of a lexical verb, then the lexical verb will be marked for tense; if the verb phrase is complex, then the first **auxiliary verb** carries the tense marker. The following sentences contain finite verb phrases: *She loves Henry; I dismantled that car; It might have been embarrassing.* See CLAUSE, FINITE, TENSE.

First language (L1) A language learned first during childhood. It is sometimes known as a 'native language' or 'mother tongue' (although these terms are perhaps slightly misleading, since 'native' has connotations of ethnicity, and not all children acquire a first language from their mothers). See NATIVE SPEAKER, SECOND LANGUAGE.

First person See PERSON.

Flap A **consonant** produced when one **articulator** (usually the tip of the tongue) makes very brief contact with another articulator, as in the **American English**

pronunciation of the middle consonant in words such as *batter* and *better*. A flap is sometimes known as a *tap*.

Floor A term used in **conversation analysis** to describe the right to speak in interaction. When a person is speaking, they are said to be 'holding the floor'. Turn-taking involves the floor 'passing' between participants in the conversation (see TURN).

Folk etymology Non-linguists' beliefs about word origins and histories. For example, the *ten gallon hat* is widely assumed to have acquired its name because of its voluminous capacity. However, 'gallon' derives from Spanish 'galón' ('braid'), which traditionally decorated this item of headwear. Many folk etymologies wrongly locate word origins in **acronyms**. For example, *news* is *not* an acronym derived from the initials of the words 'north', 'east', 'west' and 'south', nor is *golf* an acronym of 'gentlemen only; ladies forbidden'.

The term is also used to describe the way in which an unfamiliar word is re-analysed by speakers so that it comes to resemble a more familiar one. For example, the **idiom** *damp squib* is used to describe a disappointing event or occasion. *Squib* is a rather old-fashioned word for a small firework. In this extract from an online soccer magazine, the author re-analyses *squib* as *squid*, which is more semantically transparent: *It was a damp **squid** as the players didn't get stuck in enough.* Other attested examples of this kind of process include *stark raven mad* and *star-craving mad* for 'stark raving mad' and *free range* for 'free reign' in *give free range to*.

Folklinguistics Beliefs about and attitudes towards language which are widely held by 'ordinary' people (as opposed to professional linguists). There are folk-linguistic beliefs associated with many aspects of English. For example, some words have folk etymologies which are widely held but linguistically unsubstantiated (see FOLK ETYMOLOGY).

Other folklinguistic beliefs have accrued around social, regional and gender variation. For example, research on attitudes to **accent** in the UK has shown that certain qualities are routinely associated with the speakers of particular accents. People with an RP accent rate highly for intelligence, confidence and ambition, but regional accents often score more highly than RP for friendliness, sense of humour, and so on. Many people are regularly stigmatized because of the sound of their voice, particular those with working-class Birmingham, Liverpool and London accents. The repercussions of such beliefs go beyond crude stereo-typing (the 'thick' **Brummie**, the 'thieving' **Scouser**, the 'flash' **Cockney**): studies have shown that people with regional accents are more likely to be considered guilty of a crime than people who do not have a marked accent (Dixon, Mahoney and Cocks 2002). Language and **gender** is also an area where folklinguistic beliefs are common. Women, it is said, talk more than men, swear less, are more polite, more emotional, 'gossip' more, and so on.

Folklinguistic beliefs form the basis of much sociolinguistic research. **Perceptual dialectology**, for example, is centrally concerned with the attitudes of 'ordinary' people towards linguistic variation.

Foregrounding A term associated with formalist approaches to **style** (see FORMALISM). In some texts (particularly literary ones), certain patterns of language draw attention to themselves, and are therefore more prominent. In other words, they become *foregrounded* in the mind of the reader or hearer. Foregrounding is the psychological effect of stylistic choices that either depart from the norms of everyday language (see DEVIATION), or which set up noticeable patterns of **repetition** and **parallelism**.

Form [1] The shape and structure of a linguistic element (as distinct from its meaning and/or **function**). For example, the sentence *My dad liked a drink*, has structure at a number of levels. It consists of 15 **phonemes** (m, ʌɪ, d, a, d, l, ʌɪ, k, t, ə, d, r, ɪ, n, k) five **syllable**s (my│dad│liked│a│drink), six **morpheme**s (my│dad│like│d│a│drink), five **word**s (my dad liked a drink), and three **phrase**s (my dad│liked│a drink). This is a purely formal description of the utterance. Much of the **metalinguistic** vocabulary used to talk about language is concerned with formal aspects; for example, word class labels (e.g. **noun**, **verb**) and associated labels for phrases (e.g. **noun phrase**, **verb phrase**).

[2] The different 'shapes' taken by a word are sometimes referred to as 'forms'. For example, the verb *eat* consists of the forms *eat, eats, ate, eating* and *eaten* (see LEXEME).

Formalism An approach in literary studies which is particularly associated with a group of linguists and critics active in Moscow and Prague between the two world wars. Leading figures in this group include Viktor Shklovsky, Boris Eichenbaum, Vladimir Propp, Yuri Tynianov and Roman Jakobson. The Russian Formalists (as they are sometimes known) advocated a 'scientific' approach to literature, which involved close attention to the language of texts, focusing in particular on the structure of **narrative**, and formal differences between literary and non-literary language. Their work is the foundation of modern **stylistics**.

See also DEVIATION, FOREGROUNDING, PARALLELISM, REPETITION.

Formality An aspect of social behaviour (including *linguistic* behaviour) which can be conceived of as a scale, ranging from 'very formal' to 'very informal'. At one end of this continuum there is a cluster of behaviours which might be described as organized, complex, rehearsed, based on precedent, public, codified; at the other they are 'disorganized', casual, simple, spontaneous, private, fluid (compare a formal, 'black-tie' dinner with an informal family barbecue). Language is one of the most important 'social behaviours', and language use can be placed on this continuum. Any 'level' of language may be implicated as a marker of formality (**lexis**, **grammar**, **phonology**, **graphology**, and so on). External 'triggering' factors of degree of formality in language include *field* (subject matter/type of activity), *tenor* (relationship between participants in situation, their roles and status) and *mode* (the medium of communication and degree of preparedness and feedback). See REGISTER.

From such a definition it is possible to make some assumptions about where particular kinds of language use might tend to occur on the notional formality continuum. A spontaneous conversation between 'equals' in a private setting is likely to contain more informal language than a job interview, with its power differentials and pre-arranged format; a love letter will probably be expressed in more informal terms than a letter from a solicitor. See INFORMALIZATION.

Fowler's Modern English Usage An influential guide to British English **usage**, first published in 1926. The first edition, which remained in print for many years, was written by Henry Fowler, who began his career as a school teacher and then became a freelance journalist and lexicographer, contributing to the *Concise Oxford Dictionary* and the *Shorter **Oxford English Dictionary***. Subsequent editions bear his name, but they have been substantially revised and rewritten. The latest edition (*The New Fowler's Modern English Usage*, 1996) is largely the work of Robert Burchfield, who has brought it up to date and expanded its coverage.

Free direct speech   See DIRECT SPEECH.

Free indirect speech   See INDIRECT SPEECH.

Free morpheme   See MORPHEME.

French   The influence of French on the English language has been powerful and sustained. After the **Norman** Conquest, which began with the arrival of William the Conqueror in 1066, French became the language of the court, the church, education and the law, maintaining this position for some 200 years. As in modern-day situations of **language contact**, **bilingualism** must have been reasonably common. However, most ordinary native English people did not speak French.

The decline of French and the re-emergence of English probably began in the middle of the thirteenth century. From this time onwards there is a rapid increase in the production of French-teaching handbooks and wordlists, and documents from the time tell of children of the nobility who had to learn French as a second language. In 1325, William of Nassington writes that English is the language that 'men vse mast' ('men use most'): 'Boþe lered ('learned') and lewed ('unread'), olde and ӡonge, / Alle understonden English tonge'. The outbreak of the Hundred Years War between England and France in 1387 accelerated the decline

of the French language. By the end of the fourteenth century, the situation is such that, according to the clergyman John of Trevisa, writing in 1387, 'childern of gramerscole conneþ no more Frensch þan can here lift heele' ('grammar school children know no more French than their left heel') (see Crystal 2004: 131).

The impact of French on English is most obvious in vocabulary (its influence on morphology, syntax and phonology are, by comparison, trivial). There are two sources of French **loanword**s during the **Middle English** period. The first (and smaller) group of borrowings came from Norman French; later, in the thirteenth and fourteenth centuries, there was a larger influx from Central French, the dialect associated with the newly powerful Angevin dynasty. This double source often led to the same word being borrowed twice, first in its Norman form, then in its Central French form. Such **doublet**s include *catch/chase; cattle/chattel; warden/guardian; warranty/guarantee; wage/gauge; wile/guile*. The association of French with prestige and high status is reflected in the kinds of words borrowed into English. For example, the original English words for livestock were retained, such as *ox, sheep, swine, deer, calf*; but terms for their meat were introduced from French, such as *beef, mutton, pork, venison, veal*. This is because meat was a luxury food which only the French-speaking upper-classes ate regularly. This kind of prestige borrowing is also evident in other **semantic field**s, as the following examples (in modern spelling) illustrate. Government and administration: *government, parliament, people, state, crown*. Law: *court, judge, jury, crime, punish, justice, prison*. Titles: *duke, sovereign, viscount, baron, prince*. The church: *abbey, clergy, parish, prayer, religion, saviour*. Warfare: *battle, assault, siege,* *fortress, tower.* Arts and fashion: *costume, dress, fashion, art, beauty, colour, music, paint, poem, romance.* Such borrowings were at first probably pronounced in the French manner, but they were soon adapted to fit the English phonological system.

Even after the period of intense contact outlined above, French continued to be a source of new words in English. The seventeenth and eighteenth centuries, for example, see the introduction of words such as *connoisseur, envelope, premier, nuance, etiquette, elite, critique, fracas, rouge, foible, souvenir, caprice.* Arrivals in the nineteenth and twentieth centuries include *foyer, lingerie, suede, restaurant, fuselage, chauffeur, garage.*

French has had a significant influence on **English spelling**. Norman scribes often spelled English as they heard it, in the process introducing new spelling conventions derived from French. The following is a selection of changes that occurred in the written representation of certain vowels and consonants. 1) <ou> for [uː] (compare OE *hūs* and ME *hous*). 2) <ie> for [eː] (compare OE *feld* and ME *field*). 3) <u> for [y] (compare OE *bysig* and ME *busy*). 4) <o> for [u] (compare OE *sunu* and ME *son*). 5) In Old English the voiceless alveolar fricative [ʃ] was spelled <sc>, but in the Middle English period several alternatives were introduced, such as <ss>, <sch>, <sh>. 6) The consonant cluster pronounced [kw] was spelled <cw> in Old English, but by c.1300 this had been almost entirely replaced by the French-influenced <qu> (compare OE *cwen* with modern English *queen*). 7) Old English used <f> to represent [f] and [v]; Norman scribes introduced <u> or <v> for [v]. 8) The **digraph** <th> gradually replaced <þ> and <ð>.

Fricative   A **consonant** produced by a

manner of **articulation** in which the **articulator**s come close enough together to impede the **airstream**, producing audible friction. There are nine fricative consonant phonemes in most accents of English. 1) A voiceless labio-dental fricative /f/ as in *fly*. 2) A voiced labio-dental fricative /v/ as in *vow*. 3) A voiceless dental fricative /θ/ as in *thin*. 4) A voiced dental fricative /ð/ as in *these*. 5) A voiceless alveolar fricative /s/ as in *see*. 6) A voiced alveolar fricative /z/ as in *zoo*. 7) A voiceless post-alveolar fricative /ʃ/ as in *sheep*. 8) A voiced post-alveolar fricative /ʒ/ as in *leisure*. 9) A voiceless glottal fricative /h/ as in *hello*. A peripheral member of this category is the velar fricative /x/, which some speakers use in a number of specifically Scottish English words, such as *loch*, and in a small number of loanwords from German, such as *echt*. In some dialects the labial-velar fricative /ʍ/ is used in words like *whale*.

Frisian   A **Germanic** language spoken by about 700,000 people along the coast and islands of the Netherlands and north-west Germany. Of the languages indigenous to the European mainland, it is regarded as the closest to English.

Fronting   The movement of clausal material which normally occurs after the verb to initial position (also known as 'preposing'). Several types of fronting are possible. 1) Fronted object: *This I perceive plainly; Why I didn't die I don't know.* 2) Fronted adverbial: *Far below was the cobbled courtyard; Sitting on my right was Graham Manley.* 3) Fronted subject complement: *Even better is the possibility of testing things out; Equally impressive are the finds exhibited in the museum.* 4) Fronted main verb: *But change they did, and quite radically.*

Fronting has a variety of functions in discourse, especially in the maintenance of **cohesion**. It can be used to organize the flow of information in a text, express contrast, and give emphasis to particular elements. In particular, fronting serves as a device to make non-subject elements the **theme** of a sentence. Fronting is also used systematically in regular **interrogative**s in Standard English, where the *wh*-word is fronted: *What is she making?* See DISLOCATION, INVERSION.

Front vowel   A **vowel** produced with the body of the tongue positioned towards the front of the **oral cavity**, as in the vowel /ɪ/ in an RP pronunciation of *kit*.

Full stop   A punctuation mark <.> used mainly to mark the end of sentences. It also occurs at the end of some **abbreviation**s and after the initials in a person's name. The full stop is also known as the *period*, *stop* or *point*.

Function   [1] At the grammatical level, the function of a linguistic element is its role in the **clause**. For example, a **noun phrase** can function as **subject**, **direct object**, **indirect object**, **subject complement**, **object complement** and **adverbial**. Compare FORM.

[2] At the discourse level, the term refers to the function(s) of an utterance. A particularly influential typology of language functions was developed by the linguist Roman Jakobson. 1) The *referential* function focuses on conveying information about the 'world' beyond the communicative event itself. 2) The *emotive* or *expressive* function focuses on the attitude of the speaker/writer towards what they are speaking about, which may be expressed through a particular choice of words, grammar, or tone of voice. 3) The *conative* function is concerned with aspects of language which are designed to affect or influence the hearer/reader in some way. This function may be expressed

through features such as requests and commands. 4) The *phatic* function is fulfilled by language which is concerned with initiating, sustaining or closing the channel of communication, such as 'well, here we are chatting away at last' or by ritualized formulas, such as 'lend me your ears'. 5) An utterance performs a *metalingual* function when it refers to the code and how the code works. For example, whenever interactants need to check up on their mutual comprehension of the code they are using, they focus on this function of language, asking questions such as 'Do you know what I mean?' or 'What do you mean by 'ritualized formulas'?' 6) Finally, language which focuses on the message for its own sake, emphasizing the linguistic qualities of words themselves rather than any other factors in the situation, fulfils the *poetic* function.

It should be stressed that all utterances perform at least one of these functions, but most are in fact multi-functional, performing two or more simultaneously. So for example, if a weather forecaster on TV says 'Hold onto your hats! It's a breezy one today', one of the functions of the utterance is referential, since the speaker is conveying information about the world; but if a viewer rams his hat more firmly on his head before going out, a conative function is present, because it is influencing his thoughts and behaviour in some way. Furthermore, if the weather forecaster delivers this statement with an elongated vowel in 'breezy' (i.e. 'breeezy'), the utterance performs an expressive function, since in English, exaggerated prosodic patterns like this can be used to convey emotion. Finally, a poetic function is present: the repetition of the /h/ initially in the stressed syllables is a prominent piece of phonetic patterning. (See Maybin and Pearce 2006.)

In **systemic functional linguistics**, the term is used to describe the over-arching 'metafunctions' of language. See METAFUNCTION.

Function word See GRAMMATICAL WORD.

Futhorc See RUNE.

G

Gaelic See CELTIC LANGUAGES.

Gaelic English A term occasionally used to describe a variety of **Scottish English** associated with the Highlands and Western Isles (for this reason it is also known as 'Highland English' or 'Hebridean English'). The feature which distinguishes Gaelic English from other varieties of English in Scotland is the substratal influence of the Gaelic language at the level of phonology and, to a certain extent, grammar. Since the seventeenth century, Gaelic speakers in this part of Scotland had been persecuted and discriminated against because they had largely remained faithful to the Catholic church after the Protestant **Reformation**. A feature of this prosecution was a vicious attack on the Gaelic language, which became associated in the minds of Protestant lowland Scots with rebellion and barbarity. The next two hundred years or so saw continuous attacks on the Gaelic culture and way of life, with a subsequent language shift from Gaelic into English.

Today, the most marked features of Gaelic English can be found in the speech of the 60,000 or so people who are bilingual in Gaelic and English (see McArthur 2002: 95). In terms of pronunciation, there are four particularly well-known features of Gaelic English. 1) The devoicing of certain consonants, particularly /dʒ/, /f/ and /p/, so that *jest* sounds like 'chest', *alive* sounds like 'a life', and *bang* sounds like 'pang'. 2) The strong aspiration of the voiceless plosives /p/, /t/ and /k/. 3) /l/ is commonly 'clear' in all positions (see ALLOPHONE). 4) Many speakers lengthen vowels which are short in general Scottish usage, so that for example *bad* is pronounced [baːd] and *boat* is [boːt].

Characteristic features of grammar include the following. 1) The formula *to be after doing (something)*, as in *I'm just after taking the bus* ('I've just taken the bus'). 2) A non-reflexive use of *-self*, as in *I'll tell himself you are here*. 3) Cleft sentences in which the **theme** is fronted: *Isn't it her that's the smart one?* 'Isn't she the smart one?' (see CLEFTING). These features are shared by some speakers of **Irish English**.

Gender [1] A **grammatical category** which displays contrasts such as 'masculine', 'feminine' and 'neuter'. Many languages have quite a developed system of gender. For example, in Romance languages such as Spanish, **French** and Italian, gender is 'grammatical'. This means entities without biological sex are categorized as 'masculine' or 'feminine': there is nothing particularly female about a Spanish table (*la mesa*); nor is an Italian violin essentially male (*il violino*). In modern English, gender manifests itself mainly in the pronoun system, where it is based on 'natural' criteria. This means that the pronouns *she*, *her* and *hers* are used only for biologically female entities, while *he*, *his* and *him* are used for male entities. Entities which are not biologically male or female are usually referred to with *it*, *its* (singular) and *they*, *their*, *them* (plural). *Usually* but not always. English speakers will occasionally use gendered pronouns for inanimate objects. For example, ships, cars and boats are routinely personified as female, resulting in utterances such as *She's a beauty; a forty-foot ketch built of mahogany on oak.* Although boats and cars are inanimate, they do possess at least some of the attributes of a living being, and it is perhaps understandable that if people develop a close personal relationship with these things, they might want to personify them.

[2] More generally, gender is a cultural category central to the processes of social classification and organization. Because gender is reflected in (and 'constructed' by) language, it is an important area of study in linguistics. See CULTURAL DIF-FERENCE APPROACH, DEFICIT APPROACH, DOMINANCE APPROACH, FOLKLINGUISTICS, GENDERLECT, GENERIC PRONOUN, LABOVIAN SOCIOLINGUISTICS, LINGUISTIC VARIABLE, SOCIAL VARIABLE.

Genderlect A language variety associated with **gender**. The term can be somewhat misleading, because it implies that there are some communities in which men and women speak very different varieties of a language. However, in English-speaking contexts, the differences between the language use of men and women are mainly quantitative. This means that, although on average one gender may use a particular lexical, grammatical or inter-active feature more (or less) frequently than the other, there are no features which are limited entirely to the speech of either men or women.

General American A term used by some linguists to describe those accents of **American English** which do not have marked southern and north-eastern characteristics (Trudgill and Hannah 2002). The notional territory in which General American is used is vast, stretching from California in the west to Pennsylvania in the east. Unsurprisingly,

within this huge area there are some important regional differences. General American is sometimes referred to as 'network standard', which suggests that it is the accent of American English most widely heard on television and radio.

Generative grammar A general term for a system of linguistic analysis developed by Noam Chomsky in the 1950s. It has had a profound effect on the discipline, particularly in the United States. Generative grammar aims to develop theories which reveal the rules and principles governing language. It is 'generative' because it claims that a finite number of rules are capable of 'generating' all the grammatical sentences of a language. It is the purpose of so-called 'scientific' linguistics to discover these rules. The ultimate goal of Chomsky and his followers is to reveal the 'universal' grammar – the rules and principles underlying *all* language.

Generic pronoun Generic forms are those which refer to a class of objects rather than individual members of that class. In Standard English, there is no generic **pronoun** (or **possessive determiner**) which can be used to refer to an individual human being which is *not* marked for gender. For example, in the following sentence the gender of the child referred to is unknown to the writer: *When your child's sleep patterns cause a definite problem for you or for him, then he has a sleep problem.*• Traditionally, in situations like this the masculine pronoun is used, and it is 'understood' that *he, his, him* also includes female referents. This is the so-called 'generic' use of masculine pronouns. However, many people object to such usages as sexist. There are a number of ways around the problem. For example, the whole sentence could be rephrased to avoid the pronoun entirely:

When a child's sleep patterns cause a definite problem for the parent and the child, then the child has a sleep problem. Or the somewhat clumsy *he/she, him/her* construction could be used: *When your child's sleep patterns cause a definite problem for you or for **him/her**, then **he/she** has a sleep problem.* Some writers alternate between using masculine pronouns and feminine pronouns generically.

More controversially from a prescriptivist perspective is the option of using the third person pronouns *they* and *them*: *When your child's sleep patterns cause a definite problem for you or for **them**, then **they** have a sleep problem.* Some people object to this on the grounds that 'your child' (the noun phrase that the pronouns *them* and *they* refer back to) is singular, whereas *them* and *they* are plural. However, such usages have been around for a very long time and are common in both speech and writing, particularly when the antecedent of *they, them, their* or *theirs* is an **indefinite pronoun** (as in examples 2, 5 and 6): 1) *There's not a man I meet but doth salute me , / As if I were **their** well-acquainted friend* (Shakespeare). 2) *Every Body fell a laughing, as how could **they** help it* (Fielding). 3) *But to expose the former faults of any person, without knowing what **their** present feelings were, seemed unjustifiable* (Austen). 4) *A person can't help **their** birth* (Thackeray). 5) *'If everybody minded **their** own business,' the Duchess said in a hoarse growl, 'the world would go round a deal . faster than it does'* (Carroll). 6) *Experience is the name everyone gives to **their** mistakes* (Wilde). 7) *No man goes to battle to be killed. But **they** do get killed* (Shaw). 8) *He's one of those guys who's always patting **themself** on the back* (Salinger). See GENDER, PRESCRIPTIVISM.

Genitive case In inflected languages such as Russian, **Latin**, Irish and **Old**

English, the genitive case is marked by a change in the form of a noun to signal a particular grammatical relationship between the noun and other parts of the sentence, as in Latin *puella/puellae* (*a girl/of a girl*). Often this relationship is one of possession. Modern English no longer has a fully fledged genitive case. Instead, genitive relationships are shown by adding -*'s* to a noun or noun phrase, such as ***John's** suitcase.* Syntactically, English genitives usually function as determiners in the noun phrase, specifying the reference of the head noun (as in the previous example). In such cases, they can be replaced by a possessive determiner (compare ***Rushdie's** novel* with *His novel*). Genitives can also modify the head of a noun phrase: *The **novelist's** house.* Some genitives can stand alone as noun phrases. In these cases, ellipsis is usually involved, as these examples illustrate (ellipted items are in [ ]): *A. Whose turn is it? B. It's **Michael's** [turn]; The parents' interests had to be considered as well as the **children's** [interests].* Although genitives do frequently consist of a single word, syntactically they are a phrase level phenomenon. This can be seen in such constructions as *The **University of Southern California's** law school.*†

Semantically, genitives can be possessive, subjective, objective, part/whole genitives, or genitives of time/measure. 1) Possessive genitives can be paraphrased with the verbs *have* or *own*: *The **kid's** money* (The kid has/owns money). 2) Subject genitives are so-called because the relationship between the genitive word and the noun it modifies resembles the relationship of a subject to its predicate: *The **team's** success* (The team succeeded). 3) Object genitives are so-called because the relationship between the genitive word and the noun it modifies resembles the relationship between a direct object and its verb: *Ghandi's assassination* (Someone assassinated Ghandi). 4) Part/whole genitives: *The plane's wings*. 5) Genitives of measurement: *A day's work; The man's weight*.

Often, the noun phrase + *-'s* option can be used interchangeably with an *of*-phrase structure, sometimes called the periphrastic genitive (compare *The team's success* and *The success of the team*). But in many cases, one option is sometimes preferred over the other (compare *A day's work* with *?A work of a day*). Several factors influence this choice. For example, *-'s* is favoured by human beings, particularly when they are referred to with a **proper noun** (compare *John's suitcase* with *?The suitcase of John*). Abstract nouns, on the other hand, are more likely to be used with the *of*-phrase construction, as in *the collapse of communism*. Also, part/whole relationships and measurements generally prefer the *of*-phrase construction, particularly when the noun being modified is inanimate: *The roof of the building* would generally be preferred over *The building's roof*, as would *The length of the list* over *The list's length*.

Genre All texts belong to a particular 'text type' or genre. Texts characterized as belonging to the same genre generally have similar goals and purposes and share lexical, grammatical and stylistic features. The term is particularly associated with literary studies, although it is also used more widely (e.g. in media studies, film studies, and **discourse analysis**). In the West, relations between literary genres are sometimes presented as a hierarchy, with the three major genres of poetry, prose and drama being subject to further divisions: poetry – the lyric, ode, epic, ballad; prose – fiction, autobiography, essay; drama – tragedy, comedy. Further

subdivisions are also possible. For instance, fiction can be divided into science-fiction, romantic fiction, thrillers, literary fiction, and so on. Some well-known media and film genres include soap-opera, 'reality' TV, game show, war film and romantic comedy. Types of everyday interaction, such as greetings, service encounters and jokes are also described as genres by some discourse analysts. Compare REGISTER.

Geordie A commonly used name for people from the city of Newcastle-upon-Tyne in north-east England, and by extension the **dialect** of English spoken in and around the conurbation of Tyneside. Many outsiders assume that everyone in the north-east of England is a Geordie, much to the annoyance of non-Tynesiders.

Some accent features which distinguish the Geordie accent from others in the north of England include the following (see Wells 1982; Hughes, Trudgill and Watt 2005). 1) In broad Geordie, the vowel in the NURSE **lexical set** is merged to NORTH /ɔː/, so that *nurse* and *Norse*, *first* and *forced* are **homophone**s. This pronunciation, however, is in decline. 2) Words in the THOUGHT set with <al> in the spelling have the vowel [aː], such as *all, walk, talk*. 3) Vowels in words in the FACE and GOAT lexical sets tend to be the monophthongs [eː] and [oː] or the diphthongs [ɪə] and [ʊə]. 4) Vowels in words in the PRICE set are [ɛi]. 5) Word-final *-er* and *-or* is [ɐ]. 5) /p/ and /k/ (as well as /t/) tend to be glottalized when they occur in syllable-final position, giving distinctive pronunciations of words such as *happy* and *slacker*.

Some well-known lexical features of Geordie include *bairn* ('child'), *canny* ('good, kind, gentle, steady, sensible'), *bonny* ('fine, good-looking'). These words reveal the dialect's connections with varieties of English in Scotland. The most notable feature of grammar is probably the **pronoun** system. For example, forms such as '*Us*'ll do it' and 'They beat *we* four nil' occur in Tyneside English, reversing the Standard English system. There is also a plural second-person pronoun: *yous* (Thomas 1996: 244). *Wor* is commonly used where Standard English has *our* or *my*, particularly in talking about kinship relations: *wor lass*. 'Double' **modal verb**s also occur: *I **might could** get it changed though; He **wouldn't could**'ve worked* (see Beal 1993). *Divvent* is also used as an alternative to *don't*. See NORTHERN ENGLAND.

Germanic A term for the group of **Indo-European** languages descended from the now extinct *Proto-Germanic*, a language spoken by a people who originally lived in scattered groups in the forests and marshes of north-west Europe (probably in what is today northern Germany and southern Scandinavia). The Romans called these people *Germani*, hence the word 'German'. In about 300 BC, the Germans started to move outwards from their homelands, pushing further north into Scandinavia and Finland, east along the shores of the Baltic, and south into Bohemia. The dispersal of the Germans across this huge area contributed to the break-up of Proto-Germanic into three main dialect groups, which linguists call *West Germanic, North Germanic* and *East Germanic*. North Germanic (or 'Old Norse') is the parent of the modern Scandinavian languages (Icelandic, Norwegian, Faroese, Danish and Swedish). East Germanic, spoken by the Germans who moved along the Baltic coast, gave rise to Burgundian, Vandal and Gothic, which are all now extinct.

West Germanic is the ancestor of modern-day German, Dutch, Frisian and English. See OLD ENGLISH.

Gerund A term sometimes used to describe a noun derived from the *ing*-form of a verb: *We are obviously going to have to do a lot of **interviewing**.* See *ING*-PARTICIPLE.

Given and new Information which a writer or speaker assumes is already known by the intended recipients of a text or utterance is sometimes described as 'given'. The information might be known because it has already been mentioned; or it might be recoverable from the **context** of situation; or it is 'known' because it is part of general background knowledge about the world. 'Givenness' can be indicated linguistically in a number of ways. For example, **definite** reference often marks information as given. A statement such as '**The** man waved at me', which contains the definite article *the*, assumes that the person doing the waving has already been mentioned in the discourse (compare '**A** man waved at me'). Pronouns also signal givenness: '**He** waved at me' assumes that the referent of the pronoun is already known (perhaps because it has been mentioned previously, or because the speaker shares the same physical context as his addressee, and both of them can see the man who is waving). Given information usually appears at the start of a clause as the *theme* (or 'topic').

New information, on the other hand, is that which a speaker or writer assumes is *not* known by the addressee. It tends to occur towards the end of a clause, and is represented by the *rheme* (or 'comment'). Full forms and indefinite reference are associated with new information: *For my lunch I had **some fruit**.*† See THEME AND RHEME.

Global English See WORLD ENGLISH.

Glottal Of the **glottis**. The term is used in phonetics to describe sounds which are articulated at the glottis. In English, /h/ is usually described as a voiceless glottal fricative. See GLOTTAL STOP.

Glottal stop A speech sound produced by a brief and complete closure of the **glottis** (the space between the **vocal folds**). It is represented in the **International Phonetic Alphabet** by [ʔ]. In many languages (e.g. Arabic, Japanese, Maltese) [ʔ] is a consonant **phoneme**. Glottal stops are not phonemic in English, but they commonly occur variably as **allophones** of word-medial or word-final /t/ in most varieties of English in the British Isles, often preceding a consonant (as in *hit-man*) or a syllabic **nasal** (as in *button*). They also occur intervocalically (as in *butter* or *hot oil*). Less frequently, the glottal stop may be coarticulated (produced simultaneously) with the voiceless stops /p, t, k/. See GEORDIE.

The glottal stop, particularly as an allophone of intervocalic /t/, is a **shibboleth** of British working-class speech (especially in Glasgow, London and south-east England) and as such it is capable of provoking enormous class-based hostility. However, in recent years it has entered into the phoneme inventory of younger RP speakers, especially in rapid, informal speech. Although they are often labelled as 'sloppy' and 'lazy' by the linguistically ill-informed, glottal stops actually take more articulatory effort to produce than intervocalic /t/.

Glottis The space between the **vocal folds**. See GLOTTAL, GLOTTAL STOP.

Gradability A property of some **adjectives** and **adverbs**. They are gradable (i.e. variable in degree) if they take **comparative** or **superlative** forms (e.g. *Her husband*

*was **braver**; 'D'you know what you're doing?' I asked, **more bravely***), or they occur with **intensifiers** and **downtoners** (*She acted **very bravely**; Mr Brown must have been **quite brave***).

Grammar The property of language which allows meaningful structures to be built by organizing morphemes into words, words into phrases, phrases into clauses and clauses into sentences. Linguists generally divide grammar into **morphology** (morpheme–word) and **syntax** (word–phrase–clause–sentence). The term is also applied to any systematic and principled account of the structure of a language. Because there are many different approaches to language description, there are many different 'grammars', including descriptive, theoretical, pedagogical, and so on (see separate entries for DESCRIPTIVE GRAMMAR, GENERATIVE GRAMMAR).

In popular usage, 'grammar' is a body of rules laid down by various self-appointed 'authorities', who police linguistic behaviour in various ways. These rules are concerned with telling people what grammatical constructions they *should* use, rather than describing those which they actually do use. The notion of 'bad' and 'good' grammar belongs to the prescriptivist (or normative) tradition. Although academic linguists are interested in **prescriptivism** as a sociolinguistic phenomenon, they are scrupulously descriptivist in their approach.

In the past, approaches to grammatical description have usually ended with the sentence, but in recent years linguists have become interested in the grammar of longer stretches of discourse (see DISCOURSE ANALYSIS).

Grammatical boundary The boundary of a grammatical unit (a **phrase**, **clause** or sentence). In writing, these boundaries are often shown by **punctuation**.

Grammatical category See ASPECT, CASE, GENDER, MOOD, NUMBER, PERSON, TENSE, VOICE [1].

Grammatical cohesion The cohesive effects of grammatical words and structures. It is achieved mainly through *referencing, conjunction, substitution* and *ellipsis*.

1) Referencing is the means by which a speaker or writer introduces and keeps track of **participants** (people, places, concepts, entities) in a **text** (Eggins 2004: 33). When a speaker/writer mentions a participant for the first time, he or she usually 'names' it (by using a full noun phrase) but on subsequent mentions it may be indicated by a **pronoun**, **demonstrative** or **comparative**. Pronominal referencing is very common. In the following example, a proper noun (*Sombro*) is used when the main participant is first introduced, but the dog is subsequently referred to using pronouns: *Sombro was not long back from the town when **he** arrived at North Point and **he** appeared tired and wan.* Demonstrative referencing is concerned with locating elements within the text, and is most frequently realized through the demonstrative pronouns *this, that, these* and *those*. In the following example, the procedure described in the first sentence is referred to with *this* at the start of the next sentence: *A local anaesthetic is used and a little cut made in the perineum. **This** is called an episiotomy.* Comparative referencing uses adjectives or adverbs such as *similar, identical, more, similarly, identically, less* to create links with participants which have already been mentioned: *Their pride and joy is the X2000, a tilting passenger train that operates at high speed on conventional*

track. Britain abandoned a **similar** project eleven years ago.*

2) Conjunction involves the use of words and phrases (particularly **conjunctions** and linking **adverbials**) to form cohesive ties between parts of a text. Halliday and Matthiessen (2004) provide a full account of 'conjunctive relations'. They identify three main types: elaboration, extension and enhancement (for a useful summary see Eggins 2004). Elaboration involves one sentence/clause restating or clarifying another, for the purposes of exposition, exemplification, correction, summation, and so on. Words and phrases commonly performing this function include: *in other words, to put it another way, that is (to say), I mean (to say)* (exposition), *for example, for instance* (exemplification), *or rather, at least, to be more precise* (correction), *in short, briefly, to sum up* (summation). Extension involves addition (where one sentence *adds to* the meaning of another) and variation (where one sentence alters the meaning of another, by contrast or qualification): *and, also, moreover, furthermore, nor, but, yet, on the other hand, however, instead, on the contrary, alternatively.* Enhancement occurs when one sentence expands or develops in some way the meaning of another sentence, marking relations of time, comparison, result, reason, purpose, concession: *then, next, previously, finally, at once, meanwhile, soon* (time); *likewise, similarly* (comparison), *consequently, as a result* (result) *so, then, therefore, for that reason* (reason); *for that purpose, with this in view, so (that)* (purpose), *despite this, nevertheless, even so* (concession).

3) Substitution involves the replacement of a 'full' form (such as a noun phrase, verb phrase or whole clause) with a **proform** such as *one, do, so* and *not*: *Bring me the chromium tray, not the red*

*one, the chromium one** (noun phrase replaced with *one*); *You can't stink worse than you do already* (verb phrase replaced with *do*); *No other single movement has influenced American society and culture as deeply as it seems to have done±* (the clause 'influenced American society and culture' replaced with *done*); *She's poor, but the government doesn't think so** (the clause 'she is poor' replaced with *so*); *'They don't get many days off there.' 'No, I suppose not,' agreed Anthony** (the clause 'they don't get many days off' replaced with *not*).

4) Ellipsis is the omission of words, phrases and clauses which are recoverable from the textual or situational context: *Fred bought some shoes, and John a hat.* The act of recovering ellipted elements has a cohesive effect.

Grammatical metaphor A term associated with the work of Michael Halliday to describe the substitution of one grammatical class or structure by another, while preserving the core meaning of an utterance. For example, in changing an **active** sentence into a **passive** one, the grammatical structure and the grammatical relations between constituents are altered, while the essential meaning of the two sentences remains the same: *Prison officers murdered Lumumba's nephew→Lumumba's nephew was murdered by prison officers.* Halliday (1993) claims that a 'metaphorical' wording is 'non-congruent', in the sense that it is further from the 'natural' or 'congruent' way of representing the world in language. He proposes three main principles of congruency. 1) *Processes* are expressed by verbs: *The boy kissed the girl quickly* is therefore congruent, while *The boy's kissing of the girl was quick* is non-congruent, because the process is expressed by a noun (*kiss-*

ing). 2) *Participants* are expressed by noun phrases: *The boy kissed the girl quickly* is congruent, while *The boy's kissing of the girl was quick* is non-congruent, because participants are expressed by a possessive (*the boy's*) and a prepositional phrase (*of the girl*). 3) *Circumstances* are expressed by adverbs and prepositional phrases: *The boy kissed the girl quickly* is congruent, while *The boy's kissing of the girl was quick* is non-congruent, because the circumstance is expressed by an adjective (*quick*).

Grammatical metaphor is particularly associated with technical or scientific writing, where, for example, processes are routinely represented as 'things'. This leads to noun-heavy sentences such as the following from a scientific journal (processes as 'things' are in bold): *While still in its infancy, **numerical drug design** shows significant potential for **boosting experimental research productivity** by the early **identification** of promising candidates for detailed **experimental investigation**.* This style of writing has its origins in the seventeenth century. The development of science meant that the resources of language had to be adapted to accommodate new kinds of knowledge and new ways of finding out about the world.

Although grammatical metaphor is particularly common in scientific writing, it also occurs in other genres, where it often attracts the attention of critical linguists and critical discourse analysts concerned to identify the various ways in which language is used to manipulate, control and coerce. See CRITICAL LINGUISTICS, NOMINALIZATION, TRANSITIVITY.

Grammatical word A term used to describe words which, unlike **lexical word**s, have no lexical meaning. Grammatical words are members of the following word classes: **determiner**, **preposition**,

pronoun, auxiliary verb, adverbial particle, coordinator, subordinator. Because they perform various grammatical functions, they are sometimes called 'function' words. New grammatical words are very rarely coined, which is why these words are known as 'closed' class (in contrast to the 'open' class of lexical words).

Grapheme   See ENGLISH SPELLING.

Graphology   The elements of writing; and also the study of these elements. A graphological approach to a text would consider such issues as **spelling, punctuation**, font size, colour and style, layout, and so on. See ALPHABET, LANGUAGE LEVEL, ORTHOGRAPHY, PARALINGUISTIC.

Great Vowel Shift (GVS)   A change in the quality of the seven **Middle English** long **vowel**s. Broadly speaking, the mid and low vowels became 'higher' (they were articulated with the tongue closer to the roof of the mouth), and those that were already high (/iː/ and /uː/) became **diphthong**s. The term is perhaps slightly misleading, because it gives the impression of a single event that occurred quite rapidly and uniformly. In fact, it probably began in the early fifteenth century and was not complete until the early seventeenth century; and some dialects were not as affected by the shift as others. The details of the GVS are complex and its causes are much debated (see, for example, Fennel 2001, Crystal 2004). Its general impact on pronunciation is summarized in the table.

Some of the accent differences in modern British English can be traced back to the GVS. The shift probably began in south-east England, gradually

Example word	Vowel quality c. 1400	Vowel quality c. 1450–1600	Vowel quality today (RP)
time	/iː/	/əi/	/ai/
see	/eː/	/iː/	/iː/
clean	/ɛː/	/eː/	/iː/
fame	/aː/	/ɛː/	/ei/
so	/ɔː/	/oː/	/əʊ/
moon	/oː/	/uː/	/uː/
cow	/uː/	/əu/	/aʊ/

spreading north and west. But in some areas it remained incomplete. For example, some speakers in Cumbria and Northumberland pronounce the word *cow* as [kuː], preserving the pre-GVS pronunciation. Similarly, many speakers in Scotland pronounce *house* and *mouse* as [huːs] and [muːs] (see SCOTS). Further south, some speakers of the Black Country dialect in the **West Midlands** have a vowel closer to /eː/ than /iː/ in the word *meat*.

Most spellings had been fixed before the Great Vowel Shift, so they did not change to reflect the new pronunciations. This results in some of the 'irregularities' in modern English orthography. For example, the GVS lies behind the two main ways to represent the sound /iː/. Words spelled with <ee> were once pronounced differently from words spelled with <ea>. See ENGLISH SPELLING.

H

Hard palate The bony part of the roof of the mouth, located between the top teeth and the **soft palate**. It is important in the articulation of **palatal** speech sounds.

_H_-dropping A tendency for some speakers of English to drop the **glottal fricative** /h/ at the start of words. In connected speech, most English speakers do not pronounce /h/ in unstressed function words such as _he, him, her, his_. But sometimes the /h/ is dropped at the start of content words which are normally stressed, so that pairs such as _head_ and _Ed_ and _harm_ and _arm_ are **homophone**s. Most urban accents of English in the UK are _H_-drop, and the feature is present in some other varieties of English around the world. It is usually stigmatized.

Head The compulsory element in a **phrase**. For example, in the noun phrase _a very clear recollection_, the head is _recollection_, because when it is removed we are left with an ungrammatical utterance: *_a very clear_. But if the **modifier** _very_ is removed, the utterance remains grammatical: _a clear recollection_.

Headword In a **dictionary**, a word under which others are grouped. The term 'citation form' is also used. See also LEXEME.

Hedge A word or phrase which conveys imprecision: _These are **sort of** a summary of them; There are guided tours lasting **approximately** an hour_. See ADVERB, DOWNTONER, SPEECH AND WRITING.

Heteronym Words which are spelled alike but which have different pronunciations and meanings: _On the left end of_ _the back **row**; Pierre and Donna are having a humdinger of a **row**_. See HOMOGRAPH.

Hiberno-English See IRISH ENGLISH.

High-rising tone (HRT) In most accents of English, including RP, a **declarative** statement or a **_wh_-question** usually ends with falling **intonation**, whereas a yes–no question ('Do you like olives?') or an 'echo' question ('You like olives?') will often (but not always) end with rising intonation. However, some accents of English (most notably in parts of Ireland, Wales, Merseyside, Scotland and north-east England) have different statement and question intonation patterns, which means that speakers will sometimes use rising intonation in declarative statements.

A distinctive type of 'high-rising tone' (so-called because it starts near the upper limit of a speaker's pitch range, and rises slightly) has begun to appear at the end of declarative statements by speakers of accents not traditionally associated with this pitch contour. For example, in the past twenty years or so, young speakers across Britain have begun to use it, much to the annoyance of many linguistically under-informed commentators, who wrongly interpret it as a sign of uncertainty or indecision. Study of the phenomenon (which is sometimes called 'upspeak') reveals that it occurs more frequently when a speaker is telling a story or giving a description: its main function seems to be to 'question' the state of a listener's understanding and to invite empathy. The verbal equivalents of HRT might be 'do you follow me?' or 'you know what I mean, don't you?'

The origins of HRT in declaratives are much debated. Some linguists argue that it began in the 1960s in Australia and New Zealand (where it is common), spreading from there (for this reason the phenomenon is sometimes referred to as 'Australian Questioning Intonation'); others claim that it has also been well-established in the speech of some Americans for decades (see Foulkes and Docherty 2005).

Historic(al) present   A stylistic choice in which events that happened in the past are described using verbs in the present tense, usually to produce a sense of drama or immediacy. The historic present is common in anecdotes (*He **walks** into the room and he **gets** this sword and just **does** this like massive gash across someone's stomach**•**), jokes (*A man **walks** into a bar with a slab of asphalt under his arm and **says**, "A beer please, and one for the road."†*), news reports (*Embattled Kennedy **quits** as leader*) and literary texts (*Someone **raps** on the window. Pavel **is** jerked awake; he **sees** a uniform. The man **mouths** at him through the glass.*)

High vowel   A vowel produced with the body of the tongue positioned close to the roof of the mouth, as in the vowel /ɪ/ in an RP pronunciation of *kit*. High vowels are sometimes called 'close' vowels. See VOWEL.

Homograph   A set of two or more words which are spelled identically and pronounced the same, but have different origins and meanings: *pants* (item of clothing), *pants* (third person present tense form of the verb *pant*). Compare HETERONYM and HOMONYMY.

Homonym   A set of two or more **lexeme**s which share certain aspects of form but have different meanings and

origins. There are two types, represented by the following pairs. 1) Both the sound and spelling are identical: *port* (a harbour), *port* (a fortified wine from Portugal). 2) The sound is identical, but the spelling is different: *bear* (a large mammal), *bare* (naked). Homonyms of type 1) are sometimes referred to as **homograph**s. Homonyms of type 2) are also referred to as **homophone**s. Homonymy can sometimes result in **ambiguity**.

Homophone   Two or more phonologically identical word-forms with different meanings and spellings, such as *some/sum*; *beer/bier*; *pair/pear/pare*.

Hyperbole   (Greek: 'exceed') A **figure of speech** involving exaggeration. It is often achieved through analogy, simile and metaphor: *It is easier for a camel to go through the eye of a needle, than for a rich man to enter into the kingdom of God* (Matthew 19:24).

Hypercorrection   Speakers who are concerned about conforming to prescriptivist 'rules' of English **usage** will often over-correct themselves, producing utterances which either actually transgress these 'rules', and/or result in utterances which are highly unidiomatic or stilted. For example, some people may have been told that 'you and I' is preferable to 'you and me', but they may be unaware of the grammatical reasoning behind such a claim. This could result in utterances such as 'Mum's taking you and I to the zoo', where the subject pronoun *I* is being used instead of the 'correct' object pronoun *me*.

The term is also used in socio-linguistics to describe what sometimes happens when speakers wishing to change accent in the direction of a variety which they perceive as having higher **prestige** 'get it wrong' by overgeneralization. For example, in England, accents from the north and midlands do not typically have the vowel /ʌ/. This means that there is no distinction in the vowel in words belonging to the **lexical set**s of FOOT and STRUT. In these accents, words such as *put, foot, cup, drunk, strut, bun, but* and so on, all have the vowel /ʊ/. Speakers who wish to sound less northern might make the generalization that this vowel should be replaced with /ʌ/ wherever it occurs in a northern pronunciation of a word. On the whole, this will result in an appropriate pronunciation, but occasionally the form produced is a hyper-correction, such as /bʌtʃ/ for *butch*. See PRESCRIPTIVISM.

Hyphen See PUNCTUATION.

Hyponymy A type of **semantic relation** illustrated by the relationship between *rose* and *flower; table* and *furniture; orange* and *fruit*, and so on. *Orange* is a hyponym of *fruit* because it includes the meaning of the more general term 'fruit' (all oranges are fruit); and *fruit* is a 'superordinate' (or 'hypernym') of *orange*. Hyponymic relations can result in multi-levelled structures. For example, *teaspoon* is a hyponym of *spoon* which is a hyponym of *cutlery* which is a hyponym of *tableware*. Hyponymy allows for the construction of *taxonomies*: systems which classify entities and concepts at different levels of specificity. See LEXICAL COHESION.

Hypotaxis See PARATAXIS AND HYPOTAXIS.

I

Iambic pentameter A metrical pattern in poetry consisting of five iambic feet per line. A 'foot' is a unit of rhythm usually made up of one stressed and one or two unstressed **syllable**s. An 'iambic' foot consists of an unstressed syllable followed by a stressed one. After its introduction by Chaucer (see example 1 below), iambic pentameter became one of the most common metrical patterns in English verse, and was used both with and without rhyme. (In its unrhymed form, iambic pentameter is known as 'blank verse'.) During the period of **Early Modern English**, the metre was used extensively by dramatists and poets (see examples 2 and 3) and, in the form of the 'heroic **couplet**' it was characteristic of much eighteenth-century verse (example 4). Iambic pentameter remains a widely used metre (example 5).

Examples of iambic pentameter

1 *Whan that Aprill with his shoures soote / The droghte of March hath perced to the roote.* (Geoffrey Chaucer c.1390)
2 *Now is the winter of our discontent / Made glorious summer by this son of York.* (William Shakespeare c.1592)
3 *They also serve who only stand and wait.* (John Milton c.1655)
4 *True Ease in Writing comes from Art, not Chance, / As those move easiest who have learn'd to dance.* (Alexander Pope 1711)
5 *A pensioner in turban taps his stick / along the pavement past the corner shop.* (Tony Harrison 1985)

Icon (Greek: 'likeness, image, portrait') A term used in **semiotics** to describe a kind of **signifier** which resembles that

which it signifies. This resemblance can be visual (a photograph of the Pope is iconic because it looks like the Pope) and auditory (the sound of the word *quack* resembles the noise produced by ducks). It can also be gestural (as in the American **Sign Language** sign for *above*, in which one hand rises above the other). See ICONICITY, SIGN, SYMBOL.

Iconicity Similarity between a linguistic form and its meaning. The most well-known instance of iconicity in language is **onomatopoeia**, a type of **sound symbolism** in which the phonetic form of a word resembles the sound made by the word's referent. Other instances of form-meaning resemblance are sometimes expressed as three 'iconic principles' (see Ungerer and Schmid 1996). 1) *Sequential order* principle: the order in which a sequence of events is described will correspond to the order in which the events happen. This (invented) sentence follows the principle: *She woke up, got out of bed and had a shower*; this sentence does not (and as a result it sounds very odd, even though it does not violate any grammatical rules): *She had a shower, woke up and got out of bed.* 2) *Proximity* principle: closely related concepts will be close together linguistically. For example, if we consider the order of elements in complex noun phrases, the items which occur closest to the head are those which are conceptually 'closest'. This (invented) noun phrase follows the principle: *ridiculous yellow leather shoes.* Any other arrangement of elements (e.g. *yellow leather ridiculous shoes*) is not possible. *Leather* is an inherent quality of the shoes (they are made of it) so it is closest to the noun, *yellow* is next because it is descriptive of the shoes themselves, *ridiculous* is furthest from the noun because it is an evaluative term, and less intimately connected (everyone will agree that the shoes are yellow, but that they are ridiculous is subjective). 3) *Complexity* principle: if the concept being expressed is complex, then the form used to express it will also be complex. For example, in English many complex and abstract ideas are expressed using long, multi-syllabic words with Greek or **Latin** etymologies, such as *iconicity, sequential.*

Ideational metafunction See META-FUNCTION.

Idiolect A variety of language unique to an individual speaker, a sort of 'linguistic fingerprint' which distinguishes him or her from other speakers of the same **dialect**. The reality of idiolects can be confirmed by the fact that human beings are capable of identifying individuals on the basis of the voice alone.

Idiom An expression whose meaning is not immediately derivable from the individual words of which it is constituted: *You've been **barking up the wrong tree**; All right, **hold your horses** Mr Curtis; His wife changed the topic **at the drop of a hat**;± I've got a full pre-season's training **under my belt**.* Idioms share a number of semantic and syntactic characteristics. 1) They tend to behave as single semantic units, so that it is usually not possible to re-arrange their elements or insert additional items: *?His wife changed the topic at the sudden drop of a hat; ?Your horses must be held, Mr Curtis.* 2) Their grammatical structures are 'non-productive' – for example, if constituent elements are replaced with items from the same **semantic field**, the idiom is destroyed,

although some unusual **stylistic** effects can be produced: *?You've been baying up the incorrect tree; ?I've got a full pre-season's training beneath my wasteband.*

Imperative A term used in the classification of independent clauses according to **mood**. Imperative clauses typically order or request: *Put your hand under there; Be good.* Structurally, most imperative clauses lack a subject (although the subject is understood to be 'you'), and the **base** form of the verb is used. See CLAUSE, DECLARATIVE, INDICATIVE, INTERROGATIVE, SENTENCE, SPEECH ACT THEORY, SPEECH AND WRITING.

Inclusive and exclusive *we* First **person** plural pronouns (*we, us, ours, ourselves*) are often described as being either *inclusive* or *exclusive*. Inclusive *we* refers to the speaker/writer *and* the addressee(s), as when a child asks his parents 'What are **we** having for tea?' Exclusive *we* refers to the speaker/writer and to some other person or persons associated with him/her (excluding the addressee), as when a child tells his parents '**We** had pizza for dinner at school'. A text which incorporates inclusive *we* into its rhetorical strategy might be seeking to construct a set of shared interests and frames of reference. For example, we might interpret inclusive *we* in this extract from the 1970 Labour election manifesto as an attempt to unite reader and text producer (in this case a political party seeking re-election) with reference to a shared economic goal: *The answer lies in increasing **our** productivity. Only in this way can **we** keep **our** lead over **our** competitors and ensure an improvement in the real standard of life for **our** people.*

'Inclusive' *we* is often exploited in political discourse as a way of creating consensus by aligning the reader/hearer with the text producer. A text which uses inclusive *we* also implicitly claims the right to speak on behalf of others.

Indefinite See DEFINITE AND INDEFINITE.

Indefinite pronoun A pronoun with indefinite meaning: ***Everybody** danced with **anybody**; **Someone** started to clap; That **one** is the same size; Consumers prefer yellow widgets to blue **ones**.* See DEFINITE AND INDEFINITE.

Independent clause See MAIN CLAUSE.

Indian English Many accounts of the history of the English language in India begin with the establishment of The East India Company by British traders in 1600. During the seventeenth and eighteenth centuries, the influence of English grew with the fortunes of the Company. By the time British rule in India was transferred from the Company to the Crown in 1857, English had been firmly established as a language of power for some time, and was used widely in the domains of commerce, administration, government and education. The position of English was maintained after independence in 1947. It is one of the three mandatory languages in schools, English language newspapers are produced in twenty-seven out of twenty-nine states and union territories, and the percentage of books published in English is higher than the percentage of books published in any other language (see Bhatt 2004).

Although such calculations are very difficult to make, it is estimated that some 350,000 people in India speak English as a **first language**, whereas about 200 million have access to English (at widely varying levels of competence) as a **second language** (see Crystal 2003: 108–109). There is a huge range of variation in English in India. This variation can be conceived of as a continuum, with the more-or-less standard English of educated speakers at one end (see ACROLECT) and the English used by those with less (or no) formal instruction in the language at the other (see BASILECT). English in India is also influenced by its substrate languages, so that it is often possible to tell the native language or languages of a speaker by his or her accent of English (Bengalis, for example, often confuse /s/ and /ʃ/, as in *same* and *shame*, because these sounds are not **phoneme**s in Bengali). Given this diversity, the following account of the phonological, grammatical and lexical features of 'Indian English' is partial and selective, concentrating only on features which occur widely in the speech of educated speakers.

Characteristic features of pronunciation (see Trudgill and Hannah 2002: 129–130) include distinctive patterns of **stress**, **rhythm** and **intonation**. Indian English tends to be **syllable-timed**, and syllables which might be unstressed with the vowel reduced to /ə/ in other varieties of English, receive full stress. The consonants /p/, /t/, /k/ tend to be unaspirated (see ASPIRATION); the alveolar consonants /t/, /d/, /s/, /l/, /z/ often have a **retroflex** pronunciation. /r/ tends to be a **flap** [ɾ] or a retroflex flap [ɽ].

The following selected grammatical features are also characteristic: they are to be found in the speech of many educated Indians, and occasionally in some English-language newspapers. The following examples are from the ICE corpus. 1) Count and non-count **noun** distinctions: *Fixtures and fittings, electrical **installations**, **furnitures**, **cutleries**.* 2) The absence of articles in contexts where Standard English has one (*Actually, that is Indian concept; They were original inhabitants of India*), and the presence of articles where Standard English does not have one: *Though it has brought economic gain, it did harm to **the** nature.* 2) Use of **progressive aspect** with **stative verbs** (*He is **having** his own office in Palghat; Shammi must be **knowing** her sister well*) and verbs referring to completed action (*I presume you are **coming** from Karnataka*). 3) Perfect aspect used to describe completed events in the past: *Yesterday I **have seen** two guys speaking with you.* 4) *Yes* and *no* question tags: *Dravidians were in India, **yes**? Now you are doing project, **no**?* 5) *Isn't it* as an invariant question tag: *Man has passed through several stages, **isn't it**?* 6) Interrogative constructions without subject-operator **inversion**: *Why **we are** working? How **it has** come back?*

Lexically, English in India is marked by many **borrowing**s from Indian languages: *acha acha* ('all right'), *bahut* ('a lot'), *lakh* ('one hundred thousand'), *swadeshi* ('indigenous'), *yaar* ('friend'). Many words with English origins have different meanings in India compared with their meanings in other parts of the world: *colony* ('residential area'), *hotel* ('restaurant, café'), *opticals* ('spectacles'), *stir* ('demonstration').

Indicative A term used in the classification of independent clauses according to **mood**. Indicative clauses are either **declarative** or **interrogative**.

Indirect object (IO) Noun phrases which generally refer to a **recipient**, the entity which receives 'possession' of the direct object of a **ditransitive** verb: *Lady Fermoy taught **the children** card games.* Its **semantic role** as recipient usually requires that the indirect object is animate, and often human (as in the example above), or a corporate entity made up of humans: *He paid **the company** some compensation.* However, some indirect objects are clearly inanimate: *Eddie gave **the door** a shove.* In instances such as this, it is the direct object ('a shove') which actually expresses the action of the clause. See BENEFICIARY, OBJECT, SEMANTIC ROLE, VALENCY PATTERN.

Indirect speech A type of **speech presentation** (often, but not exclusively associated with **narrative** fiction) which 'reports' the words of a speaker, rather than recording them directly. Various grammatical alterations are required to turn a stretch of direct speech into indirect speech. For example, to convert *'I'm going to meet you here at six tomorrow'*, he said into indirect speech, the 'spoken' element is placed in a *that*-clause after a clause containing a **communication verb** (e.g. *say, tell, reply*): *He said that he was going to met her there at six the next day.* Notice also that in the indirect version, there is a shift of tense (*am going→was going*); the first and second **person** pronouns become third person pronouns (*I→he; you→her*); elements referring to time and place also undergo a transformation (*here→there; tomorrow→the next day*). Thought can also be represented indirectly: *She thought that Elizabeth was foolish to have married a silent countryman.*

A variant of indirect speech, known as 'free' indirect speech, combines the speech of the character with the words of the narrator, without a reporting clause, as in this passage from Virginia Woolf's *Mrs Dalloway* (1925), in which the words of Miss Kilman in conversation with Elizabeth are being represented indirectly:

> After all, there were people who did not think the English invariably right. There were books. There were meetings. There were other points of view. Would Elizabeth like to come with her to So-and-so? (a most extraordinary-looking old man).

Free indirect *thought* representation is also possible, as this further example from *Mrs Dalloway* demonstrates:

> For she could stand it no longer. Dr. Holmes might say there was nothing the matter. Far rather would she that he were dead! She could not sit beside him when he stared so and did not see her and made everything terrible; sky and tree, children playing, dragging carts, blowing whistles, falling down; all were terrible.

An even more 'indirect' form of speech presentation occurs when the **narrator** summarizes the content of the utterance; this is known as *narrative report of speech act*. In the following extract from *The Moonstone* by Wilkie Collins (1868), the narrator does not record precisely what Mr Franklin says, but he does convey the general content of his utterances:

> A chance word dropped by Mr. Franklin, when the two were alone, one day, after dinner, revealed that he had been charged by his father with a birthday present to be taken to Miss Rachel.

Indo-European languages The language family to which English belongs. Living languages with a shared Indo-European ancestry include English, Dutch, German, Danish, Swedish, Norwegian (**Germanic** branch); Irish and Scottish Gaelic, Welsh (**Celtic** branch); Italian, French, Spanish, Portuguese, Romanian (Italic branch); Persian, Farsi, Kurdish, Hindi, Urdu, Bengali, Punjabi, Gujarati, Sinhalese (Indo-Iranian branch); Russian, Ukrainian, Polish, Czech, Bulgarian, Lithuanian, Latvian (Balto-Slavonic branch); Greek (Hellenic branch); Albanian (Illyric branch); Armenian (Thracian branch); Extinct Indo-European languages include Ancient Greek, **Latin**, Gothic and Sanskrit.

The relatedness of such seemingly different groups of languages was proved by nineteenth-century philologists, who charted cross-linguistic phonological, lexical and grammatical similarities (see table below), and proposed the existence of a common ancestor, which they called Indo-European or Proto-Indo-European. No one can be certain exactly where, when and by whom this language was spoken, but a combination of linguistic and archaeological evidence has led some

Numbers 1 to 5 in five Indo-European languages (based on Fennell 2001: 23–24)

English	Gothic	Latin	Greek	Sanskrit
one	ains	unus	heis	ekas
two	twei	duo	duo	dva
three	threis	tres	treis	trayas
four	fidwor	quattuor	tettares	catvaras
five	fimf	quinque	pente	panca

scholars to the conclusion that it probably has its origins among groups of early Bronze Age semi-nomadic pastoral people living on the steppes of southern Russia (north of the Caucasus range and around the lower Volga). By c.4000 BC, these people had started to migrate from their original homelands, overrunning surrounding areas and taking their language and culture with them.

Infinitive   The non-finite, uninflected **base form** of the verb. The infinitive occurs in a range of structures. 1) With auxiliary *do: He does* **like** *almond soup; Do you* **want** *a light on?* 2) After a modal auxiliary in the verb phrase: *They think the boss should go.* 3) In *to*-clauses: *They want to* **keep** *the child.* 4) In **imperative** clauses: ***Shut** the window, please.*

Infinitive clause   See *TO*-CLAUSE.

Infix   An **affix** which is inserted within a **root** or **stem**. Infixes are rare in English, occurring mainly in constructions where an obscenity (or a euphemism for the obscenity) is infixed into an adverb: *abso**fucking**lutely*. Sometimes, infixes are inserted into proper nouns: *I don't want to see Poca**fucking**hontas*.† A 'partial' infix can occur between morphemes in a morphologically complex word: *un**bloody**believable; You're not by your **bloody** self.*

Inflection   When a **lexeme** is marked to show its grammatical role, this is known as inflection. In English, this marking usually takes place with an addition of a **suffix** to the base form. English has a rather limited system of inflection compared with some other languages: there are only eight inflectional suffixes. 1) Nouns can be marked for **number** with the addition of *-s: We've spayed one* **cat**; *My sister will be there with her two* **cats**. 2) The **genitive case** is signalled with the addition

of *-'s* (singular) or *-s'* (plural): *The* **farmer's** *wife invited us in* (singular noun); *The policy of the company is to take care of* **farmers'** *needs*± (plural noun). 3) The base form of verbs take an *-s* suffix to mark third person singular present tense: *The teacher* **writes** *on the board.* 4) The progressive is marked by adding *-ing* to the base form of the verb: *They were just* **watch***ing the game*.± 5) The past tense is marked by adding *-ed* to the base form of regular verbs: *I* **knock***ed on the hospital door and* **enter***ed*.± 6) The **past participle** is marked by adding *-ed* to the base form of regular verbs: *It is the first time an apricot toy poodle has* **walked** *the historic route*.• 7) The **comparative** form of adjectives is shown by adding *-er: He was so much* **nic***er when sober*.± 8) The **superlative** form of adjectives is shown by adding *-est: They were the* **nic***est sausages I've ever tasted in my life.* See DERIVATION.

Informalization   A term particularly associated with the critical discourse analyst Norman Fairclough which is used to describe the strategic deployment in public discourse of language practices more typically associated with everyday, 'private' life. For example, the British Prime Minister Tony Blair's use, in public contexts, of a style of speech which contains 'conversational' elements has been widely noted. Such behaviour is part of a broader strategy, designed to give the Labour government the appearance of openness and approachability. Fairclough suggests that the 'engineering of informality' (1996) has two overlapping strands: conversationalization and personalization. Conversationalization – as the term implies – involves the spread into the public domain of linguistic features generally associated with **conversation**. It is usually accompanied by 'personalization': the construction of a 'personal relationship' between the producers and receivers of public discourse. Fairclough is ambivalent towards informalization. On the positive side, it might be viewed as part of a process of cultural democratization, an opening up of 'the elite and exclusive traditions of the public domain' to 'discursive practices which we can all attain' (1995: 138). To counterbalance this positive reading of informalization, Fairclough points out that the textual manifestation of 'personality' in a public, mass media text must always be artificial. He claims that this sort of 'synthetic personalization' only simulates solidarity, and is a strategy of containment hiding coercion and manipulation under a veneer of equality. See CRITICAL LINGUISTICS, FORMALITY.

Ing-clause *Ing*-clauses are **non-finite subordinate** clauses with a variety of syntactic roles in the main clause, including subject, subject complement, direct object and adverbial. 1) Subject: *Being alone was the worst thing*. 2) Subject complement: *Looking good is **feeling good***. 3) Direct object: *My staff hate **working here***. 4) Adverbial: ***Coming home from school** he had to cross the park*.

Ing-clauses function mainly as **complement clauses**, completing the meaning of a verb or adjective in the main clause. In these cases, the *ing*-clause is said to be 'controlled' by the preceding verb or adjective. Verbs which convey the state of progress of an event or activity commonly control *ing*-clauses: *He started **feeling** queasy;*• *You keep **forgetting** the title;*• *The company will begin **searching** for another buyer.*• **Mental verbs** (particularly those concerned with emotion and attitude) also regularly control *ing*-complement clauses: *I adore **seeing John Cleese on TV as Fawlty**;*• *Michael loved **working in the soil**.*• Most adjectives

controlling *ing*-clauses convey personal feeling or attitude: *They were afraid of freezing to death*;• *I was good at **having babies**.*• The controlling adjective is nearly always followed by a preposition.

Ing-clauses also postmodify nouns: *Most research **involving octopuses** takes place outside the UK; People **working for the commission** will be vetted*.

Ing-participle A **non-finite** form of the verb constructed from the base form plus -*ing*, (also known as the *present participle*). It is used alongside **auxiliary** verb *be* to form the progressive **aspect**: *Candice is **eating** a dish of beans*. *Ing*-participles also head one of the four major types of non-finite clause, the ***ing*-clause**.

When the main verb is *sit* or *stand*, some speakers prefer auxiliary verb *be* plus *ed*-participle (past participle) to express progressive action. This usage is quite well established in speech, and it is also becoming more common in edited, written texts, as this quotation from the *Guardian* newspaper (July 2005) shows: *Passenger Mark Whitby said he **was sat** on a Northern Line train when three plainclothes officers ran on in 'hot pursuit' of an Asian man*.

Ing-participle forms can also be used as **adjectives**: *They presented him with his **glittering** prize*. See also DANGLING PARTICIPLE.

Initialism See ABBREVIATION, ACRONYM.

Inkhorn term An expression used by some contemporary commentators to criticize words with **Latin** and Greek origins which were introduced into English during the sixteenth and seventeenth centuries. The following list is a small selection of such words, which were called 'inkhorn' after the ink receptacle used by clerks: *anacephalize, adnichilate,* *eximious, exolete, fatigate, illecebrous, ingent, obtestate.* Although many of the terms introduced in the period of **elaboration** are no longer with us and appear rather odd (as do the items in the list above), hundreds have survived to the present day, to enrich the English vocabulary. See PLAIN ENGLISH.

Inner circle   See WORLD ENGLISH.

Insert   A term used in some grammars for a **word class** containing items which either stand alone or are only loosely integrated with the clause. They are normally found in speech (often at the start or finish of an utterance). Inserts include **interjection**s (*Oh wow! That's really bad*); greetings/farewells (*Hi John; Bye bye*); **discourse marker**s (*Well I'd better go and get changed*); attention-getters (*Hey what's up?±*); response forms (*Q. So you can go any night? A. Yep±*); polite formulas (*Thanks Brenda±*); expletives (*Oh Shit!±*). (See *LSGSWE:* 449–454.)

Instrument   The **semantic role** of the thing which an **agent** uses to carry out an action: *He slit the end of the envelope with a penknife;*● *Andrew used a portable phone to call the Queen.*● See SUBJECT.

Intensifier   A word or phrase which intensifies or amplifies meaning (hence they are sometimes known as 'amplifiers'): *I don't want to be a total idiot; Zhanna is exceptionally talented but very difficult.* See ADJECTIVE, ADVERB, ADVERBIAL, DOWNTONER, GRADABILITY.

Interference   See TRANSFER.

Interjection   A word whose main function is to express emotion: *oh, ah, wow, ouch, ow, ugh*, and so on. See INSERT, PROSODY, SPEECH AND WRITING.

International Phonetic Alphabet (IPA)   A system of notation used by lin-

guists for representing the sounds of speech. The alphabet uses separate symbols for each speech segment in human language, which means that sounds which are represented in standard orthography by a **digraph**, such as the voiceless post-alveolar fricative written as <sh> in English, are indicated with a single symbol (in this case ʃ). Some symbols (such as ʃ, ʌ, and ɒ) were specially invented for the IPA; others are derived from the Latin and Greek alphabets (e.g. p, t, d, θ). Further information about sound can be added by using *diacritics* (special marks placed above, below, in front of or behind the main symbol). See PHONETIC TRANSCRIPTION.

Internet   A system of linked computer networks carrying publically available information and services, such as electronic mail ('email'), online chat, and the interconnected and continuously expanding resources of the World Wide Web. The internet has had a significant impact on the English language. It has allowed for the creation of entirely new contexts in which human beings communicate and interact, such as electronic mail, chatrooms ('virtual' spaces in which participants can have written conversations with each other in real time) and blogs (online diaries which are meant for public consumption). These novel contexts have led to new ways of using English, such as the innovative graphic conventions associated with writing in an electronic medium (e.g. 'smileys' and 'emoticons'), and the 'interleaving' of messages in emails. Furthermore, the construction of texts linked with hyperlinks allows readers to move rapidly between different texts, radically altering the experience of reading. The internet, of course, has also been a rich source of **neologism**s, such as *search engine, google, browser, surf, flame, thumbnail.*

Interpersonal metafunction   See METAFUNCTION.

Interrogative A term used in the classification of sentences according to **mood** (compare with INDICATIVE, DECLARATIVE, IMPERATIVE). **Interrogative clause**s function as questions. The term is also more generally applied to any word or structure used in questions (e.g. *wh*-**words**).

Interrogative clause An **independent** clause which functions as a question. There are three main kinds of interrogative clause, which can be categorized according to structure and the kind of reply they elicit.

1) *Yes–no* interrogative clauses, as the name suggests, 'expect' the answer 'yes' or 'no': *Do you understand me?*● *Can I have these?*● *Are you still there?*● They are formed by inverting the subject and **operator**. When the verb phrase does not contain an operator (as in the first example), the 'dummy' operator *do* is used (see PERIPHRASIS [1]).

2) *Wh*-interrogative clauses start with *wh*-**word**s and are used to elicit a wide range of answers. Because of this, they are sometimes known as 'open' or 'information-seeking' questions, in contrast to 'closed' *yes–no* questions: *Who ate it? What are you giggling about, Flavia? Where are the lettuces? When will you marry me? Why did you attack them? Whose dog was it? Which one do you like? How is infection transmitted?* As with *yes–no* interrogatives, if there is no operator in the verb phrase, 'dummy' *do* is used, *unless* the *wh*-word is the subject, as in the first example. The word order in *wh*-interrogatives is as follows: the *wh*-word goes before the operator and the

operator goes before the subject: *Where* (*wh*-word) *are* (operator) *the lettuces* (subject)?* In other words, subject–operator inversion takes place (except, once again, in cases where the *wh*-word is already the subject). *Wh*-words in interrogatives perform a variety of grammatical roles. *Who* and *what* are pronouns and can therefore occupy any noun phrase slot (e.g. subject, object and complement): *Who's there?* (*who* as subject); *What are you looking for?* (*what* as direct object); *Who has she left the other half to?* (*who* as prepositional object/indirect object); *What is that blue box?* (*what* as subject complement); *What did you give him?*● (*what* as object complement). *When, where, how* and *why* have an adverb function in interrogatives: *When will my acne finally disappear?*● (adverb of time); *Where do you live?*● (adverb of place); *How does it work?*● (adverb of manner); *Why does Father Connolly tickle Granny's feet?*● (adverb of reason). Some *wh*-words function as determiners: *Which book of the Bible follows Jeremiah?*● *What things should a potential greenhouse buyer consider?*

3) Alternative questions resemble yes–no interrogative clauses, but present options to choose between: *Would you like a tea or coffee?*

'Interrogative' is a **form** label. It should be pointed out that interrogative structures can function, for example, as **exclamation**s (*What have I done!*) and suggestions (*Why don't we get a microwave?*), as well as questions. See SPEECH ACT THEORY, TAG QUESTION.

Intertextuality A general term for the different kinds of relationship a text has with other texts. Intertextual relations exist on a continuum, ranging from the intangible (one text 'influences' another) to the concrete (one text quotes directly from another). Between these extremes is a range of intermediary positions (e.g. **allusion**). The potential complexity of the phenomenon can be seen in the title of Robert Liddell's novel *Unreal City* (1952), which is a direct quotation from T.S. Eliot's poem *The Waste Land* (1922). In turn, Eliot's description of London as 'Unreal city' is a compressed translation of Baudelaire's 'Fourmillante cité, cité pleine de rêves' ('Swarming city, city full of dreams'). Intertextuality is, of course, not simply a literary phenomenon. Everyday conversation is full of fragments of other voices and other texts, as are popular television programmes and advertising. See also DEVIATION, PARODY, PASTICHE.

Intervocalic   A term used to describe a **consonant** occurring between vowels. For example, /t/ is intervocalic in *pity*.

Intonation   A **prosodic feature** of speech. Intonation consists of patterned **pitch** changes. These patterns are sometimes known as intonation 'contours'. Intonation has a wide range of functions. Most obviously, in combination with other prosodic features such as **tempo** and **volume**, it can be used to express emotion, attitude or **stance** (wide pitch changes can convey surprise, excitement, shock, and so on; a steady level tone can convey boredom, sarcasm, and so on). It is also used to signal grammatical contrasts: a declarative sentence can be turned into a question by changing the intonation contour (note the contrast when you say the following sentences aloud: *He's getting married; He's getting married?*).

Accents of English sometimes have distinctive patterns of intonation associated with them, impressionistically captured in terms such as 'lilting' or 'sing-song' (some Welsh accents) or 'flat' and 'monotone' (some accents from

the English midlands). See HIGH RISING TONE.

Intransitive   Said of a verb which is being used without an **object**: *She snores*. Some verbs can be used intransitively and transitively (with an object): *Strike her if she resists; The Chancellor resists the temptation*. See also DITRANSITIVE, MONOTRANSITIVE, VALENCY PATTERN.

'Intrusive' /r/   See LINKING /r/.

Inversion   A re-ordering of the basic clause pattern so that the verb phrase, or a part of it, is placed before the subject. There are two main types of inversion. 1) Subject–verb inversion (subject in bold, verb underlined): *On the top was a pole wrapped in straw* (compare *A pole wrapped in straw was on the top*); *Along the line of her brow lay a seam of piercing pain* (compare *A seam of piercing pain lay along the line of her brow*). These two examples illustrate one of the main contexts for subject–verb inversion: an adverbial of place or direction in initial position. Such inversion is often associated with more formal kinds of writing, and is used as a cohesive device (and also gives end-weight to a long subject). 2) Subject–**operator** inversion involves placing the operator (rather than the whole verb phrase) before the subject. It is regularly used in the formation of questions: *Are you experienced?* (see INTERROGATIVE CLAUSE). It also occurs after a fronted negative element: *Never will I send for him; No way could he tolerate young children.*• In such cases, the negative element is emphasized by the inversion. See END-WEIGHT, EXTRAPOSITION, FRONTING, GRAMMATICAL COHESION, WORD ORDER.

Irish English   The varieties of English spoken in Ireland, an island off the north-west coast of Europe forming part of the **British Isles**. The island of Ireland consists of the Republic of Ireland (which gained independence from the UK in 1921) and the Province of Northern Ireland (which is politically part of the United Kingdom of Great Britain and Northern Ireland). The English language was introduced into Ireland (alongside Norman French) when English rule was imposed by the Anglo-Normans, who began their colonization of the island in the late twelfth century. By the late fifteenth century, the colonists had largely adopted the culture and language of the indigenous population: English was limited to an arc of territory surrounding Dublin (known as 'The Pale'); Irish was spoken everywhere else. This situation lasted until the middle of the sixteenth century. Then, under the Protestant Tudor monarchs, a second wave of colonization, known as the 'Plantations', began. Land was seized from the indigenous Catholic Irish and granted to Protestant settlers from Britain. The Plantations continued throughout the seventeenth century, and have had a profound effect on the politics, culture and language of Ireland. For example, most of the settlers in the north-east of Ireland were from south-west Scotland, resulting in the variety of Irish English known as 'Ulster Scots'. The Plantations forced the Irish into the poorer west of the country, and today the parts of Ireland where Irish is still spoken as a community language are mainly along the Atlantic coast in the counties of Donegal, Mayo, Galway and Kerry (the area known as the 'Gaeltacht'). Ireland is now predominantly English-speaking – only 1–2 per cent of the population have Irish as a **first language**. In the nineteenth century, the Irish language went into rapid decline. Depopulation, as a consequence of famine and emigration (par-

ticularly to the United States of America) reduced the number of Irish speakers, and there was massive **language shift** from Irish into English. The causes of the shift are various and complex. By the end of the eighteenth century, English had become the sole language of government and administration, and an 'English only' education system had been imposed. English, therefore, was a **prestige** language, a prerequisite of social and economic advancement, whereas Irish was stigmatized as the language of the poor and ignorant (although the language underwent a revival in the early twentieth century as part of the movement for Irish independence, and it is now a compulsory subject in schools in the Irish Republic).

English in Ireland is, of course, subject to regional and social variation. The most immediately recognizable regional difference is between the 'southern' and 'northern' varieties. Southern varieties are used mainly in the Irish Republic, and may be further subdivided into *Anglo-Irish* (associated mainly with middle-class speakers in the Dublin area) and *Hiberno-English* (associated mainly with working-class Catholic speakers). Speakers of the Scots-influenced Northern varieties live mainly in the province of Northern Ireland (the territory of Ireland which is still politically part of the United Kingdom). The following overview lists some of the most characteristic features of southern and northern Irish English, and is based on Trudgill and Hannah (2002: 98–104) and Hughes, Trudgill and Watt (2005: 110–120).

In southern English there are typically fifteen vowel phonemes. Some of the most obvious features of the system are as follow. 1) The vowel in words in the LOT lexical set is typically [ɑ] (as it is in most varieties of American English).

2) The vowel in the FACE set is typically [eː]. 3) The vowel in the PRICE set is typically [ɜɪ]. 4) The vowel in the GOAT set is typically [oː]. 5) The vowel in the MOUTH set is typically [ɜʉ]. 6) Some words in the FLEECE set (e.g. *tea, please, see*) have the vowel [ei], so that to many English speakers outside Ireland they sound like *Tay, plays* and *say*. 7) Words such as *old, cold* and *bold* often have the vowel [ɜʉ], and rhyme with *fouled*.

Characteristic features of consonants of English in the south of Ireland include the following. 1) Preservation of the contrast between /ʍ/ and /w/, so that *which* is pronounced /ʍɪtʃ/ ('hwich') and *witch* is /wɪtʃ/. 2) /l/ is 'clear' in all positions (see ALLOPHONE). 3) Many speakers do not preserve a contrast between /θ/-/t/ and /ð/-/d/, but use the dental stops [t̪] and [d̪] throughout. This means that word pairs such as *tin/thin* and *dare/there* are **homophone**s.

Some well-known characteristics of the grammar of southern Irish English include the following. 1) Stative verbs can be used with progressive **aspect**: *I'm seeing it very well; This is belonging to me*. 2) The adverb *after* can be used with a progressive where a perfective would be used in other varieties: *I'm after seeing him* ('I've just seen him'). This is a **loan translation** from Irish. 3) **Clefting** is common, and it is extended to use with copular verbs: *It was very ill that he looked; Is it stupid you are?* Again, this shows a **substrate effect** from Irish.

As far as vocabulary is concerned, the most characteristic items can be placed in two main categories. 1) General words with distinctive senses: *bold* ('naughty'), *doubt* ('believe strongly'), *backward* ('shy'). 2) Words taken from Irish: *boxty* ('mashed potato'), *smig* ('chin') *crubeen* ('pig's trotter'), *streel* ('slovenly girl'), *acushla* ('my dear').

Because of the history of English in Ireland, northern Irish English is similar in many respects to **Scottish English**. Features of a typical northern Irish accent include the following. 1) The vowel in words belonging to the lexical sets of FOOT and GOOSE is the same [u], which means that the following words all share the same vowel: *put, boot, pull, pool, poor*. 2) The vowel in words belonging to the FACE and SQUARE sets is the same [e], which means that the following words all share the same vowel: *bay, bear, plate, weight, mate*. Sometimes this vowel is **diphthong**ized to [ɛə] or [iə] when it occurs before a consonant, e.g. *mate* [miət]. 3) In words belonging to the MOUTH set (e.g. *house, mouse, Scouse*) the vowel can have a range of realizations, such as [œu], [ɛʉ], [æʉ], [ɐʉ]. 4) Intervocalic /t/ (as in *better, butter*) is often an alveolar **flap** [ɾ].

Most of the non-standard grammatical features of English in the north of Ireland can also be found in English in Scotland, or English in the south of Ireland.

Many of the non-standard lexical items in northern Irish English are shared with Scottish English. These include *bairn* ('baby', 'child'), *greet* ('cry', 'weep'), *pinkie* ('little finger'), *wee* ('small'), *ken* ('know').

Irish Gaelic   See CELTIC LANGUAGES.

Irregular verb   A **verb** which does not follow the regular pattern of inflection. For example, to form the past tense and past participle of a regular verb such as *borrow*, the *-ed* ending is used: *borrow***ed**. But the past tense and past participle of an irregular verb such as *swim* are *swam* and *swum*, not **swimmed*. The nine most common lexical verbs in English are all irregular: *say, get, go, know, think, see, make, come, take* (*LSGSWE:* 110). Compare REGULAR VERB.

Isogloss   A line drawn on a **dialect** map which purports to show the geographical distribution of variants of a linguistic form. In English **dialectology**, there are a number of well-known isoglosses. For example, many dialect maps show an isogloss running from the Severn Estuary in the west to the Wash in the east (see Chambers and Trudgill 1998: 107). North of this line, words from the **lexical set** of STRUT are pronounced with the vowel /ʊ/; south of the line they are pronounced with /ʌ/. A line marking the limits of the 'northern' pronunciation of the vowel in the BATH set (/a/) follows a similar route, but does not extend quite so far south in the Midlands.

J

Jamaican creole An English-based creole spoken in Jamaican, sometimes known as **Patois** or Patwa. It is the most well-known and well-studied of the Caribbean creoles, and has had wide international exposure through music (particularly reggae), poetry and other forms of cultural expression, including the Rastafari movement. Jamaican creole has also played an important part in the development of **British Black English**.

Like speakers of all Caribbean creoles, speakers of Jamaican creole have access to a 'span' of the **creole continuum**, and are capable of **style shifting** when it is required by the context. In what follows, some grammatical features are listed which are associated with the **mesolect**, the 'central' section of the continuum lying between the highly vernacular **basilect**, and the **acrolect**, which is closest to Standard English (for a description of general features of pronunciation in Caribbean varieties of English, see the entry on the CARIBBEAN). All of the examples are from the World Wide Web. 1) Nouns are not usually marked with -*s* to form the plural: *six man*. 2) Possession is marked by **apposition**, rather than -'*s*: *Ring ina di man hase* ('ring in the man's ears'). 3) The system of personal pronouns contrasts with Standard English: *Im mean every word* ('He means every word'); *Dem si red* ('They see red'). 4) The **base** form of the verb is used with all persons in the present tense: *Im pick har up a work* ('He picks her up from work').

5) The **base** form of the verb is used for past tense meaning: *One time it rain and rain.* 6) Absence of the copula *be* (see COPULA DELETION): *If she small an slim* ('if she is small and slim'). 7) Absence of *be* as an **auxiliary** verb: *We living ere.* 8) Verb negation with *no*: *She no mek no pramiss.*

Jargon [1] The distinctive vocabulary of a particular profession, activity or group. For example, the jargon of doctors might include terms such as *stent*, *phlebotomy*, and *arthralgia*, while the jargon of builders has *arris*, *corbelling*, and *purlin*. Because this kind of terminology is often impenetrable to outsiders, jargon sometimes attracts criticism, especially when it is used deliberately to obscure or mislead. However, such technical vocabularies are essential if professions or organizations are to operate efficiently. Compare SLANG.

[2] A term used to describe a pidgin language which is not yet stabilized. See PIDGIN.

Jutes An ethnic label for a group of Germanic people, some of whom migrated to Britain about 1500 years ago. The original homeland of the Jutes is thought to be Jutland, in northern Denmark (which is probably named after them) and the **Frisian** coast. The Jutes settled in Kent and along parts of the south coast, including the Isle of Wight. See ANGLES, ANGLO-SAXON, KENTISH, OLD ENGLISH, SAXONS.

K

Kentish One of the four generally recognized dialects of **Old English**, alongside **West Saxon**, **Mercian** and **Northumbrian**. It is thought to have descended from the language of the **Jutes**. There are only a few surviving documents in Kentish, most of them are charters from the eighth and ninth centuries.

Koiné A language variety which emerges when speakers of different dialects come into contact. The new variety shows fewer 'local' features than its constituent varieties, and is often used in a wider area. Because koinés arise in situations of **language contact**, they are often associated with geographical mobility. New towns in England and Scotland, for example, have been identified as places where these levelled varieties develop, as people from different parts of the country mix together in newly established settlements (see Kerswill and Williams 2000). On a larger scale, some linguists regard the situation of dialect contact brought about by colonial migrations to Australia, North America and Southern Africa as fertile ground for the development of koinés. The process by which a koiné is formed is called koineization. See DIALECT LEVELLING.

Kriol [1] An English-based **creole** spoken by about 10,000 people in the north of **Australia**, from western Queensland, across the north of the Northern Territory and into Western Australia. It is used mainly in Aboriginal communities. Like most creoles, Kriol is a continuum of varieties ranging from **basilectal** 'hebi' Kriol to **acrolectal** 'lait' Kriol.

[2] The preferred term for the English-based creole spoken in Belize in Central America.

L

Labiodental A term used in the description of **consonants** referring to a place of **articulation** (the point in the **vocal tract** where a constriction of the **airstream** occurs). Labiodental consonants are produced when the upper teeth come into contact with or come close to the lower lips. There are two labiodental consonant phonemes in most varieties of English: /f/ and /v/. Many varieties of South Asian English also have a labiodental approximant [ʋ], used in words such as *wish, wand*.

Labovian sociolinguistics A methodology developed by the American sociolinguist William Labov (1927-) involving the correlation of linguistic variation with social factors, such as **gender**, **social class**, **ethnicity** and so on. One of the main aims of Labovian (or 'variationist') sociolinguistics is to understand **language change**. Labov's most influential work is *The Social Stratification of English in New York City* (1966), which pioneered survey and quantitative methods, and revealed that linguistic variation and change is *structured* according to factors such as the social background of a speaker or the speech **style** which he or she adopts in particular contexts. His *Language in the Inner City: Studies in the Black English Vernacular* (1972) did much to discredit the widely held notion that speakers of **African American Vernacular English** were somehow verbally deprived, by showing how this variety was as logical and expressive as Standard English.

Language [1] A system of communication used by human beings which has certain characteristics distinguishing it from forms of communication found elsewhere in the animal kingdom (most animals communicate, but only people communicate with *language*). The most important of these are: *productivity* – a feature which allows humans to produce and understand an infinite number of completely new utterances; *displacement*, which enables language users to refer to things remote in time and space from the site of the communication; and *duality*, which allows a large number of meaningful elements to be constructed from a small number of meaningless elements (e.g. the sounds /p/, /n/ and /ɪ/ mean nothing by themselves, but when combined and ordered as /pɪn/ they convey meaning in English). There are three **modes** of language: speech, writing and sign (see SIGN LANGUAGE, SPEECH AND WRITING).

[2] But the word 'language' is not applied simply to the general human accomplishment outlined above. It is also used to refer to particular instances of this system, such as **French**, Arabic and Bengali. However, defining this sense of the word 'language' is not as straightforward as it might at first seem. For example, we might regard a 'language' as a set of linguistically similar and mutually intelligible **varieties** (that is, if two people speaking different but linguistically related dialects can understand each other, they are therefore speaking the same language). This works quite well for some languages, but not for others. For example, the so-called 'dialects' of Chinese are not linguistically similar enough for speakers of, say, Mandarin and Cantonese to understand each other; and although Norwegian and Swedish are

regarded as separate languages, their linguistic similarities make them mutually intelligible. In the words of Janet Holmes 'in order to define a language it is important to look to its social and political functions, as well as its linguistic features' (2001: 141). 'Norwegian' and 'Swedish' are languages (and not dialects of some notional 'Scandinavian') because they are used by people who *choose* to call them separate languages for political and social reasons. Similarly, some people regard **Scots** as a separate language from English; others as a dialect of English. The choice of label is bound up with people's attitudes and also depends on the distribution of political power. Elites usually have the power to decide what is a language and what is a dialect, a fact captured in this popular saying amongst sociolinguists: 'a language is a dialect with an army and a navy'.

Language change All languages change over time. The study of language change is concerned with identifying the changes which have occurred, and discovering why they have happened. Change can occur at any **language level**: morphological (compare Old English *helpende* with modern English *helping*); grammatical (compare Early Modern English *Heard you that?* with modern English *Did you hear that?*); semantic (modern English *cringe* is related to an Old English word which meant 'to fall in battle'); lexical (the first citation for the word *cyberspace* in the **Oxford English Dictionary** is dated 1982); phonological (the vowel in the word *time* was once pronounced /iː/, so that it sounded like modern English *team*). Language change can arise from the nature of language itself (in which case the change is said to be 'internally' motivated), or the nature of society (it is 'externally' motivated).

Examples of internal change include what happens when natural processes involved in speech production such as **assimilation** (where adjacent sounds come to resemble one another), **syncope** (loss of a medial sound in a word) and **apocope** (loss of an initial or final sound) become conventionalized, so that eventually they occur in slow and careful speech as well. Internal language change also proceeds by **analogy**: speakers abandon irregular forms in favour of regular ones, as has happened in English with the spread of plural *-s*. For example, until the sixteenth century some nouns could be made plural with the *-en* ending, as in *one paire of shoen*, but this option is no longer available (although it is preserved in a few words, such as *children* and *oxen*). Similarly, there has been a generalization of the *-ed* ending to some verbs which were once irregular. For example, *clomb* was being used as a past tense and past participle form of *climb* well into the nineteenth century, but it has now been replaced by the regular form *climbed*.

External change derives from a number of sources. Some changes might have their origins in language learning. Children grow up speaking the language or languages of people around them, but the language each child acquires is never identical to that of its adult carers. Through processes of simplification and generalization, small changes are introduced which can accumulate over time. Other changes come about when – as a result of trade, colonialism, war or migration – speakers of one language come into contact with speakers of another. In such situations of **language contact**, where **multilingualism** is common, speakers will often import sounds, words and grammatical structures from one language into another, and these will spread through the language generally (see TRANSFER). A further source of external linguistic change arises from the fact that all human languages display various kinds of social differentiation. In particular, some varieties of a language are perceived as having more **prestige** than others, and some speakers will alter their language (either consciously or subconsciously) so that it contains more prestige and fewer non-prestige features (see OVERT PRESTIGE). Conversely, the language of some speakers will change in the other direction, so that more non-standard vernacular features appear in their speech (see COVERT PRESTIGE).

Language change is universal and unstoppable. Only dead languages do not change.

Language contact Contact between speakers of different languages (or varieties of the same language). This contact usually comes about when one group of people moves into another group's territory, either by conquest (e.g. the Norman French coming into contact with the English after 1066), or immigration (e.g. the mass immigration of people from Europe to the United States during the late nineteenth and early twentieth centuries). Immigration is not always voluntary. Language contact can also be brought about when people are used as forced labour (see ATLANTIC SLAVE TRADE).

Language contact is a dynamic process, and its social and linguistic consequences can be complex and various, ranging from lexical and structural **borrowing** to **language shift** and, occasionally, language death. The outcome depends on a range of factors, such as the intensity of contact between speakers, speakers' attitudes towards the languages involved, and the social and political contexts of the contact situation. Language contact has influenced vari-

ation and change in English in numerous ways. See BORROWING, CONTACT VARIETY, CREOLE, LANGUAGE CHANGE, LANGUAGE SHIFT, PIDGIN.

Language level Any stretch of spoken or written language can be analysed from different perspectives (i.e. on different levels). Linguists generally recognize four main levels: **phonetics** (the physical facts of pronunciation), **phonology** (the way a language organizes sound to convey meaning), **grammar** (the way meaningful units are organized to convey wider and more varied patterns of meaning) and **semantics** (the patterns of meaning themselves). These levels are often further subdivided. For example, within grammar it is common to distinguish between **morphology** and **syntax**; and within semantics, a distinction is often made between the study of **lexis** (vocabulary) and the study of **discourse** (larger patterns of meaning) (see Crystal 1997: 82–83).

Language shift A process in which speakers in a situation of **language contact** abandon their original language in favour of the 'new' language. Usually, the shift occurs in an 'unstable' situation of language contact, where a less powerful minority group co-exists alongside a more powerful majority group. Because the language of the dominant group is perceived as more prestigious and useful than the language of the subordinate group, over a period of time the subordinate group's original language will be replaced in all contexts and for all functions. Many speech communities have experienced language shift into English. For example, the descendants of millions of people whose ancestors emigrated from Europe to the USA in the late nineteenth and early twentieth centuries now have little or no knowledge of the language of their ancestors. As this example demonstrates, language shift is particularly common in second or third generation immigrants. Typically, adult first generation immigrants will learn the 'new' language (e.g. English) so that they can function in the wider community, but will also maintain their ancestral language. Second generation immigrants will learn English as children, alongside their ancestral language. But third generation children are sometimes brought up in families where, even though the parents are bilingual, the ancestral language is rarely used. If they acquire this language at all, it is often only to a basic level. See SUBSTRATE EFFECT.

Larynx   A structure of muscles and cartilage in the throat housing the **vocal folds** and **glottis**. It is sometimes known as the 'voice box'.

Lateral   A term used in the description of consonants to describe those which are produced by allowing the **airstream** to flow over the edges of the tongue. There is one lateral consonant phoneme in English – the alveolar lateral approximant /l/.

Later Modern English (LModE)   The period in the history of the English language which follows **Early Modern English**, extending from c.1700 to the present day. Since the early eighteenth century, there have been no major changes to the structure of the language of the kind that marked earlier periods. By 1700 the main changes in pronunciation associated with the **Great Vowel Shift** were more-or-less complete, third person forms like *loveth* had disappeared from educated speech, as had the pronouns *thou* and *thee*. All in all, the language differed only in minor ways from present-day English (Barber 1993: 199). The opening of Jonathan Swift's *Gulliver's Travels* (1726) provides no serious problems for the modern reader, despite having been written nearly 300 years ago:

> MY FATHER had a small Estate in *Nottinghamshire*; I was the Third of five Sons. He sent me to *Emanuel-College* in *Cambridge*, at Fourteen Years old, where I resided three Years, and applyed my self close to my Studies: But the Charge of maintaining me (although I had a very scanty Allowance) being too great for a narrow Fortune; I was bound Apprentice to Mr. *James Bates*, an eminent Surgeon in *London*, with whom I continued four Years.

Morphology, syntax and vocabulary differ very little from modern English. Two differences stand out: current English usually introduces time adverbials expressing duration with the preposition *for* (preferring *where I resided **for** three years* and *with whom I continued **for** four years*); and in present-day Standard English *closely* rather than *close* is the accepted adverb form. As far as spelling and punctuation is concerned, there are some differences between texts produced at the beginning of the LModE period and later texts, but because orthography had become more or less standardized (especially in print) by the end of the **Early Modern English** period, these differences are minor. In the Swift passage, the first letter of all the nouns is capitalized (a practice which had all but died out by the end of the eighteenth century), and there are slight differences in the use to which punctuation marks such as the colon and semicolon are being put. Only one spelling <applyed> is different from current English, and the vocabulary is entirely familiar (although the meaning of at least one of the words – *apprentice* – has changed slightly, in the sense that it is no longer applied to a trainee professional such as a doctor).

The last three hundred years have seen important changes in the social and cultural contexts shaping the English language. As Britain extended its overseas territories in the eighteenth and nineteenth centuries, the vocabulary of English grew richer (see BORROWING). Examples of loanwords which entered the general vocabulary of English during this period include *ketchup* from China, *jungle, pyjamas* and *shampoo* from India, and *taboo* from Polynesia. The language also acquired new speakers and new 'non-native' varieties of English developed in Asia and Africa. English in America continued to diverge from British English, particularly after the American Revolution, which resulted in independence for the United States of America in 1776. The geographical expansion of English during the period was accompanied by profound social and economic change. These changes have left their mark on the language, particularly at the level of lexis. For example, there has been an enormous expansion in the vocabularies of science and technology over the last three hundred years. The eighteenth century saw a huge increase in words associated with the life sciences, because this was the age of biological description and classification. From this period come words such as *albino, anther, fauna, habitat, ovate*. In the nineteenth century, many specialized fields were developing rapidly, and each had its own vocabulary. Some of these words have come into common use, including *cereal, conifer, hibernate, isobar, metabolism, ozone* and *pasteurize*. New scientific and technological frontiers have opened up in the twentieth and twenty-first centuries, resulting in the formation of words such as *isotope, neutron, antibiotics, penicillin, vitamin, biodegradable,* *biosphere, ecosphere, virtual reality* (see Barber 1993: 215–219).

The growing diversity of English was accompanied by vigorous attempts to regulate it. The eighteenth century is widely regarded as a period of 'linguistic anxiety', during which a number of concerns about the state of the English language were expressed. Increasing numbers of dictionaries and grammars were produced in an attempt to codify English (see CODIFICATION), and many guides to 'correct' **usage** appeared (see PRESCRIPTIVISM). A strand of prescriptivism has continued to the present day, but in general attitudes to linguistic diversity and change have become more tolerant and accepting, perhaps as a consequence of the massive social changes which came about after World War Two.

Latin An **Indo-European language** originally spoken in the first millennium BC in and around Rome. Between the first century BC and the fourth and fifth centuries AD, Latin, as the language of the Roman Empire, accompanied colonial expansion and conquest across a vast territory, stretching from North Africa to Britain and from Portugal to Armenia. Members of the Romance family of languages, which include **French**, Spanish, Italian and Portuguese, are descended from the **vernacular** Latin which was spoken from around the third century AD across this territory. After the collapse of the Roman Empire, Latin continued to exercise a profound influence on Western culture, as the official language of the Roman Catholic Church, and as a medium of **Renaissance** culture.

The most obvious way in which Latin has influenced English is in the vocabulary. Throughout the late Roman period, Latin speakers came into contact with speakers of **Germanic** languages and some words which were borrowed into these languages (mostly from rather 'domestic' **semantic fields**) survived into **Old English**, such as *weall* (wall), *pytt* (pit), *mangere* (monger), *win* (wine), *cytel* (kettle), *cuppe* (cup), *disc* (dish), *pipor* (pepper), *butere* (butter), *pise* (pea), *minte* (mint), *cealc* (chalk), *copor* (copper), *pic* (pitch), and *tigele* (tile). The **Anglo-Saxons** also borrowed a few words of Latin origin from the Celts: these were mostly elements of place names or geographical features, such as *porta* (port), *munt* (mountain), *wic* (village). However, it was during the period in which Christianity was introduced to Britain that the Latin influence on Old English was at its strongest. Words introduced by the Christian missionaries are often associated with ecclesiastical matters, and include *abbot*, *alms*, *altar*, *angel*, *candle*, *canon*, *cleric*, *disciple*, *hymn*, *martyr*, *mass*, *minster*, *nun*, *priest*, *psalm*, *shrine*. But not all the Latin borrowings from this period were religious in flavour; some, for example, indicate the extent to which the Church was involved in scholarship and education: *school*, *master*, *grammatical*, *verse*, *meter*, *gloss*. As well as presiding over an influx of new vocabulary, the Christian missionaries radically altered the appearance of written English. Before the arrival of Christianity, English had been written (usually in the form of inscriptions on stone and wood) using runic script. But Christian scribes produced documents in English using the Latin **alphabet** (supplemented with a few additional letters derived from **runes**).

In the **Middle English** period, Latin loanwords associated with religion and scholarship continued to enter the lexicon, together with terms associated with law and administration. Some survivals include *immortal*, *pulpit*, *scripture*, *equator*, *history*, *solar*, *allegory*, *conspiracy*, *custody*, *homicide*. However, it is sometimes not clear whether a word has been introduced directly from Latin, or whether it enters English through French. In contrast, the Latin origins of many **Early Modern English** borrowings are more obvious. In the sixteenth and seventeenth centuries, as part of the **elaboration** of English, hundreds of words were either borrowed directly from the classical languages or coined using elements from Latin and Greek, a trend particularly encouraged by the large number of English translations from Latin sources which were made during the Renaissance. Some Latin-based words from this period include *agile*, *abdomen*, *anatomy*, *area*, *compensate*, *excavate*, *expensive*, *fictitious*, *gradual*, *insane*, *meditate*, *notorious*, *orbit*, *peninsula*, *physician*, *ultimate*, *vindicate*.

Beyond the lexicon, Latin has had a particular influence on the normative tradition of English **usage**. During the seventeenth, eighteenth and nineteenth centuries, for example, grammars of English were produced by scholars who based their descriptions of English (and recommendations for English usage) on prestigious Latin models. As a result, various 'rules' were promulgated which often seem to go against what many English speakers regard as 'natural' English syntax. Some of the most well-known of these include the prescriptions against ending sentences with prepositions (as in *You would need to practice those two sounds with the words they go **with***), or 'splitting' infinitives (as in *It is rare for a Royal **to openly criticize** Government policy*). See BIBLE, INKHORN TERM, POLYGLOSSIA, PRESCRIPTIVISM, REFORMATION, SPLIT INFINITIVE.

Latino English A cover term for varieties of English spoken by people of

Latin-American descent in the USA (the term 'Hispanic English' is sometimes used). See CHICANO ENGLISH.

Lax See TENSE AND LAX.

Lect A **backformation** from words such as **idiolect**, **dialect** and **sociolect** which is occasionally used as a synonym for **variety**.

Left-dislocation See DISLOCATION.

Lemma See LEXEME.

Lexeme A grouping of one or more word-forms. A lexeme can be made up of several word-forms, or it might have only one member. Word-forms 'represent' or 'realize' lexemes, so for example the lexeme *GO* (lexemes are conventionally written in upper case) is realized by the word-forms *go*, *goes*, *went*, *going*, *gone*; the lexeme *AND* is realized solely by the word-form *and*. **Dictionary** makers employ the concept of the lexeme: it is more or less equivalent to the terms 'citation form' or **headword**. Lexemes are sometimes referred to as **lemmas**, particularly in **corpus linguistics**.

Lexical bundle A term associated mainly with **corpus linguistics** to describe stereotyped, prefabricated sequences of words which occur frequently. In speech, lexical bundles are common because such 'ready-made' chunks of language are easily retrievable from memory and can be used as 'building blocks' in the course of an ongoing conversation. The following examples give some idea of the range of structures of common lexical bundles in speech: *I don't know what, well I don't know, I don't know how, oh I don't know, have a look at, let's have a look, going to be a, going to have to, was going to say, thank you very much, do you want to, do you want a, are you going to, what do you mean, what do you think* and so on. In writing,

different lexical bundles are associated with different genres. For example, structures consisting of a noun phrase + the start of a prepositional phrase are common in academic writing: *the end of, the case of, the nature of, the relationship between* and so on (see *LSGSWE:* 443–449).

Lexical cohesion The cohesive effects of vocabulary choice. The simplest type of lexical cohesion is **repetition** of a word or **lexeme**. More complex cohesive ties are a product of the **semantic relations** that exist between words (e.g. **synonymy**, **antonymy**, **hyponymy** and **meronymy**). Repetition and semantic relations work together to produce the 'continuity of lexical meaning' (Halliday and Hasan 1976) which is a characteristic of cohesive texts. 1) Repetition: *She saw her father walking a **dog** on the road. The **dog** was under leash. This **dog** saw a **goat**. He (the **dog**) instantly wrestled himself free and ran off. He tore up the **goat** into pieces.*± 2) Synonymy: *She still lives to recount her **tale**. This is her **story**.*± 3) Antonymy: *The **big** ones get noticed; the **small**, silent ones die out without a whimper.*± 4) Hyponymy: *Egyptians did not weaken in their worship of the **cat**. We know from the observations of Herodotus nearly a century later that they were still treating the **animal** with the utmost respect.* 5) Meronymy: *He kept his **face** near the open window to get as much fresh air as possible, but the dust kept getting into his **mouth** and **eyes**.*± Compare GRAMMATICAL COHESION.

Lexical density A measurement of the proportion of **lexical words** (nouns, verbs, adjectives and adverbs) to the total number of words in a text, usually expressed as a percentage. If L is the number of lexical words in a text and T is the total number of words, then the lexical density is $L \div T \times 100$. The following sentences both have the same number of words, but their lexical density is different (lexical words in bold). *The* **red safety indicator line** *on* **extension ladders** *should be* **vertical**• ($7 \div 11 \times 100 = 63.6$); *But he was* **using** *it all the* **time** *wasn't he?* ($2 \div 11 \times 100 = 18.2$). Writing is generally more explicit and detailed than speech, and therefore has a higher information load, making it more lexically dense. See SPEECH AND WRITING, TYPE-TOKEN RATIO.

Lexical diffusion A change in pronunciation which first appears in a single word or set of phonologically related words, and then spreads by **analogy** to all the phonologically similar words in the lexicon. For example, in New Zealand English, a vowel merger is currently in progress affecting words in the NEAR and SQUARE **lexical set**s, so that for most speakers, word pairs which were once distinct (such as *beer* and *bear*) are now **homophone**s. However, the change is not yet complete, since some speakers maintain the distinction in other word pairs, such as *fear* and *fair* (see Holmes 2001: 222–223).

Lexical field See SEMANTIC FIELD.

Lexical gap The absence in a language of a word for an object or concept. Cross-linguistic comparisons can reveal lexical gaps. For example, there is no single word in English which refers to the father of your daughter-in-law or son-in-law; a relationship which is economically expressed in Russian as *svat*. The presence of a lexical gap is often a motivation for **borrowing**. For example, in English there is no word which captures the meaning of 'the kind of pleasure you feel at another person's misfortune', so the German *Schadenfreude* is used for this purpose.

Lexicalization The process by which a word is coined for a new entity or concept. A 'lexicalized' meaning is one for which a word exists. Different languages lexicalize the world differently. For example, the exact quality of the snug cosiness conveyed by the German word *gemütlich* cannot be rendered in English with a single word. See also OVERLEXICALIZATION AND UNDERLEXICALIZATION.

Lexical semantics The branch of **semantics** concerned with the meaning of words.

Lexical set An influential concept developed by the English phonetician John Wells. A lexical set is a group of monosyllabic words whose members tend to share the same vowel. Wells identifies twenty-four standard lexical sets, 'based on the vowel correspondences which apply between British Received Pronunciation and (a variety of) General American' (Wells 1982: xviii). Each set is represented by a 'keyword' (conventionally written in upper case) intended to be identifiable no matter which accent they are said in. These are KIT, DRESS, TRAP, LOT, STRUT, FOOT, BATH, CLOTH, NURSE, FLEECE, FACE, PALM, THOUGHT, GOAT, GOOSE, PRICE, CHOICE, MOUTH, NEAR, SQUARE, START, NORTH, FORCE and CURE. Lexical sets are a convenient way of comparing vowels in different accents of English. For example, for most English speakers, words in the STRUT set have a different vowel from words in the FOOT set. But some speakers in the north of England have the same vowel in both sets (usually /ʊ/). The concept of lexical sets provides a convenient way of describing such systemic differences.

Lexical verb One of the four lexical word classes. Lexical verbs express actions, events, activities, processes, states and so on, and function as the **main verb** in a verb phrase. Lexical verbs are often categorized according to their semantic properties. See separate entries for ACTIVITY VERB, CAUSATIVE VERB, COMMUNICATION VERB, EXISTENCE VERB, MENTAL VERB, OCCURRENCE VERB.

Lexical word A word which carries lexical meaning. Lexical words are **nouns**, **lexical verbs**, **adjectives** and **adverbs**. They are **open class**, because new coinages can be added to them. Lexical words are sometimes known as 'content' words. Compare GRAMMATICAL WORD.

Lexicogrammar The interface between **lexis** and **grammar**. Vocabulary and grammatical structures are interdependent; so much so that it is possible to say with some justification that words have their own grammar. This interdependency of lexis and grammar is evident everywhere in language. For example, lexical verbs have **valency patterns**: some verbs can be used with a direct object (*I made some oven gloves•*), or with both a direct object and an indirect object (*The government awarded them a pay rise•*), others need no object at all (*The Colonel was laughing•*). Lexical verbs also have 'preferences' in terms of the kind of **complement clause** they select. For example, *like* and *enjoy* are semantically related, but only *like* can occur with both an *ing*-clause and a *to*-clause: *I like playing bingo games; The babies liked to play quietly; Humans enjoy playing with animals;* but not **Humans enjoy to play with animals.* The advent of **corpus linguistics** has made the identification of lexicogrammatical patterns much easier than it once was. See COLLIGATION.

Lexicography The compilation and design of **dictionaries**, glossaries, thesauruses, usage guides, concordances and so on.

Lexicology A branch of linguistics concerned with the study of **lexis** (words) and the lexicon (vocabulary).

Lexicon See LEXIS.

Lexifier language The language from which a **pidgin** or **creole** derives all or most of its vocabulary.

Lexis A term with a number of related meanings. At its broadest it is used to describe the **language level** concerned with words and their meanings. More narrowly, it is used to refer to the words (vocabulary) of a **language**, **variety** or **register**, such as *the lexis of New Zealand English; the lexis of advertising* (the term *lexicon* is occasionally used for this purpose). See also FORMALITY, LANGUAGE LEVEL, LEXEME, LEXICAL COHESION, LEXICAL DENSITY, LEXICALIZATION, LEXICAL SEMANTICS, LEXICAL WORD, LEXICOGRAMMAR, LEXICOLOGY, OVERLEXICALIZATION AND UNDERLEXICALIZATION, SEMANTIC FIELD, SLANG, TYPE-TOKEN RATIO, WORD, WORD-CLASS, WORD FORMATION.

Lingua franca A language used as a medium of inter-group communication across a wide geographical area. Languages which have served this function around the world and at different times include **Latin** in Western Europe (first as the language of the Roman Empire, then as the language of scholarship and the church); **French** as the language of diplomacy in the nineteenth century; Russian and German in parts of eastern Europe after World War Two; Russian in the countries which once made up the Soviet Union; Kiswahili in East Africa; Hindu/Urdu in India. English currently has a major role as a lingua franca in all domains of international communication (see WORLD ENGLISH). The term is derived from Lingua Franca, a *lingua franca* which was used (mainly by sailors and traders) in lands bordering the Mediterranean from the Middle Ages to the nineteenth century.

Linguistic atlas   See DIALECT ATLAS.

Linguistic insecurity   Negative attitudes held by a person about aspects of their own speech. As a result of linguistic insecurity, a speaker might consciously alter their way of speaking so that it more closely resembles a prestigious variety of a language. Sometimes, this can lead to **hypercorrection**. See CHANGE FROM ABOVE.

Linguistic marketplace   A term coined by Pierre Bourdieu (*marché linguistique*) to describe the way in which the 'symbolic capital' represented by language is converted into economic capital. In some contexts, the value of an utterance is increased if it is made in a standard variety; in others it has more market value if it is made in a local dialect. Nevertheless, standard language varieties, with their associations with education and high status, are generally more 'marketable' than vernacular dialects, and much language variation can be explained by the economic 'requirement' to use prestigious forms of speech in the workplace and other public settings.

Linguistic typology   Linguists sometimes group languages according to shared structural similarities. Languages can be categorized according to their morphological or syntactic features. The most well-known categories into which languages can be placed according to **morphology** are *analytic* and *synthetic*. 1) In analytic languages (also known as 'isolating' languages), most words consist of a single **morpheme**, and most morphemes are 'free' (there are no 'word endings' in such languages). Examples of analytic languages include Chinese, Vietnamese and Thai. 2) In synthetic (or 'fusional' languages) such as German, Russian and Korean, words usually contain two or more morphemes.

Present-day English (PDE) is mainly analytic. For example, in PDE the **subject** and **object** in a clause containing a **transitive verb** are distinguished by their position in the clause: *The king* (S) *greets* (V) *the thane* (O). If the order is reversed, the meaning is changed: *The thane greets the king.* In a synthetic language, such as **Old English**, the grammatical role of a noun phrase is marked inflectionally, so that *se cyning greteð ðone ðegn* and *ðone ðegn greteð se cyning* mean the same thing ('The king greets the thane'). This is because the information about which noun phrase is the subject and which is the object is carried by the determiners *se* ('the'-subject) and *ðone* ('the'-object).

Languages can also be categorized according to their syntactic characteristics, such as the 'preferred' or 'typical' order in which the subject (S), verb (V) and object (O) elements occur in the clause. Most languages prefer SVO order (e.g. English, French, Vietnamese), or SOV (Japanese, Tibetan, Korean). Between 10 and 15 per cent of the world's languages (including **Welsh** and Tongan) have VSO order (see Crystal 1997: 98).

Linguistic variable   A linguistic unit with more than one variant which can occur in the same context without altering meaning. Linguistic variables can be grammatical (e.g. *I don't have any money, I have no money, I haven't got any money, I ain't got no money*) and lexical (e.g. *I need the toilet, I need the lavatory, I need the bog*), but they are most often phonological (e.g. the word *butter* can be pronounced in a variety of different ways, for example ['bʌtə], ['bʊtə], ['bʌʔə], ['bʊʔə], ['bədəɹ], and so on). Sometimes, the choice of variable is related to 'purely' linguistic factors. For instance, there are a set of **grammatical words** in English which are pronounced in one way in connected speech and another way when they are spoken in isolation or being emphasized. Examples include *to* (/tə/ and /tuː/), *that* (/ðət/ and /ðat/) and *from* (/frəm/ and /frɒm/). But in many other cases, the choice of variable is related to the class, age, gender, regional background or ethnicity of the speaker. In other words, linguistic variables can be regarded as linguistically equivalent but socially different ways of saying the same thing (Chambers and Trudgill 1998: 50). See SOCIAL CLASS.

Linking /r/ In some accents of English, /r/ is no longer pronounced in words with <r> in the spelling, where it occurs after a vowel (these are known as non-rhotic accents). For example, RP speakers do not usually have an /r/ in *car, fear, near, star, fur* and so on. However, in connected speech, the 'historic' /r/ at the end of such words is pronounced when it precedes a vowel (so that the 'near' in 'near Ashford' would be pronounced /nɪər/). By **analogy**, some speakers of non-rhotic accents insert an /r/ even when there is no <r> in the spelling, resulting in pronunciations such as /lɔːr/ for *law* in *law and order*. Some people object to this so-called 'intrusive' /r/, but it is extremely common in speakers of non-rhotic accents, such as **Received Pronunciation**. See RHOTIC ACCENT.

Literal and non-literal Traditionally, the 'literal' meaning of a word is its basic meaning, which is usually captured in its primary dictionary definition. If you presented someone with a single word devoid of any context and asked for its definition, they would probably provide a literal meaning. 'Non-literal' meanings involve a semantic extension beyond a word's basic meaning, and include **metaphor** and **connotation**. Sometimes **figurative language** is regarded as the 'opposite' of literal language.

Loan translation A process of word formation in which a word or phrase is acquired from the 'source' language, but instead of being borrowed into the 'target' language directly it is translated morpheme-for-morpheme or word-for-word. The result of this process is sometimes known as a **calque**. Loan translation is the source of some quite well-known English words and phrases, including *standpoint* (from German *Standpunkt*), *flea market* (from French *marché aux puces*), *wisdom tooth* (from Latin *dēns sapientiae*).

Loan translation is common in contexts of sustained contact between speakers of different languages, and is sometimes a source of vocabulary in **pidgins** and **creoles**. See BORROWING, CODE-SWITCHING.

Loanword See BORROWING.

Locative The **semantic role** of a noun phrase specifying the place where the state or action denoted by the verb takes place. In the following examples, locatives are in bold: *The computer lab is in **the library**; He lives near **Newcastle***. The term can also be used more generally to describe any word or structure denoting location.

Long passive A passive construction which includes the *by*-phrase: *Trepper was interrogated **by the Gestapo***. See PASSIVE VOICE.

Low vowel A vowel produced with the body of the tongue positioned as far as possible from the roof of the mouth, as in the vowel /ʌ/ in an RP pronunciation of *cup*. Low vowels are sometimes called 'open' vowels. See VOWEL.

M

Main clause   A clause which is capable of standing independently as a complete sentence (and which is therefore sometimes known as an *independent clause*).

In a **simple sentence**, the entire sentence consists of a main clause: *They were very solid doors*. In a **compound sentence**, there is a sequence of two or more main clauses, linked by coordinating conjunctions: *I like my job and I like my life.*• In a **complex sentence**, the main clause is the structure on which the subordinate clause or clauses are dependent: *When my sons went to the village school there was respect*. All main clauses are **finite**.

The following examples illustrate some of the most typical main clause structures in English (elements are indicated in brackets): 1) Subject + Verb: *I* (S) *fainted* (V). 2) Subject + Verb + Direct Object: *Egyptian commandos* (S) *devoured* (V) *live chickens* (DO). 3) Subject + Verb + Subject Complement: *British justice* (S) *is* (V) *a myth* (SC). 4) Subject + Verb + Adverbial: *The books* (S) *were* (V) *on the shelves* (A). 5) Subject + Verb + Indirect Object + Direct Object: *Dad* (S) *had bought* (V) *him* (IO) *a tarantula* (DO). 6) Subject + Verb + Direct Object + Object Complement: *Marjorie* (S) *named* (V) *her* (DO) *Lizzie* (OC). 7) Subject + Verb + Direct Object + Adverbial: *I* (S) *placed* (V) *the parcels* (DO) *on the table* (A).

Main verb   The **head** of a **verb phrase**. The main verb is either a **lexical verb** or one of the **primary verbs** (*be, have, do*). The main verb occurs alone in a simple verb phrase, or alongside modal verbs and/or auxiliary verbs in a more complex verb phrase, where it is placed at the end. In the following examples, the main verb is in bold and the verb phrase is underlined: *I **sorted** it out; Hatton had been living like a king; I will **bless** you; They're young*. Main verbs are important in the clause because they 'select' subsequent clause elements, as seen in the following examples. A **transitive** main verb selects a **direct object**: *Eileen **enjoys*** (transitive verb) *swimming* (direct object). A ditransitive verb selects an **indirect object** and a direct object: ***Give*** (ditransitive verb) *Michael* (indirect object) *the thingybob* (direct object). A **copular verb** selects a subject **complement**: *Sarah **is*** (copular verb) *innocent* (subject complement). See LEXICOGRAMMAR, VALENCY PATTERN.

Markedness   When two **phonemes** are distinguished from each other with respect to a single feature, one is said to be 'marked' for that feature, while the other is 'unmarked'. For example, in English the consonants /t/ and /d/ are identical, except that /d/ is 'marked' for voice and /t/ is voiceless. The concept has been extended to morphology. For example, in English, the 'unmarked' form of a word is its **base form** (e.g. *table, lion*) while the addition of **affix**es results in 'marked' forms (e.g. adding *-s* to the noun *table* marks it for number; adding *-ess* to the noun *lion* marks it for **gender**). It is usually the case that the unmarked term in a pair is the more 'neutral' item. In the case of *lion* and *lioness*, *lion* can be used to refer to animals of either sex (*Lions habitually hunt in teams*), whereas *lioness* can only be used to refer to female lions

(*While a lioness is lactating for her cub, she will not produce another*). Where male/female pairs exist, it is always the female term which is marked, usually by affixation (e.g. *prince/princess, author/authoress, actor/actress, host/hostess, usher/usherette* and so on). Since the advent of the feminist movement there has been a tendency to use the unmarked form for both sexes (see GENDER).

The term 'markedness' is more generally applied to any linguistic feature or structure which is being used in an unexpected or unusual way (compare DEVIATION). For example, in English the unmarked order of the **clause elements** in a declarative sentence containing a transitive verb is S (Subject) V (Verb) DO (Direct Object), as in *I saw that one*. Placing the object at the front of the clause results in a clause with marked word order: *That one I saw* (see FRONTING, INVERSION).

Material process   See TRANSITIVITY.

Melanesian Pidgin English   A general term for three varieties of **Pidgin** spoken in Melanesia (a region in the western Pacific consisting of Papua New Guinea, the Bismarck Archipelago, the Solomon Islands, Santa Cruz, Vanuatu, New Caledonia and Fiji). **Tok Pisin** is spoken mainly in Papua New Guinea, while Bislama is a national language of Vanuatu, and Pijin is spoken in the Solomon Islands.

Mental process   See TRANSITIVITY.

Mental verb   A **lexical verb** which refers to internal mental activities and states: *believe, consider, expect, feel, hear, know, like, listen, love, mean, need, remember, see, think, want* and so on. Some mental verbs convey a sense of deliberate psychological action on behalf of the **agent** subject (they are **dynamic**); others describe

somewhat 'passive' mental states undergone by an **experiencer** subject (they are **stative**). Compare *The children* **listened** *carefully* (dynamic) with *They* **heard** *the back door slam* (stative).

Mercian   The **Old English** dialect associated with Mercia, one of the Kingdoms of the **Anglo-Saxon** heptarchy. The Mercian dialect was probably spoken from the Thames in the south to the Humber in the north. Surviving documents in the dialect include a collection of charters of the Mercian kings and part of the tenth-century Rushworth Gospels. See KENTISH, NORTHUMBRIAN, WEST SAXON.

Meronymy   A type of **semantic relation** involving a 'part–whole' relationship between words. X is a meronym of Y if X is 'part of' Y. For example, *finger* is a meronym of *hand*. See LEXICAL COHESION.

Mesolect   A term coined by the sociolinguist Derek Bickerton to describe the variety of a creole which lies somewhere between the **acrolect** and the **basilect**. See CREOLE CONTINUUM.

Metafunction   In **systemic functional linguistics**, human utterances can be classified according to which of three broad functions they fulfil. These are the *ideational, interpersonal* and *textual* metafunctions (it should be stressed that a single utterance is capable of performing more than one metafunction simultaneously). 1) The ideational metafunction refers to the way in which language is used to *represent* human beings' experiences of the real world, and also the inner world of consciousness. Halliday argues that this representation is expressed through the system of **transitivity**, which organizes the world of experience into process types (see Halliday and Matthiessen 2004). 2) The interpersonal metafunction refers to the way in which we use language to communicate with others, to forge and maintain social relationships, and to express thoughts, judgements, feelings and attitudes. Halliday argues that the interpersonal metafunction is expressed through the systems of **mood** and **modality** (see also **stance**). 3) The textual metafunction refers to the way in which language is used to form and organize the **text** itself, to hold it together (see COHERENCE and COHESION).

Metalanguage Language 'about' language. Any word or expression which is used to describe, categorize or explain a linguistic phenomenon is performing a metalinguistic **function**. Metalanguage can range from commentary on the everyday and familiar (*Her squeaky voice is a bit of a shock at first*) to highly technical accounts of language (*The adjective provides the syntactic-semantic condition under which the relation between the verb and its object holds*).

Metalinguistic See METALANGUAGE.

Metaphor (Greek: 'transference') A **figure of speech** which involves a semantic 'transfer' from one field of reference to another. So, if someone says 'John is a tiger', some of the qualities of a tiger (its strength, viciousness, implacability and so on) have been transferred metaphorically to 'John'. Traditionally, literary criticism has analysed metaphor in terms of a relationship between the *tenor* (the 'topic' of the metaphor, in this case 'John'), the *vehicle* (the conceptual source of the metaphor, in this case 'tiger') and the *ground* (the semantic basis of the comparison). Although metaphor is often associated with literary language, it is pervasive in all domains of spoken and written language: *I was a pizza faced geek* (cycling website).

Conceptual mappings from one domain to another can be characterized according to the cognitive effort required to process them (see Stockwell 2000, 2002). The most straightforward and easily recoverable mappings are **similes** of the type 'X is like Y', and copula constructions of the type 'X is Y' ('The brain is like a city'; 'The brain is a city'). Other constructions which make the mapping visible are **apposition**s ('The brain, that teeming city'), and **genitive** expressions ('Paris is the city of my mind'). Some metaphorical expressions, however, are 'invisible', because either the tenor or the vehicle is not explicitly stated. For example, in the expression 'His brain was gridlocked' the vehicle (the city) is present only in the form of a state *associated* with cities (that of being gridlocked).

See also ANALOGY [1], CONCEPTUAL METAPHOR, DEVIATION, FIGURE OF SPEECH, LITERAL AND NON-LITERAL, SIMILE.

Metathesis (Greek: 'transposition, change') A process of **sound change** in which adjacent sounds are re-ordered, as in the following pairs of Old English words and their modern English equivalents: *briddl/bird; hross/horse; thridda/ third; aks/ask* (in some varieties of English, *aks* remains unmetathesized).

Metonymy (Greek: 'change of name') A **figure of speech** in which a word or phrase is replaced by another with which it is associated in some way: *Mock me and you mock **the crown**!* In this example, an item of headwear *associated* with royalty stands for the entire institution of monarchy. Metonymic expressions, like other figures of speech, are conventionally regarded as features of literature and rhetoric, but they are also widespread in language generally, as this list of types which occur frequently in English shows (see Lakoff and Johnson 1980). 1) The part for the whole (see SYNECDOCHE): *Move your **butt**; We need a fresh **pair of legs**.* 2) The whole for the part: *We locked **the house** up; I'll fill up **the car**.* 3) Producer for product: *I always enjoyed reading **Shakespeare**; He drives a **BMW**.* 4) Container for contained: ***The toilet** overflowed; **The car** decided to turn left.*† 5) Institution for people responsible: ***The company** sacked workers; **Exxon** is closing its gas stations.*• 6) Controller for controlled: ***Hitler** attacked the Soviet Union; **Saddam Hussein** killed thousands of people.*† 7) Place for institution: ***Downing Street** tried to dampen down the story; **Belgrade** will have to accept our terms.* 8) Place for the event: ***Iraq** is turning into **another Vietnam**.*† 9) Possessor for possessed: *I'm parked out back.*•

Metre   Patterns of **rhythm** in poetry. Metre organizes **stress**ed and unstressed **syllable**s into regularly occurring and repeated units. These units are known as *feet*. A foot consists of at least one stressed syllable and one or more unstressed syllables. Some of the most commonly occurring types of feet in English poetry are the *iamb*, *trochee*, *anapest* and *dactyl*. Iambs and trochees consist of two syllables. An iamb contains an unstressed syllable followed by a stressed one (stressed syllables in bold): *Shall **I** | compare | thee **to** | a **summ** | er's **day**?* A trochee is a reversed iamb, consisting of a stressed syllable followed by an unstressed one: ***Peter** | **Piper** | **picked** a | **peck** of | **pickled** | **pepper***. Anapests and dactyls consist of three syllables. An anapest has two unstressed syllables followed by a stressed one: *I am **mon** | arch of **all** | I sur**vey**.* A dactyl is a reversed anapest, consisting of a stressed syllable followed by two unstressed ones: ***One** for the | **master** and | **one** for the | **dame***.

In poetry, feet are organized into lines, and poetic lines are labelled according to how many feet they contain. A *monometer* is a line with one foot; a line with two feet is a *dimeter*, with three feet a *trimeter*, with four feet a *tetrameter*, with six feet a *hexameter*, with seven feet a *heptameter* and with eight feet an *octameter*.

This terminology allows for the categorization of metre according to line length and foot type. The following examples illustrate some common metrical patterns in English verse.

1   This **grave** | yard **stands** | above | a **worked** | out **pit** | **(iambic pentameter)**

2   I **heard** | a **fly** | buzz **when** | I **died** | (iambic tetrameter)

3   **Willows** | **whit**en, | **asp**ens | **quiv**er (trochaic tetrameter)

4   Not a **crea** | ture was **stirr** | ing, not **ev** | en a **mouse** (anapestic tetrameter)

Middle English (ME)   The period in the history of the English language which follows **Old English** and precedes **Early Modern English**, extending from the mid-eleventh to the late fifteenth century. Although the start of the period is often given as the **Norman** Conquest (1066), some of the differences between Old English and Middle English are a consequence of changes which were already under way before the arrival of William the Conqueror. The most important of these is the reduction in the system of grammatical **inflection**s, which was a consequence of several linked processes. In Old English (as in modern English), the main stress was usually placed on the first syllable of a word. This sometimes led to the grammatical information contained in the more weakly stressed inflected syllable at the end of the word becoming difficult for a listener to recover, especially when so many of the inflectional endings of Old English were so similar (e.g. *glofe, glofa*). The distinctive endings probably became indistinguishable in fast connected speech, and were therefore redundant. Further motivation for the loss of inflections was the period of sustained contact between the English and Scandinavians. Speakers often 'simplify' aspects of their language when trying to make themselves understood to speakers of another language (see LANGUAGE CONTACT). This could have happened in the context of interaction between English and **Norse** speakers, who might have relied less on inflectional endings to convey grammatical information, and used word order and prepositions instead. During the Middle English period, all inflections consisting only of a vowel, or a vowel plus a nasal were lost. The main classes of verb inflection survived, but all noun inflections gradually disappeared apart from *-s*.

The Norman Conquest brought about a period of close contact between the English and the French which also had important consequences for the English language. This can be seen in the following extract from a translation of the New Testament made in the late fourteenth century (see Görlach 1997):

> And whanne Jhesu cam into the hous of the prince, and say mynstrallis, and the puple makynge noise, he seide, Go Ze a wei, for the damysel is not deed, but slepith.
>
> (Wyclif Bible, c.1380)

In the years following the Conquest, the vocabulary of English took on the mixed Germanic and Romance nature that it has today. It is estimated that about 35 per cent of the most common, non-technical words in present-day English are Germanic in origin. In the passage, *and*,

whanne ('when'), *cam* ('came'), *into, the, hous* ('house'), *of, say* ('saw'), *he, seide* ('said'), *go, Ze* ('you'), *a wei* ('away'), *for, is, not, but* and *slepith* ('sleeps') fall into this category. But *prince, mynstrallis* ('minstrels'), *puple* ('people'), *noise* and *damysel* all have French etymologies. The use of the preposition *of* in *the hous of the prince* might also be traced to French influence. **English spelling** was also influenced by French. By the end of the fourteenth century, the letters þ (*thorn*) and ð (*eth*), which had been used indiscriminately in Old English texts to represent the sounds [θ] and [ð], had fallen out of use. For these sounds, the Middle English scribes used the **digraph** <th>, which they imported from French via Latin (<th> had been used in Latin to represent the sound [θ] in Greek loanwords). Middle English spelling is much more diverse in comparison with the relative stability of Old English, as these variant spellings of *might* demonstrate: *math, mahte, mihhte, mayht, mihte, micht, micthe*. One of the main reasons for this is that throughout most of the Middle English period there was no standard variety of English used in texts, nor a dominant scribal tradition: documents were simply written in the local dialect of the writer. Indeed, Middle English is the only period in the history of the English language where regional variety is reflected in written language so widely and unselfconsciously (Crystal 2004: 194).

The following tables (based on Crystal 2003: 42) give some indication of how vowels and consonants were pronounced in the dialect of south-east England – the variety used by the poet Geoffrey Chaucer (c.1343–1400).

Middle English vowels

Spelling	Sound	ME word
y	iː	ryden
ee	eː	sweete
ee	ɛː	heeth
a	ɑː	name
ou	uː	houre
oo	oː	good
o	ɔː	holy
i	ɪ	this
e	ɛ	men
a	a	can
a	ə	aboute (in unstressed syllables)
u	ʊ	but
o	ɔ	oft
ay	æɪ	day
oy	ɔɪ	joye
oi	ʊɪ	joinen
ew	ɪʊ	newe
ew	ɛʊ	fewe
aw	aʊ	lawe
ow	ɔʊ	growe

Middle English consonants

Spelling	Sound	ME word
p, b	p, b	pin, bit
t, d	t, d	tente, dart
k, g	k, g	kin, good
ch	tʃ	chirche ('church')
gg	dʒ	brigge ('bridge')
m, n, ng	m, n, ŋ	make, name, song
l, r	l, r	lay, rage
w, y	w, j	weep, yelwe ('yellow')
f, v	f, v	fool, vertu
s, z	s, z	sore, Zephirus
th	θ, ð	thank, the
h	h	happen

Middle voice See ERGATIVE VERB, VOICE [1].

Mid vowel A vowel produced with the body of the tongue positioned between where it would be for a **high vowel** and a **low vowel**. The vowel /ɛ/ in *bed* is a mid vowel. See VOWEL.

Mind style A term coined by Roger Fowler in *Linguistics and the Novel* (1977) to describe the way in which **stylistic** choices construct the interior mental world, perceptions, beliefs and so on of an author, **narrator** or character.

Minimal pair   Two words that contrast in only one sound, with the contrastive element occurring in the same position in both words, as in the RP pronunciation of the following pairs: *bad/mad; tap/tip; cod/cot*. Because the difference between the items in a minimal pair always signals a difference in meaning, they are helpful to linguists drawing up a **phoneme** inventory for a language or language variety (if the two different sounds result in two different meanings, then the sounds must be phonemes).

Minor sentence   A sentence which has one or more elements of canonical sentence structure missing, but which nevertheless conveys meaning: *One week of authentic spring, one rare sweet week of May, one tranquil moment between the blast of winter and the charge of summer* (Sinclair Lewis, 1920). Highly elliptical utterances might be termed minor sentences, as would a **verbless clause**. Minor sentences are also known as 'sentence fragments'. See ELLIPSIS.

Modality   A term used to describe a speaker or writer's attitude towards a) the truth of the propositional content of an utterance, and b) his or her attitude towards the situation or event described in the utterance. A variety of forms can convey modality, including **modal verb**s, **stance** adverbs, evaluative nouns and adjectives, and lexical verbs. In English, modality is usually divided into two types: *epistemic* and *deontic*. 1) Epistemic modality is concerned with levels of certainty; it conveys the extent of a speaker's commitment to the truth of a proposition, ranging from slight possibility (*It **might** have been a wig*) to complete certainty (***She is sure** that we are lovers*). 2) Deontic modality communicates meanings such as permission, obligation, requirement, commitment, intent. This is

often done through modal verbs (*You **must** talk to the patient•*) and **directive**s (***Shut up**, Doreen; **I insist** that we have a re-vote*). Expressions of **volition** also convey deontic modality: *I **want** to read my newspaper; I **will** feed my flock*.

Modal verb   A member of a set of **auxiliary verb**s consisting of nine 'central' modal verbs (*can, could, may, might, must, shall, should, will* and *would*) and several **semi-modal verb**s such as *have to, be going to*. Formally, the central modals are invariant (they do not take inflections to show distinctions of person or tense). Four of them, however, can be grouped into pairs which distinguish between present and past time: *can/could, may/might, shall/should, will/would*. (Compare the following invented sentences: *I **may** go tomorrow/I **might** have gone if I'd known about it*.) Syntactically, modal verbs function as an auxiliary verb in verb phrases, combining with a bare infinitive main verb. They can form part of complex **verb chain**s: *George **must have been carrying** it in his hand.•*

The central modal verbs are used to express *epistemic* and *deontic* **modality**. Epistemic modality is concerned with levels of certainty, and modal verbs can be used to express meanings on a continuum from doubt to absolute certainty, as the following invented examples show: *You **could** be right; You **may** be right; You **might** be right; You **must** be right.* Deontic modality is the modal system of 'duty', and is concerned with ordering, obliging, requiring, allowing and so on. Modal verbs can be used to express meanings on a continuum which shows increasing degrees of obligation, as these invented examples show: *You **may** go; You **should** go; You **can** go; You **must** go; You **will** go*.

Mode   See REGISTER.

Modern English   See EARLY MODERN ENGLISH, LATER MODERN ENGLISH, PRESENT-DAY ENGLISH.

Modifier   A modifier is an element in a **noun phrase**, **adjective phrase** or **adverb phrase** which provides additional information about the **head**, by describing or classifying it. Unlike a **complement**, modifiers are not needed to *complete* the meaning of another form, and can therefore be omitted without affecting grammaticality (although their omission will, of course, affect meaning).

When modifiers occur before the head, they are called *premodifiers*. In noun phrases, premodifiers are adjectives, nouns and participles (in the following examples the heads are underlined and the modifiers are in bold): *the **smelly** duck; **brick** walls; the **broken** windows.* Premodifiers in adjective and adverb phrases are most commonly adverbs: ***really** lovely; **so** slowly.*

Modifiers occurring after the head are called *postmodifiers*. In noun phrases, postmodifiers are phrases or clauses. The main phrasal types of postmodification are prepositional phrases (*a box **of dates***); appositive noun phrases (*the Chancellor, **Norman Lamont***), and – less commonly – adjective phrases (*congregationalists **keen on disestablishment***). The main clausal types of postmodification are finite **relative clauses** (*men **who have suffered repeated attacks***), and non-finite **to-clauses**, **ing-clauses** or **ed-clauses** (*the most difficult stuff **to sell**; aircraft **flying in the area**; new fares **proposed by the big airlines***). In adjective phrases, postmodifiers are usually prepositional phrases: *late **for breakfast;**• big **for my age.**•* Postmodifiers of adverb phrases are rare, but when they do occur they are usually prepositional phrases: *luckily **for him.**•*

Monolingualism   At the individual level, the term is used to describe the condition of being able to speak only one language. Sociolinguistic situations in which a single language is used can also be described as monolingual. It comes as some surprise to many people in **Anglophone** countries such as Britain and the USA that a minority of the world's population is monolingual. Compare BILINGUALISM, MULTILINGUALISM.

Monophthong   A **vowel** whose quality does not change as it is produced (compare DIPHTHONG and TRIPHTHONG). For this reason, monophthongs are sometimes called 'pure' or 'stable' vowels.

Monosyllable   A word containing one **syllable**. Compare POLYSYLLABLE.

Monotransitive   A **valency pattern** which selects a **direct object**: *He licked **his thumb***. Compare DITRANSITIVE.

Mood   A grammatical category concerned with the classification of clauses according to whether they are **indicative**, **imperative** or **subjunctive** (although the subjunctive mood is now rarely used in English). See CLAUSE, DECLARATIVE, INTERROGATIVE, SENTENCE, SPEECH ACT THEORY, SPEECH AND WRITING.

Morpheme   The smallest unit of meaning in a language. Morphemes can be *free* or *bound*. A free morpheme is a unit of meaning which constitutes a single word: *fish, anvil, habitat, they*. In English, bound morphemes are either **inflectional** or **derivational** affixes which, unlike free morphemes, cannot stand alone as meaningful **words**: ***un**known, **dis**interested, **re**considered, **de**thrones, walk**ing**, warm**ly**, great**ness**.*

Morphology   The part of **grammar** which is concerned with word structure and the rules governing the way morphemes combine into words. See AFFIX,

BASE FORM, BLENDING, CLIPPING, CONTRACTION, DERIVATION, FORM, GRADABILITY, GRAMMAR, LEXEME, MONOSYLLABLE, MORPHEME, POLYSYLLABLE, REANALYSIS, REDUPLICATION, ROOT, SUFFIX, WORD.

Multilingualism The use of several languages by an individual or society. Sometimes, bilinguals are described as multilingual, but usually the term is reserved for speakers or sociolinguistic situations in which more than two languages are used. Nearly all nation states are multilingual, in the sense that speakers of different languages live in them. It is estimated, for example, that over 300 different languages are spoken by London schoolchildren (Baker and Eversley 2000). Some nations endorse multilingualism at a constitutional level. For example, India has two official national languages (Hindi and English) and fourteen languages with official status in certain regions. See BILINGUALISM, POLYGLOSSIA.

Multiple negation Two or more negative forms occurring in a single clause. The following sentences all contain multiple negation: *They don't want no crisps;*• *I never seen nobody cook as quickly as you do;*• *They never said nothing about wanting it back.*• Although such forms are often stigmatized, they are very common in most **non-standard** varieties of English.

Multiple sentence See SENTENCE.

Multi-word verb A type of verb which consists of a **lexical verb** plus one or more other words and behaves more or less like a single verb. There are four main types of multi-word verb: *phrasal verbs*, *prepositional verbs*, *phrasal–prepositional verbs* and *semi-modal verbs*.

1) Phrasal verbs consist of a **lexical verb** and an **adverbial particle**: *The plane*

took off; Camp breaks up in a day or two; Confravision never really caught on. In most cases, the adverbial particle in a phrasal verb is formally identical to a preposition: *off, up, on, down, in* and so on. Many phrasal verbs are **transitive** (that is, they can take a **direct object**): *Mayer had the power to bring about Gilbert's downfall; Middlesbrough have called off a proposed tour to Australia.* In most phrasal verbs, the adverbial particle can be moved to a position after the direct object: *He put out the light/He put the light out; Arsonists burned down the warehouse/Arsonists burned the warehouse down; We tracked down the drivers/We tracked the drivers down.* Interestingly, when the direct object is a pronoun, it must always precede the adverb: *He put it out* / **He put out it; Arsonists burned it down* / **Arsonists burned down it.*

The meanings of phrasal verbs are often idiomatic (that is, they cannot be derived from combining the meanings of the lexical verb and the accompanying adverbial particle): *The bombs went off at lunchtime; We won't give in.* Sometimes, the meaning is more or less equivalent to a single lexical verb: *The bombs exploded at lunchtime; We won't surrender.* When a phrasal verb and a lexical verb are semantically 'equivalent' like this, the phrasal verb generally has a more informal quality (see FORMALITY).

2) Prepositional verbs are made up of a fixed combination of a lexical verb and a **preposition**: *listen to, look after.* Prepositional verbs always occur with a 'prepositional object' (the noun phrase which occurs after the preposition): *He won't listen to his critics; John is looking after a sizeable vegetable garden.* Some prepositional verbs take a direct object and a prepositional object (direct object underlined, prepositional object in bold): *Mr Kinnock accused them of*

negative campaigning; I've based it on the photograph of Rosa Ponselle. When prepositional verbs can take two objects, they commonly occur in the **passive** voice: *Mrs T* **was accused of** *infidelity; Early American cultures* **were based on** *maize.*

Phrasal and prepositional verbs look similar, but there are some important differences between them. For example, the preposition in a prepositional verb must come before the prepositional object (*Gertie cared for Hilary*), whereas the adverbial particle in a phrasal verb can be placed either before or after the direct object (*Nicola made the whole thing up; They made up the whole story*). Also, a prepositional verb allows an adverb between the lexical verb and the preposition (*He cared deeply for the countryside*), whereas a phrasal verb does not (**She made quickly up the story about finding the creature*).

3) Phrasal–prepositional verbs combine a lexical verb with a preposition *and* an adverbial: *Margaret* **looks down on** *people like me; I can* **put up with** *mosquitoes; We* **got away with** *it.* Adverbs can be placed between the adverb and the preposition, but not between the preposition and the object: *We got away* **completely** *with it; *We got away with* **completely** *it.*

4) Semi-modal verbs ('periphrastic' modals) are semantically similar to the 'central' **modal verbs**, but have a different grammatical form. The main semi-modals are *had better, have (got) to, need to, ought to, be supposed to, be going to.* The meaning of each of these semi-modals can usually be captured by one of the 'central' modal verbs. Most semi-modals express obligation and necessity, as the following paired examples demonstrate: *I* **had better** *go | I* **should** *go; They* **have to** *keep fighting | They* **must** *keep trying; This man* **has got to** *be caught | The culprit* **must** *be caught; We* **need to** *appoint a female | They* **should** *appoint four trustees;•* *You* **ought to** *be ashamed of yourselves | They* **should** *be ashamed of themselves; You're* **supposed to** *call Picone in Las Vegas | You* **should** *call the police.•* One semi-modal (*going to*) expresses volition and prediction: *I'm* **going to** *go home | I'll* *go home; I think it's* **going to** *rain | Do you think it* **will** *rain?* All of these semi-modals, with the exception of the invariant *had better* and *ought to*, can be marked for tense and person; and some can be incorporated into quite lengthy constructions containing other modals and semi-modals: *I* **was supposed to** *meet him in the park; Alison* **would have had to** *decide where to put her own clothes;•* *The bridging fund has not been applicable to many of the circumstances farmers* **have been needing to** *apply for; Mother and father* **were going to have to** *find someplace else to stay.•*

Some semi-modals have a phonologically reduced form in speech. For example, *had better* is often contracted to *'d better* or even just *better* (*You'd* **better** *put something on it; You* **better** *watch out what you're saying*). *Going to* becomes *gonna* (*They're* **gonna** *beat Walsall*); *have got to* becomes *gotta* (*I* **gotta** *transcribe this into my book±*). Such reduced forms are frequently represented in informal styles of writing.

N

Narrative The representation in words and/or images of a real or fictional sequence of events. Non-fiction narratives occur in newspaper reports, anecdotes, biography, history and so on. Fictional narratives can be found in novels, short stories, comics, plays, films and so on. A distinction is usually made between the 'abstract' storyline or plot (the sequence of real or imagined events that takes place) and the 'concrete' representation of these events in the narrative, which might use various techniques to disrupt chronological order (see ANALEPSIS) and manipulate point of view (see NARRATOR).

This distinction becomes clear when two different versions of the 'same' story are compared. In *Exercices de Style* (1947, translated as *Exercises in Style*), the French novelist Raymond Queneau presents ninety-nine versions of a minimal plot which consists of a young man on a bus having an argument with another passenger. Later that same day, outside a railway station, the man receives advice from his friend about getting an extra button on his coat. Although each of the ninety-nine versions has the same basic *plot*, each of the *narratives* is different. One version of the story begins 'One day at about midday in the Parc Monceau district, on the back platform of a more or less full S bus (now No. 84), I observed a person with a very long neck who was wearing a felt hat which had a plaited cord round it instead of a ribbon'; another begins 'I was not displeased with my attire this day. I was inaugurating a new, rather sprightly hat, and an overcoat of which I thought most highly'. Here the main difference is one of point of view: in the first version the events are told by an observer on the bus; in the second one, the perspective is the young man's.

Various attempts have been made to identify the structural properties of narratives. One of the most well known of these is Labov's account of conversational narratives (1972). He claimed that a narrative usually contains at least some (and often all) of the following elements: *abstract* (which signals that the story is about to begin and says what it's about); *orientation* (which provides information about context, such as who's involved and where it takes place); *action* (which tells what happened); *resolution* (which concludes the sequence of events); *coda* (which signals the end of the story); *evaluation* (which justifies the point or value of the story). The elements usually occur in this order, but evaluation is dispersed throughout the narrative.

Narrator In a **narrative**, the events are always presented to readers from a particular perspective, or point of view. This viewpoint is that of the *narrator*. Narrative perspectives can be 'internal' to the world of the story or 'external' to it. There are two main types of narration: *first person* and *third person*.

In first person narration, the main perspective is that of a character 'inside' the fictional world. The narrating character usually participates in the events of the story, often as the chief protagonist. Ishmael in Herman Melville's *Moby-Dick* (1851) exemplifies this type of narrator. Participants can also be minor characters, 'observing' the events of the story as they unfold, or reporting on them after they have happened. A well-known example of this perspective is Nick Carraway in F. Scott Fitzgerald's *The Great Gatsby* (1925). First person narration can also switch between characters, to give multiple perspectives on a story, as in William Faulkner's *As I Lay Dying* (1930), which builds up a picture of the events surrounding the death of an elderly woman in fifty-nine chapters from the perspective of fifteen internal narrators.

In third person narration, the main perspective is that of a narrator who is 'outside' the fictional world in which the events of the story take place. Third person narrators can be 'omniscient' – free to move anywhere within the fictional world, including in and out of the minds of characters and backwards and forwards in the time-frame of the story. Although the omniscient third person narrator is very common, it is not the only kind of third person perspective found in narrative fiction. 'Semi-omniscience' is also a popular option, in which the narrator's perspective is 'limited' to the minds of only a few characters, or even a single character, as in James Joyce's short story 'The Dead' (1907). Finally, so-called 'objective' third person narration appears to function like a camera, 'recording' the events of the story as they occur, and not revealing anyone's thoughts. Ernest Hemingway's story 'A Clean, Well-Lighted Place' (1933), adopts this perspective.

Narrators vary in other respects. For example, some first person narrators are more 'reliable' than others, in the sense that they are more credible and trustworthy. An 'unreliable' narrator's perspective is slanted in some way, perhaps because of mental illness or instability, criminality, or lack of knowledge. Famously unreliable narrators in literature include Holden Caulfield in J.D. Salinger's *The Catcher in the Rye* (1951) and Humbert Humbert in Vladimir Nabokov's *Lolita* (1955).

Narrowing (of meaning) A process of **semantic change** (also known as 'specialization') where the denotational meaning of a word becomes less general and inclusive. For example, in **Old English** *deor* (*deer*) meant animals in general, rather than the particular kind of ruminant mammal it refers to today. Similarly, the meaning of *meat* has narrowed over time: it once meant 'food', but now means 'the flesh of an animal used as food'.

Nasal A **consonant** produced by a manner of **articulation** in which the **articulators** make a complete obstruction in the **oral cavity**, while the lowered **soft palate** allows the **airstream** to escape into the nasal cavity. There are three nasal consonant phonemes in English. 1) A voiced labial nasal /m/ as in <u>m</u>at. 2) A voiced alveolar nasal /n/ as in <u>n</u>eck. 3) A voiced velar nasal /ŋ/ as in si<u>ng</u>.

Native language The language (or languages) acquired by an individual before the acquisition of any other languages. A native speaker of a language is someone who has acquired that language in infancy. Compare FIRST LANGUAGE.

Negation Negation is generally associated with the **clause**, which has either positive or negative **polarity**. A positive clause is typically made negative by inserting *not* after the **operator**: *He could **not** afford a camera.* For this reason it is sometimes known as *not*-negation. If there is no auxiliary verb, the semantically empty *do* auxiliary is used as a 'dummy' operator: *The price **does not** include lunch.*• This rule only applies when the main verb is not *be*. When it is *be*, *not* is inserted after the verb: *We are **not***

criminals. In speech, and increasingly in writing, *not* can be contracted to *n't* and attached to the operator (see CONTRACTION): *She couldn't have four bridesmaids; Bruno doesn't like his father.*● The modal auxiliaries *will* and *shall* have special forms when they are used with negative contraction: *won't, shan't*.

Another way of expressing negation is by using 'negative' words such as *no, nowhere, never, nobody, nothing* and so on. This is sometimes known as *no-negation*. As the following examples show, a clause with *no*-negation can be converted into one with *not*-negation by inserting *not* after the operator and including a 'non-assertive' form, such as *any, anybody*, or *anything*: *His wife has no income* (compare *His wife doesn't have any income*); *There's nobody here* (compare *There isn't anybody* here); *They have given me nothing at all* (compare *They haven't given me anything at all*).●

There are several widely dispersed **non-standard** grammatical constructions associated with negation. The most well-known of these is **multiple negation**: *I hope nobody ain't been swearing*. This example also contains the common non-standard negative **contraction** *ain't*, which is used where Standard English has *isn't, aren't, hasn't, haven't, 'm not*.

Neologism   A new word. See WORD FORMATION.

New   See GIVEN AND NEW.

New Zealand English   New Zealand is an island country in the South Pacific, about 1900 km from the east coast of **Australia**. People from eastern Polynesia began arriving in the islands c. AD 800, naming their discovery Aotearoa ('Land of the Long White Cloud'). English speakers, in the form of sealers from Port Jackson (now Sydney), first arrived there

in 1792. New Zealand was administered from New South Wales, Australia until it became a colony in its own right in 1840. Throughout the nineteenth century, the population of the colony grew steadily as a result of migration – mainly from Australia, Britain (in particular Scotland) and Ireland. By the middle of the century, people of European descent outnumbered the indigenous people (called Maori). Today, approximately 14 per cent of the population are of Maori ethnicity, compared with 80 per cent of European ethnicity (2001 census).

It was once thought that, given the level of immigration from Australia, English in New Zealand was merely an 'offshoot' of Australian English, but current research suggests that a complex process of **dialect levelling** has taken place there, giving rise to its characteristic features (see Gordon and Sudbury 2002).

For outsiders, the vowels are the most well-known aspect of the New Zealand **accent**. For example, the vowel /ɪ/ as in *hit* and *pin* is moving towards [ə] (in contrast to Australia, where it is moving towards [i]). One of the easiest ways to tell whether someone is from New Zealand or Australia is to ask them to say a phrase like 'six thick bricks'. If it sounds a bit like /səks θək brəks/ they are probably a New Zealander, but if they produce something resembling /sɪːks θɪːk brɪːks/ they are likely to be Australian. Another **shibboleth** of the New Zealand accent concerns the front vowels /ɛ/ and /æ/, which are approximately [i] and [ɛ]. This means that *dead* and *mess* could be mistaken for *did* and *miss* by outsiders, while *pat* and *bat* could be confused with *pet* and *bet*. There is also a tendency for /ɪə/ and /ɛə/ to merge, making *fear* and *fair* **homophone**s: the direction of the merger is subject to variation, but most speakers seem to favour [ɪə] (Crystal 2003; Trudgill and Hannah 2002). See also HIGH RISING TONE.

The grammar of Standard English in New Zealand is practically identical to Standard British English; and there are few, if any, non-standard features which are not also found in other **inner circle** territories around the world. The characteristic lexis of New Zealand derives mainly from the Maori language (some examples include *kiwi, haka, Pakeha, moa* and *iwi*). English words have also undergone shifts of meaning in New Zealand, including *tramp* ('hike'), *section* ('building plot'), *front* ('turn up, appear'). Much of the colloquial lexis is shared with Australian English, including *creek* ('stream') and *crook* ('ill'), but some items are distinctly New Zealand: *greasies* ('fish and chips'), *pingers* ('money'), *chilly-bin* ('insulated food container').

Nigerian Pidgin English See WEST AFRICA.

Nominal clause See COMPLEMENT CLAUSE.

Nominalization A process in which a verb or adjective is converted into an **abstract noun**. The most common way of doing this is to add a **suffix** to the base form of the verb or adjective (*educate-education*; *dense-density*; *mad-madness*; *terror-terrorism*; *establish-establishment*). Words can also be converted into nouns without the addition of suffixes. Compare *That's where they* **change** *their outfits* with *A* **change** *took place in Alejandro±* (see CONVERSION). Nominalization is often used when the **agent** is not known, not relevant, or deemed to be unimportant: *As we all know,* **killings** *beget more* **killings**. See GRAMMATICAL METAPHOR.

Nominative See CASE.

Nonce word A word which comes into existence to serve a temporary purpose and then vanishes. Their ephemeral nature makes them difficult to exemplify. The following examples come from internet postings containing the search string 'I invented the word': *egotesticle, gothnoir, boomerangutan, grammomancy, orthorexia, homoracial, snarkasm*.

Non-finite Said of a verb phrase or clause which is not marked for tense or does not contain a modal verb. **Infinitives**, **present participles** (*ing*-participles) and **past participles** (*ed*-participles) are all non-finite constructions. The following sentences all contain non-finite verb phrases: *Dolphins need to* **eat** *considerable quantities of food; I've grown up* **believing** *in God*. Non-finite constructions can occur in finite verb phrases, where they come after the finite verb: *My heart* **has** (finite) **stopped** (non-finite); *Women and children* **were** (finite) **stopping** (non-finite) *traffic*. See FINITE, NON-FINITE CLAUSE.

Non-finite clause In this type of **subordinate** clause, the verb phrase is **non-finite**. There are three main types of non-finite clause: *to***-clause**, *ing***-clause** and *ed***-clause**. To- and ing-clauses have a wide range of syntactic roles. For example, they can act as subject (***To know the Bible*** *was to trace divine and human action in this world through history;* ***Drinking alcohol*** *is an important part of foreplay*), extraposed subject (*It is ridiculous* ***to be vindictive towards a fictional character***; *It was horrible* ***being in one tiny room***), subject complement (*To know the Bible was* ***to trace divine and human action in this world through history***; *His hobby is* ***playing golf***), direct object (*I still enjoyed* ***singing 'Love Divine'***; *Some people like* ***to sing***), adverbial (*I phoned* ***to invite you this morning***; *She stopped walking and stood still,* ***folding her arms resolutely across her chest***). *Ed*-clauses are less versatile, mainly having an adverbial function: ***Transfixed with terror***, *Melissa dragged her eyes from the edge*. See FINITE CLAUSE.

Non-restrictive relative clause See RELATIVE CLAUSE.

Non-standard Said of any grammatical structure or word which is not recognized as part of a 'standard' variety of a language. See BIDIALECTALISM, COVERT PRESTIGE, PATOIS, REGULARIZATION, SOCIAL NETWORK, SOLIDARITY, SPEECH AND WRITING, STANDARD ENGLISH, VERNACULAR.

Normans The Scandinavian people (mainly **Danes**) who began to settle in the part of northern France now known as Normandy in the late ninth century, where they converted to Christianity and became French-speaking. Once the Duchy of Normandy had been established in 911 AD, the Normans ('Northmen') turned their attention abroad, exercising their influence in territories as far apart as Ireland and Sicily. But they are perhaps best known for the role they played in English political and cultural history. See FRENCH, MIDDLE ENGLISH.

Normative See PRESCRIPTIVISM.

Norse A term used as a label for a **Germanic** language spoken across Scandinavia and its overseas settlements (including Iceland and parts of the **British Isles**) between about the eighth and twelfth centuries. The influence of Norse (sometimes known as 'Old Norse') on English has been profound. The sustained period of contact between **Anglo-Saxon**s and Scandinavians during the early Middle Ages resulted in an influx of hundreds of Norse **loanword**s, including such everyday terms as *both*, *same*, *seem*, *get*, *give*, *they*, *them*, *their*, *skirt*, *sky*, *skill*, *skin*, *awkward*, *birth*, *dirt*, *gap*, *ill*, *root*, *rotten*, *rugged*, *scowl* and *wrong*. Some borrowings from Norse have not spread into general usage, but are found in **Scottish English** and the dialects of **northern England**, such as *bairn*, ('child'), *brigg* ('bridge'), *greet* ('cry'), *laik* ('play'), *spelk* ('splinter'). Norse influence is also evident in place names in Scotland and the north and east of England, such as *Lerwick*, *Thurso*, *York*, *Lowestoft*.

Language contact between speakers of Norse and Old English also affected English grammar. For example, the third person -*s* ending on verbs in the present tense probably arose when Danes learning English had difficulty with the unstressed, voiceless /θ/ verb ending (e.g. *tellað*), substituting it with an /s/. Another possibility is that English speakers adopted the -*s* after hearing Danes use a -*sk* ending in constructions such as *hann telsk* ('he tells himself') and *þeir teljask* ('they tell each other'). Both processes, of course, were probably under way at the same time. The new ending spread south and west, eventually becoming part of Standard English (see Crystal 2004: 218–221).

Northern cities vowel shift A vowel shift currently taking place in northern metropolitan areas of the USA, in particular the cities of Cleveland, Detroit, Chicago, Milwaukee, Buffalo, Syracuse and Minneapolis. The shift is affecting six vowel phonemes, and can be summarized as follows. 1) The vowel in KIT is backed and/or lowered, so that it approaches [ə] in some cases. 2) The vowel in DRESS shifts towards the vowel in STRUT, so that to speakers with an 'unshifted' accent of **American English**, *guess* sounds like *Gus*. 3) The vowel in STRUT shifts towards the vowel in THOUGHT, so that *cut* sounds like *caught*. 4) The vowel in the TRAP, BATH and DANCE lexical sets becomes a diphthong [eæ], so that *Ann* sounds like *Ian*. 5) The vowel in LOT/ PALM shifts towards the vowel in TRAP, so that *Don* sounds like *Dan*. 6) The vowel in CLOTH/THOUGHT shifts towards the vowel in LOT, so that *Dawn* sounds like *Don* (see Gordon 2004).

Northern England The part of England consisting of the modern counties of Northumberland, Cumbria, Tyne and Wear, Teesside, Humberside, Yorkshire, Merseyside, Greater Manchester and Lancashire. As anyone familiar with English in England knows, there is considerable variation between English in different parts of the north: people from Liverpool sound different from people in Newcastle. However, it is possible to make some general statements about the phonology, grammar and lexis of the dialects of the north of England which give a flavour of the English used there.

The following overview of the phonology of northern English is based on Hughes, Trudgill and Watt (2005), and Beal (2004a). The first two items are widely seen as the 'most salient markers of northern English' (Beal 2004a: 122). 1) Typically, the vowel /ʌ/ does not occur in accents of the north: /ʊ/ is used in words belonging to the STRUT **lexical set** (occasionally, younger middle-class speakers will use a vowel resembling [ə]). This means that words such as *hut, bun* and *come* share the same vowel as *put*. 2) The vowel in the BATH set is /a/, not /ɑː/ as it is in RP and some accents of southern England, which means that words such as *grass, laugh* and *path* share the same vowel as *pat*. 3) Some speakers have /uː/ rather than /ʊ/ in certain words in the FOOT set, such as *cook, look, book* (so that these words rhyme with *spook*). 4) Words in the GOAT lexical set have a range of pronunciations across the north: most of the region has the **monophthong**

/oː/, while in Tyneside and Northumberland, some speakers have the **diphthong**s /uə/ or /ɪə/ (although these pronunciations are in decline amongst younger speakers). In Merseyside /oʊ/ is common. 5) Across the north, the most common vowel in the FACE lexical set is the monophthong /eː/. Some speakers in Tyneside and Northumberland have /ɪə/, so that the word *pace* sounds quite like an RP pronunciation of the word *pierce*. 6) For some speakers in the far north, the vowel in the MOUTH set is /uː/, so that *mouse* and *moose* are **homophone**s. In Tyneside and Northumberland this pronunciation is used mainly by older working-class males, although 'in certain words which are strongly associated with local identity this pronunciation has been lexicalized and reflected in the spelling' (Beal 2004a: 124). This can be seen in the phrase *The Toon* ('town'), a local name for Newcastle United FC. In South Yorkshire, the MOUTH set is pronounced with /aː/. 7) The SQUARE and NURSE lexical sets are merged in some parts of the north, making word pairs such as *pair/purr* and *fair/fur* into **homophone**s. The vowel shared by the merged sets is usually either /ɛː/ or /ɜː/. 8) In most parts of northern England, the unstressed vowel at the end of words such as *happy, city, coffee* and *money* varies between **tense and lax** realizations. Tense realizations (usually [i] or [iː]) are typically associated with the North East, Liverpool and Hull. Elsewhere, lax realizations (usually [ɪ] or [ɛ]) are heard. The lax variant is generally stigmatized. 9) The unstressed vowel at the end of words such as *letter, butter* and *traitor* is usually realized as [ə], but some speakers in Manchester and Sheffield have [ɒ], and Tynesiders and Wearsiders have [ɐ]. 10) ***H-dropping*** is widespread in the accents of northern England, although /h/ is generally retained at the start of stressed syllables in the North-east. This does seem to be changing, however. *H*-dropping is now being reported in Sunderland and Newcastle, as 'young north easterners' converge 'with their northern peers' (Beal 2004a: 128). 11) Throughout the north, /t/ is pronounced as /r/ in certain environments, usually between vowels, as in *get off* [gɛɹaf] and *put it* [pʊɹɪt]. /t/ glottalization is also common, particularly in towns and cities (see GLOTTAL STOP). 12) Glottalized forms of /p/ and /k/ are present in the North-east (see GLOTTAL STOP). 13) In Liverpool, /t/, and /k/ are sometimes heavily aspirated or even affricated, resulting in pronunciations such as *can't* [kxɑːnt], *straight* [stɹeɪts] and *back* [bakx].

As Beal points out, as far as the morphology and syntax of dialects of northern England are concerned, 'there are very few features which both distinguish northern dialects from those of the South and Midlands, and can be found throughout the North' (2004b: 114). However, there are two features which, in the British Isles, are exclusively or predominantly found in the dialects of northern England. These are special forms for the second person pronoun (*thou*/*thee* is used by some speakers, particularly in Yorkshire; while in Tyneside, Liverpool and Manchester the plural form *yous* is common); and the double-modals which occur in the speech of some North-easterners, when the second modal verb is *can* or *could*: *I might could manage it* (see Kortmann 2004).

For historical reasons, the lexis of the dialects of northern England has been influenced more strongly by **Norse** than have varieties of English in other parts of England (see DANELAW). Words with Norse origins include *aye* ('yes') and *nay* ('no'), *beck* ('stream'), *lop* ('flea'), *garth*

('yard'), *gate* ('street'), *gawp* ('stare with open mouth'), *greet* ('weep'). Another prominent feature of northern lexis is the range of terms of endearment used. The most widespread of these is *love*, as in *You have what you like love, don't you?*. More localized terms include *pet* (North-east), *chuck* (Lancashire) and *duck* (South Yorkshire). See GEORDIE, SCOUSE.

Northumbrian The **Old English** dialect associated with Northumbria, one of the Kingdoms of the **Anglo-Saxon** heptarchy. The territory of Northumbria stretched from the Humber to the Forth. Surviving documents in the dialect include Caedmon's Hymn, glosses on the Lindisfarne and Rushworth Gospels, and runic inscriptions on the Franks Casket and the Ruthwell Cross (see RUNE).

Noun One of the four **lexical word** classes. Nouns refer to objects, entities, places and concepts: *I gripped the **chair** hard;*± *The **eagle** circled around him;*± *Let's talk about **feminism**;*± *The **United States** has renewed a **threat** of **sanctions**.*± Nouns are either *proper* or *common*. A proper noun refers to specific people, places, organizations and so on. They are usually written with an initial capital letter (*Shakespeare, Belize, Ford*), and because of the specificity of their referent, proper nouns do not need an article or plural form (*Belizes; *a Belize). However, proper nouns are occasionally used as if they were countable, to produce particular stylistic effects: *That's what sets apart the **Chelseas, Manchester Uniteds** and **Arsenals** from the rest*.† A common noun is any noun which is not a proper noun, such as *dog, rainbow, liposuction*. Common nouns can be countable or uncountable. Countable nouns refer to things which can be enumerated, and they nearly always have a singular and plural form: *chair*/*chairs*; *child*/*children*.

Countable nouns can also be marked as **definite** or **indefinite** with the articles *the* and *a/an*: *the chair*; *a chair*. Non-count nouns refer to things and concepts which are not generally countable: *flour*; *music*; *health*. Non-count nouns do not usually have a plural form. They cannot occur with the indefinite article (**a flour*; **a health*), although they do allow a contrast between definite and indefinite with the **zero-article** (*the flour*; *flour*). Some common nouns can be both countable and uncountable, usually with a difference in meaning: *Brazil re-opened coffee exports for registration* (non-count)/ *Bring me two coffees* (count); *The smell of the steaming meat tormented them* (non-count)/ *They are particularly good with cold meats* (count). Sometimes, nouns which are generally uncountable are treated as countable, as in the opening sentence of *The War of the Worlds* by H.G. Wells (1898): *No one would have believed in the last years of the nineteenth century that this world was being watched keenly and closely by intelligences greater than man's and yet as mortal as his own.*

Syntactically, nouns occur as the **head** of a **noun phrase**.

Noun phrase One of the five major **phrase** types. The **head** is a **noun** (or **pronoun**): *Thérèse is asleep; She is asleep*. The head can be preceded by **determiners** (specifying the reference of the head noun): *the puppy*; *my mum*. It can also be accompanied by **modifiers** (describing or classifying it): *His good leg*; *the green lizard*.

When modifiers precede the head (as in the examples above) this is known as premodification (see MODIFIER). There are four main types of premodification in the noun phrase. 1) **Adjective** premodification: *old cottages*. 2) **Ed-participle** premodification: *motivated people*. 3) **Ing-participle** premodification: *revealing dress*. 4) Noun premodification: *bus depot*. Lengthy structures can be built up with strings of premodifiers: *Sgt. Pepper's Lonely Hearts Club Band*; *lower metamorphic grade Lewisian sediments*.

When modifiers follow the head, this is known as postmodification. Structures used to postmodify nouns include **relative clauses** (*the teacher who knows all the answers*), **non-finite clauses** (*the plane flying low*), **prepositional phrases** (*the plates on the calyx*) and appositive noun phrases (*Harold Brighouse, the author of the play*).

The most important functions of the noun phrase are **subject** (*Both knees hit the ground*), **direct object** (*Both knees hit the ground*), **indirect object** (*He gave the man two dollars*), subject **complement** (*The doctor is a fool*) and object complement (*They called him a liar*).

Number A grammatical category (associated in English mainly with **nouns**, **demonstratives**, **personal pronouns** and **verbs**) showing contrasts of singular, plural, dual and so on. In English, there are basically two distinctions: singular and plural. The plural of nouns is usually formed by adding *-s* or *-es* to the singular (*legs*). Demonstratives are also singular (*this* table, *that* table) and plural (*these* tables, *those* tables). Personal pronouns also mark singular and plural, but only in the first and third persons: *I* (singular) *we* (plural); she (singular) *they* (plural). Number contrast in verbs (with the exception of the highly irregular verb *be*) is limited to the third person present tense form (*eats*).

O

Object (O) One of the five **clause elements**. Objects are either *direct* or *indirect*. **Direct objects** are noun phrases which usually refer to a **patient**, the entity affected by the process or action of a **transitive** verb: *He slapped **Jack***. **Indirect objects** are usually noun phrases which generally refer to a 'recipient' or **beneficiary**, the entity which receives 'possession' of the direct object of a **ditransitive** verb: *He gave **the man** a knife*.

Objective See CASE.

Obsolescence The loss of words, usually because the things or concepts they refer to are obsolete or redundant: *gramophone*; *telegraph*. **Archaism** is the deliberate attempt to revive obsolete words and expressions.

Occurrence verb A type of lexical verb which can be used to report an event or action which takes place separate from the willed activity of a conscious entity: *The rate of evaporation **increases** with increasing surface area*; *By late summer temperatures **became** a uniform 4–5°C at all depths*. Other examples include *develop, die, change, happen, occur*. Often, occurrence verbs can be used *ergatively*. This means that the action they denote affects the subject: *John Galt **died** in Greenock*. See ERGATIVE VERB.

Old English A label used to describe the earliest form of English, brought to Britain by settlers from the European mainland in the form of mutually intelligible **Germanic** dialects. The Old English period is generally considered to have lasted from c. AD 500 to c. AD 1100.

Throughout the period of Roman occupation (c. AD 43 – c. AD 436), small numbers of **Germanic** people had settled in the British Isles, but during the period of Roman withdrawal, their ranks increased dramatically. This influx came about as a consequence of the power vacuum left by the Romans. Unprotected by legionaries, the Celtic tribes came under attack from marauding Picts and Scots. This prompted the Celtic King Vortigern to conscript mercenaries from across the North Sea. The first arrivals (c. AD 449) were the **Jutes**, who are thought to have come originally from what is now northern Denmark. After helping to see off the Picts and Scots, the Jutes settled by force in Kent. The **Angles**, who came from southern Denmark arrived later, settling across a huge swathe of territory from the River Thames to southern Scotland. And the **Saxons**, from the coastal lowlands of northern Germany, settled in what became Wessex and Sussex. The original pattern of settlement contributed to the development of the dialects of Old English, which modern linguists have labelled **Kentish**, **Mercian**, **Northumbrian** and **West Saxon**.

The Old English period was marked by two major influences from overseas, both of which had consequences for the language: the arrival of Christianity and the settlement of large parts of northern and eastern England by Scandinavians. The Christianization of Britain, from the sixth century onwards, resulted in many Latin words entering the language (see LATIN). The Christian missionaries also introduced the Latin alphabet; until then, English had been written down (intermittently) using **runes**. Between the ninth and eleventh centuries, the Scandinavians introduced hundreds of new words into the English lexicon, many of them very basic in character – evidence of close and sustained contact between the settlers and the original inhabitants: *birth, egg, root, sister, sky* (see DANE, DANELAW, NORSE, VIKING, LOANWORD). A third external influence came in the form of the **Norman** invasion, which marked the end of the Old English period (although texts continued to be produced in what is recognizably Old English for up to a hundred years after 1066).

Old English, of course, only survives in the form of documents. The entire corpus of Old English consists of about 3.5 million words – the equivalent of about thirty modern novels. Everything that is known about the language comes from examining these texts. A flavour of Old English can be gleaned from the following extract, which comes from an eleventh-century translation of the Lord's Prayer in West Saxon (a word-for-word translation is given in brackets).

> fæder ure þu þe eart on heofonum
> (father our thou that art in heaven)
> si þin nama gehalgod (be thy name hallowed)
> to becume þin rice (come thy kingdom)
> gewurþe ðin willa (be done thy will)
> on eorðan swa swa on heofonum (on earth as in heaven)
> urne gedæghwamlican hlaf syle us todæg (our daily bread give us today)
> and forgyf us ure gyltas (and forgive us our sins)

Many of these words – *fæder, ure, on, heofonum, nama, to, becume, willa, eorðan,* *us, todæg, and, forgyf* – are recognizably 'English' (even though in some cases their meaning appears to be slightly different from present-day English). Other aspects of the text, however, seem strange to the modern reader. For example, **word order** is different – both at the level of the phrase ('Father our'), and at the level of clause elements ('Be thy name hallowed, come thy kingdom, be done thy will'). Furthermore, words which in modern English have a single form (e.g. *our*) seem to have more than one form in Old English *(urne gedæghwamlican hlaf; ure gyltas)*. These textual features illustrate some important characteristics of Old English. 1) The vocabulary was essentially Germanic in character (with some input from **Latin**). 2) Unlike present-day English, Old English was a synthetic language (see LINGUISTIC TYPOLOGY): inflections were used to mark grammatical relations, rather than word order. This means that word order could be relatively free, as it seems to be in the prayer. 3) Because it was a synthetic language, nouns, verbs, adjectives, determiners and pronouns were highly inflected. For example, *urne* ('our') is the masculine objective case of *ure* ('our').

The 1000-year-old prayer is legible to the modern reader because Old English was written down using the Latin alphabet. Only three letters in the text are no longer in general use: <æ, þ, ð>. The **digraph** <æ> (called *ash*) was originally used in Latin, and adopted by scribes to represent the vowel /æ/. The consonant /θ/ did not exist in Latin, so the runic letters *thorn* <þ> and *eth* <ð> were used to write the sound (see RUNE).

The following tables (based on Fennell 2001) give some indication of the sounds of Old English, together with the spellings used to represent those sounds.

Old English consonants

Spelling	Sound	OE word	Meaning	*Notes*
p	p	pipor	pepper	
t	t	tam	tame	
b	b	beald	bold	
d	d	drinc	drink	
m	m	mann	person	
n	n	nama	name	
l	l	land	land	
r	r	ræt	rat	
w	w	willa	mind	
cg	dʒ	brycg	bridge	
sc	ʃ	disc	dish	
c	k	cyning	king	The sound spelled with <c> was /k/ before a consonant or back vowel e.g. *cwic* ('alive'); or [ç]/[tʃ] next to a front vowel e.g. *ceosan* ('choose').
c	tʃ	ceosan	choose	
g	g	god	good	The sound spelled with <g> was either [j] before or between front vowels e.g. *gear* ('year'); or [g] before consonants, back vowels, and some front vowels e.g. *ges* ('geese'). An allophone of [g] was a voiced velar fricative [ɣ] between back vowels and after /l/ or /r/ in words such as *sagu* ('saw') and *fylgan* ('follow').
g	j	gear	year	
f	f	fæder	father	The letter <f> represented two separate sounds [f] and [v]. Voicing was predictable by context: between voiced sounds /f/ is voiced e.g. the consonant represented by <f> in *seofon* ('seven') is pronounced [v].

Spelling	Sound	OE word	Meaning	*Notes*
þ, ð	θ	eðel	native lord	The letter <ð> represented two separate sounds [θ] and [ð]. Voicing was predictable by context: between voiced sounds /θ/ is voiced e.g. the consonant represented by <þ> in þegn ('thane, attendant') is pronounced [θ], while <þ> represents [ð] in baþian ('bathe').
s	s	strang	strong	The letter <s> represented two separate sounds [s] and [z]. Voicing was predictable by context: between voiced sounds /s/ is voiced e.g. the consonant represented by <s> in *nosu* ('nose') is pronounced [z].
h	h	hlaf	loaf	<h> represented the following sounds: [h] initially as in *ham* ('home'); [x] after back vowels as in *leoht* 'light'.

Old English vowels

Spelling*	Sound	OE word	Meaning
a	ɑ	camp	battle
ā	ɑː	wa	woe
æ	æ	hæft	captive
ǣ	æː	lǣst	last
e	ɛ	tellan	count
ē	eː	eðel	native lord
i	ɪ	hit	it
ī	iː	is	ice
o	ɔ	from	from
ō	oː	hrof	roof
u	ʊ	hund	dog

Spelling*	Sound	OE word	Meaning
ū	uː	ful	foul
y	y	yrre	anger
ȳ	yː	ystig	stormy
ea	æə	heall	hall
ēa	æːə	eage	eye
eo	ɛo	seolc	silk
ēo	eːo	beo	be

* The marks above certain vowels indicate that they are long. They are used by modern scholars but are not present in the original Old English texts.

Onomatopoeia (Greek: 'the making of words') A type of **sound symbolism** in which the phonetic form of a word resembles the sound made by the word's referent: *quack*, *splash*, *bong*. See ICONICITY.

Onset See SYLLABLE.

Open class This term is sometimes used to describe **lexical word**s (nouns, verbs, adjectives and adverbs). The class is 'open' because new words are almost always lexical. Conversely, **closed class** words have a limited membership (e.g. determiners, conjunctions, prepositions).

Operator A term used to describe a particular function carried out mainly by auxiliary verbs, although *be* and *have* as main verbs can also have an operator function (see below). Operators are the first auxiliary verb in a verb phrase. In the following sentences, the operator is in bold: *The fund* **will** *take out insurance; Victoria* **is** *living in my flat; Sails* **would** *have been a hindrance*. In English, the operator is particularly important in the formation of negative and interrogative clauses. In negative clauses, *not* is inserted after the operator: *The United States* **will not** *take these people; He* **is not** *living in the real world; A reasonable person* **would not** *have been frightened*. In interrogative clauses, subject–operator **inversion** takes place: *Where* **have you** *been? What* **are you** *drinking?*

In negative clauses which do not contain an auxiliary verb, the *do* auxiliary is used as a 'dummy' operator: *The price* **does not** *include lunch.*• This rule only applies when the main verb is not *be*. When it is *be*, *not* is inserted after the verb: *We* **are not** *criminals* (in such cases, *be* as a main verb is functioning as an operator). In *yes–no* interrogative clauses and *wh*-interrogatives where the *wh*-word is *not* the subject, 'dummy' *do* is also used: **Do** *you want an ice-cream? What* **did** *Alan Parker say to you?* The main verbs *be* and *have* also function as operators in interrogative clauses: **Are** *you mad? Who* **is** *he?* **Have** *you any bread?* See NEGATION.

Oral cavity A term used in phonetics to refer to what is essentially the inside of the mouth.

Orthography The aspect of language study broadly concerned with **spelling** and **punctuation**.

Outer circle See WORLD ENGLISH.

Overlexicalization and underlexicalization Terms associated with the linguist Roger Fowler. *Overlexicalization* describes a proliferation of **synonym**s or quasi-synonyms for the same entity, concept or activity. Overlexicalization is often an indicator of concern with a particular area of meaning. For example, the huge number of terms for sexual intercourse in English points to an area of intense preoccupation. **Slang** and **antilanguage**s often employ overlexicalization to an unusual extent, as does **jargon**. *Underlexicalization* signifies the opposite: a lack of words for a particular object or idea. Natural speech is often 'underlexicalized': the pressures faced by speakers means they do not draw on the full resources of the lexicon, and rely instead on repetition and the use of vague terms, such as *thingy*, *stuff*.

Overt prestige A term used in **Labovian sociolinguistics** to label the **prestige** associated with what is publicly acknowledged as 'correct' English (in terms of pronunciation, grammar and vocabulary). Speakers will often alter their speech so that it contains more of these overtly prestigious features and fewer **vernacular** features, in the belief that standard forms confer higher social status. Compare COVERT PRESTIGE. See LANGUAGE CHANGE.

Oxford English Dictionary (OED) The largest and, arguably, the most important and influential **dictionary** of the English language. Its origins go back to 1857, when the Philological Society of London decided that current dictionaries of the language were inadequate in terms of coverage, consistency and accuracy, and that a new dictionary of English was needed which would address these deficiencies. The production of the first edition of the OED was a vast undertaking. The first installment was published in 1884 by Oxford University Press, but the entire work, consisting of ten volumes, was not completed until 1928. In 1933, the original work was reprinted in thirteen volumes containing definitions for nearly 415,000 words. In 1989, the second edition was published, with an additional 200,000 definitions. The second edition is now available online, and the electronic format allows the editors to update the dictionary much more rapidly than they were able to in the past. A third edition is currently in preparation.

The dictionary is based on 'historical principles', which means that each entry contains, according to the preface to the 1933 edition, 'all the relevant facts concerning [a word's] form, sense-history, pronunciation, and etymology'. Each word is also accompanied by quotations from printed sources illustrating usage over time.

P

Palatal A term used in the description of **consonant**s referring to a place of **articulation** (the point in the **vocal tract** where a constriction of the airstream occurs). Palatal consonants are produced when the middle or back of the tongue is raised against or towards the **hard palate**. There is only one palatal consonant phoneme in most varieties of English: /j/.

Palate See HARD PALATE and SOFT PALATE.

Paralinguistic A paralinguistic feature is any *non-verbal* element of spoken or written language which carries meaning. Paralanguage in speech includes **prosodic feature**s such as **pitch**, **volume**, and **intonation**, together with voice quality (e.g. husky voice, breathy voice, whisper), gesture and facial expression. Paralanguage in writing includes punctuation, choice of font style and colour, and so on. These can be manipulated to convey a variety of meanings. For example, some fonts suggest *antiquity* while others have a more contemporary feel. The physical form of writing can also be manipulated to mimic aspects of the speaking voice: *This looks sooooo cool!*†

Parallelism A stylistic device involving prominent patterns of **repetition** at the level of sound, grammatical structure or meaning. 1) *Phonological parallelism* is the combining of the same or similar sounds. There are four main types of phonological parallelism: **alliteration** (the repetition of word initial consonants), **assonance** (the repetition of similar vowel sounds), **rhyme** (the repetition of similar syllables) and **metre** (the repetition of rhythmic patterns). 2) *Grammatical parallelism* is the repetition of phrase and/or clause structure: *Shape without form, shade without colour, / Paralysed force, gesture without motion* (T.S. Eliot 1925). 3) *Semantic parallelism* involves the repetition and sometimes extension of the meaning of words, phrases and images. The example of grammatical parallelism above also contains semantic parallelism, in the setting up of a series of paradoxes (formless shape, colourless shade, paralysed force, motionless gesture).

Parataxis and hypotaxis A pair of terms used to describe contrasting ways of linking clauses. In traditional grammatical descriptions, *parataxis* is the combining of clauses through simple juxtaposition, rather than by **coordination** or **subordination**: *I came, I saw, I conquered.* However, some grammars also regard clauses linked by coordinating conjunctions as paratactic sequences: *I came, and I saw, and I conquered.* Parataxis is often associated with an unsophisticated or naïve style of writing. Stories written by children, for example, often contain long paratactical sequences, as do children's rhymes. However, literary writers often use parataxis as a stylistic device, as in this passage from 'Cat in the Rain' by Ernest Hemingway (1925): 'There were big palms and green benches in the public garden. In the good weather there was always an artist with his easel. Artists liked the way the palms grew and the bright colors of the hotels facing the gardens and the sea.'

Hypotaxis, on the other hand, is used to describe grammatical relationships between clauses involving **subordination**.

Hypotaxis is particularly associated with kinds of writing in which it is important to make clear the logical, temporal and syntactic relations between elements. For this reason, a hypotactic style is often a feature of **expository prose**.

Parody An imitation of a particular style of writing or speech, usually for the purposes of ridicule or satire. Compare PASTICHE.

Participant, participant role See TRANSITIVITY.

Participle The -*ed* and -*ing* forms of a **verb**: *walked, walking*. (Note that the term *ed*-participle is also used with an irregular verb e.g. *broken* is the *ed*-participle of the verb *break*. Some grammars, however, call the *ed*-participle the *en*-participle.) The *ing*-participle is also known as the 'present participle' and the *ed*-participle is also known as the 'past participle'. See *ED*-PARTICIPLE, *ING*-PARTICIPLE.

Part of speech See WORD CLASS.

Passive voice The marked choice in the system of **voice** which allows the speaker or writer to de-emphasize the **agent**: *I have been told* (by whom?) *that your ship has been destroyed* (by whom/what?). The process of transforming a clause in the **active voice** into one in the passive voice (sometimes known as 'passivization') involves turning the **direct object** of the active clause into the **subject** of the passive clause. This is usually achieved by combining the *be*-**auxiliary** with the past participle. For example, *Bonnie ate the money* (active) becomes *The money was eaten by Bonnie* (passive). In this example, the agent is present in the *by*-phrase, but if the speaker or writer wishes to exclude the agent entirely, the *by*-phrase can be omitted: *The money was eaten*.

The passive can also be formed by using *get* as an auxiliary, rather than *be* (compare *The main school building was hit by a bomb* with *Your home got hit by a tornado*). The *get*-passive is more usual in colloquial speech than in writing, and interestingly it is more common when the subject suffers from the action of the verb in some way. See AGENTLESS PASSIVE, LONG PASSIVE, VOICE [1].

Pastiche An imitation (usually light-hearted) of a particular style of writing or speaking. When pastiche is done for the purposes of ridicule or satire, it is **parody**. The origins of the word can be traced (via French) to the Italian *pasticcio* – a pie made from lots of different ingredients. This etymology is reflected in a more specific sense of *pastiche*: a work consisting of a medley or hotch-potch of pieces put together from various sources. See also ALLUSION, INTERTEXTUALITY.

Past participle See *ED*-PARTICIPLE.

Past tense See TENSE.

Patient The **semantic role** of the being or entity affected by an event or undergoing a process: *John Fletcher repaired the transom on his boat.*[*] See OBJECT, SUBJECT, VOICE [1].

Patois A common term for **Caribbean** (particularly Jamaican) **creole** (sometimes spelled 'Patwa'). The word is often avoided, however, because of its negative associations (it is sometimes used pejoratively to refer to any non-standard variety of a language, particularly if it lacks **prestige**, a meaning which is captured in expressions such as *criminal patois*). See also BRITISH BLACK ENGLISH.

Pejoration A process of semantic change in which the **connotations** of a word 'worsen' over time. For example, in **Old English** *sælig* ('silly') meant 'blessed, blissful', and *cnafa* ('knave') meant 'a youth, child'. Samuel Johnson in his *Dictionary* (1755) defines *awful* as 'that which strikes with awe, or fills with reverence'. Pejoration is sometimes called 'degeneration'. See SEMANTIC CHANGE.

Pentameter See METRE.

Perceptual dialectology The study of how 'ordinary people' (i.e. non-linguists) classify dialects, and the attitudes they hold towards regional and social variation. The term is particularly associated with the work of the American linguist Dennis R. Preston. See FOLKLINGUISTICS.

Perfect See ASPECT.

Periphrasis (Greek: 'circumlocution') [1] In grammar, the use of a lengthier or less compact construction where a shorter construction is an option. In English, the most well-known periphrastic constructions are the *of* **genitive** (compare *the beak of the bird* with *the bird's beak*); periphrastic *do* (compare *I do like a challenge* with *I like a challenge*); and the use of *more/most* in the construction of **comparative** forms of adjectives and adverbs (*You're more clever*; *We are cleverer*). [2] In **rhetoric**, the term is a synonym of 'circumlocution': using more words than might be strictly necessary.

Person A **grammatical category** associated in English mainly with **personal pronouns**. There are three grammatical persons in English: *first person*, *second person* and *third person*.

The *first person* is the speaker or writer in discourse. The personal pronouns associated with the first person in Standard English are *I* (subjective case), *me* (objective case), *mine* (genitive case), *myself* (reflexive pronoun) in the singular, and *we*, *us*, *ours*, *ourselves* in the plural. The plural first person pronouns can be used *inclusively* and *exclusively* (see INCLUSIVE AND EXCLUSIVE *WE*).

The *second person* is the addressee in discourse. The personal pronouns associated with the second person in Standard English are: *you* (subjective case); *you* (objective case); *yours* (genitive case); *yourself*, *yourselves* (reflexive pronouns). In some non-standard varieties of English, *you* has a plural form when more than one person is being addressed: *And did **youse** get any sort of protective clothing or anything?* (Scotland); *Now I hope **y'all** don't mind if we stop at K-Mart first•* (USA). Historically, English made a distinction between *you* and *thou* (subjective case) and *you* and *thee* (objective case). *You* (originally a plural form) was used to address social superiors or strangers while *thee* and *thou* (originally singular forms) were reserved for social equals, subordinates and close friends and family, a contrast which will be familiar to anyone who speaks a language such as French, Spanish or German, where the so-called T/V (*tu/vous*) distinction is preserved. Although these pronouns are often regarded as **archaism**s, they are still used in some dialects of English. *You* can also function as an indefinite pronoun. Its 'generic' flavour (evident in sayings such as '**You** can't teach an old dog new tricks' and '**You** only live once') means that it is often used to reflect conventional wisdom and 'common sense' values. It is also used with some degree of first person reference, as in the following comment about dolphins: ***You** just feel that they understand what **you** are going on about. And while **you** don't understand them, **you** feel you're in the presence of greater intelligence.* In situations like this, *you* seems to stand for the speaker (who is reporting on an inner mental state); but by choosing a second person form rather than *I*, the speaker/writer is economically implying that this is also what 'everyone' would feel or think in similar circumstances. It is a powerful means of creating 'common ground' between speaker and addressee.

The *third person* refers to the participant or participants other than the speaker/writer or addressee in the discourse. In Standard English, the third person pronouns are: *he, she, it, they* (subjective case); *him, her, it, them* (objective case); *his, hers, its, theirs* (genitive case); *himself, herself, itself, themselves* (reflexive pronouns). *He, she, him, her, his, hers, himself* and *herself* are used when the **gender** of the (animate) referent is known. Some inanimate objects and entities are traditionally referred to using gendered pronouns: *The* Titanic *sank on her maiden voyage*; *There are many, priests too, who would wipe out in a day all the familiar things about Mother Church that endear her to us all.* See CONCORD.

Personal pronoun Speakers and writers use personal pronouns to refer to themselves or other people and entities. They typically 'stand in' for a **noun phrase** (see PROFORM): *You know why I think they do it?* The form of personal pronouns varies according to **case**, **person** and **number**.

This table shows Standard English pronouns. But there is great variation among different varieties of English, as these corpus examples illustrate. 1) *He, she* and *they* as object pronouns: *Don't talk to she about grub*; *I did talk to they* (south-west England). 2) *Him, her, them* and *us* as subject pronouns: *Us'll do it* (northern England). 3) *Y'all* and *yous/youse* as a second person pronoun: *I forgot y'all were here‡* (southern USA); *I want yous to be quiet* (Ireland). See POSSESSIVE PRONOUN, REFLEXIVE PRONOUN.

Phatic See FUNCTION [2].

Phonaesthesia See SOUND SYMBOLISM.

Phoneme A contrastive phonological segment in a language. For example, in English the initial sounds of the words *pit* and *bit* are phonetically different: the first is unvoiced and the second is voiced. Because this contrast serves to differentiate the two words from each other we can say /p/ and /b/ are separate phonemes (see MIMIMAL PAIR). However, not all sound differences are meaningful in this way. The words *pin* and *spin* contain a sound which speakers of English would recognize as a /p/, but the two sounds are in fact phonetically different. The /p/ in *pin* is accompanied by a puff of breath: in phonetic terms it is aspirated. But the /p/ in *spin* is unaspirated. The **International Phonetic Alphabet (IPA)** marks aspiration with a diacritic: [pʰɪn]. Someone who

Standard English personal pronouns

	First person		Second person		Third person	
	Singular	Plural	Singular	Plural	Singular	Plural
Subject	*I*	*We*	*You*	*You*	*He, she, it*	*They*
Object	*Me*	*Us*	*You*	*You*	*Him, her, it*	*Them*
Genitive	*Mine*	*Ours*	*Yours*	*Yours*	*His, hers, its*	*Theirs*

pronounced the word *spin* as [spʰɪn] might be regarded as talking rather strangely, but they would still be understood as uttering the word *spin*. In English, we can say that [p] and [pʰ] are **allophone**s of the phoneme /p/. But in some languages, /p/ and /pʰ/ are separate phonemes. For example, in Hindi the words [pal] 'take care of' and [pʰal] 'knife blade' are distinguished by the contrast between an unaspirated bilabial plosive and an aspirated bilabial plosive. This difference is phonemic in Hindi, but not in English. Hindi speakers have no problem telling these words apart, whereas those unfamiliar with Hindi might hear them as the 'same' word. Conversely, sounds that are different phonemes in English are sometimes allophones of a phoneme in other languages. For example, in English /r/ and /l/ are separate phonemes, but in Korean they are allophones of a single phoneme, with [ɹ] produced between vowels and [l] produced everywhere else. This means that Koreans often have problems producing the [l] in English words like *belly* and *hollow*.

Phonemic change   See SOUND CHANGE.

Phonemic transcription   See PHONETIC TRANSCRIPTION.

Phonetics   The scientific study of the production and reception of speech sounds. The discipline has three main branches. 1) *Articulatory phonetics* studies how speech sounds are produced. 2) *Acoustic phonetics* studies the physical properties of these speech sounds. 3) *Auditory phonetics* studies how speech sounds are perceived. Mainstream linguistics has traditionally concentrated on articulatory phonetics. Compare PHONOLOGY. See AIRSTREAM, ALLOPHONE, ASSIMILATION, INTERNATIONAL PHONETIC ALPHABET, PHONEME, PHONETIC TRANSCRIPTION, PROSODY, STRESS.

Phonetic transcription   A means of representing in written form the sounds of human speech. Depending on their purpose, phonetic transcriptions vary in the amount of detail they contain. A 'narrow' phonetic transcription is a precise and detailed symbolic representation of the actual sounds made by a speaker, using the full resources of the **International Phonetic Alphabet** to record all contextual variants of phonemes (see ALLOPHONE), together with the speaker's unique habits of speech. Such a transcription is conventionally signalled by the use of square brackets, as in these transcriptions of speakers from Perth, Australia and Tokyo, Japan saying the word 'please': [pʰliːz], [pəriz]. A 'broad' phonetic transcription ignores much of the detail, focusing mainly on the phonemes a speaker uses. Properly speaking, a 'broad' phonetic transcription is in fact a 'phonemic' transcription, and it is conventionally enclosed between slants, as in /pɛt/.

Phonology   A term used to describe the sound system of a language (and also the study of sound systems). The human **vocal tract** is capable of producing an infinite range of sounds, and the study of the physiology and acoustics of speech-sound production and reception is called **phonetics**. But in any one language, only a relatively small number of speech sounds are used. The study of the particular sounds of a language or variety, and the way in which these sounds are structured, is called phonology. Linguists generally include phonology as one of the **language levels**. See ALLOMORPH, PHONEME, PHONETICS, PHONOTACTIC, SYLLABLE.

Phonotactic   All languages have a set of phonological rules concerning the ways in which **phoneme**s can be arranged to form **syllables**. These are known as phonotactic constraints. Phonotactic constraints determine the syllable structure of a language. For example, in some languages (e.g. Japanese) the only consonant which can occur at the end of a syllable is /n/; in other languages, syllable-final consonants are forbidden completely (e.g. Hawaiian). Some languages (e.g. English) allow **consonant clusters**, others (e.g. Maori) do not. English consonant clusters are themselves subject to a number of phonotactic constraints. There are constraints in terms of length (four is the maximum number of consonants in a cluster, as in *twelfths* /twɛlfθs/); there are also constraints in terms of what sequences are possible, and where in the syllable they can occur. For example, although /bl/ is a permissible sequence at the start of a syllable, it cannot occur at the end of one; conversely /nk/ is permitted at the end, but not the start.

Phrasal verb   See MULTI-WORD VERB.

Phrase   A grammatical structure consisting of a compulsory **head** and one or more optional **modifiers**. There are five phrase types: the **noun phrase**, **verb phrase**, **adjective phrase**, **adverb phrase** and **prepositional phrase**. The term 'phrase' is a **form** label: phrases perform a range of **functions** at clause level.

Pidgin   A language created to act as a means of communication between groups of people (typically more than two) who do not have a language in common. Pidgins have no native speakers; however, if a pidgin eventually acquires them it becomes a **creole**. Pidgins often develop in situations where people need to communicate for purposes of trade. This is why many (but not all) pidgins arose as a result of European colonial expansion. The vocabulary of a pidgin (which is

limited) usually derives from the language of one of the groups in contact (the **lexifier language**), and it leads to pidgins being classified by linguists as 'English-based', 'French-based', 'Portuguese-based' and so on (although the languages have their own local names).

A prototypical pidgin will begin life as a *jargon*: an unstable system of communication displaying a high degree of variation between speakers. Eventually, if the situation of **language contact** is sustained, a jargon might become 'stabilized'. This involves a reduction of variability and the establishment of lexical norms. The morphology and syntax of stabilized pidgin languages are usually 'simple'. Pidgins rarely show the kind of morphological complexity found in the languages of the people who created the pidgin. Nouns are not normally marked, as they are in many languages, with endings which show plurality; and tense and aspect is not indicated by endings on verbs, as these examples from **Tok Pisin** demonstrate: *wanpela pik* ('one pig'); *sikspela pik* ('six pigs'); *shirt em werim asde* ('the shirt he wore yesterday'); *shirt em werim nau* ('the shirt he's wearing now'). Word order is often invariant, so that questions are signalled by intonation rather than **inversion**. Clauses are usually linked by **coordination**, rather than **subordination**. Semantically, pidgins tend to be 'transparent', which means that they often contain compounds whose meanings are derivable from combining the meanings of their component parts, and **reduplication** is common (see Sebba 1997: 54).

Some stabilized pidgins enter a third stage of development in which speakers begin to use the language for a wider range of functions than those for which it was originally intended. During the 'expansion' phase its stylistic resources are developed, so that it can be used as means of cultural expression in songs and story-telling, for example. One of the best known examples of a fully expanded pidgin is **Tok Pisin**. Expanded pidgins can be distinguished from **creoles** by the fact that they have no native speakers. See also CONTACT VARIETY, CREOLE, LANGUAGE CONTACT, LEXIFIER LANGUAGE, MELANESIAN PIDGIN ENGLISH, WEST AFRICA.

Pitch   The auditory sensation of the rate of vocal fold vibration during speech production. 'High' pitch is associated with a rapid rate of vibration; 'low' pitch with a slow rate. The linguistic use of pitch is called **intonation**.

Plain English   English that is clear and easy to understand. The term is particularly associated with various pressure groups in the UK, USA, Canada and Australia, who define plain English as 'something that the intended audience can read, understand and act upon the first time they read it'. They promote plain English by publishing writing guides and endorsing organizations which use it in their documents (in the UK, the 'Crystal Mark' on a text indicates approval from the Plain English Campaign). On the other hand, English which is regarded as being exceptionally unclear, misleading and evasive might receive a *Doublespeak Award* in the USA, or a *Golden Bull Award* in the UK. A recent UK winner was an email from a phone company which described laying a cable as: 'physically installing the metallic facility path between the customer's line and the equipment'.

Plain English can be seen as a contemporary form of linguistic **prescriptivism** concerned with 'democratizing' public language. In his introduction to *The Plain English Guide*, Martin Cutts claims that 'clearer documents can improve people's access to benefits and services, justice and a fair deal', and that 'plain language should ... become an accepted part of plain dealing between consumers and business, and between citizens and the State' (1995).

Plosive   A **consonant** produced by a manner of **articulation** involving the following stages. First, the vocal tract is closed at some point, preventing air from escaping through the **oral cavity**. This results in a build up of air pressure behind the closure. When the blockage is removed and the air released, a small 'explosion' occurs (hence 'plosive'). In English there are six plosive consonant phonemes. 1) A voiceless labial plosive /p/ as in *pet*. 2) A voiced labial plosive /b/ as in *bag*. 3) A voiceless alveolar plosive /t/ as in *tap*. 4) A voiced alveolar plosive /d/ as in *dig*. 5) A voiceless velar plosive /k/ as in *cat*. 6) A voiced velar plosive /g/ as in *goal*. Plosives are also known as *stops*.

Plural   See NUMBER.

Poetic diction   Words and phrases which occur frequently in poetry, but are not common elsewhere. From a twenty-first century perspective, this concept seems rather unusual: in contemporary English verse there is no lexical item which could not be found in other contexts (and, conversely, no word from other contexts which could not occur in poetry). Yet there are moments in the history of English literature when just such a specialized vocabulary existed. For example, **Old English** poetry contains many words which are rarely found in prose texts of the period (and which were presumably not common in speech). For example, there are a variety of terms denoting 'man', 'warrior': *beorn, guma, hæleð, rinc, secg*. All five words are virtually confined to verse. Such an abundance of **synonym**s probably derives from the stylistic device at the heart of Old English poetry: variation. Variation is the multiple statement of the same thing in different words. This device requires a large number of synonyms, especially in those areas which are central to OE poetry, such as the sea, ships, warriors and so on. Poetic diction is also associated with the eighteenth century, during which period a style developed which was characterized by the use of stock poetic words and phrases (*verdant vales, azure main, solemn hour*), adjectives formed by adding the suffix *-y* to nouns (*bloomy, plumy, wingy, finny*) and formulaic epithets (*finny tribe, scaly flocks, wingy swarm, fleecy wealth*).

Point of view See NARRATOR.

Polari A lexicon used mainly by gay men, particularly in the UK in the 1930s to the 1970s. The sources of the vocabulary are various, but include **rhyming slang**, backslang (pronouncing a word as if it were spelled backwards), Italian, French, American Airforce slang and words derived from criminal **argot**. Because Polari was often used for purposes of concealment by a criminalized social group (homosexual acts between men were illegal in Britain until 1967), it is sometimes described as an **antilanguage**. Core Polari vocabulary items include *eek* ('face'), *cod* ('bad', 'fake'), *lally* ('leg'), *omi* ('man'), *palone* ('woman'), *omi-palone* ('gay man'), *bona* ('good'). Some Polari terms have entered colloquial British English: *naff* ('awful', 'tasteless'), *camp* ('effeminate'), *send up* ('to make fun of').

Polarity A way of describing certain linguistic phenomenon according to whether they are *positive* or *negative*. Polarity can be expressed syntactically

(*Jim is very ambitious/Jim is not very ambitious*) and morphologically (*intelligent/unintelligent*). See NEGATION.

Politeness In general usage, a display of good manners or etiquette. Linguistic politeness is shaped by three main factors: face needs, social distance/solidarity, and social and cultural contexts. 1) *Face needs* are either positive or negative. *Positive* face relates to the desire to be liked, respected and approved of. When we greet, compliment, or give a direct expression of approval to someone, we are supplying their *positive* face needs: *Oh what a lovely jumper!* *Negative* face needs are associated with the desire not to be constrained or imposed on. When we accompany a request or order with hedges, apologies and indirect expressions, we are supplying the negative face needs of the addressee: *What I was going to ask you is would you mind if I had a party while you were in Dieppe?* 2) Strategies of politeness are influenced by the relationships between people in a conversation. For example, terms of address and levels of formality and directness vary according to the social distance between speakers and their relative status. 3) Social and cultural factors also influence politeness. Speakers need to be aware of appropriate levels of formality in a particular social context, and follow the 'rules' governing behaviour such as the acceptance or rejection of invitations, giving and receiving hospitality, greetings, the use of taboo language and so on.

Polyglossia A situation in which two or more languages exist side by side in a multilingual society, but are used for different purposes. Typically, one of the languages (usually labelled the 'H' or 'high' variety) has greater **prestige** than the others, and is used in formal, public contexts such as education and administration. The other languages in a polyglossic situation (usually labelled the 'L' or 'low' varieties) tend to be used in informal, private contexts (and also in popular culture).

During the **Middle English** period, England was a *triglossic* society, with English as the 'L' variety, and **French** and **Latin** as 'H' varieties. As French died out, England became *diglossic* in English and Latin (which was maintained as the language of education and the Church).

Polysemy Two or more distinct meanings associated with a single **lexeme**: *They gave me a **shot** and took me to the operating room;*• *Gomez was a **shot** behind the Australian;*† *Venice, God help us, was introduced by a **shot** of gondoliers.* See AMBIGUITY.

Polysyllable A word containing more than one **syllable**. Longer polysyllables are often words with **Latin** and Greek etymologies: *telescope, monogamy, detumescence.* Compare MONOSYLLABLE.

Possessive determiner A type of **determiner** which indicates who or what 'possesses' the referent of the head noun in the noun phrase. The seven possessive determiners in Standard English are *my, our, your, his, her, its* and *their*: *I started **my** car*; *Enter **our** fantastic competition*; ***Your** prints will be ready this evening*; *Celia hoped to live with **her** mother in Birmingham*; ***Their** house was the tallest on Thrush Green.* There is considerable variation in the form of possessive determiners in non-standard varieties of English, as these examples demonstrate: *Where's **me** money for **me** crisps?* (south-west England); ***Wor** Peter's a marvel*• (north-east England); *I'll fetch them like for **us** dinner* (Yorkshire); *Sitting on **ma** daddy's knee* (Scotland); *When we have no ozone layer left, **y'all's** stories will be more important*‡ (southern USA). See GENITIVE.

Possessive pronoun A type of **personal pronoun** which marks 'possession'. In Standard English, the possessive pronouns are *mine, ours, yours, his, hers* and *theirs*. As the following examples show, they 'stand in' for a whole noun phrase, which means that they can perform the same functions as noun phrases in the clause: ***Mine** is glittering and blue* (possessive pronoun as subject); *Vitor's brown eyes trapped **hers*** (possessive pronoun as object); *They were strong and the future was **theirs*** (possessive pronoun as subject complement). See POSSESSIVE DETERMINER, GENITIVE.

Post-alveolar A term used in the description of **consonant**s referring to a place of **articulation** (the point in the **vocal tract** where a constriction of the air-stream occurs). Post-alveolar consonants are produced with the tip of the tongue between the palate and the **alveolar ridge**. There are four post-alveolar consonant phonemes in most varieties of English: /ʃ/, /ʒ/, /tʃ/, /dʒ/.

Post-determiner See DETERMINER, NOUN PHRASE.

Postmodifier A modifier occurring after the phrase **head**. See MODIFIER.

Post-vocalic See PRE-VOCALIC AND POST-VOCALIC.

Post-vocalic r See LINKING /r/, RHOTIC ACCENT.

Pragmatics A branch of language study which focuses on the relationship between meaning and situational, social and cultural **context**s. See AMBIGUITY, ASYMMETRY, CODE-SWITCHING, COHERENCE, CONVERSATION ANALYSIS, CO-OPERATIVE PRINCIPLE, DEIXIS, DISCOURSE,

GIVEN AND NEW, POLITENESS, PRESUPPOS-
ITION, SPEECH ACT THEORY, SPEECH AND
WRITING, STYLE SHIFTING.

Predicate   A term used to describe everything which comes after the **subject** of a clause. The predicate must contain a verb; other elements (e.g. **object, complement, adverbial**) are optional. In the following examples, the predicates are in bold: *I **like chicken**; He **sways around helplessly**.*

Predicative   A term used in some grammars as a synonym for the **complement** (as **clause element**).

Predicative adjective   An **adjective** functioning as the **subject** or **object complement**. Predicative adjectives functioning as subject complement follow a **copular verb**: *These big old country houses are **beautiful**; She seems **nice**.* Predicative adjectives functioning as object complement occur with 'complex transitive verbs' – verbs which can take a **direct object** and an **object complement**. In the following examples, the object is underlined and the predicative adjective functioning as object complement is in bold: *He proved <u>them</u> **wrong**; They declared <u>the game</u> **null**;†They were aware of the allegations, but considered <u>them</u> **unfounded**.*

Most adjectives can occur predicatively and attributively (*He still suffers from **smelly** feet; The diesel fumes are **smelly***), but there are some which can *only* occur predicatively. For example, adjectives with an *a-* prefix, such as *afraid, asleep, afloat, alive* and so on cannot premodify nouns, as the following pairings demonstrate: *The child was afraid / *The afraid child; The doctor was alive / *The alive doctor.* See ATTRIBUTIVE ADJECTIVE, COMPLEMENT.

Preface   See DISLOCATION, SPEECH AND WRITING.

Prefix   An **affix** which comes before the **morpheme**(s) to which it is attached, as in the following examples: ***un**pleasant; **re**organize; **de**limit; **co**operate.* In English, prefixes are usually **derivation**al (that is, they are used to modify the meaning of the **stem**). Compare SUFFIX.

Premodifier   A modifier occurring before the phrase **head**. See MODIFIER.

Preposing   See FRONTING.

Preposition   Function words which serve as the **head** of **prepositional phrase**s, expressing relations of place, time, possession and agency. In the following examples, the preposition is in bold and underlined, and the noun phrase to which it is linked is in bold: *We were staying **<u>in</u> Escondido**; The wedding's going to be **<u>in</u> February**; The growing indebtedness **<u>of</u> the USA** is regarded as unacceptable; He is refused hospitality **<u>by</u> the rich village priest**.* Prepositions usually consist of a single lexical item: *about, above, against, at, below, by, from, in, on, of, with* and so on. But complex prepositions also exist, made up of two and three words: *such as, apart from, in spite of, as far as.* There is considerable overlap between the class of prepositions and **adverbial particle**s. Forms having both a prepositional and an adverbial function include *about, above, below, by, in, on.*

Prepositional phrase   One of the five major **phrase** types, consisting of a preposition followed by a noun phrase: *at the zoo, by the door, on a microscope slide.* The **head** of a prepositional phrase is sometimes preceded by an adverb indicating place or degree: ***down** by the river, **precisely** at midnight.* The two main roles of prepositional phrases are **adverbial**s at clause level, and as a modifier following a noun at phrase level. The first main role is illustrated in the following examples:

T'zin was standing **at the far end***; Bracken rose up steeply* **behind the house***.* At phrase level, prepositional phrases commonly postmodify nouns: *The boys and girls* **in the green uniforms***; He was a student* **of divinity***.* Prepositional phrases can also postmodify certain adjectives: *He's scared* **of the dark***.*

Prepositional verb See MULTI-WORD VERB.

Prescriptivism An attitude towards language which endorses certain usages because they are 'correct', and outlaws others because they are 'incorrect'. Correctness, of course, is never a linguistic judgment; it is always a social one, because 'correct' forms are almost always the forms favoured by the dominant social group. Anxieties about 'correct' and 'incorrect' English are particularly associated with the eighteenth century, a period which saw the rapid growth of the middle class. Traditionally the most insecure of all social classes, the bourgeoisie needed to demarcate itself from its social 'inferiors'. One of the ways it did this was through language: use of the 'correct' forms was a marker of social superiority. During this period a number of grammars were produced which people could consult for guidance. Two were particularly influential: Robert Lowth's *Short Introduction to English Grammar* (1762) and Lindley Murray's *English Grammar* (1795). Both were remarkable works of scholarship that provided generally accurate descriptions of the grammar of English – it is simply wrong to characterize them, as some do, merely as guides to linguistic propriety. Nevertheless, they do contain criticisms of current and past usage (Shakespeare, Milton, Dryden and Pope do not escape censure), together with prescriptive rules about what one should or should not say or write. Many of these rules (such as the prohibition on **multiple negation**, or the rule outlawing sentences which end with a **preposition**) have been handed down by generations of school teachers and survive to provoke anxiety in English speakers around the world. See also ACADEMY, AUTHORITY, GENERIC PRONOUN, GRAMMAR, HYPERCORRECTION, LATER MODERN ENGLISH, PLAIN ENGLISH, SPLIT INFINITIVE.

Present-day English (PDE) A term sometimes used in discussions of the history of the language to describe English as it is currently spoken.

Present participle See *ING*-PARTICIPLE.

Present tense See TENSE.

Prestige A language or variety is said to have linguistic prestige if it is highly valued. Social and linguistic prestige is interrelated. The language of powerful social groups usually carries linguistic prestige; and social prestige is often granted to speakers of prestige languages and varieties. See COVERT PRESTIGE, OVERT PRESTIGE, STIGMATIZATION.

Presupposition Facts, beliefs or opinions which are not actually asserted in an utterance but which are implied. Take the following examples. 1) *Fornication in the kitchen is surely not allowed.* 2) *Come in out of the rain.* 3) *Maria's sister is ill.* What is 'taken for granted' as **given** information in these three sentences? The first sentence presupposes that there is fornication going on in the kitchen. A way of saying this without using presupposition would be to *assert* that there is fornication in the kitchen first, as in *There is fornication in the kitchen and it is surely not allowed.* Similarly, the second sentence presupposes that it is raining – to avoid using presupposition we would have to say something like *It is raining, so come in out of the rain.* Finally, the presupposition in the third sentence is that Maria has a sister. A defining feature of presuppositions is that they remain the same when the **polarity** of the sentence is reversed. For example *Maria's sister is not ill* still contains the presupposition that Maria has a sister. *Don't come in out of the rain* still presupposes that it is raining. And *Fornication in the kitchen is allowed* still contains the presupposition that there is fornication going on. Presuppositions are often associated with particular lexical items or grammatical structures, sometimes known as presupposition 'triggers'. Common triggers include **definite** descriptive and referring expressions: *I heard the church clock strike nine* (there exists a church clock); 'factive' constructions: *That really makes me regret changing schools* (I changed schools); change-of-state verbs: *Jane stopped the chainsaw* (the chainsaw had been running); temporal clauses: *She ate a bowl of custard before she went to bed* (she went to bed); **cleft sentences**: *It wasn't me who tempted you* (someone tempted you); iteratives: *I didn't try again* (I tried before); comparisons and contrasts: *I'm not as clever as Stan* (Stan is clever).

Sometimes what is presupposed is uncontentious (as in the examples above). But many presuppositions take for granted what is questionable, as in this extract from a speech by the US Secretary of Defense Donald H. Rumsfeld (October 2002). Contentious presuppositions have been underlined and glossed in brackets:

The war on terrorism (there is a war on terrorism) began in Afghanistan, to be sure, but it will not end there. (it is continuing) It will not end (it is continuing) until terrorist networks (there are terrorist networks) have been rooted out, (they are 'hidden') wherever they exist. It will not end (it is continuing) until the state sponsors of terror (there are state sponsors of terror) are made to understand (they do not understand) that aiding, abetting and harboring terrorists (they are doing these things) has deadly consequences for those that try it. It will not end (it is continuing) until those developing nuclear, chemical and biological weapons (they are developing these weapons) end their threat (there is an ongoing threat) to innocent men, women and children.

Pre-vocalic and post-vocalic Occurring before a vowel (*pre-vocalic*) and after a vowel (*post-vocalic*).

Primary auxiliary verb When the **primary verb**s *be* and *have* (which are used to construct the perfect and progressive **aspect** and passive **voice**) are used as **auxiliary verb**s they are known as primary auxiliary verbs: *Workplace stress is sweeping across industry; A wind of change has swept Ellesmere Port town.* *Do* is also sometimes included in this category, when it functions as an **operator**: *I do want a little break.*

Primary verb The verbs *be, have* and *do* are known as primary verbs because of their central grammatical role. *Be* and *have* can function as both a **main** and an **auxiliary verb**: *The world is mad* (main verb); *The world is turning* (primary auxiliary verb); *Visual aids have several advantages* (main verb); *An eagle-eyed referee may have sabotaged their cup run* (primary auxiliary verb). *Do* can function as a main verb and as an **operator** in questions and negative statements: *I do French and German* (main verb); *Does she* *make bread pudding often?* (operator); *I don't know* (operator). See INTERROGATIVE CLAUSE, NEGATION.

Process type See TRANSITIVITY.

Productivity [1] One of the so-called 'design features' of language. This property allows speakers to produce an infinite number of novel utterances from the finite resources of the language system.

[2] In **lexicology**, the term is used to describe the extent to which a particular process of **word formation** is productive. For example, the suffix *-able* is highly productive because it can be added to the **base form** of many verbs to denote 'capable of (or fit for the purpose of) undergoing or experiencing the action or state denoted by the verb' (e.g. *lovable, salvageable, downloadable*). Slightly less productive is the suffix *-er*, which can be added to the base form of an **activity verb** to denote 'the entity performing the action of the verb' (e.g. *walker, talker, stalker*). See BACKFORMATION.

Proform An item which can stand in for a phrase, clause constituent or clause. Proforms are usually pronouns, adverbs or verbs, as the following examples illustrate. 1) Pronouns as proforms: *Esther sent a card to Alix; **She** sent it to **her*** (pronouns substituting for noun phrases). 2) Adverbs as proforms: *'I wonder if he'll be very hurt?' 'I hope he is!'; 'I wonder if he'll be very hurt?' 'I hope **so**!*' (*so* substituting for an elliptical clause). 3) Verbs as proforms ('pro-verbs'): *He wants to see him. Yes he **does*** (*does* substituting for a verb phrase + complement: 'does want to see him'). See GRAMMATICAL COHESION, PRONOUN, SPEECH AND WRITING.

Progressive See ASPECT.

Pronoun A **proform** which stands in for a noun phrase: *He gives way to **them** so much that **they** actually bully **him**.*± See the following separate entries: DEMONSTRATIVE, INDEFINITE PRONOUN, PERSONAL PRONOUN, POSSESSIVE PRONOUN, QUANTIFIER, RECIPROCAL PRONOUN, REFLEXIVE PRONOUN, RELATIVE PRONOUN, QUANTIFYING PRONOUN.

Proper noun See NOUN.

Prosody Those aspects of speech which convey meaning but are non-verbal. The main prosodic features of speech are **tempo, volume, pitch, stress, intonation**.

Pun A type of word-play which depends on phonological **ambiguity**. A 'pure' pun relies on **homophone**s (two words which sound the same but have different meanings): Q. *Why couldn't the foal talk?* A. *Because he was a little **hoarse***. Other puns rely on a phonological resemblance: Q. *What do you call a monkey in a minefield?* A. *A **baboom***. As these children's jokes show, puns are often regarded as a rather minor form of wit. As well as being a staple of jokes, puns are also common in light-hearted newspaper headlines and shop names as in *BASQUE IN CHARL'S GLORY* (accompanying a picture of a singer called Charlotte in revealing lingerie); *Tanfastic* (the name of a tanning salon).

Punctuation Marks used to help clarify the meaning of written text. In present-day written English, the most commonly used punctuation marks are the **full stop, comma, semicolon, colon, hyphen, brackets, quotation mark, question mark, exclamation mark, apostrophe**.

Q

Quantifier Quantifiers are either **determiner**s or **pronoun**s. Quantifying determiners specify nouns according to quantity, extent or amount, as these examples demonstrate: *All families are different;* **Both** *men had to be restrained;* **Each** *district had only one biochemical pathology laboratory;* **Every** *child had a gas mask and a suitcase;* **Many** *people have to use a car to get to work.* Quantifying pronouns usually have the same form as the determiners. For example: **Both** *shared a love of collecting antiques; When* **all** *were aboard, the storm broke;* **Each** *gave birth to a baby on the same day.* See INDEFINITE PRONOUN.

Question See INTERROGATIVE.

Question mark The **punctuation** mark <?>, early versions of which appear in eighth-century manuscripts. It is used to indicate that the word, phrase, clause, or sentence which precedes it is a direct question (*What is the capital of South Africa?*); but it is not used to mark questions in **indirect speech** (*She asked what he was selling*).

Quotation marks These **punctuation** marks (which are also known as *inverted commas*) are either single <'. . .'> or double <". . .">. They are used to enclose **direct speech**: *'Yes Bob', she said.* American usage tends to favour the double quotation mark, while British usage prefers the single. Single quotation marks are also used to enclose words or phrases which writers want to draw attention to, perhaps because they wish to distance themselves from the word or phrase, or because they are pointing out a non-standard usage or a figurative expression: *A history of imperialism and Western economic dominance has enabled white men to pursue technological progress at the expense of the so-called 'third world'.*

R

Reanalysis A process of **word formation** (also known as 'recutting') in which words are reanalysed into components which are different from their original parts. For example *apron, umpire* and *adder* were once *napron, noumpere* and *nadder*. But at some point (probably during the fourteenth century), the word boundaries were reanalysed so that the initial /n/ became attached to the definite article (*an*). See FOLK ETYMOLOGY.

Rebus A written word or sentence consisting of a combination of letters, numerals and symbols. Often, a single letter (such as U or C) stands for the word which the letter name resembles. Rebuses are common in text messages and other form of electronic communication: *L8R* ('later'), *B4N* ('bye for now'), *RU* ('are you').

Received Pronunciation (RP) A minority **accent** of English used mainly in England. Unlike most accents of English, RP is not a regional **variety**; its speakers can be found all over the country. The variety of informal descriptions it has attracted – including the Queen's (or King's) English, Oxford English, public school English, 'talking posh' – indicate that the accent is often associated with speakers of a high **social class** and status. However, in present-day English society the accent is much more widely based than it once was (Upton 2004b). RP is particularly important for linguists, because it is often used as a point of reference against which other accents of English can be compared.

One of the earliest uses of the term is by the phonetician Alexander Ellis (1869), who points to the existence of a '*received pronunciation* all over the country, not widely differing in any particular locality, and admitting a certain degree of variety. It may be especially considered as the educated pronunciation of the metropolis, of the court, the pulpit and the bar.' In 1917, Daniel Jones in the introduction to his *English Pronouncing Dictionary* writes that the model accent 'used in this book is that most usually heard in everyday speech in the families of Southern English persons whose men-folk have been educated at the great public boarding-schools. This pronunciation is also used by a considerable proportion of those who do not come from the South of England but who have been educated at these schools.' Both Ellis and Jones point to London and the south-east as the probable point of origin of the accent, but are at pains to point out that it is not limited geographically. RP is, however, an accent strongly associated with social elites of various kinds (educated 'men-folk' and their families, the royal court, the Church and the legal system), which developed through a system of 'levelling' as members of these elites came into contact in the public schools and universities (see DIALECT LEVELLING). Interestingly, Ellis writing in the 1860s acknowledges that a certain amount of variety was then present in the accent, which he described as a 'thread' of colouring from the local regional variety. But by the time Jones wrote his dictionary, this 'thread' was less evident: RP speakers were much less likely to provide clues to their geographical background in their speech. However, this is not to say that at any point in its history RP has been entirely uniform. Linguists have attempted to capture this variation by identifying and describing different kinds of RP. In the 1960s, Gimson identified 'conservative' RP (used by the older generation), 'general' or 'mainstream' RP, and 'advanced' RP (used by young upper-class and professional people). The 1960s also saw the re-emergence of regional colouring in RP which Ellis had remarked on a hundred years earlier. This phenomenon is sometimes known as 'modified' RP (see Crystal 2004: 472). Upton (2004b) distinguishes between 'RP' and 'traditional RP'. RP is the label he uses for an accent 'that will not be the object of comment as regards elevated upbringing or social pretension. Furthermore, it is not to be associated with any one geographical region in England.' For Upton, contemporary RP is exemplified by the 'scarcely remarked upon "background" accent of the media newsreader'. On the other hand, 'traditional RP' is a more socially restricted accent, which many British people associate with the upper classes (hence the pejorative label 'posh'), regarding it is affected and old-fashioned. The reference to the newsreader is important, since it points to one of the most important means by which British people in the twentieth century were exposed to RP: through the broadcast media. The association between RP and the British Broadcasting Corporation (BBC) became so strong that the term 'BBC English' was sometimes used as a synonym for RP. Even today, announcers and newsreaders on the BBC are still more likely to speak with an RP accent than a regional variety of English, although few, if any, are speakers of 'traditional' RP.

The vowels of RP (see Upton 2004b and Trudgill and Hannah 2002)

Vowel	RP and 'trad' RP	'Trad' RP only	Notes
KIT	ɪ		
DRESS	ɛ	e	
TRAP	a	æ	The movement from 'trad' RP [æ] to RP [a] is possibly one of the most striking changes in the accent in recent years. Now only elderly speakers preserve the [æ] sound (which is often mimicked as 'trep' for *trap* and 'het' for *hat*).
LOT	ɒ		
STRUT	ʌ		
FOOT	ʊ		

Vowel	RP and 'trad' RP	'Trad' RP only	Notes
BATH	ɑː ~ a	ɑː	Some RP speakers now have [a] in words where traditionally [ɑː] occurred. The shortened vowel is more likely to occur in words where a nasal follows the vowel (e.g. *chance, dance, sample*).
CLOTH	ɒ	ɒ~ ɔː	[ɔː] as a pronunciation of the vowel in words like *cloth* and *off* is associated only with the most conservative speakers of RP – it is rarely heard.
NURSE	əː	ɜː	
FLEECE	iː		
FACE	eɪ		
PALM	ɑː		
THOUGHT	ɔː		
GOAT	əʊ	əʊ ~ oʊ	
GOOSE	uː		
PRICE	ʌɪ	aɪ	
CHOICE	ɔɪ		
MOUTH	aʊ		
NEAR	ɪə		
SQUARE	ɛː	ɛə	In RP the SQUARE vowel is a long monophthong [ɛː]. The vowel is a dipthong [ɛə] in trad-RP.
START	ɑː		
NORTH	ɔː		
FORCE	ɔː		
CURE	ʊə ~ ɔː	ʊə	The vowel in the CURE set is often heard as the monophthong [ɔː] in RP, whereas the diphthong [ʊə] is a more usual realization in trad-RP.

The consonant phonemes of RP are p, b, t, d, k, g, f, v, θ, ð, s, z, ʃ, ʒ, h, tʃ, dʒ, m, n, ŋ, l, r, j, w. This twenty-four phoneme system is shared with many other varieties of English. However, there are some features of the realization of consonants which are characteristic of (though not necessarily unique to) RP. 1) Most accents of English in England have lost the /w/:/ʍ/ contrast (e.g. *witch* and *which* are usually **homophone**s). However, some more conservative RP speakers preserve the distinction. 2) Syllable-final /t/ is often realized as the glottal stop [ʔ] when it precedes a consonant, as in *Gatwick, hatbox, Batman* and so on, particularly in the speech of younger RP speakers. 3) RP is a non-**rhotic accent**, so that /r/ is *not* pronounced after a vowel in words with an <r> in the spelling (e.g. *farm, car*). However, in common with other non-rhotic accents, **linking /r/** and so-called 'intrusive' /r/ are widely used, resulting in the orthographic /r/ being sounded in *far away*, and an /r/ being inserted after the /ə/ in *China* in *China and Japan*.

Recipient See BENEFICIARY.

Reciprocal pronoun A **pronoun** which shows that the action or state expressed by the verb is reciprocated by a (plural) subject. There are only two reciprocal pronouns in Standard English, and they are exemplified in the following sentences: *We phone **each other** every day;*• *Their parents love **one another**.*•

Reduplication A morphological process involving the repetition of words or parts of words to create new meanings. In many languages reduplication is used **inflection**ally (to signal grammatical meaning) or **derivation**ally (to derive new words). Although reduplication is productive in some English-based **pidgin**s and **creole**s, it is of only limited produc-tivity in English more generally, where it is mainly associated with colloquial and informal styles of speech and writing, or speech directed at young children. Reduplication consists of exact repetition (*fifty-fifty, goody-goody, wee-wee*); rhyming repetition (*claptrap, gang-bang, sci-fi*); or repetition involving a vowel contrast (*flip-flop, zig-zag, riff-raff*).

Reference, referent A referent is a person, entity, place, concept, experience and so on in the real (or an imagined) world which is designated by a word or phrase. For example, the word *cat* 'refers to' a feline domestic animal, while *hobbit* refers to a small human-like creature with hairy feet and pointed ears (in the fictional universe of J.R.R. Tolkein). Reference is often contrasted with 'sense' – **semantic relations** *between* words (e.g. antonymy, synonymy) which are internal to language.

Not all linguistic elements 'refer to' objects and entities in the outside world; some refer to other parts of the text in which they occur: *In **this section** we summarize our findings* (see GRAMMATICAL COHESION). See also ARTICLE, DEFINITE AND INDEFINITE, DEIXIS, DETERMINER, ZERO-ARTICLE.

Reflexive pronoun A pronoun which signals that the subject undergoes the action or state denoted by the verb: *Deidre might hurt **herself**.*• If two noun phrases occur in the same clause, and refer to the same person, object or entity, the second noun phrase must be a reflexive pronoun, and this pronoun must reflect the same person and number as the first noun phrase: *I grin at **myself** in the mirror; They might find **themselves** on the same side.* Reflexive pronouns can also be used to mean 'alone': *I'm going to do it **myself**;*• *She sang it all by **herself**.*• Sometimes reflexives are used to 'intensify' the preceding noun or pronoun: *I myself am a policeman;* • *But meeting John himself was more than enough for me.* •

In Standard English, the reflexive pronouns are formed by adding *-self* and *-selves* to the possessive pronoun in the case of *my, your* and *our* (*myself, yourself/selves, ourself/selves*). On the other hand, *himself, herself, itself* and *themselves* are formed by adding these endings to the object pronoun. Many non-standard varieties of English attempt to regularize this inconsistency by adding *-self/-selves* uniformly to the possessive: *Perhaps Nicodemus has helped **hisself** to them* (northern England); *They cut **theirselves*** (London); *They don't help **theirself*** (south-west England); *Young folks want to be by **theirselves*** • (USA). See REGULARIZATION.

Reformation A sixteenth-century movement for the reform of Catholicism based in Northern Europe. It is sometimes known as the Protestant Reformation, because its advocates 'protested' against the centralized authority of the Pope in Rome, and these protesters eventually established the Protestant churches. The Reformation's influence on the **vernacular** languages of Europe was profound. Across Europe, Protestants looked to scripture as the main source of religious authority, not to tradition or the Pope. The linguistic outcome of this shift in outlook was the decline of ecclesiastical Latin. Translations of the **Bible** were produced and church services were conducted in the language of their congregation. In England, as writers and scholars strove to make English a suitable instrument for religious and intellectual discourse, the number of publications in English increased rapidly.

Register A term used mainly in **stylistics** and **sociolinguistics** to refer to a variety of language defined according to its *use*. We can talk about the 'register' of scientific English, religious English, business English and so on. Register is determined by the interaction of three variables in the linguistic situation: *field* refers to what is taking place, what the participants are engaged in; *tenor* refers to who is taking part, the relationships between participants, the status and role of participants; *mode* refers to the part language plays in the situation, the channel used (spoken or written, or a mixture of the two), and what is being achieved by the text (is it expository, persuasive, didactic and so on?). Each register has associated with it a particular combination of linguistic features; in other words, each register has a particular **style**.

Regular form An item which conforms to the most common pattern. For example, plurals in English are normally created by adding *-s* to the base form (*dogs*), and the past tense of verbs is usually marked by adding *-ed* to the base (*talked*). Irregular forms do not conform: *children*; *went*.

Regularization A process in which irregular forms are changed so that they become more regular and/or simplified. For example, in Standard English there is only one inflectional verb ending in the present tense: the *-s* ending on the third person singular verb form (*he runs*). In some non-standard varieties of English, the process of regularization has led to all present tense verbs having the same form: *He **say** we got to keep moving till we find her* (USA); '*You have a baby boy,' I **says*** • (USA). For many English speakers, the past participle of **irregular verbs** has the same form as the past tense: *He's **took** a bite out of it.*

The tendency towards regularization is quite strong. When new words enter the language they usually conform to regular morphological patterns. For example, the plural of *lowlife* is not **lowlives*, but *low-lifes*: *It's just those **lowlifes** selling that shit.*[•] And the plural of *Walkman* is usually *Walkmans*, not ** Walkmen*: *Top of my list would be people with **Walkmans.**[•]* However, irregular plurals can also occur: *Smokers are marshalling their computer **mice.**[•]*

Regular verb A verb with the following pattern of inflections (examples are from the CWEC):

walk	*The window seemed thick enough to **walk** on; You must **walk** south.*	base
walk	*You **walk** around with it; I **walk** in there just to browse.*	first and second person present
walks	*She **walks** over to the table.*	third person present
walked	*She **walked** over to the window.*	past
walked	*The refugees have **walked** for hundred of kilometres.*	past (*-ed*) participle
walking	*I was **walking** along the bay.*	present (*-ing*) participle

Most verbs in English are regular. However, many of the most frequently occurring verbs are not. See IRREGULAR VERB, REGULARIZATION.

Relative adverb An **adverb** used to introduce a **relative clause**. Three adverbs can perform this function: *where, when* and *why*. *Where* occurs at the start of a clause postmodifying a noun of place: *Faliraki is a lively town **where** you'll find a host of tavernas.* *When* introduces a clause postmodifying expressions of time: *The fun began on Monday **when** a giant sandcastle was built on the beach.* And *why* introduces a clause postmodifying nouns of 'reason': *That's the reason **why** they want to get me back.*

Relative clause A finite or non-finite subordinate clause which postmodifies a noun phrase and is therefore sometimes referred to as an adjectival or adjective clause. Finite relative clauses usually begin with a **relative pronoun** (*who, which, whom, whose, that*) or a **relative adverb** (*where, when, why*). In the following examples, the relative clause is in bold and the head of the noun phrase it postmodifies is underlined: *There are so many <u>people</u> **who have no jobs at all**;±️ I use <u>plants</u> **which are good oxygenators**; One of the food hawkers was our seventh <u>grand-aunt</u>, **whom I remember very well**; <u>Professor Leder</u>, **whose research field is molecular genetics with special focus on cancer cell growth**, is a highly regarded scientist in the USA;±️ He must run a motor <u>car</u> **that doesn't drink petrol like tapwater;** The officers were particularly interested in a <u>spot</u> **where she had uprooted a banana tree**;±️ There was a <u>time</u> **when he spent his personal money with abandon**;±️ This is the reason **why I bought this ticket**.±️ In some circumstances the relative pronoun can be omitted – this is known as a *zero relative clause*: *She could make no sense of the books Ø **she was given**.* This omission can only occur in certain types of restrictive relative clauses (see below). A further category is the reduced relative clause. These have no relative pronoun or adverb, and the verb is non-finite: *She saw the woman* **standing by the reception desk**; *No severe or moderate dysplasia was seen in any of the patients* **examined**. The elements in bold can be expanded to a full relative clause: *the woman* **who was standing**; *the patients* **who were examined**.

Relative clauses are either *restrictive* or *non-restrictive*. Restrictive relative clauses are used to identify the referent of the noun phrase (*These are likenesses of the* <u>man</u> **who committed those attacks**); non-restrictive relative clauses do not identify the referent, but provide additional information about it (*The* **man**, **who was** **about forty**, *came to meet me*). In writing, a non-restrictive relative clause is usually preceded by a comma. In speech, the difference between a restrictive and non-restrictive relative clause is signalled by **intonation**.

Relative pronoun   A pronoun used to introduce a **relative clause**. In Standard English, these are *who*, *which*, *that*, *whom*, and *whose*. *Who* is used when its antecedent is either human or has quasi-human characteristics: *I'm a woman* **who** *completely supports herself*; *A dog* **who** *has high self-confidence is never worried by strangers*. *Which* is used when the antecedent is a non-human creature or an inanimate entity or idea: *They stick out their tongue and snap at any* <u>insect</u> **which** *flies by*; *Petwood is a long, low* <u>building</u> **which** *exudes an air of absolute tranquility*; *A lipogram is a literary* <u>composition</u> **which** *omits a certain letter of the alphabet*. *That* is used with human, non-human animate, and inanimate antecedents: *She decided on private treatment from a* <u>doctor</u> **that** *a friend recommended*; *A* <u>horse</u> **that** *pulls with his ears forward tends to be just eager*; *They're making* <u>cars</u> **that** *will run on water*; *It is a pervasive* <u>ideology</u> **that** *bolsters the*

global political economy. *Whom* is used when the antecedent is a human **object** in the clause: *The young* <u>revolutionary</u>, **whom** *they had been trailing for sixteen hours a day, was proving less useful than Cowley had hoped*. *Whose* is used when the pronoun is in a genitive relationship with its antecedent, as in *Mr Norris is a* <u>man</u> **whose** *face was not that well known to the public*;• *More framed photographs decorate a side* <u>table</u> **whose** *cover matches the floral* <u>curtains</u>.• When the antecedent is non-human (as in the second example), some speakers feel uneasy about using *whose*. This is probably influenced by the prescription limiting the use of *who* to human antecedents. Consequently, they will replace *whose* with the periphrastic genitive construction *of which*: *More framed photographs decorate a side* <u>table</u>, *the cover* **of which** *matches the floral curtains*. However, this sounds rather stilted and formal, so many people avoid using *whose* with inanimate antecedents all together. Another option is rapidly gaining ground in colloquial English: *He drove this monster truck* **thats** *wheels were so huge it floated on water*;† *Sarah and Mary discovered a butterfly* **thats** *wings were not a symmetrical pattern*.† These examples show a 'new' relative pronoun, formed by adding *-s* to *that* (by **analogy** with *who* and *whose*).

The relative pronoun can be omitted in Standard English in restrictive relative clauses when its antecedent is *not* the subject: *He had found a manuscript of a book* Ø *he had written*;• *She will be grieving for the man* Ø *she loved*.•

Relative pronouns often attract the attention of prescriptivists. This is perhaps not surprising since there is so much variability in their use. For example, many speakers in different parts of the world routinely use *what* as a relative pronoun: *She's got the book* **what** *I had* *last week*. Some speakers (particularly in the southern USA) also omit the relative pronoun when its antecedent is the subject, as in this (invented) example: *That's the boy hit me*.

A further usage is *which* as a **coordinating conjunction**: *I have two rats, a very large male adult and a tiny little baby **which** I don't even know what sex it is.*† Here *which* seems to be conveying something like 'regarding which' or 'as for that'.

Renaissance [French: rebirth] The revival of Classical learning in Europe that started in Italy in the fourteenth century. Its influence began to be felt in Britain in the mid-fifteenth century, and it lasted for about two hundred years. Its most direct effect on the English language was a massive influx of new words derived from the Classical languages (see ELABORATION). The period is also characterized by an exuberant literary style (this is the age of Spenser, Shakespeare and Milton) and a growing confidence in English as a medium for serious writing, particularly as a consequence of the **Reformation**. See EARLY MODERN ENGLISH, LATIN.

Repetition Saying or writing something more than once. In everyday **conversation**, repetition is very common, as a response to the pressures of speaking in 'real time': *No she she she she enjoyed it*. The repetition of words is also used to give texts **lexical cohesion**: *My father was taking a stroll to the store. The cat was in sole occupancy. The rocket destroyed the house and blew the cat's fur off. My father met the poor creature, who fled at his approach*. When repetition is used for creative and artistic purposes it is known as **parallelism**. See also FIGURE OF SPEECH, FOREGROUNDING, REDUPLICATION, SPEECH AND WRITING, TRANSCRIPTION.

Retroflex A manner of articulation of consonants (especially /r/) in which the tip of the tongue is curled back slightly behind the **alveolar** ridge. See INDIAN ENGLISH.

Retronym Phrases such as *black and white television, landline telephone, silent movie*. Such items are created because an existing term which was once used by itself (in these cases *television, telephone* and *watch*) requires modification as a result of technological or social change. At first, all movies were silent, and they were just called *movies*. Then came talking pictures, which meant that the retronym *silent movie* had to be coined to distinguish between the two types of film. The general term *movie* is applied to the technological advancement, while the marked term *silent movie* is applied to the original form of film. Other retronyms include *snail mail, hard copy, acoustic guitar, World War One*.

Rheme See THEME AND RHEME.

Rhetoric The art of effective speaking and writing. Rhetoric has its origins in Ancient Greece, where it initially referred to the skills required for persuasion in courtroom debate. Later, as Athenian democracy developed, rhetoric became associated with the art of public oratory more generally, particularly in the domain of politics.

According to Aristotle (384–322 BC), persuasion is brought about by three kinds of appeal: the appeal to reason (*logos*); the appeal to emotion (*pathos*) and the persuasive appeal of the speaker's character (*ethos*). These three appeals work together for persuasive ends. Various stylistic devices ('rhetorical figures', or more generally **figures of speech**) are used for persuasive purposes. Several hundred of these figures were identified and classified by the classical rhetoricians. Many of these are well-known and widely used today. See ANAPHORA, BATHOS,

HYPERBOLE, METAPHOR, METONYMY, PERIPHRASIS, SYNECDOCHE.

Rhotic accent   Accents of English can be classified according to whether they are 'rhotic' or 'non-rhotic'. A rhotic accent is one in which the pronunciation of /r/ is permitted after a vowel (that is, post-vocalically). For example, a speaker of a rhotic accent will pronounce *star* as /star/ and *start* as /start/. Non-rhotic accents do not permit pronunciation of /r/ after a vowel, giving the pronunci-ations /staː/ and /staːt/. Post-vocalic /r/ is, however, preserved in non-rhotic accents when it is followed by a vowel, as in words such as *starry, Mary* and *sorrow*. It is also preserved across word boundaries, as in the RP pronunciation of *her axe*, which for most RP speakers would be /həːr aks/ (compare this with *her saw*, which would be pronounced /həː sɔː/). Where /r/ is preserved in response to the vowel at the start of the next word, it is known as **linking** /r/.

In North America, most accents are rhotic, with the exception of the southern Atlantic coastal areas of the United States, metropolitan New York City and parts of eastern New England. In the British Isles, Scotland, Ireland and south-west England are rhotic areas (there is also a small pocket of rhoticity in central Lancashire); most of England and Wales is non-rhotic. Speakers of English with non-rhotic accents can also be found in Australia, New Zealand, South Africa, West Africa, India and Singapore.

Rhyme   A matching of sounds at the end of words (e.g. *ban, plan, saucepan*). The most well-known kind of rhyme involves sound correspondence between final vowels (e.g. *boo, zoo, taboo*), or final vowel + final consonant sequences (e.g. *rat, cat, wombat*). These are sometimes known as 'full' rhymes. Half-rhymes,

on the other hand, involve a phonetic *closeness* between words rather than an exact correspondence. This closeness can involve final vowels (as in *deep* and *ship*) or final consonants (as in *send* and *hand*). Sometimes rhymes extend over more than one syllable, producing pairs such as *sailing*/*wailing* (two rhyming syllables); *weariness*/*dreariness* (three rhyming syl-lables). When rhymes involve unstressed syllables (e.g. *running*/*eating*) they are sometimes known as 'feminine' rhymes, in contrast to 'masculine' rhymes, which are on stressed syllables (e.g. *confine*/ *entwine*).

From the early medieval period until the twentieth century, rhyme was a characteristic feature of English poetry. Various ways of distributing rhymes across lines of verse, known as 'rhyme schemes', have been developed (con-ventionally, the letters a, b, c, d and so on are used to indicate these schemes). Some-times, adjacent lines rhyme, forming a couplet (aa, bb and so on): *What beck'ning ghost, along the moon-light shade* / *Invites my steps, and points to yon-der glade?* Common patterns associated with the four-line stanza known as the *quatrain* include abab (*Love seeketh not itself to please,* / *Nor for itself hath any care,* / *But for another gives its ease,* / *And builds a Heaven in Hell's despair*); and aabb (*I was angry with my friend.* / *I told my wrath, my wrath did end.* / *I was angry with my foe.* / *I told it not, my wrath did grow*).

Rhyme, of course, is not limited to literature. It is also a common feature of song lyrics, slogans of various sorts and language play (particularly by children).

Rhyming slang   A process of **slang** word-formation involving, at its simplest, the replacement of a word with a rhyming phrase, such as 'Rosie Lee' for 'tea' and 'butcher's hook' for 'look'. However, speakers rarely utter the full rhyming phrase; it is usually shortened to its first element ('Rosie Lee' becomes 'Rosie' and 'butcher's hook' becomes 'butchers'). The target word can sometimes be made even more difficult to trace. For example, 'Judith Chalmers' (a British TV presenter) = 'farmers' = 'farmer Giles' = 'piles'. The origins of rhyming slang are obscure, although it is often claimed that these unusual formations originated in the **argot** of nineteenth-century London criminals and street vendors, as a method of concealment. The connection with London is still strong (hence **Cockney** rhyming slang), but it is also heard in other parts of the world, including Australia, New Zealand and the United States. It is now no longer associated with criminality, but remains one of the many creative ways in which slang vocabulary is replenished. See ANTILANGUAGE.

Rhythm In the flow of speech, some **syllable**s are perceived as more prominent than others because they receive more **stress**. Rhythm is the recurring pattern of stressed and unstressed **syllable**s in speech. The rhythm of the **inner circle** varieties of English (e.g. **British English, American English, Australian English**) is *stress-timed*, which means that the stressed syllables occur at roughly regular intervals. In the phrase 'many of the new students', it takes roughly the same amount of time to say 'many of the' as it does to say 'new' ('many of the' contains one stressed syllable, as does 'new'). On the other hand, when all the syllables in the stream of speech take up roughly the same amount of time, this is known as a *syllable-timed* rhythm. Syllable-timed (or near syllable-timed) varieties of English include **Caribbean English, Chicano**

English, Indian English, Singapore English, and varieties of English in **West Africa**. Patterns of rhythm in poetry are known as **metre**.

Right-dislocation See DISLOCATION.

Root A 'bare' lexical **morpheme** which has no **derivation**al or **inflection**al affixes attached to it. For example, the root of *unselfishly* is *self*. It is what remains when the derivational affixes *un-*, *-ish* and *-ly* have been removed. A root can usually stand alone as a word (as in *self*), although some roots cannot (e.g. *ceive* in *conceive, couth* in *uncouth, chalant* in *non-chalant*). See BASE, STEM.

Root creation A comparatively rare process of word formation involving the creation of an entirely new **root**. There are two types. 1) Root creations which are 'motivated' in some way; that is, they resemble or are somehow related to a word or words which already exist, or they are echoic or onomatopoeic (*bang, splash, cuckoo*). 2) Root creations where no such resemblance is immediately obvious (*pooch, snob, orc*). The second type is often associated with fiction (particularly science fiction or fantasy) where new words need to be invented to refer to novel objects (*phaser, tardis*), species (*phagor, dalek*), concepts (*cranch, kemmer*) and places (*Mordor, Mesklin*). Arguably, there are very few 'pure' root creations, in the sense that the neologism has no relationship *whatsoever* with existing words, or does not exploit the phonaesthetic associations of particular sounds (see SOUND SYMBOLISM). This can be seen in the coining of brandnames, which are carefully designed to evoke particular associations for potential consumers by exploiting the connotations of the words they echo, as these car names illustrate: *Lexus, Acura, Lumina, Achieva*.

Rounded   See VOWEL.

RP   See RECEIVED PRONUNCIATION.

Rune   A character in a group of related alphabets which were used to write Germanic languages from about the third century AD, mainly in Scandinavia, Iceland and the British Isles. These alphabets were known as the *futhark/futhorc*, after the sounds symbolized by their first six letters. The origin of the runes is obscure, though their resemblance to letters in the Etruscan and Latin alphabets point to southern Europe as a probable source. The Anglo-Saxons employed a version of the alphabet consisting of between thirty-one and thirty-three symbols, which they developed to cope with the sound system of their language. Most runic inscriptions survive on stone, wood, metal and bone artifacts. Perhaps the most famous example is the extract from the poem 'The Dream of the Rood', carved into a stone cross housed in Ruthwell Church near Dumfries (Scotland).

Runes were eventually superceded by the Latin alphabet introduced by the Christian missionaries.

S

Sapir–Whorf hypothesis The label often used as a shorthand way of referring to a body of work by the American linguists Edward Sapir (1884–1936) and Benjamin Lee Whorf (1897–1941), which explored the relationships between language, reality, thought and culture. The hypothesis is made up of two principles: *linguistic determinism* (thought is dependent upon language) and *linguistic relativism* (speakers of different languages perceive and understand the world in different ways). The 'strong' versions of linguistic determinism and relativity have few adherents – if it were true that language entirely determined thought, then translation between different languages would not be possible. Furthermore, there is no empirical evidence which supports the claim that *all* thought is a linguistic phenomenon. However, the idea that language has no effect at all on cognition is equally false. For example, experiments have shown that the ability of people to discriminate between different colours may be influenced by the way in which their language divides up the colour spectrum. Colours are more easily distinguishable as separate if they are labelled as such (e.g. *green* and *blue*) in the test subject's language.

Saxons An ethnic label for a group of **Germanic** people whose original homeland is thought to be in northern Germany near the mouths of the Elbe and Weser rivers. About 1500 years ago, migrants from this region began settling in Britain, mainly in what became Wessex (home of the West Saxons), Sussex (South Saxons), Essex (East Saxons) and Middlesex (Middle Saxons). See ANGLES, ANGLO-SAXON, JUTES.

Schwa A term sometimes used for the most common **vowel** sound in English, the mid-central unrounded vowel represented in the **International Phonetic Alphabet** by /ə/. In most accents of English, it usually occurs in unstressed syllables, as in the following words: /əˈdrɪft/ (*adrift*), /kənˈdɛm/ (*condemn*), /ˈlɛsən/ (*lesson*). In spelling, all the orthographic vowels can be used to represent /ə/: <b**a**nan**a**, rott**e**n, stat**io**n, o**u**r>.

Scots The vernacular, non-standard varieties of English spoken in Scotland. It is sometimes used in contrast to **Scottish English**, although the term Scottish English is often taken to include Scots. An overview of the history of Scots can be found in the entry on SCOTTISH ENGLISH. Linguists generally divide the current dialects of Scots into *Central Scots* (the Central Lowlands, including Edinburgh and Glasgow); *Southern Scots* (the Borders); *Northern Scots* (from Caithness to Aberdeenshire and Angus); and *Orkney and Shetland* (a variety of Scots in the Northern Isles, with a substantial Scandinavian component). Some of the characteristic phonological, grammatical and lexical features of mainland Scots are outlined below (based on Crystal 2003; McArthur 2002). For illustrative purposes, vernacular spellings have been included – although it should be pointed out that modern Scots is generally tolerant of spelling variation.

Pronunciation. 1) The retention of /uː/ in *hoose* ('house'), *oot* ('out'), *doon* ('down'), *coo* ('cow') (see GREAT VOWEL

SHIFT). 2) Final /l/ was replaced by a [u]-type vowel in late Middle English. This is reflected in the Scots spelling of words such as *foul/fu* ('full'), *baw*, ('ball') *pu* ('pull'). 3) There is no lip rounding in words such as *home* and *stone*, giving Scots *hame, stane*. 4) The velar fricative [x] is often heard in words with <-ch-> in the spelling, such as *loch, nicht* ('night'), *dochter* ('daughter'). 5) The voiceless bilabial fricative /ʌ/ is widespread, allowing a contrast between *witch/which* and *Wales/whales*.

Grammar. 1) Irregular plural nouns: *eye/een* ('eye/eyes'); *shuin* ('shoe/shoes'); *cauf/caur* ('calf/calves'); *coo/kye* ('cow/cows'). 2) Some pronouns are distinctive: *thae* ('those') and *thir* ('these'); *mines* ('mine'); *they* ('these'). 3) Distinctive verb forms include *gae/gaed/gan(e)* ('go, went, gone'); *gie/gied/gien* ('give, gave, given'); *griet, grat, grutten* ('weep, wept, wept'). 4) The regular past forms of the verb are *-it, -t*, or *-(e)d* depending on the preceding consonant or vowel: *hurt/hurtit* ('hurt, hurt'); *dee/deed* ('die, died'). 5) Negation is either by the adverb *no*, as in *Ah'm no comin* ('I'm not coming'); or with *-na/nae* (equivalent to Standard English *-n't*), as in *canna* ('cannot') and *didnae* ('did not'). 6) Double modal verbs are often heard, as in *He'll no can come the day* ('He won't be able to come today') and *Ah micht could dae it the morn* ('I might be able to do it tomorrow'). 7) The definite article is often used distinctively, as in *the day* ('today') and *the now* ('just now'). 8) Verbs of motion are sometimes dropped before an adverb or adverbial of motion: *Ah'm awa tae ma bed* ('I'm off to my bed').

Many words with Scots origins have entered the general vocabulary of English, often via Gaelic, such as *bog, cairn, clan*. Vocabulary items which are largely restricted to Scots include *airt* ('direction'), *ay* ('always'), *dominie* ('teacher'), *dreich* ('dreary'), *fash* ('bother'), *swither* ('hesitate'), *birl* ('whirl'), *donnert* ('dazed, stupid'), *couthey* ('homely, homey'), *braw* ('fine, excellent').

Scottish English   The English language as spoken in Scotland, a country making up the northern two-thirds of the island of **Britain**. Scotland consists of a mainland divided into three regions (the Highlands, the Lowlands and the Southern Uplands), and three island regions (the Hebrides, the Orkneys and the Shetlands). Until the sixth century, much of the territory now known as Scotland was inhabited by Celtic people belonging to three main groups. The Picts lived in the area north of the Firths of Forth and Clyde. The Britons lived in what is now known as Strathclyde and the Borders. Both people spoke languages belonging to the Brythonic Celtic group (see CELTIC LANGUAGES). In the fifth century, Celtic people from Ireland began settling in the Western Isles and along the west coast. These were the Goidelic Celtic-speaking people whom the Romans called the 'Scotti' (hence 'Scotland'). Their language is the ancestor of modern Scottish Gaelic. The English language was introduced in the sixth century, by **Angles** spreading northwards from **Northumbria** into the south. In the late eighth century, **Viking**s (mainly from Norway) began raiding and then settling in parts of the country.

Until the eleventh century, most people in Scotland spoke a form of Celtic, with pockets of English speakers in the south-east and **Norse** in the far north. The number of English speakers increased in the eleventh century as displaced English noblemen fled north after the **Norman** Conquest. They were welcomed by Malcolm III (reigned 1058–93), who spoke English and was married to Margaret, a dispossessed member of the Saxon royal house who had herself sought refuge in Scotland after the Conquest. Malcolm, and later his sons and grandsons, reformed the Scottish monarchy in ways which increased the **prestige** of the English language. A system of trading settlements known as 'burghs' were established, based on Anglo-Norman models, with English as a *lingua franca*. English also became the language of the law courts, guilds and other institutions (although French had been taken up amongst the court and aristocracy, as it was elsewhere in Western Europe). The influence of English increased further when the Celtic royal line died out in the thirteenth century, to be replaced by new royal lines from English-speaking families from the Lowlands (e.g. Balliols, Bruces and Stewarts). By the end of the thirteenth century, the English of Scotland and the English of England had diverged markedly. One reason for this divergence was the Three Hundred Years' War – a period of conflict between Scotland and England which followed Edward I's invasion in 1296. In these circumstances, there was little motivation for speakers of Scottish English and English English to accommodate to each other's speech patterns, and every motivation to diverge (Crystal 2004: 204). By the late fifteenth century, English in Scotland was being referred to as 'Scottis', or **Scots** (previously it had been known as 'Inglis'). The change acknowledges the growing distinctiveness of English north of the border, and also reflects a shift in Scottish national self-awareness: until this point Scottishness had been associated with the Gaelic languages. From the end of the fourteenth century to the beginning of the seventeenth, Scots flourished as a medium of literary expression in works by writers

such as Robert Henryson, William Dunbar and Gavin Douglas. It was also used extensively in sermons, diaries, letters, pamphlets, contracts and other public and private forms of writing (Fennell 2001: 193). However, Scots did not become a separate standard language. By the mid-sixteenth century, Scots had begun to undergo a process of 'Anglicization', in which 'southern English word forms and spellings progressively invaded written and later spoken Scots' (Aitken 1992: 894). One of the main reasons for this was the decline in Scottish political autonomy in the sixteenth century, culminating in the Union of the Crowns in 1603, when James VI of Scotland became James I of England, and moved his entire court to London. In 1707, the parliaments of Scotland and England were united. As a consequence of political union, the Scottish upper classes often adopted southern English patterns of speech, regarding these as more prestigious than Scottish patterns. By the start of the eighteenth century, there is little evidence of a distinctive variety of Scots in published works. Nevertheless, Scots did not die out, and is still widely used, mainly as a spoken vernacular (see SCOTS). The eighteenth century also saw the development of what is sometimes referred to as Scottish Standard English (SSE), which is basically Standard English spoken with a Scottish accent.

In Scotland today, English exists on a continuum with broad Scots at one end and SSE at the other. Scots is associated mainly with working-class people, while SSE is generally used by educated middle-class speakers (Stuart-Smith 2004). The following overview of typical phonological, grammatical and lexical features of current Scottish English (based on Trudgill and Hannah 2002; McArthur 2002) focuses on Scottish Standard

English. For information on other varieties of Scottish English, see SCOTS and GAELIC ENGLISH.

The phonology of SSE is characterized by a radically different vowel system from other varieties of English. As the following table shows, there are fewer vowels in this system than in any other 'inner circle' variety of English. There are five main reasons for this. 1) Scottish English is **rhotic**. This means that vowels such as RP /ɪə/ and /ɜː/ which arose in RP after the loss of **post-vocalic /r/**, do not occur. Words like *bee* and *beer* have the same vowel, but are distinguished by the presence or absence of /r/. 2) Length is not generally a distinctive feature of Scottish vowels. This means that word pairs such as *cot/caught*, *pull/pool* and *Pam/palm* are **homophones**, pronounced

Scottish English vowels (based on Trudgill and Hannah 2002: 92)

/i/	*bee, peer*
/e/	*bay, plate, weight, pair*
/ɛ/	*bed, merry, fern*
/ɪ/	*bid, bird, wanted*
/ʌ/	*putt, hurry, fur, sofa*
/a/	*bad, marry, bard, path, father, calm*
/u/	*put, boot, poor*
/o/	*boat*
/ɔ/	*pot, long, cough, fork, paw*
/ai/	*buy*
/au/	*bout*
/ɔi/	*boy*

/kɔt/, /pul/ and /pam/. 3) Scottish English vowels are **monophthongs**, although for some middle-class speakers /e/ and /o/ may be **diphthongs** similar to those found in RP (/ei/ and /ou/). 4) /ɪ/ tends to be central [ə]. 5) All vowels are approximately the same length. However, there is a complication known as the *Scottish Vowel Length Rule*. Vowels occurring word-finally, and before /v/, /ð/, /z/ and /r/ are longer than they are elsewhere. For example, the /i/ in *breathe* is longer than the /i/ in *breed* and the /e/ in *pave* is longer than the /e/ in *pale*.

The main features of Scottish English consonants are as follow. 1) The distinction between /w/ and /ʍ/ is preserved, so that *witch* is pronounced /wɪtʃ/ and *which* is pronounced /ʍɪtʃ/ ('hwich'). 2) /r/ is usually a **flap** [ɾ], as in *fern* [fɛɾn]. 3) /t/ is frequently realized as a **glottal stop** [ʔ], in medial or final position. 4) /l/ is often 'dark' in all positions (see ALLOPHONE). 5) The velar fricative /x/ occurs in a number of specifically Scottish English words such as *loch* [lɔx] 'lake' and *dreich* [drix] 'dull'. In **Scots** /x/ occurs in many other words, such as *nicht* 'night'.

The grammar of current Scottish Standard English is, of course, almost identical to Standard English in general. Any differences which occur are usually in informal speech. Some of the most well known include the following. 1) The absence of *do* in constructions where *have* is the main verb: *Had you a good time?* (compare 'Did you have a good time?'). 2) *Will* has replaced *shall* in most contexts: *Will I put out the light?* (compare 'Shall I put out the light'). 3) *Need* can occur with the past participle form of a verb as its object, whereas in other varieties *need* occurs with the present participle, or passive infinitive: *My hair needs washed* (compare 'My hair needs washing' and 'My hair needs to be washed'). 4) Some stative verbs can occur in the progressive aspect: *Rest is all he's needing; I'm wanting one in the kitchen.* 5) *Yet* can occur with non-perfective forms of the verb (as it can in **American English**): *Did you buy one yet?* (compare 'Have you bought one yet?'). 6) There is a preference for *not* instead of the **contraction** *n't*. In the following paired examples, a speaker of Scottish English would be likely to prefer the first: *He'll not come/ He won't come; Is he not coming?/ Isn't he coming?* 7) *Amn't I?* is preferred to *Aren't I?*

The lexis of Scottish Standard English overlaps with the lexis of Standard English generally. However, there are many words which sometimes occur in the speech and writing of speakers of SSE which are characteristically Scottish. The following list gives a flavour of these items: *bonnie, braw, cairn, ceilidh, dreich, glaikit, gloaming, kilt, kirk, och, wee.* The source of these words is mainly **Scots**, with some input from Scottish Gaelic, such as *cairn, ceilidh.* Some words which are used generally in English have a special meaning in Scotland: *stay* ('reside, live'), *sort* ('mend'), *through* ('across').

Scottish Gaelic   See CELTIC LANGUAGES.

Scouse   A colloquial term for an inhabitant of the city of Liverpool in Merseyside, north-west England. By extension, the term has come to be used for the dialect of the area. See FOLK-LINGUISTICS, NORTHERN ENGLAND.

Second language (L2)   A language learned by someone after they have acquired their first language or languages, in order to fulfil a particular communicative need. Second languages are often accorded official status by governments, and are used widely in public contexts

such as education, the media and administration. They are also an everyday medium of communication for some people around the world (e.g English in India). See ENGLISH AS A SECOND LANGUAGE (ESL).

Second person   See PERSON.

Semantic change   Meaning change. See AMELIORATION, BROADENING OF MEANING, NARROWING OF MEANING, PEJORATION, SUBREPTION.

Semantic field   A particular area of meaning and the subset of the lexicon (the set of words and expressions) associated with it. Examples include 'vehicles' (*truck, car, tyre* and so on) 'buildings' (*school, factory, house* and so on), 'emotions' (*anger, sorrow, fear* and so on), 'plants' (*cabbage, rose, tree* and so on), 'colours' (*red, blue, green* and so on). Although it is not possible to devise a complete list of semantic fields for any language, the concept is a useful one because it can provide an insight into what a linguistic community regards as socially and culturally important: a proliferation of terms within a particular field would suggest that the domain is of particular significance (see OVERLEXICALIZATION AND UNDERLEXICALIZATION). There is also evidence to suggest that semantic fields dó have some psychological reality (people learning foreign languages, for example, often retain more vocabulary when words are presented to them in thematically arranged groups); and they are certainly useful in the organization of encyclopedias and other reference works.

Semantic prosody   A term associated with **corpus linguistics** which describes the tendency for certain words to be related to a particular area of evaluative or attitudinal meaning, even when the meaning of the word itself appears to be evaluatively neutral. For example, corpus studies have revealed that the verb *cause* is used much more frequently in relation to unpleasant events than pleasant ones, as these corpus examples illustrate: *Atmospheric pressure may **cause damage** to some instruments*; *He intended to **cause** grievous bodily **harm**; Membranes may develop in the throat, **causing death** by asphyxiation.* Other words with attested 'negative' semantic prosodies include *impending* ('doom', 'disaster', 'danger'); *potentially* ('dangerous', 'disastrous', 'harmful'). The British Prime Minister Tony Blair revealed a lack of appreciation of semantic prosody in the run up to the 2005 General Election when he promised an '*unremittingly* New Labour third term'. A corpus search reveals that when 'unremittingly' is used as a modifier in this way, the adjective it modifies is almost always negative, sometimes highly so, as this list indicates: *hostile, pessimistic, critical, scabrous, tedious, gloomy, vile, evil, critical, bad*. 'Positive' semantic prosodies also exist, but they seem to be rarer. Examples include *provide* ('opportunity', 'assistance', 'support') and *derive* ('benefit', 'pleasure', 'satisfaction'). See Stubbs (2001) for further examples.

Semantics The study and analysis of meaning in language. See LEXICAL SEMANTICS, SEMANTIC CHANGE, SEMANTIC FIELD, SEMANTIC RELATIONS.

Semantic relations The various ways in which words and their meanings relate to each other. For example, this relationship can be one of inclusion (a *haddock* is a kind of *fish*); sameness (*pistol* has a similar meaning to *handgun*); and opposition (*hot* is the opposite of *cold*). Semantic relations are also called 'sense relations' and 'meaning relations'. See ANTONYMY, HOMONYMY, HYPONYMY, LEXICAL COHESION, MERONYMY, POLYSEMY, SYNONYMY. Compare REFERENCE.

Semantic role The clause elements of **subject**, **direct** and **indirect object**, **subject complement** and **object complement** can be categorized according to their semantic role in relation to the **verb element**. For example: *Peter* (experiencer) *died*; *The cat* (agent) *chased the dog* (patient). Semantic roles are also known as *theta roles* or *thematic roles*. The main semantic roles are **agent**, **beneficiary**, **causer**, **experiencer**, **instrument**, **locative**, **patient**.

Semicolon The **punctuation** mark <;>, which was first used in the fifteenth century to mark a pause midway in length between a comma (shorter) and a colon (longer). In present-day English writing, the semicolon has two main uses. 1) It can link two independent clauses that are not joined by a coordinating conjunction: *A good plan, she thought; it could really work.* 2) It can also be used to separate items in a list, particularly when the listed items are quite lengthy: *Historical Geography; Geography of Russia and its relations with the successor states of the former USSR; Southern Africa; Biogeography; Hydrology; Quaternary Environments.*

Semi-modal verb See MULTI-WORD VERB.

Semiotics The study of **sign**s in communication. What differentiates semiotics from linguistics more generally is that semiotics looks not only at language, but also at *anything* which can function as a sign. The remit of a semiotician, then, is extremely broad, ranging from traffic signals to architecture, hair styles to dancing.

Sentence A unit of language consisting of one or more **clauses**. Sentences can be classified using **formal** or **functional** criteria (the following comments refer to **major sentences**; see also the entry on MINOR SENTENCES).

Formally, sentences can be simple or multiple. 1) Simple sentences consist of a single finite clause (i.e., a clause containing a **finite verb** form): *I **lost** my wallet*; *Into his small cup he **ladled** a measure of fresh goat's milk from a jug on the window-ledge*. 2) Multiple sentences contain more than one clause. There are two types. Multiple **compound sentences** consist of two or more simple sentences linked by the **coordinating conjunctions** *and*, *or* or *but*: *Betty bought a beginner's quilling set **and** set out to make a card*; *It was exceptionally arduous this year, **but** we did survive*. Multiple **complex sentences** consist of two or more clauses, where at least one of the clauses is **subordinate**, which means that it cannot stand alone as a complete sentence (subordinate clauses in bold): *They do it **because their fathers did**;• **After she left me**, I found out the truth*.• In these examples, the subordinate clause is introduced by a **subordinating conjunction**: *after, although, as, because, before, if*. But not all subordinate clauses are connected to the **main clause** like this. For example, non-finite subordinate clauses have no overt link: *She hated **living in England**.*

Functionally, simple sentences (i.e. sentences consisting of a single clause) can be **declarative** (*Sunderland have lost their last five league matches*), **interrogative** (*How long have you lived here?*), **imperative** (*Put the gun down*) or **exclamation**s (*What a goal!*).

In writing, sentences are generally bounded by punctuation such as <.>, <?> and <!>, which makes them easy to identify. In speech, it is often much more difficult to decide whether a stretch of language is a sentence, because the grammar of speech is influenced by various real-time production constraints, which result in apparently 'incomplete' structures, and what appear to be 'unusual' clause linkages (when seen from the perspective of writing). See SPEECH AND WRITING.

Shibboleth [Hebrew: Stream] According to the Old Testament Book of Judges, the pronunciation of this word was used as a test of identity in a conflict between two Jewish tribes, the Gileadites and Ephraimites. Gileadite troops, unsure of the identity of soldiers attempting to cross the River Jordan, forced them to say the word 'shibboleth'. If they could only manage 'sibboleth' they were summarily executed as enemy Ephraimites. In contemporary usage, a *shibboleth* is a word, phrase, grammatical structure or pronunciation which marks out its user as having a particular social or regional background.

Short passive See AGENTLESS PASSIVE.

Sibilance The effect produced by the repetition of the fricative consonants /s/ and /ʃ/ and /z/: *His soul stretched tight across the skies* (T.S. Eliot 1917).

Sign Anything which conveys meaning by being interpreted as standing for or referring to something else. Signs are not just linguistic phenomenon; pictures, gestures, sounds, scents and textures can all be signs. For example, signs of fire include a photograph of a fire, the smell (as well as the sight) of smoke, and the sound of an alarm bell. These examples exemplify the three kinds of sign proposed by the American philosopher Charles Sanders Peirce (1839–1914). A photograph of a fire is an **icon**: the sign resembles in some way the thing it represents (a photograph of a fire looks like a fire). Smoke for fire is an *index*, because there is a direct physical relationship between smoke and the phenomenon to which it refers (smoke points to the thing it represents). A fire alarm is a **symbol**: here the relationship between *signifier* (the sign) and *signified* (the object or concept symbolized by the signifier) is arbitrary – the connection between a loud ringing bell and a fire only exists because as members of a culture we all agree that, in certain circumstances, that is what a loud ringing bell conventionally refers to. In language, where signs are words, most words are symbols. The only reason the sequence of sounds making up the word 'fire' stands for the real-world phenomenon of flames, smoke heat and so on is because as speakers of English we 'agree' that that is what this sequence means. Only a small number of words have an iconic relationship with their referents (see ICON, ICONICITY).

Signifier and signified   See SIGN.

Sign language   A language of comparable complexity to spoken language consisting of a system of symbols made up of hand gestures and other forms of visual signalling, and a set of rules (a *grammar*) for combining these symbols to make meaningful utterances. Sign languages develop as a means of communication amongst deaf people. Different communities of deaf people use different sign languages. For example, American Sign Language (ASL) and British Sign Language (BSL) are mutually unintelligible.

Simile   (Latin: 'like') A type of **metaphor** in which an *explicit* comparison is made between one object, entity or concept and another, often (but not always) using 'like' or 'as': *My mind's like a sieve;*• *I feel like a dry riverbed;*± *Whitney*

Houston is as cool as a cucumber.± See FIGURE OF SPEECH.

Simple sentence   See SENTENCE.

Singapore Colloquial English ('Singlish')   See SINGAPORE ENGLISH.

Singapore English   A variety of English spoken in Singapore, an island state at the tip of the Malay peninsula in Southeast Asia. In 1819, Sir Stamford Raffles, keen to establish a strategic trading post in the region, claimed the island for the East India Company. Singapore was a British colony between 1867 and 1963, and was briefly part of the Federation of Malaya until gaining independence in 1965. During the period of British rule, the labour force was swelled by immigration, mainly from India, Ceylon and southern China. The ethnic make-up of Singapore, as recorded in the 2000 census, is 76.8 per cent Chinese, 13.9 per cent Malay, 7.9 per cent Indian and 1.4 per cent other.

The English language is part of a complex ethnic and linguistic mix. The four official languages are Malay, Mandarin, Tamil and English, and most inhabitants are multilingual from infancy. English is the only language which is not directly affiliated with a particular ethnic group, and is 'intended by the government to be a "neutral" language, serving as the lingua franca for international and inter-ethnic communication' (Wee 2004a: 1019). Since 1987, all children have been educated through the medium of English, and the language is commonly spoken in the home.

The situation of English in Singapore is one of **diglossia**. The H (or 'high') variety is a localized Standard English; the L (or 'low') variety is Singapore Colloquial English (a **contact variety** commonly known as *Singlish*). The H variety confers prestige and is associated with the public domain, while the L variety is a badge of Singaporean cultural identity. The following overview of Singapore Colloquial English is based on Gupta (Language Varieties website) and Wee (2004a, 2004b).

Some distinctive pronunciation features include **TH-fronting** and **TH-stopping**. The initial consonants in words like *this* and *these* tend to be [t] and [d], and the final consonants in words like *bathe* and *with* are sometimes realized as [v] and [f]; post-vocalic /r/ in words like *car* and *farm* is absent; consonant clusters are reduced at the end of syllables, resulting in pronunciations such as [mis] for *mist* and [mɛn] for *meant*; plosives in final position are often unreleased, causing the glottalization of the preceding vowel in words such as *make, lip, fat*; word-final fricatives are voiceless, making **homophone**s of the following word pairs: *etch/edge, rice/rise, leaf/leave, bus/buzz*. Singapore Colloquial English has fourteen vowel phonemes (nine monophthongs and five diphthongs), which means that some of the distinctions made in other accents of English (e.g. RP) do not exist. For example, long and short vowels are not distinguished, making homophones of the following word sets and pairs: *marry/merry/Mary* [ɛ]; *pull/pool* [u]; *knot/nought* [ɔ]; *come/calm* [ʌ]; *sit/seat* [i]. Prosodic features include a syllable-timed **rhythm**, which gives a somewhat 'staccato' feel to the accent, and an equal **stress** placement in words which in other varieties of English often receive primary and secondary stress.

The following examples from ICE illustrate some of the characteristic features of morphology and syntax associated with the **verb phrase**. These include the absence of marking for **tense**

and **number** on the verb (*Sure she like me lah*); the use of *already* to convey **aspect**ual information (*Your niece came back already* 'Your niece has come back'); use of the invariant **tag** *is it?* (*You want to kill me is it?*); the absence of copula *be* (*She very fun-loving*); the use of *got* as a possessive and existential marker (*They got CD player and all*; *Look, there got shoes and everything down there*). As far as the **noun phrase** is concerned, articles are often omitted (*He's very pally one you know*); there is a tendency for nouns which in other varieties are uncountable (e.g. *equipment, staff, furniture, luggage*) to be to treated as **count noun**s (*She won't have those like the angle* **equipments** *attached*). At the level of the **clause**, subject and/or object pronouns are often omitted (*Must say it loud*), and *wh-***question**s often have the following pattern (examples from Wee 2004b): *You buy what?* ('What did you buy'); *This bus go where?* ('Where's this bus going?'); *You go home for what?* ('Why are you going home?').

Singapore Colloquial English also uses a wide range of particles (borrowed from Chinese) which communicate a speaker's attitude to the content of his or her utterance. The three most common are *ah* (a question marker) *lah* (which marks a strong assertion) and *lor* (which conveys obviousness and resignation): *So you don't want to go ah?*;± *Very ugly lah*;± *Doesn't matter lor*± (see Gupta 1992).

Singular   See NUMBER.

Slang   A term which is widely used to identify a sub-set of the vocabulary of a language. This sub-set consists of new words (or old words with novel meanings) at the informal end of the **formality** continuum, which are used by certain closely knit social groups as markers of solidarity. While it is true to say that all slang is informal lexis, it should be stressed that not all informal lexis is slang.

All social groups develop their own slang: students, surfers, lawyers, criminals, drug addicts, city traders and so on. However, it is particularly associated with younger speakers (e.g. teenagers and university students), and those who are, perhaps, outside of the 'mainstream'. Slang is used both to *include* and to *exclude*: if you know the slang, you are part of the group (or you aspire to be); if you don't know it, then you're not. Slang, then, is part of the lexical component of a **sociolect**.

Although some lexical items with slang origins have entered the general vocabulary of colloquial English (e.g. *dough* for 'money', *flunk* for 'fail'), most slang is short-lived. This is because slang is valued when it is new and current (rather like fashion). And it is particularly appreciated when the processes of its formation display wit, humour and creativity. This is why so many slang terms are a product of semantic, etymological and phonological playfulness, as these examples of current British student terms for being drunk illustrate: *bladdered*, *gattered*, *mashed*, *hamstered*. See ANTI-LANGUAGE, ARGOT, COLLOQUIAL, RHYMING SLANG.

Social class An important **social variable** used in **sociolinguistics**. Prestige, power, wealth and education are distributed unevenly in a society. Social classes are made up of people who share similar social and economic status. In the West, status is particularly associated with occupation, so many models of social class rank people according to the jobs they do. For example, in the UK the Office of National Statistics has seven socio-economic classes: 1. Higher managerial and professional occupations. 2. Lower managerial and professional occupations. 3. Intermediate occupations. 4. Small employers and own account workers. 5. Lower supervisory and technical occupations. 6. Semi-routine occupations. 7. Routine occupations. 8. Long-term unemployed (including those who have never worked). The hierarchical arrangement of social classes or status groups is sometimes known as 'social stratification'. **Linguistic variables** sometimes correlate with social stratification. The earliest work exploring this relationship was Labov's *The Social Stratification of English in New York City* (1966). Among its findings is clear evidence that the presence or absence of **post-vocalic /r/** in the speech of New Yorkers is related to social class. See LABOVIAN SOCIOLINGUISTICS, SOCIOLECT.

Social dialect See SOCIOLECT.

Social network An anthropological concept which has been applied in **sociolinguistics** to study dialect maintenance and change (see in particular Milroy 1980). A social network is the pattern of social *relationships* between people in a community. Such networks are assessed according to two main dimensions: 'density' and 'plexity'. Density concerns the extent of interaction amongst members of the community. In a high-density network, everyone is linked to everyone else, and knows each other. In a low-density network, this is not the case. Plexity concerns the extent to which the same individuals interact with each other in different contexts (e.g. in the local neighbourhood, at work, taking part in leisure activities). A very close-knit community will be both high-density and multiplex; a less close-knit community will be low-density and 'uniplex', where individuals interact with each other in different contexts (e.g. at work *or* in the neighbourhood, but not both). Sociolinguists have discovered that 'network strength' can influence the extent to which non-standard forms of speech are maintained. High-density, multiplex communities are much more likely to retain vernacular forms than low-density uniplex ones.

Social stratification See SOCIAL CLASS.

Social variable Social categories such as **age**, **ethnicity**, **gender** and **social class**. Many sociolinguistic studies attempt to correlate social variables with **linguistic variable**s.

Sociolect The dialect of a particular social group defined according to social class, rather than geographical origin (for this reason it is also known as a 'social dialect'). The term is sometimes used more broadly to refer to the dialect of any group, not just groups defined in socio-economic terms: *The sociolect of repentant criminals;*† *A sociolect of women and eunuchs in Mesopotamia.*† See AGE, ETHNOLECT, GENDERLECT.

Sociolinguistics The study of the relationship between language and its social, political and cultural contexts. Sociolinguists combines insights from a range of disciplines including linguistics, sociology and anthropology, to explore topics such as language variation and change, and the way speakers use language to convey social meaning. See ACCENT, ACCOMMODATION, ACROLECT, AGE, ANTILANGUAGE, APPROPRIATENESS, BIDIALECTALISM, BILINGUALISM, CHANGE FROM ABOVE, CHANGE FROM BELOW, CODE-SWITCHING, CONTACT VARIETY, COVERT PRESTIGE, CREOLE CONTINUUM, CROSSING, DIALECT, DIALECT LEVELLING, DIALECTOLOGY, ETHNICITY, ETHNOLECT, FOLKLINGUISTICS, GENDERLECT, HYPER-CORRECTION, IDIOLECT, KOINÉ, LABOVIAN SOCIOLINGUISTICS, LANGUAGE CHANGE, LANGUAGE CONTACT, LANGUAGE SHIFT, LECT, LINGUISTIC INSECURITY, LINGUISTIC MARKETPLACE, LINGUISTIC VARIABLE, MESOLECT, MONOLINGUALISM, MULTI-LINGUALISM, OVERT PRESTIGE, PERCEPTUAL DIALECTOLOGY, POLYGLOSSIA, PRESTIGE, SOCIAL CLASS, SOCIAL NETWORK, SOCIAL STRATIFICATION, SOCIAL VARIABLE, SOCIOLECT, SOLIDARITY, STIGMATIZATION, STYLE SHIFTING, SUBSTRATE EFFECT.

Soft palate A flap of muscular tissue located behind the **hard palate** towards the back of the mouth. The soft palate (which is also known as the *velum*) can be lowered to allow the **airstream** to flow into the **nasal cavity**. This is necessary for the production of **nasal** sounds, such as /m/ and /n/. When it is raised, the air flows only into the **oral cavity**, producing oral sounds.

Solidarity Human beings are in a relationship of solidarity when their aims and interests coincide. Solidarity can influence language in a number of different ways. Speakers often alter their speech so it sounds more like that of people they wish to show solidarity with, and less like those with different aims and interests (see ACCOMMODATION and CROSSING). Some stylistic choices are also associated with solidarity. For example, in many languages, speakers can choose between different forms meaning 'you' (the so-called 'T' and 'V' **second person** pronouns). 'T' pronouns (such as *tu* in French) are typically used by speakers to signal intimacy and social solidarity towards the person being addressed; 'V' pronouns often signal social distance or respect.

The term is also used in the study of language attitudes, in particular attitudes towards **accents**. Researchers have shown that people tend to rate speakers with regional accents of English quite highly on the 'solidarity' dimension (friendliness, honesty, integrity), while speakers with less regionally marked accents (such as RP in England) are generally accorded higher status, intelligence and competence. The desire to show solidarity is a factor behind the **covert prestige** associated with non-standard varieties of English.

Sound change Over time, the sounds of a language change. Sounds can be lost (see ELISION, APOCOPE, SYNCOPE, APHESIS); modified (see ASSIMILATION, METATHESIS) or new sounds can be added (see EPENTHESIS). Sound change which alters the phonemic system of a language or variety is known as *phonemic change*. The most well-known example of this is the **Great Vowel Shift**. Other examples of phonemic change in English include the 'split' of the Old English fricative phonemes. In Old English, /f/, /θ/ and /s/ were voiced to [v], [ð] and [z] when they occurred between voiced sounds: in other words, [f] and [v], [θ] and [ð], [s] and [z] were **allophone**s of the same phoneme. In the **Middle English** period, they split into separate phonemes: /v/ and /f/, /θ/ and /ð/, /s/ and /z/. This fact helps to explain some 'anomalies' in **English spelling**, such as <busy>, <weasel>. See also NORTHERN CITIES VOWEL SHIFT.

Sound symbolism Most of the time, the relationship between the form of a word and its **referent** is arbitrary. For example, the sequence of sounds making up the word *dog* in English bears no phonetic resemblance to a four-legged domestic pet (nor does the written form of the word visually resemble the creature). However, there is evidence to suggest that some degree of sound symbolism – a phenomenon which can be described as a non-arbitrary relationship between sound and meaning – is present in many human languages. There are two main types of sound symbolism: *imitative* and *phonaesthetic*. 1) Imitative sound symbolism (or **onomatopoeia**) involves the sound of an utterance somehow mimicking its referent, as in *splash, moo, howl* and so on. 2) Phonaesthetic sound symbolism does not involve imitation. It is concerned with the way in which certain sounds (in English, particularly **consonant cluster**s) seem to become associated with certain meanings. For example, words containing the cluster /sl/ are often associated with wetness and slipperiness (*slip, slippery, slick, slide, slither, sloppy, slimy, slick, slather* and so on); words containing /gl/ are often associated with light and vision (*glitter, glimmer, glint, glow, glitzy, glamour, gleam* and so on). See ICONICITY.

South African English A general term for the English spoken in South Africa. The first permanent European settlements were established at the Cape of Good Hope by the Dutch in 1652. The British seized the Cape in 1795, adding English speakers to a complex cultural mix which included Dutch speakers and speakers of Bantu and Khoisan languages.

South African English is not a homogenous variety: at least five types of South African English have been identified which can be categorized (albeit crudely) according to the ethnicity of their speakers. Within each variety there is considerable social variation (see Gordon and Sudbury 2002). 1) *White South African English* is the variety spoken as a first language mainly by white people of British descent. 2) *Afrikaans English* is spoken as a second language, both by white people of Dutch descent and coloured people, who have Afrikaans as a first language. 3) *Cape Flats English* is spoken (mainly as a second language, but increasingly as a first language) in and around Cape Town by members of the historically Afrikaans-speaking, mixed-race coloured community (for this reason it is sometimes known as 'coloured' English). 4) *Black South African English* is spoken by black South Africans (the majority of the population). 5) *South African Indian English* is spoken by people of Indian descent. The following overview of phonology, grammar and lexis concentrates mainly on White South African English, and is based on Trudgill and Hannah (2002) and Bowerman (2004).

The most salient features of the accent involve the vowels in the KIT, DRESS TRAP and PRICE **lexical set**s. 1) The KIT vowel is realized as [i] when it occurs at the start of a word; before or after the **velar** consonants /k/, /g/ and /ŋ/; before /ʃ/, and after /h/. Elsewhere it is realized as [ə]. Thus *bit* is pronounced [bit] while *big* is pronounced [bəg]. 2) The vowel in the DRESS set is usually realized as [e]. 3) The vowel in the TRAP set is usually realized as [ɛ], so that to an outsider, the word *bad* might resemble *bed*. 4) The diphthong in the PRICE set is sometimes realized as a monophthong [ɑː], so that to an outsider, the word *shy* might resemble the word *Shah*. Other characteristic features are its non-rhoticity (see RHOTIC ACCENT), and a tendency for intervocalic /t/ to be realized as an alveolar **flap** [ɾ].

Characteristic grammatical features of White South African English include the following. 1) The omission of the object of transitive verbs in certain contexts: *Oh good, you've got ø*; *Did you bring ø?* 2) The preposition *by* is sometimes used where Standard English would have *near*, *at* or *with*: *I live by the station* ('near');

I left it by my friend's house ('at'); *He stays by his parents* ('with'). 3) Use of *is it?* as an invariant response to a statement: A: *The kittens ran away?* B: *Is it?* ('Did they?'). 4) *One* as a non-specific determiner: *My one cat is sick* ('One of my cats is sick'). There is some debate over the origins of these (and other) non-standard features. Some have been linked to the influence of Afrikaans; others were probably well-established in the English of the British settlers before they arrived in South Africa.

The lexis of White South African English has been enriched in particular by Afrikaans and the indigenous languages of southern Africa such as Zulu, Xhosa, Bantu, Sotho and Pedi. Examples from Afrikaans include *stoep* ('porch'), *dorp* ('village'), *veld* ('flat open country'), *braai* ('cooking fire'). Zulu has provided *impi* ('group of warriors'), *sangoma* ('traditional healer'), *suka* ('go away').

South-east England Dialectologists generally divide southern England into two main areas: South-east England (London, Kent, Surrey, East and West Sussex, Essex, Hertfordshire, Hampshire, Buckinghamshire, Berkshire and Bedfordshire); and **South-west England**. Dialect boundaries are notoriously difficult to demarcate. Altendorf and Watt (2004) discuss the particular problems associated with identifying dialect areas in southern England. However, it is possible to make some general statements about the phonology and grammar of the dialects of South-east England which give a flavour of the English used there. In particular, the focus here is on those features which are salient in distinguishing South-eastern varieties from other varieties spoken in England.

The following overview of phonology is based on Altendorf and Watt (2004) and Upton (2004a). 1) The vowel in words in the STRUT **lexical set** (which is usually [ʌ]) contrast with the vowel in the FOOT lexical set (usually [ʊ]). In **northern England** the vowel in both sets of words is the same, [ʊ]. 2) Words in the BATH set usually have [ɑː], in contrast with most other accents of English which have something like [a] or [æ]. 3) The diphthong in the FACE set is sometimes realized as [ʌɪ], so that words like *pay*, *lace* and *stale* sound similar to RP pronunciations of *pie*, *lice* and *style*. 4) The vowel in the GOAT set is usually a diphthong [əʊ] or [oʊ], whereas monophthongs (e.g. [oː]) are usual elsewhere in Britain and Ireland. A common vernacular pronunciation in the South-east is [ʌʊ]. 5) **TH-fronting** (where /θ/ is realized as [f] and /ð/ is realized as /v/) is quite common in the South-east, particularly in London. Vernacular orthography reproduces this phenomenon in spellings such as <fink> *think* and <bruvva> *brother*. 6) Post-vocalic /l/ is often realized as a vowel ('vocalized') in the South-east, resulting in pronunciations such as [mɪʊk] for *milk* and [ʃɛʊf] for *shelf*. 7) The accents of South-east England are generally **non-rhotic** (/r/ is not pronounced after vowels in words such as *her*, *car*, *harm*). 8) **H-dropping** and /t/ glottalization are widespread.

The grammar of the dialects of South-east England contains few features which are not also found in other varieties of English in the British Isles. However, Kortmann's analysis (2004) does reveal several features which seem to be predominantly (but not exclusively) associated with the dialects of South-east England. These are the use of *ain't* as the negated form of *be* and *have* (e.g. *He's so thick **ain't** he, really?*; *I **ain't** got no paper*); invariant non-concord **tags** (e.g. *innit*, as in *You're so cool you beat your dog, innit?*);

and *what* as a **relative pronoun** (e.g. *The one about that bloke **what** was living with her*). See also COCKNEY.

South-west England Dialectologists generally divide southern England into two main areas: South-west England (Gloucestershire, the former county of Avon, Somerset, Devon, Cornwall, Dorset, Wiltshire, parts of Hampshire and parts of Oxfordshire) and **South-east England**. In the following overview, the focus is on those features of phonology and grammar which are salient in distinguishing South-western varieties from other varieties spoken in England. Material on phonology is drawn mainly from Altendorf and Watt (2004) and Upton (2004a), while the grammar material is mainly from Wagner (2004) and Kortmann (2004).

1) The vowel in the LOT lexical set is frequently [ɑ], as it is in varieties of **American English**. 2) In rural parts of Devon and Cornwall, the vowels in the FACE and GOAT lexical sets are [eː] and [oː]. 3) The quality of the vowel in the PRICE set is often close to RP realizations of the vowel in the CHOICE set, so that a South-western pronunciation of *ties* sounds like RP *toys*, and *tile* sounds like *toil*. 4) The South-west generally has post-vocalic /r/ in words such as *car*, *bar* and *charm* (in other words, the accents are generally **rhotic**). This rhoticity (sometimes referred to as the 'West Country Burr') is a stereotypical feature of English in the South-west. 5) Some older, rural speakers voice the fricatives /f, θ, s, ʃ/ to [v, ð, z, ʒ] respectively, a feature captured in vernacular spellings such as <varmer> *farmer* and <zeez> *sees*. Again, this is a stereotype of the region, although it is now very rare.

According to Wagner (2004) the grammar of the dialects of South-west

England contains some features which are not found in other varieties of English in the British Isles. 1) The use of a subject **personal pronoun** (e.g. *I, he, she, they, we*) in instances where Standard English would use an object personal pronoun (e.g. *me, him, her, them*): *Don't talk to she about grub.* 2) The use of 'gendered' pronouns to refer to inanimate objects: *He have been a good watch.* 3) Unemphatic periphrastic-*do* as tense carrier: *The hooter did blow at the finish.*

Speech act theory A theory developed by the British philosopher of language J.L. Austin (1911–60), who was interested in the kinds of actions performed by utterances. He initially distinguished between constative utterances (which report things about the world) and performative utterances (which are used to do things), but later abandoned this distinction on the grounds that, in fact, *all* utterances are performative. Austin identified three types of actions which utterances perform. 1) A *locutionary* act is the saying of something with linguistic meaning; the act of speaking itself. 2) An *illocutionary* act is performed *in* saying something (e.g. stating, questioning, commanding, and so on). 3) A perlocutionary act is the effect produced *by* saying something. So, when someone says *Get down Rosie*, the speaking of the words themselves is the locutionary act; the act of commanding is the illocutionary act; and Rosie getting down is the perlocutionary act. Speech act theory focuses mainly on illocutionary acts, in particular the kinds of *illocutionary force* that an illocutionary act might carry. For example, the illocutionary force of *It's freezing in here* varies depending on a range of factors. In certain contexts it could be a *statement* about the temperature, in others it could be a *request* for

someone to close the window or *advice* not to come into the room. Many kinds of speech act have been identified. Searle (1975) provides the following categories: assertives (e.g. stating, suggesting, claiming, reporting); directives (e.g. ordering, commanding, requesting, advising); commissives (e.g. promising, vowing, offering); expressives (e.g. congratulating, thanking, blaming, praising); declaration (e.g. resigning, dismissing, naming, sentencing).

Speech acts can be *direct* or *indirect*. A direct speech act is one in which the surface form of the utterance matches the intended illocutionary force. For example, *Get down Rosie* is a direct speech act, since it is a **directive** employing the imperative **mood**. An indirect speech act is one where this is a 'mismatch' between surface form and intended illocutionary force. For example, *It's freezing in here*, uttered in an attempt to get someone to close a window or turn the heating on is an indirect speech act, since this is a directive using the **declarative** mood. See COMMUNICATION VERB, IMPERATIVE, PRAGMATICS.

Speech and writing The two main **modes** of human language. Traditionally, linguistics has regarded writing as purely derivative of speech. A comment by one of the most important figures in North American linguistics, Leonard Bloomfield (1887–1949) is typical of this attitude: 'Writing is not language, but merely a way of recording language by means of visible marks.' However, more recent thinking has emphasized that, although speech and writing are, of course, historically related, they 'function as independent methods of communication': writing is something more than simply speech written down (Crystal 2003: 291).

Most accounts of the differences between the two modes set up a series of contrasts, as in the table below.

Speech	Writing
phonic medium	graphic medium
time-bound	space-bound
temporary	permanent
dynamic	static
interactive	one-way
personal and social	public and informational
errors cannot be corrected	errors can be corrected
complex advanced planning not possible	complex advanced planning possible
usually involves shared physical context	physical context not shared

However, it is important to stress that such a presentation simplifies the situation in a number of ways. The characteristics presented here (and this is by no means an exhaustive list) are not polar opposites. There are many counter examples. For example, the performance of a famous political orator stored in a sound archive (permanent speech); a scribbled note on the fridge door (temporary writing); a lecture (one-way speech); internet chatroom discourse (interactive writing); a message on a greetings card (personal and social writing); a TV news bulletin (public and informational speech).

Differences between speech and writing are best thought about in terms of a scale, with its extreme points occupied by 'prototypical' forms of the two modes. The most typical form of speech is spontaneous conversation, since this is the language activity that the vast majority of human beings engage in most often. 'Typical' writing is perhaps slightly more difficult to identify, **expository prose** of the kind found in serious analytical journalism and academic writing probably fits this description best. What are the **lexicogrammatical** characteristics of these prototypical forms of speech and writing? One of the most important recent grammars of English – *The Longman Grammar of Spoken and Written English* (Biber et al. 2002) – attempts to answer this question by considering the contextual factors influencing the spoken and written modes.

	Conversation	Expository prose
1	shared context	remote context
2	low elaboration of meaning	high elaboration of meaning
3	high interactivity	low interactivity
4	high online processing constraints	low online processing constraints
5	high repetition	low repetition
6	non-standard	standard

Contextual factors influence the differences between conversation and expository prose in a number of ways. 1) Conversation is typically face-to-face interaction in a shared physical, social and cultural context. Therefore, speakers can use posture, facial expression, gesture, intonation and contrasts of loudness, tempo and rhythm to add meaning. Less obviously, shared context influences lexicogrammar. Because participants are constantly referring to themselves and each other, conversation has a relatively high frequency of **first** and **second person** pronouns compared with expository prose. Speakers also use linguistic features which rely on shared knowledge of the surroundings for their interpretation. For example, situational **ellipsis** is common in conversation, as are substitute **proforms** and deictic items (see DEIXIS). In expository prose, on the other hand, the writer is usually distant from the reader, and only has a notional audience in mind. This means that writers must usually be more explicit than conversationalists, since they cannot rely as heavily on shared context. 2) Shared knowledge of context also means that participants in a conversation do not have to elaborate on and specify meaning to the same extent as writers of expository prose. Writing, on the other hand, packages information much more densely. Therefore, conversation has a lower **lexical density** than prose, and speakers tend to avoid **noun phrase** structures with lengthy sequences of pre- and postmodification. Additionally, conversation often uses 'purposefully vague language' (Carter 2004: 31). In writing, **hedges** such as *kind of, sort of* and *like* would probably provoke criticism for their imprecision. However, in conversation precision is less important, particularly when it might hold things up, so speakers often make 'hints and rough indications, relying on shared knowledge' (*LSGSWE:* 431). Shared knowledge and socio-cultural context also means that speech tends to use more **non-standard** and **colloquial** forms than writing.

3) Conversation is interactive, and a number of its typical features reflect this, such as **adjacency pairs**, questions, **imperatives**, **stance** adverbials, **discourse markers**, **backchannel** devices, attention getters (such as *hey, yo, say*) and **vocatives**. 4) Conversation takes place 'live', in real-time; expository prose is usually produced with considerable delay between production and reception. The production and processing constraints of conversation result in various kinds of dysfluency. For example, pauses (filled and unfilled) and repetition provide the speaker with time to plan an utterance. Sometimes utterances are left incomplete; sometimes 'syntactic blends' occur, where a sentence 'finishes in a way that is grammatically inconsistent with the way it began' (*LSGSWE:* 437). Various features associated with reducing effort are also common in conversation, including **elision**, **assimilation** and **contraction**. Real-time production and processing constraints also help to account for the prevalence of **dislocation** in conversation. 'Prefaces' highlight the **theme** for the benefit of listeners, and **tags** reinforce or clarify what is being said, as in these examples: *That man, he did his job* (preface);[•] *A friend of mine, she had a leg operation* (preface);[•] *He's great, my dad* (tag).[•] 5) Repetition is also a response to production constraints. Conversation tends to be far more repetitive than expository prose. Speakers repeat themselves and each other, often to relieve real-time planning pressure, sometimes for emphasis. They also rely on prefabricated chunks of language, known as **lexical bundles** to a greater extent than writers. Production constraints also mean that **type-token ratio** is lower in speech than in writing. 6) Finally, speech contains far more **non-standard**, **vernacular** grammatical constructions than writing.

Speech presentation A general term for the ways in which speech is portrayed in writing. There are two main types of speech presentation: see separate entries on DIRECT SPEECH and INDIRECT SPEECH.

Spelling See ENGLISH SPELLING.

Spelling pronunciation A change in the pronunciation of a word so that it corresponds more closely to the way it is spelled. For example, in the **Early Modern English** period, as rates of literacy increased, spelling began to play a more influential role in speakers' pronunciation, particularly of more unusual words. Some French **loanword**s, such as *humble*, *human*, *habit*, *hectic* and *history* are pronounced with an initial /h/ in English, in accordance with spelling, even though these words are 'h-less' in French. (The process is uneven, though. *Hour*, *honour*, *honest* retain the original French pronunciation, despite the presence of <h>.)

Split infinitive The placing of a word or phrase (usually an adverb) between the particle *to* and the **infinitive** form of a verb. Such constructions attracted the censure of prescriptivist grammarians in the nineteenth century, on the grounds that you could not split an infinitive in Latin, so you should not do it in English. Today, most people neither know what a split infinitive is nor care, and produce sentences such as the following with impunity: *You will find it hard to find people to openly talk about it.* The most famous split infinitive comes from the US TV show *Star Trek*. In the original 1960s series, the voice-over accompanying the opening credits ends with *to boldly go where no man has gone before*. For the 1990s version of the show, the gender specific 'man' was excised, but the split infinitive remained: *to boldly go where no one has gone before*.

Stance A broad cover-term (often used interchangeably with 'evaluation' and 'appraisal') to describe the expression by speakers and writers of their personal feelings towards, and value judgments of the 'content' and the 'form' of the utterance (*LGSWE*: 966). For example, a comment such as *That was a great idea* can be uttered in such a way as to convey the exact opposite of what the words would appear to mean. In this instance, the speaker would be using tone of voice to convey his or her 'stance' towards the propositional content of the utterance. Non-verbal devices for marking stance include **volume**, **pitch**, voice quality, gesture, body-language, facial expression (see PARALINGUISTIC). Stance can be marked verbally by using overtly evaluative lexis (*That was a **wonderful** book*), stance **adverbial**s, stance **complement clause**s, and **modal** and **semi-modal verb**s. The following examples from CWEC have been annotated to show the structural device being used and the kind of stance being marked: *Something is **definitely** wrong with Teddie* (stance adverb expressing certainty); *I **doubt** that the guys I would date are shooting up* (verb+ complement clause expressing doubt); *They **must** have known I wasn't in hospital* (modal verb expressing certainty); ***Unfortunately**, we used up most of our reserve funds* (stance adverb expressing attitude); *I'm **delighted** to do favors for my friends* (adjective+complement clause expressing emotion); ***Honestly**, you teenagers today think you invented uncertainty* (stance adverb commenting on style of speaking). See MODALITY.

Standard English (SE) A **dialect** of English typically used by the most well-educated and influential people in

English-speaking communities around the world. Standard English is an unusual variety for a number of reasons. 1) It is purely a **social dialect**: this means that it is not confined to any geographical area. 2) This lack of a local base means that Standard English can be spoken in any **accent**. 3) It is the 'official' dialect of nearly all institutions and organizations in English-speaking contexts (e.g. government, the law, the media, education, business and so on). 4) Only a minority of English users *speak* Standard English, although it is widely understood. 5) Standard English is strongly associated with writing, particularly print.

Because of its associations with writing, the effects of Standard English can be felt particularly strongly at the level of spelling, where clear-cut rules have developed regarding 'correct' and 'incorrect' forms – and if there is any debate about how to spell a particular word, we can turn to the **dictionary** for the 'right' answer. Similarly, if we are unsure about the 'standardness' or otherwise of certain grammatical structures, we can consult a grammar book, where features which millions of English speakers use every day attract the label of 'nonstandard' or **vernacular** (*Are y'all telling me you just lost every coin flip? These are funky, **ain't** they?‡*) Notions of standardness are less secure when it comes to vocabulary. As Trudgill (1999) points out, while there is no such thing as Standard English vocabulary (in the sense of lexical items which *only* occur in Standard English), there *is* such a thing as nonstandard English vocabulary (in the sense of lexical items which occur *only* in non-standard varieties of English).

Although terms such as Standard American English, Standard Australian English and Standard British English are sometimes used, the differences between 'national' standard varieties are quite minor, consisting of some well-known vocabulary items (*tap* or *faucet*; *pavement* or *sidewalk*) and a small set of grammatical contrasts (*Have you got any money? Have you any money?*). This uniformity ensures mutual intelligibility between all speakers of Standard English, wherever they are in the world.

Indeed, the drive to establish mutual intelligibility in written texts is one of the factors behind the development of Standard English in the first place. The origins of the variety lie in fifteenth-century England. Before then, all written texts were produced in the local dialect. This must have led to problems in comprehension, a fact acknowledged by Chaucer who is concerned that 'the gret diversite in Englissh and in writing of oure tonge' means that his works might not be widely understood. A second impetus behind the development of a standard was the decline of **French** and **Latin**. As English began to be used for a wider range of purposes, its great variability began to be perceived as a shortcoming, particularly in its written form. So, by the fifteenth century the conditions were suitable for a standard to develop. It has its origins in London, a thriving political, commercial and administrative centre which was home to powerful social groups such as lawyers, physicians, court officials, civil servants, merchants and so on, whose professional lives depended on the production and distribution of various kinds of documents. In this context, consensus over aspects of usage developed. The consensus would have been secured further by the development of printing, as printers settled on usages which would give their books the widest commercial appeal.

It is important to stress that during the period when a standard was becoming established in London, the character of the London dialect was changing. The fourteenth century had seen extensive migration to the capital, particularly from the East Midlands. The dialect of this part of the country had a number of prestigious associations, because of the region's relative prosperity (it was a rich agricultural area and the centre of the wool and cloth industries), and the presence of the University of Cambridge. The East Midland dialect influenced the incipient standard to such an extent that it is often characterized as 'an upper-class dialect developed in London . . . mainly on the basis of the influential dialect of East Midlands immigrants' (Fennell 2001: 124–125). See also CHANCERY ENGLISH.

Standardization   The process by which a language becomes standardized. Haugen's (1972) model consisting of the following four stages has been influential. 1) Selection of an existing language or variety as the basis of the standard, usually that of the dominant social group. 2) **Codification**, involving the establishment of norms and the reduction of variability. 3) **Elaboration**, ensuring that the variety selected can be used for a variety of functions. 4) Implementation, whereby texts in the standard are produced and disseminated, and alternatives to the standard in official domains are discouraged. See STANDARD ENGLISH.

Stative verb   Verbs with stative meaning are used to refer to ongoing processes or states of being with no easily identifiable start or finish, such as *like*, *mean*, *contain*, *see*. In Standard English, stative verbs do not normally occur in the **progressive** or the **imperative**: **I am liking mayonnaise*; **Contain this!* Stative verbs are often contrasted with **dynamic verb**s. See ASPECT.

Stigmatization   The negative evaluation of a language, variety or linguistic form, usually because of its association with low-status social groups. Stigmatization can play an important part in **language shift** (as speakers abandon a stigmatized language or variety) and **language change** (as speakers avoid stigmatized words, pronunciations and grammatical structures).

Stress   In English speech, some **syllable**s are stressed, which means that they are phonetically more prominent than others. In general, stressed and unstressed syllables may be distinguished using the following criteria. 1) Stressed syllables have greater duration and are therefore perceived as longer than unstressed syllables. 2) Stressed syllables have a higher pitch than unstressed syllables. 3) Stressed syllables are produced with greater articulatory force than unstressed syllables, which means that they are perceived as being louder. 4) The full vowel quality is retained in stressed syllables, whereas vowels may be weak in unstressed syllables.

Typically, stressed syllables occur in monosyllabic **lexical word**s: *fish*, *head*, *box*; and in the prominent syllable of polysyllabic words: *'payslip*, *fla'mingo*, *de'lay* (when a word contains more than one syllable, one of them is always stressed). Note that the conventional way of indicating stress is by using ['] before the stressed syllable. In English, stress patterns vary from word to word. For example, the first syllable is stressed in *'domino*, the second is stressed in *fla-'mingo*, and the third is stressed in *con-ste'llation*. Contrasting stress patterns also distinguish some words which are otherwise identical: compare *'convert* (noun) and *con'vert* (verb); *'increase* (noun) and *in'crease* (verb). Unstressed syllables usually occur in **grammatical words** (in connected speech), e.g. *that* /ðət/, *to* /tə/, *of* /əv/; and in the least prominent syllable of polysyllabic words. A distinction is also made between *primary* and *secondary* stress. In longer words the most prominent syllable receives primary stress, while another syllable often receives weaker, or secondary stress. For example, in the word *polysyllable* the first syllable has primary stress, while the third has secondary stress (which is conventionally marked [ˌ], as in ˈpolyˌsyllable).

Stress is also used to express contrasts of meaning (this is sometimes known as 'sentence' or 'contrastive' stress). For example, the utterance 'Peter called Jane yesterday' can convey at least four different meanings depending on which syllable is given prominence. 1) **Peter** called Jane yesterday (not Martin, or Sam or Tom). 2) Peter **called** Jane yesterday (he didn't visit her, or email, or attach a note to a carrier pigeon). 3) Peter called **Jane** yesterday (not Lucy, or Hilda, or Sharon). 4) Peter called Jane **yesterday** (not this morning, on Tuesday, or last week).

Stress-timed   See RHYTHM.

Style   In English generally, the word *style* refers to a particular and distinctive way of doing something: *In a rage at Leeds' **style** of play*; *Mr Morton's Rottweiler **style** of management*. The implication here is that there is an element of choice involved in style: Leeds could choose to play differently if they wanted to, and Mr Morton doesn't have to run his company like a large, vicious dog. In language too, the notion of choice is central to style. Speakers and writers are continually making choices amongst the potentially available options in pronunciation, grammar and word choice, in response to various contextual factors. For example, the decision to say 'Would

you mind if I borrowed your pen?' or 'Chuck us your biro' is a style choice motivated by various contextual factors (is the person being addressed known to the speaker, a social equal or 'superior', considerably older than the speaker, and so on?). Style can vary according to medium (e.g. **speech and writing**), **context** of situation, **genre** and historical period. Compare REGISTER.

Style shifting   Variations in an individual's style of speech. These 'shifts' are triggered by **context**ual factors, such as audience, level of **formality**, the purpose of the utterance and so on. They provide a means by which speakers can associate themselves with some social groups and distance themselves from others. There are three main models which have been developed to account for style shifting: the *accommodation* model; the *audience design* model and the *speaker design* model (see Wolfram and Schilling-Estes 2006: 266–293 for an overview).

1) The **accommodation** model ascribes style shifts to the speaker's evaluation of the addressee's social identity. A positive evaluation results in 'convergence', where a speaker begins to sound more like the addressee (conversely, a negative evaluation results in 'divergence', where the speaker marks social distance by sounding less like the addressee).

2) The 'audience design' model, which is particularly associated with the New Zealand sociolinguist Allan Bell (1984, 2001), develops the accommodation model by extending the notion of audience to include 'participants' who are in fact physically absent from the immediate context of the speech event. Bell used this refinement to the accommodation model to explain a style shifting phenomenon he discovered amongst news readers working in the same radio studio in New

Zealand. When they read bulletins which were to be broadcast by a *local* station, the presenters tended to voice /t/ when it occurred between vowels, making words such as 'writer' and 'latter' sound more like 'rider' and 'ladder'. But when the same news readers, in the same studio read bulletins meant for the *national* station, **intervocalic** /t/ was voiced much less frequently. Bell concluded that the presenters were, in a sense, accommodating to the perceived speech norms of an *absent* audience (with vernacular pronunciations being associated with the less prestigious local station).

3) The 'speaker design' model focuses on the speaker's concern with projecting a desired social image, role or identity to hearers. For example, people might 'perform' exaggerated versions of their own vernacular dialects in certain contexts, or they might even adopt styles which do not 'belong' to them, as when features of **African American Vernacular English** appear in the speech of people of other ethnicities who wish to associate with certain aspects of hip-hop culture (see CROSSING).

See also CODE-SWITCHING.

Stylistics At its broadest, the study of any aspect of **style**, that is, any aspect of linguistic variation motivated by contextual factors, such as audience, purpose, mode and so on. The term is also used more specifically to refer to a method of textual interpretation which uses insights and techniques from linguistics in the study of poetry, drama and the novel. Stylistic approaches to literature involve relating literary effects to 'linguistic "triggers"', where these are felt to be relevant' (Wales 2001: 373). In the context of literary studies, stylistics is occasionally referred to as *literary linguistics* or *linguistic criticism*. See DEVIATION, FORE-GROUNDING, FORMALISM, NARRATIVE, NARRATOR, PARALLELISM, POETIC DICTION, REGISTER, SPEECH PRESENTATION.

Subject (S) One of the five **clause elements**. The most typical function of the subject is the performer of the 'action' of an activity verb (the **agent**). Agent subjects are usually animate entities: *The camel plods slowly; The policemen fingered their rifles.* However, subjects have other **semantic roles**. For example, they can be **instrument**, **experiencer**, **causer**, **patient**, identified and located subjects. 1) Instrument subjects are inanimate entities used by agents to perform an action: *Bombs damaged the Spanish embassy.* 2) Experiencer subjects are animate entities which receive a sensory impression or undergo a psychological state: *She heard Benedict swearing; They love each other.*• 3) Causer subjects are inanimate entities lacking intention or volition: *The storm cut power.* They are also animate entities acting without volition: *Tom bumped his head.* (It can often be difficult to distinguish animate causer subjects from agents. If Tom *deliberately* bashed his head against the wall, he is the agent subject; if it was an accident, he is the causer subject.) 4) Patient subjects are animate or inanimate entities to which things happen: *The door banged open*;• *Uccello died in his eighties.* 5) Identified subjects are described or characterized by the predicate, and co-occur with copular verbs: *David seems very happy.* 6) Located subjects are positioned in space: *The butcher is on the back doorstep.*

Formally, subjects are **noun phrases**. They can range in complexity from a single pronoun or noun to highly complex structures involving lengthy strings of pre- and postmodification, including clauses: *He adores your cake; The clown and the man with the big bow-tie were out* *for a drive; **The men who had not heard them arrive in the courtyard** looked up in surprise.* They normally precede the verb phrase, except in the case of **inversion**, such as questions: *Were **you** brought up religiously?* Subjects can also be clauses: ***To view this situation as 'normal'** is unacceptable.*

Subjects have a powerful influence on the rest of the clause, determining, through **concord**, the **number** of the verb phrase.

Subject complement See complement.

Subjunctive A rarely used verb form with two main uses. 1) The 'mandative' subjunctive is a special kind of **directive** which occurs in *that*-complement clauses, when the main verb makes some sort of demand (i.e. verbs such as *suggest, beg, demand, ask, insist, require* and so on). Because the mandative subjunctive consists of the base form of the verb, it is only recognizable in the third-person singular form of the present tense (unless the verb is *be*): *We **insisted** that he **spend** the days at the centre;* ● *We and the rest of the civilized world **demand** that he **release** all innocent civilians;* ● *I **requested** that he **have** psychotherapy;* ● *The government **requires** that they **be** fitted with suitable clothes.* ● 2) The 'past' subjunctive is used to express hypothetical or unreal meaning. Only the verb *be* has a past subjunctive form, which is *were* for all persons, making it recognizable only in the first and third person singular. This form occurs after the verb *wish* (*I **wish** he **were** working with me*) and conjunctions such as *if, as though* and *whether*: *If she **were** right, his life depended on this practice;* ● *Margaret watched his face **as though** he **were** a holy man;* ● *Paul wondered **whether** he **were** destined always to shiver in the black night outside.* ● The subjunctive is mainly associated with formal, written English.

Subordinate clause A **clause** (also known as a dependent clause) which is part of a larger clause, and cannot stand alone (but see MINOR SENTENCE). Subordinate clauses can be **finite** or **non-finite**. The main types of finite dependent clause are *that*- and *wh*-**complement clauses** (*I think **that she will be a reasonably useful nurse**; Now I know **why he whacked me***); **adverbial clauses** (***When the man's shift was over**, he was replaced by a shabby flute player*); **relative clauses** (*This is not the place **where I can make my career**); **comparative clauses** (*I'm as happy **as I can be***). The main types of non-finite dependent clause are *to*-**clauses** (*He's there **to play football**); **ing**-clauses (*I love **making stupid noises on this**); **ed**-clauses (*Sex need not be a big loaded word, **burdened with anxieties and fears and emotions***). See also VERBLESS CLAUSE.

Subordinating conjunction A function word which introduces **subordination**. Words which can perform this function include *after, although, as, because, before, if, how, however, like, once, since, that, till, unless, until, when, whenever, wherever, whereas, whereby, whereupon, while.* Subordinating conjunctions can also consist of multi-word units, such as *in that, so that, in order that, except that; as far as, as soon as.* Subordinating conjunctions are also known as 'subordinators'. See SUBORDINATION, SUBORDINATE CLAUSE.

Subordination The linking together of **clauses**, so that one unit is subordinate to (or 'dependent' on) another: *He believes **that Hell is a state of mind**.* The units linked in this way are of unequal grammatical status (compare COORDINATION). See HYPOTAXIS, SUBORDINATE CLAUSE.

Subreption A process of **semantic change** in which objects, entities, social roles, concepts, institutions and so on change over time, but the words for them remain the same. Take, for example, the phrase 'the *driver* of the *car* looked at the *dashboard*'. The emphasized words have their English origins at a time when all wheeled vehicles were powered by horses: the original meaning of *drive* (a meaning which it still retains) was 'to force to move before one' (which is what a 'driver' did with horses); *car* is derived from an earlier word meaning 'chariot', and *dashboard* originally referred to the wooden board located at the front of a horse-drawn carriage to prevent objects kicked up by the horses' hooves from hitting the driver.

Substrate effect   A type of linguistic **transfer** which occurs in a situation of **language shift**. Phonological, morphological and syntactic features of a group's native language are preserved in the speech of members of that group who have shifted into the new language. The substrate effect can explain certain features in many varieties of English around the world (see, for example, AFRICAN AMERICAN VERNACULAR ENGLISH, CHICANO ENGLISH, IRISH ENGLISH, WELSH ENGLISH).

Suffix   An **affix** which comes after the **morpheme(s)** to which it is attached, as in the following examples: *selection*, *realism*, *clearly*, *hats*, *clamped*. In English, suffixes can be **derivation**al or **inflection**al. Compare PREFIX.

Superlative   One of the 'degrees' of adjective and adverb comparison. It is marked by the suffix -*est* (*Britons are facing their* **bleakest** *Christmas for years; Strongly advise that you come* **soonest**) or by the adverb *most* (*He was one of her* **most enthusiastic** *supporters; Radical change was embraced* **most enthusiastically** *in Poland*). See COMPARATIVE.

Superordinate   A linguistic unit which is higher in a hierarchy than another. In syntax, for example, the term is sometimes used to refer to the **main clause** in relation to any **subordinate** clauses. In semantics, it describes the word at the top of the hierarchy in a relationship of **hyponymy**.

Suppletive form   In English, the past tense of the verb *go* is *went* and the past tense of *be* is *was/were*. These are examples of suppletion, whereby one word form is historically unrelated to other forms. In these cases, different forms of the same verb are unrelated. There are also three adjectives in English which display suppletion: *good/better/ best*; *bad/worse/worst*; *little/less/least*.

Survey of English Dialects (SED)   The first systematic survey of dialects of English in England. The project leaders, Harold Orton (University of Leeds) and Eugen Dieth (University of Zürich), believed that such a survey was necessary in order to record the traditional rural dialects of England before they vanished as a result of social and demographic change in the post-war period. Between 1950 and 1961, fieldworkers were sent out to 313 mainly rural locations across the country to conduct interviews with people who were thought likely to maintain 'traditional' features in their speech (usually older males). The wealth of information on the lexis, grammar and phonology of English dialects collected in the survey has led to a number of important publications, including *The Linguistic Atlas of England* (Orton, Sanderson and Widdowson 1978) and *The Survey of English Dialects: The Dictionary and Grammar* (Upton, Parry and Widdowson 1994). The sound recordings have been digitized and are held in the

Leeds Archive of Vernacular Culture at the University of Leeds.

Survey of English Usage   Founded in 1959 by Professor Randolph Quirk and based at University College London, the Survey was the first centre in Europe to carry out corpus-based research on English. The most well-known corpora constructed by the Survey are the 'London' component of the London–Lund Corpus (based on Quirk's original Survey of English Usage Corpus), and ICE-GB, the British component of the International Corpus of English (ICE). Important recent work includes the Diachronic Corpus of Present-day Spoken English (DCPSE). See CORPUS LINGUISTICS.

Survey of Regional English (SuRE)   An ongoing project based at the universities of Leeds and Sheffield designed to collect up-to-date and comparable data on language variation in the British Isles. Like the **Survey of English Dialects** (its predecessor), SuRE depends on fieldworkers collecting data from informants all over Britain and Ireland. But unlike the SED (which relied largely on structured interviews based on a questionnaire), SuRE is keen to capture the natural, informal speech of informants, and has pioneered new methods for achieving this. Eventually the data will be made available in an electronic database. Research has been completed or is currently in progress in Middlesborough, the Black Country, Southampton and Sunderland (see Upton and Llamas 1999).

Syllable   A phonological unit consisting of one or more phonemes. Every syllable contains a 'nucleus', which is usually a vowel. Syllables consisting of just a nucleus (as in the first syllable of the word

adrift) are allowable. The other constituents are the 'onset', which precedes the nucleus and the 'coda', which follows it. Onsets and codas are made up of either single consonants (*pan*), or **consonant clusters** (*spank*). The nucleus and coda together form the 'rhyme' (sometimes spelled 'rime'). This is an appropriate term, since in rhyming syllables, only the nucleus and coda are identical (*pot, hot, dot, cot, lot*). Syllables are sometimes categorized according to whether they are 'open' (with no final consonant, e.g. *sea*) or 'closed' (with a final consonant, e.g. *swim*).

The **phonotactic** rules of English allow for a wide range of syllable structures. There are three allowable structures where there is a single consonant in the onset or coda: CV (as in *no*), VC (as in *on*) and CVC (as in *not*). The fact that English, unlike many other languages, permits consonant clusters in onsets and codas greatly extends the range of possible structures, allowing CCVC (*spot*), CVCC (*pant*), CCVCC (*plots*), and so on. English can have up to three consonants in the onset and four in the coda (CCCVCCCC), as in some pronunciations of *strengths* /strɛŋkθs/.

In English (and in many other languages) one or more syllables in every **lexical word** (i.e. nouns, verbs, adverbs and adjectives) is stressed. Stressing a syllable involves changing its pitch, increasing its volume, or lengthening it. This means that a stressed syllable is perceived as more prominent than an unstressed syllable. See METRE, RHYTHM, STRESS.

Syllable-timed   See RHYTHM.

Synchronic variation   Linguistic variation in space. Compare DIACHRONIC VARIATION.

Syncope   (Greek: 'cutting short') A process of **sound change** involving the loss of a sound or sounds (usually a vowel) in a word. Compare the following Old English and present-day English pairs: *munuc/monk*;   *heall/hall*;   *cylene/kiln*; *mynet/mint*. See ELISION.

Synecdoche (Greek: 'understanding one thing with another') A type of **metonymy** in which the part is used for the whole or the whole is used for the part: *All **hands** on deck*;† ***England** won the World Cup*;† *How do the **string** players know which way to bow?*† See FIGURE OF SPEECH, RHETORIC.

Synonymy A type of **semantic relation** involving similarity of meaning. The **folk linguistic** view is that synonyms are words with the same meaning, but in fact this sort of 'absolute' synonymy is rare. 'Same meaning' suggests a correspondence in all aspects of meaning and use, including connotative meaning as well as denotative meaning. Most synonyms are, in fact, partial synonyms: *house*, *dwelling*, *abode*, *domicile*, *residency* and so on.

The claim is often made, with some justification, that modern English is a language rich in synonyms. This richness is largely due to the mixed origins of the English vocabulary. At its core is a stock of **Germanic** (see OLD ENGLISH and NORSE) and **French** words. But words with **Latin** and Greek origins also figure prominently. For example, *house, dwelling* and *abode* have Old English roots, whereas *domicile* and *residency* are French. See CONNOTATION, DENOTATION, FORMALITY, LEXICAL COHESION, OVER-LEXICALIZATION, STYLE.

Syntax **Grammar** is usually divided into two broad fields: **morphology** and syntax. Syntax refers to the way in which words are arranged into **phrases**, phrases are arranged into **clauses**, and clauses arranged into **sentences**.

Synthetic language See LINGUISTIC TYPOLOGY.

Systemic functional linguistics (SFL) An approach to language description and analysis mainly associated with the British linguist Michael Halliday (1925–). SFL places at its centre the social context of language, and explores how language is used and how it is structured for this use (Hewings and Hewings 2005: 50). See separate entries on TRANSITIVITY and METAFUNCTION.

T

Taboo An area of human experience about which a particular culture has certain prohibitions. Words and phrases associated with these topics are often avoided by speakers and writers in certain contexts because of their power to shock, upset and offend. In English, these expressions are frequently to do with sex, excretion and religion: *Fucking hell, this is really crap*. Speakers and writers sometimes employ a variety of means to avoid taboo language. For example, a non-taboo substitute with some phonological resemblance to the original term is sometimes used: '*Oh Sugar!*' *Sally said; Jeepers! You get about all over the place.* In writing, asterisks or dashes can be employed in an attempt to lessen the force of a taboo term (or in some cases to avoid legal repercussions): *Oh! Happy F---ck, thou alone art he, / From jealous Stings and forked Antlers free* (Thomas Brown, 1720). This practice is becoming less common than it once was, as prohibitions surrounding such words and phrases diminish.

Tag An item added to the end of a clause, and only loosely attached to it in terms of grammar. Tags occur more frequently in speech than in writing. They perform a variety of functions and consist of a wide range of structures.

1) Tag questions are added to the end of statements, and their function varies according to whether they, or the statement, are positive or negative. A negative tag on a positive statement signals that the speaker is seeking confirmation for a positive proposition: *The locals are very determined, aren't they?* A positive tag on a negative statement signals that the speaker seeks confirmation for a negative proposition: *The locals aren't very determined, are they?* When both the tag and the statement are positive, the speaker is not seeking confirmation. Instead he or she is possibly repeating something that has been said earlier, perhaps in a slightly threatening way: *The locals are very determined, are they?* The process of forming a tag question involves identifying whether the statement is positive or negative (adding the negative particle where necessary), turning the subject of the statement into a pronoun (in the above example, *the locals* become *they*), and inverting the subject and operator. If the statement contains auxiliaries, as in *Your mum would be pleased, wouldn't she?* only the auxiliary occurs in the tag. Some speakers of English use invariant tags: *But not many people can see, isn't it?*± (**Singapore English**); *If you tell them you won't, you just get a caution, innit?* (London English). 2) Noun phrase tags have a clarifying function. In the following example, the tag serves to make clear the referent of the initial pronoun: *He's got backbone, that boy* (SEE DISLOCATION). 3) Declarative tags reinforce the speaker's commitment to the proposition and are formed from a noun phrase and either *do, be,* or *have*: *I liked that bit, I did*. See SPEECH AND WRITING.

Tag question See TAG.

Tempo A prosodic feature of speech. Varying the tempo (speed) of an utterance can communicate different meanings. A rapid delivery might convey excitement, enthusiasm or nervousness; a slow delivery boredom, thoughtfulness or equivocation. Grammatical boundaries are also signalled by changes in tempo. For example, parenthetical elements and asides can be marked by increased tempo.

Tenor   See REGISTER.

Tense   A **grammatical category** usually associated with the verb. It is used to relate the time of the event or state expressed by the verb to some other time. Tense is usually divided into past, present and future. Some languages mark all three distinctions on the verb through inflection, e.g. Spanish *canto* ('I sing'), *canté* ('I sang') and *cantaré* ('I will sing'). In English, however, tense is used to make a distinction only between past and present. For example, *She teaches history* (now); *She taught history* (at some time in the past). Future meanings are expressed through *will, shall* and *be going to* (see MODAL VERB, SEMI-MODAL VERB), together with particular uses of the present tense (see below).

There are two forms in the present tense in Standard English lexical verbs (with the exception of *be*). First person and third person plural subjects take the base form (*I run, you run, they run*); third person singular subjects take base form + *-s* inflection (*he runs, she runs, it runs*). Present tense (or 'simple' present tense) forms are used to express seven main meanings. 1) Permanent state: *Jupiter is a very massive planet.* 2) General truth: *The earth is round.* 3) Habitual action: *Her daughter works in Rome.* 4) 'Live' commentary: *In each case I add the two numbers: three plus three gives six, one plus three gives four, three plus one gives four.‡* 5) Performative: *I pronounce you man and wife* (see SPEECH ACT THEORY). 6) Past time (see HISTORIC PRESENT): *He moves to the window alongside, and sees her inside the office moving away from the door. He shoots twice through the window and kills her.* 7) Future time: *My flight leaves at four thirty this afternoon.* As these examples demonstrate, it is quite unusual for the simple present tense to report an event which is ongoing in present time (only 4 above falls into this category). A fluent English speaker would be unlikely to say 'I go home now'. In such cases, the present progressive is used: 'I'm going home now' (see ASPECT).

The past tense in English is marked on regular verbs by adding the ending *-ed* to the base form. The same form is used in each person (*I walked, you walked, he walked, she walked, it walked, they walked*); and this form is also used as the past participle (*I walked* and *I have walked*). **Irregular verb**s have special forms of the past tense (e.g. *break–broke, sing–sang*). The past tense is used mainly to describe completed events that are in the past: *They ate chicken, peas and chips* (and they are not still eating them). Often, the past tense form is accompanied by an **adverbial** which provides a time-frame: *I was up at the Grange last night*.

In **non-standard** English there is considerable variation in present and past tense forms. Some speakers use one form invariantly throughout the present tense: *I likes a bit of ice-cream; They likes to see us;• She love her chocolate, innit?* Other processes of 'levelling' include the generalization of the past participle to the past tense (*I seen him last night; I know she done that*) and invariant use of either *was* or *were* (*We was running late;• I didn't know if you was ever coming back;• He were in there eight weeks*).

Tense and lax   **Vowel**s can be classified according to the amount of muscular effort expended in their production. A tense vowel is produced with relatively greater effort than a lax vowel. Examples of tense vowels are high front or high back vowels (e.g. the vowels in RP pronunciations of *heat* and *hoot*). Examples of lax vowels are centralized vowels (e.g. the first and last vowel in an RP pronunciation of *banana*).

Term of address See ADDRESS, TERM OF.

Text Any stretch of language that forms a unified whole, often with a definable communicative **function** in a specific **context**. A text, therefore, can be as brief as a road sign and as lengthy as a novel. The term is sometimes limited to language in the written **mode**, although many **discourse** analysts also use it to refer to spoken passages. See also COHERENCE, COHESION, CONTEXT, GENRE, INTERTEXTUALITY, METAFUNCTION, REGISTER.

Textual metafunction See METAFUNCTION.

That-clause *That*-clauses are finite **subordinate** clauses with a variety of roles. Most commonly, they are **complement clauses** and **relative clauses**.

That-clauses as **complement clauses** are linked to their main clause with the subordinator *that*. They complete the meaning of a verb, adjective or noun in the main clause, and function as direct object, complement or subject.

1) *That*-clauses completing the meaning of a verb. A limited number of verbs allow for a *that*-clause as direct object. These are mostly **mental verbs** (e.g. *think, know, believe, see, feel*) and **communication verbs** (e.g. *say, suggest, write*): *I believe that the government must increase the tax*; *Sharon said that Jewish settlement was not an obstacle to peace*. The subordinator *that* can be omitted when the *that*-clause is the direct object: *I know you're not asleep*. In a limited range of contexts, *that*-clauses can function as subject

complement to a copular verb (generally describing problems and presenting reasons, results, truths and facts): *The central problem was that the chronically unemployed could not be covered by insurance; The fact is that organic cheese is fine*. *That*-clauses are sometimes subjects in the main clause: *That he had a thumb in many pies was undeniable*.

2) *That*-clauses completing the meaning of an adjective convey **stance** (the thoughts, feelings and attitudes of the speaker). Adjectives which commonly control *that*-clauses include *sure, certain, happy, glad, proud* and so on. *He is certain that the city is not becoming ungovernable; I'm glad that we all went*.

3) *That*-clauses completing the meaning of a noun also convey stance. For example, many of the nouns controlling *that*-complement clauses communicate something about the certainty of the proposition in the complement clause: *There is a possibility that the event may not occur*; *We also recognize the fact that Oxford's a marvelous place*. There is another group of nouns controlling *that*-complement clauses which indicate something about the source of the information in the complement clause: *The study is based on the hypothesis that basic research is increasingly important in technological innovation; It is my opinion that nothing can be done*.

That-clauses also function as **relative clauses**: *A blind man fought off a bull terrier that attacked his guide dog*.

Theme and rheme The *theme* (or 'topic') is what a **clause** is 'about'. 'Typical' themes have the following characteristics. 1) They are usually the first element in the clause. 2) They are often (but not always) the **subject**. 3) They usually represent *given* information (i.e. information that has been mentioned in the preceding **discourse**). In the following examples, the theme is in bold: *Colin had always nursed a horror of death;*[•] *This diminution in bore size was made possible by two developments;*[•] *She considered the question for a moment.*[•]

Not all themes, however, share these characteristics. Elements other than the subject can function as theme when they are moved to the front of the clause (see FRONTING). *Also important are beer brewing and the manufacture of cement* (complement as theme);[†] *English I don't like* (object as theme);[†] *By the door was a tall man dressed in a full tuxedo* (adverbial as theme).[†]

The *rheme* (or 'comment') is everything which follows the theme in a clause. In the following examples, the rheme is in bold and the theme has been underlined: <u>George</u> **ate a pizza at every road stop**;[†] <u>Quickly,</u> **George raised his rifle**.[†] The rheme is the part of the message which contains *new* information.

Theme and rheme are important for **cohesion**, since the rheme of one clause often becomes the theme of the following clause. See GIVEN AND NEW.

TH-fronting A tendency for some speakers of English to replace the **dental** fricatives /θ/ and /ð/ with the **labiodental** fricatives /f/ and /v/, so that *thin* is pronounced *fin* and *lithe* is pronounced *live*. Although *TH*-fronting (so-called because /f/ and /v/ are produced further forward in the mouth than /θ/ and /ð/) is particularly associated with accents from London and south-east England, it has also been recorded in the speech of people from as far apart as Norwich, Derby, Hull, Middlesborough and Glasgow. It is also present (though not widespread) in **New Zealand English** and **African American Vernacular English**.

Third person See **person**.

TH-stopping A tendency for some speakers of English to replace the **dental** fricatives /θ/ and /ð/ with the **alveolar** plosives /t/ and /d/. This pronunciation is captured in vernacular spellings, such as <ting> for *thing* and <dem> for *them*. *TH*-stopping is widespread, occurring in the Caribbean, the USA (e.g. in **African American Vernacular English** and **Cajun English**), Orkney and Shetland, Ireland, and contact varieties in the Pacific.

To-clause *To*-clauses (sometimes called infinitive clauses) are **non-finite subordinate** clauses with a variety of roles. They are mainly **complement clause**s, completing the meaning of a verb, adjective or noun in the **main clause**.

1) *To*-clauses completing the meaning of the verb function as direct object, subject complement or subject in the main clause. They are particularly common in direct object position: *He <u>likes</u> to knit quickly; She hadn't <u>planned</u> to cook tonight; She always <u>remembers</u> to smile*. Less frequently, *to*-clauses function as subject complement to a copular verb: *Your only hope <u>is</u> to find Madame V; The best solution will <u>be</u> to demolish them*. Even more uncommonly, they can function as subject: **To have flags** *is not important;*[±] **To offer an explanation of this view** *doubtless seemed unnecessary*. Subject *to*-clauses are frequently extraposed, as in *It is not important* **to have flags** and *It doubtless seemed unnecessary* **to offer an explanation of this view**. See EXTRAPOSITION.

2) *To*-clauses also complete the meaning of an adjective in the main clause. These controlling adjectives generally express levels of certainty (*Job cuts are almost certain* **to follow**); ability or willingness (*He was eager* **to learn**); emotion or stance (*I feel very proud* **to be a feminist**); ease or difficulty (*He was tough*

to handle); evaluation (*I'm sorry to disappoint you*).

3) *To*-clauses also complete the meaning of a noun in the main clause. These controlling nouns commonly refer to goals (*I knew about the plan to publish it*), opportunities (*I'm thrilled by the opportunity to join its team*) and actions (*Mrs Frizzell made an effort to sound normal*).

Not all *to*-clauses are complement clauses. In the following examples they are functioning as **adverbial clauses**: *To consolidate his power, he needed new members*; *I only cheat to win*.

Token   See TYPE-TOKEN RATIO.

Tok Pisin   A variety of pidginized English spoken in Papua New Guinea and its offshore islands. Although its name in English means 'talk pidgin', it is fully stabilized and expanded and used in a much wider range of contexts than most pidgins. Furthermore, an increasing number of people are acquiring it as a first language. See MELANESIAN PIDGIN ENGLISH, PIDGIN.

Transcription   The process of representing real speech in written form. Ways of transcribing speech vary depending on the purpose of the transcription. Some transcriptions provide 'tidied-up' versions of what was said. For example, *Hansard*, the official record of proceedings in the British Houses of Parliament, states that MPs' words are reported 'with repetitions and redundancies omitted and with obvious mistakes corrected'. This is adequate for the purposes of historical record, but for many researchers undertaking **conversation analysis**, such 'repetitions', 'redundancies' and 'mistakes' might be a central concern, and therefore they are often included in transcriptions.

A highly specialized form of transcription is a **phonetic** transcription, which uses the symbols of the **International Phonetic Alphabet** to accurately capture the sounds uttered by speakers.

Transfer   Sometimes known as 'interference', transfer occurs when speakers import elements from another language or variety into the one they are currently speaking. When we describe someone as 'speaking English with a French accent', for example, we are acknowledging the existence of transfer at the level of phonology. Words and grammatical constructions can also be transferred. See BORROWING, LANGUAGE CHANGE, LANGUAGE CONTACT, LANGUAGE SHIFT, SUBSTRATE EFFECT.

Transitive   Said of a lexical verb which is being used with an **object**: *Tabitha stroked the bird's head*. When a transitive verb is used with a **direct object** only, it is **monotransitive** (as in the previous example); when it is used with a direct object and an **indirect object**, it is **ditransitive**: *The clerk handed him the envelope*. Transitive verbs co-occur with agent, instrument, experiencer and causer **subjects**. Some verbs can function both transitively and intransitively: *The baby is growing* (intransitive); *They also grow potatoes* (monotransitive). See VALENCY PATTERN.

Transitivity   A term used mainly in **systemic functional linguistics** to refer to the system of grammatical choices available in language for representing actions, events, experiences and relationships in the world (see IDEATIONAL METAFUNCTION).

There are three components in a transitivity process: the *process type* (the process or state represented by the **verb phrase** in a clause), the *participant(s)* (people, things or concepts involved in a process or experiencing a state) and the *circumstance* (elements augmenting the clause, providing information about extent, location, manner, cause, contingency and so on). So in the clause 'Mary and Jim ate fish and chips on Friday', the process is represented by 'ate', the participants are 'Mary and Jim' and the circumstances are 'on Friday'.

Halliday and Matthiesen (2004) identify three main process types, *material*, *mental* and *relational*, and three minor types, *behavioural*, *verbal* and *existential*. Associated with each process are certain kinds of participants. 1) Material processes refer to actions and events. The verb in a material process clause is usually a 'doing' word (see ACTIVITY VERB): *Elinor* **grabbed** *a fire extinguisher; She* **kissed** *Marina*. Participants in material processes include *actor* ('Elinor', 'she') and *goal* ('a fire extinguisher', 'Marina'). 2) Mental processes refer to states of mind or psychological experiences. The verb in a mental process clause is usually a **mental verb**: *I can't* **remember** *his name; Our party* **believes** *in choice*. Participants in mental processes include *senser(s)* ('I'; 'our party') and *phenomenon* ('his name'; 'choice'). 3) Relational processes commonly ascribe an attribute to an entity, or identify it: *Something* **smells** *awful in here; My name* **is** *Scruff*. The verb in a relational process clause is usually a **copular verb**. Participants in relational processes include *token* ('something', 'my name') and *value* ('Scruff', 'awful'). 4) Behavioural processes are concerned with the behaviour of a participant who is a conscious entity. They lie somewhere between material and mental processes. The verb in a behavioural process clause is usually **intransitive**, and semantically it refers to a process of consciousness or a physiological state: *Many survivors* **are** **sleeping** *in the open;• The baby* **cried**.• The participant in behavioral processes is

called a *behaver*. 5) Verbal processes are processes of verbal action: *'Really?', said Septimus Coffin; He told them a story about a gooseberry in a lift*. Participants in verbal processes include *sayer* ('Septimus Coffin', 'he'), *verbiage* ('really', 'a story') and *recipient* ('them'). 6) Existential processes report the existence of someone or something. Only one participant is involved in an existential process: the *existent*. There are two main grammatical forms for this type of process: **existential** *there* as subject + copular verb (*There are thousands of examples*); and existent as subject + copular verb (*Maureen was at home*).

See also GRAMMATICAL METAPHOR.

Triphthong   See DIPHTHONG.

Turn   A term used in **conversation analysis** to describe a single contribution of a participant in a conversation. The process by which speaker change occurs is known as *turn-taking*. It is a coordinated and highly-ordered activity, governed by 'rules' determining who may speak (and when they may begin speaking), how participants can achieve (and hold onto) their turn, and how the transition to the next speaker is made. See also ADJACENCY PAIR, FLOOR.

Type-token ratio (TTR)   The ratio of word *types* to word *tokens* in a text. The number of word tokens is simply the total number of words the text contains. The number of word types is the number of *different* words used. The following text contains fifty-eight words (types) and forty-five different words (tokens). Therefore the type-token ratio is $45 \div 58 \times 100 = 77.59$ (or $45 \times 100 \div 58$).

As soon as it became clear that Miss Trunchbull had completely disappeared from the scene, the excellent Mr Trilby was appointed Head

Teacher in her place. And very soon after that, Matilda was moved up into the top form where Miss Plimsoll quickly discovered that this amazing child was every bit as bright as Miss Honey had said.

A property of the type-token ratio is that shorter texts will generally have higher ratios than longer texts. This is because in each successive chunk of text, there is more chance of a word being repeated. Therefore, in order to make the measurement applicable to longer texts, and to allow comparisons between texts of different lengths to be made, *standardized* type-token ratio is calculated. This is done by working out the ratio for each consecutive 1000 words of the text, and then generating a running average.

TTR is a measurement of lexical richness. A high TTR indicates that the speaker or writer is paying careful attention to selection of vocabulary. Because such a task requires considerable cognitive effort, a high TTR is often associated with writing, where there is usually time to dwell on vocabulary choice and to revise and redraft work. Spontaneous speech, on the other hand, is produced under what are sometimes quite severe time constraints, and speakers generally find it more difficult than writers to exploit the full resources of the lexicon. TTR is not only affected by the constraints of production (and reception). It is also influenced by the **function** which a particular text is performing. Informationally dense texts have a high TTR, and such texts tend to be written rather than spoken. See SPEECH AND WRITING.

U

Underlexicalization See OVERLEXI-CALIZATION AND UNDERLEXICALIZATION.

Upspeak, uptalk See HIGH-RISING TONE.

Usage A term in language study which refers to the ways in which a particular linguistic feature is used. Usage varies according to who is speaking or writing, who the audience is, and where the speech event is taking place (see CONTEXT). Some usages are common and conventional in some contexts, and rare and unusual in others. See also ACADEMY, ACCEPTABILITY, APOSTROPHE, AUTHORITY, CODIFICATION, COLLOQUIAL, FORMALITY, *FOWLER'S MOD-ERN ENGLISH USAGE*, GENERIC PRONOUN, HYPERCORRECTION, OXFORD ENGLISH DICTIONARY, PRESCRIPTIVISM, REGISTER, STANDARD ENGLISH, VERNACULAR.

V

Valency pattern The pattern of elements in a clause determined by the main verb. There are three main valency patterns: **intransitive**, **transitive** and copular. The intransitive pattern consists of S+V (*He died*). The transitive pattern is either S+V+DO, in which case it is **monotransitive** (*She hit him*), or S+V+ DO+IO, in which case it is **ditransitive** (*He gave him a violent blow*). The copular pattern requires a **complement** for grammatical completion (*Your coypu is crazy*).

Variety A useful, though somewhat vague sociolinguistic term to describe a distinct form of a language. There are various ways of identifying and categorizing varieties of English. It is quite common to distinguish between *user-based varieties* (regional and social **dialect**) and *use-based varieties* (**register**). User-based variation is related to the social and geographical background of a speaker, and is the origin of variety labels such as *American English, British English, Geordie, Jamaican Creole, Black English, urban working-class English, Anglo-Indian* and so on. Regional and social variation is generally defined in terms of **phonology**, **grammar** and **lexis**. Varieties of English are also identifiable according to use. This gives rise to labels such as *literary English, legal English, journalese, scientific English.* The defining features of use-based varieties are often **stylistic**.

Velar A term used in the description of **consonants** referring to a place of **articulation** (the point in the **vocal tract** where a constriction of the **airstream** occurs). Velar consonants are produced when the back of the tongue touches or approaches the **soft palate** (velum). There are three velar consonant phonemes in most varieties of English: /k/, /g/ and /ŋ/.

Velum See SOFT PALATE.

Verb Verbs may be divided into two categories: **lexical verbs** and **auxiliary verbs**. Lexical verbs express actions (*make, go, come*), mental states and processes (*know, think, mean*), acts of communication (*say, tell, write*), existence (*stay, live, exist*), occurrence (*happen, change, occur*) and so on. They function as the main verb in a verb phrase: *They **glared** at the screen.* Auxiliaries are a **closed class** of verbs which include **modal verbs** and **primary verbs** (although the primary verbs *be, have* and *do* can also function as lexical verbs). They can be added to a **main verb** to build **verb phrases** (verb phrases in bold, auxiliaries underlined): *You **will write** a feature article; We **would have been going** to Sydney.*

Verbal process See TRANSITIVITY.

Verb chain A **verb phrase** consisting of one or more **auxiliary verbs** and a main **lexical verb**. The following examples contain progressively longer verb chains: *Mrs Chalk **is cooking** pheasant; Western society **has been eating** too much fat; The grandparents **could have been living** a few houses away.* See ASPECT, MODAL VERB.

Verb element (V) The verb element is the only obligatory **clause element**. Other elements can be omitted without making a sentence ungrammatical. For example, starting with the (invented) sentence *My pet cat eats fish regularly*, we can omit the adverbial (*My pet cat eats fish*); the object

(*My pet cat eats regularly*) and even the subject – in a situation where the cat in question is visible and the speaker is pointing to it (*Eats fish regularly*). However, we cannot normally omit the verb (** My pet cat fish regularly*). Minimally, a clause can consist of just the verb element (*Eat!*). The verb element is always a **verb phrase**, and can therefore range in complexity from a single lexical verb (*She **lies** on her back*) to lengthy structures (*You **could have been lying** out there in the farmyard all night*). See MINOR SENTENCE, VERBLESS CLAUSE.

Verbless clause   Clauses which do not contain any surface verb form: ***When in doubt**, shove on a mini-series;*• ***If possible**, please give 24-hours notice;*• *Indicate quantity, color or size **where appropriate**.*• Expressions such as these can be regarded as clauses, despite having no verb, because they are generally analysable as adverbial clauses with ellipsis of the verb *be* and the subject. See MINOR SENTENCE.

Verb phrase (VP)   One of the five major **phrase** types. Its **head** (i.e. the **main verb**) is either a **lexical** or **primary verb** (*be, do* or *have*). As the following set of examples from a potentially much longer list show, the VP can consist solely of a main verb, or be preceded by **auxiliary verb**s, which add information about **tense**, **aspect** and **modality**: *Tom **walks** over to a pizza stall; She **walked** past the sugar-beet factory; This retriever **is walking** to heel; Mrs Holt **was walking** swiftly; He **has walked** the length and breadth of it; She **had walked** many miles; You **must walk** very carefully; They **must have walked** miles that day; He **must be walking** up to your school.*

Verb phrases are sometimes split into two parts (they are 'discontinuous'). This happens in questions, where the subject is placed after the first auxiliary verb: *Where*

*are you **going**? When **will** he **be joining** us?* Verb phrases can also be split by adverbials, as in 'can also be split' and *Adding fish water to your compost bin will **certainly** improve the result.*

All the examples so far have been **finite** verb phrases (they are marked for tense and/or contain a modal verb). Clauses containing **non-finite** verb phrases are usually subordinate to a main clause: *It's so hard **being rootless in a foreign country**; Birds have an instinct **to build nests**.* See VERB CHAIN.

Vernacular   (from Latin *vernaculus*: domestic, native) [1] A label sometimes applied to the distinctive usage of a particular place or community. Vernacular forms are typically **non-standard**, **dialect**al, **colloquial** and informal.

[2] The term is also used to describe the 'national' languages of Europe, such as French, Spanish and English, especially when they are contrasted with Latin: *The Catholic Church ended the Latin epoch by introducing **vernacular** languages into the liturgy.*†

Viking   A term used for the Scandinavian sea-farers who raided and settled many parts of northern Europe between the ninth and eleventh centuries, including parts of Scotland and the north and east of England. See DANE, DANELAW, NORSE.

Vocal folds   Two bands of muscular tissue stretching from the front to the back of the **larynx**. Their tension, elasticity and shape can be altered to modulate the flow of air from the windpipe into the **larynx**, pharynx and **oral cavity**. This modulation produces a variety of effects, including the audible vibration known as voicing, which in English is required to produce all the vowels and many of the consonants. The rate of vibration can also be changed, resulting in variations in **pitch** and **volume**, and different voice qualities (e.g. 'breathy' voice, 'husky' voice).

Vocal tract   The parts of the human body involved in the production of speech sounds. It consists of the respiratory tract (from the lungs to the nose), together with the mouth. See GLOTTIS, LARYNX, VOCAL FOLDS.

Vocative   A noun phrase used by a speaker or writer to refer directly to the person being addressed. Vocatives are usually, but not always, proper nouns: *Sarah, do you know what they're looking for? It was good, wasn't it Kevin? You are part of me now, my dear*. See SPEECH AND WRITING.

Voice   [1] The system of voice in English allows speakers and writers to present the **subject** of a clause as either **agent** or **patient**. When the subject has the **semantic role** of agent, the clause is in the **active voice** (*He opened the door*); when the subject is the patient, the clause is in the **passive voice** (*The door was opened*). Some grammars recognize the existence of the 'middle voice', in which the subject can be the semantic patient without the passive voice being used (*The door opened*). See ACTIVE VOICE, ERGATIVE VERB, PASSIVE VOICE.

[2] In **phonetics**, **consonants** are classified according to three main parameters: place and manner of **articulation**, and voice. A voiced consonant is one whose production is accompanied with a vibration of the **vocal folds**. If you place your fingertips lightly on your throat and say the sounds /s/ and /z/ one after the other, you should be able to feel vibration on the /z/. In English, the following consonants are identical apart from the absence or presence of voice (the second consonant in each pair is voiced): /p/ and /b/; /t/ and /d/; /k/ and /g/; /f/ and /v/; /θ/ and /ð/; /s/ and /z/; /ʃ/ and /ʒ/; /tʃ/ and /dʒ/.

Volition   An expression of wanting, willingness, intention, wishing, promising or threatening by a conscious entity exercising its will. See EXPERIENCER, MODALITY, MODAL VERB, STANCE, SUBJECT.

Volume   A **prosodic feature** of speech. Variations in volume can communicate different meanings. Affection and intimacy are often associated with a quiet voice, whereas loudness often conveys anger or excessive enthusiasm. Alterations in volume are also used to mark the difference between stressed (louder) and unstressed (quieter) syllables. See STRESS.

Vowel   A category of speech sound produced when the **airstream** passes through an open **vocal tract**, in contrast to **consonants**, whose production involves a total or partial closure of the vocal tract. Variation in the position of the tongue and the shape of the lips alters the quality of the vowel being produced. Therefore, vowels are generally categorized according to these two main articulatory parameters.

Tongue position has two dimensions: the height of the body of the tongue in relation to the roof of the mouth (the vertical dimension), and how far forwards or backwards the tongue is in the **oral cavity** (the horizontal dimension). Vowels are categorized according to whether they are 'high' or 'close' (produced with the body of the tongue close to the roof of the mouth), 'low' or 'open' (produced with the body of the tongue distant from the roof of the mouth) or 'mid' (produced with the tongue in an intermediate position between high and low). The effect of the vertical dimension on vowel production can be seen in the contrast between the vowels in the words *bid* (high) and *bad* (low). If you say these words one after the other, you can feel your tongue moving from a higher to a lower position in your mouth. Vowels are further categorized by tongue position according to whether they are 'front' (produced with the body of the tongue forward in the mouth), 'back' (produced with the body of the tongue near the back of the mouth) or 'central' (produced with the tongue in an intermediate position between front and back). The effect of the horizontal dimension on vowel production can be seen in the contrast between the vowels in the words *pat* (front) and *put* (back). If you say these words one after the other, you can feel your tongue moving from the front to the back of your mouth.

Vowels are also categorized according to the shape formed by the lips when the vowel is produced: they are either 'rounded' or 'unrounded'. In most varieties of English, front vowels tend to be unrounded, while back vowels are rounded. This is best appreciated by watching yourself in a mirror as you alternate between unrounded and rounded vowels; for example, by saying *pat* (unrounded) and *put* (rounded). See BACK VOWEL, FRONT VOWEL.

W

Welsh   See CELTIC LANGUAGES.

Welsh English   A general term for the varieties of English spoken in Wales, one of the three nations (along with Scotland and England) sharing the island of **Britain**. The word *Wales* is derived from an Old English word *wealh*, meaning 'foreigner' or 'slave'. In the Welsh language (*Cymraeg*), which is a direct descendant of the **Celtic language** spoken throughout most of Britain before the **Anglo-Saxons** arrived, the country is called *Cymru*. Wales was the only area of southern Britain to remain an autonomous Celtic territory during the period of Anglo-Saxon expansion between the fifth and ninth centuries (although the first communities of English speakers were probably established in the Wye valley as early as the eighth century). This autonomy was threatened in 1282, when the English king Edward I invaded. In 1301, Edward's son was crowned *Prince of Wales*, and Wales became England's first colony. Wales was effectively incorporated into England with the Acts of Union of 1536 and 1542, accelerating the decline of the Welsh language which had begun at the start of the colonial period in the fourteenth century. In present-day Wales, there are hardly any monolingual speakers of Welsh, although about 20 per cent of the population is bilingual. The proportion of bilingual people varies according to region. In Gwynned in the north-west of Wales, for example, the figure is as high as 60 per cent (Crystal 2003).

Welsh English has been shaped by three main influences: the Welsh language; dialects of English in neighbouring counties of England; and Standard English, as taught in schools and used in the media (McArthur 2002). Present-day Welsh English has at least three regional varieties: the dialect associated with the industrial south, the south-west and the north. The influence of Welsh is at its strongest in the northern counties; this decreases the further south you go. In the industrial south, a substratal Welsh influence is present (see SUBSTRATE EFFECT), but there is no **transfer** from the contemporary Welsh language, as there is in the north.

Notable pronunciation features of Welsh English include the following (see Thomas 1994). 1) The vowel in words in the STRUT **lexical set** is usually **schwa** [ə], resulting in pronunciations such as /kəp/, /bəd/ and /kəm/ for *cup*, *bud* and *come*. 2) Words in the FACE and GOAT sets are more likely to be pronounced with a diphthong than a monophthong, e.g. /feːs/, /goːt/. 3) Consonants in the middle of a word following a short vowel tend to be lengthened, resulting in pronunciations such as /mənni/ (*money*), /səppə/ (*supper*). 4) Two consonants from Welsh occur: the voiceless lateral fricative [ɬ], as in the sound represented by <ll> in *Llandudno*, and the voiceless velar fricative [x], as in the sound represented by <ch> in *bach*.

The grammar of Welsh English bears the traces of substratal Welsh influence (see Penhallurick 2004). For example, generalized *isn't it* as a confirmatory **tag** (as in *We saw some the other day, isn't it?*) is possibly a transfer of the all purpose Welsh tag *ydy fe?* Similarly, the Welsh construction *dyna* ('there is') + adjective is reflected in exclamations such as *There's nice to see you!* The **fronting** of the subject complement (*A weed it is; Coal they're getting out*) seems to be more common in Welsh English than in other varieties, and this is probably also a transfer from Welsh. Other features of Welsh English grammar are shared with neighbouring dialects of English in England. These include constructions such as *He do go to the cinema every week*.

Distinctive features of Welsh English vocabulary include words taken from Welsh, which often relate to culture and behaviour (*eisteddfod* 'a cultural festival'; *iechyd da* 'good health'). Terms of affection such as *bach* and *del* are also common. Some general English words take on additional meanings in Welsh English, e.g. *tidy* 'good, attractive'. *Boyo* (from 'boy') is a popular term of address and reference for men, which is often used negatively: *Listen, boyo, I've something to say to you* (McArthur 2002).

West Africa English is used widely in West Africa, and has official status in Cameroon, Gambia, Ghana, Liberia, Nigeria and Sierra Leone. Europeans first arrived in West Africa in the fifteenth century as traders, but the first European colonies did not become established until the late nineteenth century. During this period, the influence of European languages (especially Portuguese, Dutch, French and English) was limited to the coast, where a number of pidgins developed, in the interaction between European traders and the indigenous population. Several of the English-based contact varieties were the ancestors of pidgins and creoles which are spoken today.

The situation of English in West Africa is complex. It is present in a continuum ranging from Standard English, which is used for official purposes and in the media (alongside the main state languages), to **basilect**al varieties such as *Nigerian Pidgin English*, which shares features with *Kamtok* (in Cameroon) and *Krio* (in Sierra Leone). In between there are a number of 'local' Englishes, which are influenced by the native language(s) of the speaker. English is generally acquired as a **second language**, mainly through the education system.

Some typical pronunciation features of English in West Africa include the following. 1) A tendency towards syllable-timing rather than stress-timing, which means that vowels are rarely reduced to /ə/, and polysyllabic words receive equal stress on all syllables (see RHYTHM). 2) Absence of post-vocalic /r/, so that *ten* and *turn* are **homophone**s. 3) A reduced vowel system (compared with '**inner circle**' varieties of English), which means that words which in RP have different vowels often share the same vowel in the speech of people from West Africa. For example, words in the KIT and FLEECE **lexical set**s have the vowel [i], so that the pairs of words *sit/seat*, *bin/bean* are homophones; words in the LOT, THOUGHT and STRUT sets have the vowel [ɔ], making *cot*, *caught* and *cut*, and also *shot*, *short* and *shut* homophones; words in the DRESS and NURSE sets have the vowel [ε], making *lend* and *learned* homophones. 4) Final consonants are often devoiced, so that the following pairs are homophones: *robe/rope, bed/bet, pig/pick*. (See Trudgill and Hannah 2002.)

Typical non-standard grammatical forms in 'general' West African English include the following. 1) Nouns which are often considered to be uncountable in Standard English are countable: *advices, furnitures, aircraft*. 2) Articles are sometimes omitted: *Waziri played ø crucial role to secure victory for the president.* 3) Use of progressive **aspect** with *have* to express a temporary state: *LG is having global leading position in third generation mobile phone.* 4) Invariant question tags, such as *is it?* and *isn't it?*: *You like that, isn't it?* 5) Formation of comparative clauses without *more*: *He has ø money than his brother.* (See Alo and Mesthrie 2004.)

The distinctive vocabulary of English in West Africa has three main sources. 1) Loanwords from local languages: *akara* ('beancake'), *obanje* ('spirit child'), *kwi* ('foreigner'). 2) Loan-translations: *to have long legs* ('to exert influence'), *to throw water* ('to offer a bribe'). 3) Local coinages: *decampee* ('a person who changes political parties'), *cash madam* ('wealthy woman'). (See McArthur 2002.)

West Midlands A region of England consisting of the city of Birmingham and an area to the west known as the Black Country (made up of Dudley, Walsall, West Bromwich and Wolverhampton). The dialects of Birmingham and the Black Country are related, but different in several respects.

In the following overview of the phonology of West Midlands English (based on Clark 2004), only those features which are particularly salient in distinguishing these varieties from other varieties spoken in England are described. 1) The vowel in the KIT **lexical set** tends to be very high at [i]. 2) The vowel in the LOT set is sometimes realized as [ʊ], particularly by older, working-class speakers from the Black Country in words where the vowel precedes a nasal. This pronunciation is reflected in the following vernacular spellings noted by Clark: <lung> *long*; <sung> *song*; <(w)rung> *wrong.* 3) The vowel in the STRUT set is typically realized as [ʊ] (as it is in accents of **northern England**), but

there is evidence of [ɒ] occurring, especially before nasals (a pronunciation captured in the common West Midlands vernacular spelling of <mom> *mum*). 4) The vowel in the FLEECE set is often realized as something approaching [əi], so that the following word pairs are near-**homophone**s: *meet/mate; piece/pace; key/Kaye* (this feature is particularly associated with the Black Country). 5) For some speakers, the vowel in the PRICE set is realized as [ɔi], making near-homophones of *buy/boy* and rhyming pairs of *pie/Roy* and *wild/boiled.*

The grammar of the dialects of the West Midlands shares many features with other non-standard varieties of English (e.g. multiple negation; *what* introducing a relative clause). But the Black Country dialect contains grammatical features unknown in other varieties of English. For example, modal and primary auxiliary verbs have special negative forms, which can be captured with the following vernacular spellings: *ay* (haven't, isn't, aren't); *bay* (am not, isn't, aren't); *cor/caw* (can't); *dae* (didn't); *woe* (won't); *wor* (wasn't).

West Saxon The **Old English** dialect associated with Wessex, one of the kingdoms of the **Anglo-Saxon** heptarchy. The territory of Wessex was centred on the modern-day counties of Hampshire, Dorset, Berkshire, Wiltshire and Somerset, with its capital at Winchester. The earliest documents in the dialect date from the mid-ninth century. The fact that most of the surviving corpus of Old English is in West Saxon, including the *Anglo-Saxon Chronicle,* is a reflection of the cultural and political hegemony of Wessex in the ninth and tenth centuries. A great deal of material written in other Old English dialects was translated into West Saxon, and writers as far away as

Northumbria were producing material in West Saxon (as well as in their local dialect). This has led some scholars to describe West Saxon as a 'standardized' written form of Old English (although the use of this term is controversial and can be confusing, since West Saxon is *not* the basis of present-day **Standard English**).

Wh-clause A subordinate finite clause introduced by a **wh-word**. *Wh*-clauses can function as direct object (*Kee saw* **what was happening**); indirect object (*I shall tell* **whoever comes in** *to get my tea*•); subject complement (*The problem is* **where to put it**•); object complement (*Hell, call it* **what you want!**•); adjectival complement (*They were not sure* **who fired the first shot**); prepositional complement (*We'll send you information on* **how you can receive your Photocard**•); adverbial (*They laughed* **when they saw her**). *Wh*-clauses can also function as subjects, but usually only when they precede copular verbs and verbs expressing a mental reaction of some sort: **What we need** *is a definition of Marxism*; **What surprised them both** *was Rosemary's reaction*. *Wh*-clauses as subjects are often extraposed: *It is not clear from the evidence* **how catalogue usage could be increased**; *It is not known* **whether they had any children** (see EXTRAPOSITION).

Wh-question A question beginning with a **wh-word**. See INTERROGATIVE CLAUSE.

Wh-word A set of grammatical words belonging to several word classes which all begin with *wh-* (with the exception of *how*). They have three main functions: introducing **interrogative clauses** (**Who** *are they?*•); introducing **relative clauses** (*It's the town* **where** *Victor Hugo was born*•); introducing **complement clauses** (*I don't care* **what** *you say*•). See *WH*-CLAUSE.

Word A widely used definition of *word* is the 'smallest unit of grammar which

can stand alone as a complete utterance' (Crystal 1992: 419). For example, *road* (consisting of one free **morpheme**) is a word, and *roads* (consisting of the free morpheme *road* and the bound morpheme *-s*) is a word; but the bound morpheme *-s* is not a word. In English, this rule works in most cases, but not for items such as *the* or *an* which, although they do not usually occur 'meaningfully' by themselves, are certainly words. For this reason it is useful to distinguish between **lexical words** (e.g. *fish*, *run*, *blue*) and **grammatical words** (e.g. *to*, *by*, *a*). Linguists also use the concept **lexeme** to describe a grouping of 'word forms' (e.g. *swim*, *swam*, *swum* and *swimming* belong to the lexeme *swim*). See also WORD CLASS, WORD FORMATION.

Word class Words are traditionally grouped into two broad categories which are then subdivided into classes (or 'parts of speech') according to their grammatical and/or semantic characteristics. These are **lexical words** (**nouns**, **lexical verbs**, **adjectives** and **adverbs**) and **function words** (**determiners**, **pronouns**, **auxiliary verbs**, **prepositions**, and **conjunctions**). Some grammars identify **inserts** as a third category.

Word formation The creation of new words. See ABBREVIATION, ACRONYM, ANALOGY [2], BACKFORMATION, BLENDING, BORROWING, CLIPPING, COINING, COMPOUNDING, CONVERSION, DERIVATION, EPONYM, FOLK ETYMOLOGY, LEXICALIZATION, LOAN TRANSLATION, NEOLOGISM, NONCE WORD, PRODUCTIVITY, REANALYSIS, RETRONYM, ROOT CREATION.

Word order The sequence of elements in a clause. Languages are often classified according to the order in which **clause elements** most frequently occur. In English, the subject usually precedes the verb and the verb precedes the other elements, resulting in sequences such as SV (*You stink*); SVO (*I like Quakers*); SVC (*They're lovely*); SVA (*My bathroom tiles are coming on Tuesday*), and so on. In **interrogative clause**s, however, the verb (or the **operator**) precedes the subject: *Are you Cantonese?*± *What does that mean?*±

It is important to stress that SV(O/C/A) is the *typical* order in declarative clauses; it is not the *only* order. The re-ordering of clause elements is usually marked, as in the following examples: *This I did not mind*± (fronted object); *Far more surprising*, *however, is the amount that has been retained*± (fronted subject complement); *On the controls was Charles Muiruri*± (subject–verb inversion). See FRONTING, INVERSION, MARKEDNESS.

World English   A term sometimes used in talking about the English language as a global phenomenon. Largely as a consequence of British imperialism in the nineteenth century and the economic, military and technical dominance of the USA in the twentieth and twenty-first centuries, English has achieved a geographical reach unparalleled in the history of human language. But 'World English' is far from being a monolithic entity. Speakers of English around the world have acquired the language in different ways and use it for different purposes. Linguists have constructed various 'models' in an attempt to understand this complexity; one of the most influential of these has been Braj Kachru's 'Circles of English' model. This describes the spread of world English as a series of concentric circles: the 'inner circle', 'outer circle' and 'expanding circle' territories. The inner circle consists of areas which are the traditional cultural and linguistic bases of English (Kachru 1985), such as USA, UK, Canada, Australia, New Zealand, and Ireland. Next comes the outer circle, territories in Asia and Africa where English was first introduced as a language of colonialism, and is now used mainly as a **second language** (often with an official role) for purposes of internal communication in a multilingual setting, such as India, Pakistan, Nigeria, Philippines, Singapore, Tanzania, Zambia. Areas where English has been used as a second language have developed their own distinct varieties of English. Finally there is the expanding circle, a growing collection of nations where English has no special status but is recognized as an important medium of international communication, such as China, Russia, Japan, Indonesia. In such contexts, English is often described as a 'foreign language'.

Like all linguistic models, this simplifies the actual situation. For example, some people in the outer circle have English as a **first language** (e.g. Singapore) which they speak at home and do not use solely for official purposes. And an increasing number of speakers in the expanding circle are using English in ways that seem to be going beyond what might be expected of a 'foreign language' (e.g. Denmark, Sweden, Norway and Holland). In effect, they are becoming second language speakers: using English for communication *within* their own country, in higher education, for example, or even in certain social and personal contexts. Despite these caveats, the model remains valuable because of the attention it draws 'to the different historical and social issues raised by the notion of world English' (Crystal 2003: 107).

Z

Zero-article Not all noun phrases require an **article**. 'Zero-article' is used to signal indefiniteness with uncountable nouns and plural countable nouns: *I don't take **sugar**; I hate **books**.* In these examples, zero-article is being used for non-specific and generic reference. Other uses include places as institutions (*That's what we learnt at **college****); means of transport (*I go by **train****); methods of communication (*Return it by **fax** or **post****); certain time references (*See the Big Apple at **sundown****); **vocative**s (*Hey **dad**! Come out*). It is also common in forms of abbreviated or condensed language, such as newspaper headlines and notices: *KEEP OFF GRASS; BOTTLE OF JUICE KILLS PENSIONER.* See DEFINITE AND INDEFINITE.

Zero relative clause See RELATIVE CLAUSE.

Bibliography

Aitken, A.J. 1992. 'Scots', in Tom McArthur (ed.) *The Oxford Companion to the English Language.* Oxford: Oxford University Press, pp. 893–899.

Alo, M.A. and Rajend Mesthrie 2004. 'Nigerian English: morphology and syntax', in Edgar W. Schneider, Kate Burridge, Bernd Kortmann, Rajend Mesthrie, Clive Upton (eds) *A Handbook of Varieties of English Volume 2: Morphology and Syntax.* Mouton de Gruyter: Berlin, pp. 813–827.

Altendorf, Ulrike and Dominic Watt 2004. 'The dialects in the South of England: phonology', in Edgar W. Schneider, Kate Burridge, Bernd Kortmann, Rajend Mesthrie, Clive Upton (eds) *A Handbook of Varieties of English Volume 1: Phonology.* Mouton de Gruyter: Berlin, pp. 178–203.

Austin, John L. 1962. *How to Do Things with Words.* Oxford: Oxford University Press.

Baker, Philip and John Eversley 2000. *Multilingual Capital.* London: Battlebridge Publications.

Barber, Charles 1993. *The English Language: A Historical Introduction.* Cambridge: Cambridge University Press.

Bauer, Laurie 1983. *English Word-formation.* Cambridge: Cambridge Univeristy Press.

Bayley, Robert and Otto Santa Ana 2004. 'Chicano English: morphology and syntax', in Edgar W. Schneider, Kate Burridge, Bernd Kortmann, Rajend Mesthrie, Clive Upton (eds) *A Handbook of Varieties of English Volume 2: Morphology and Syntax.* Mouton de Gruyter: Berlin, pp. 374–390.

Beal, Joan 1993. 'The grammar of Tyneside and Northumbrian English', in Milroy, J. and Milroy, L. (eds) *Real English: The Grammar of English Dialects in the British Isles.* London: Longman, pp. 187–213.

Beal, Joan 2004a. 'English dialects in the north of England: phonology', in Edgar W. Schneider, Kate Burridge, Bernd Kortmann, Rajend Mesthrie, Clive Upton (eds) *A Handbook of Varieties of English Volume 1: Phonology.* Mouton de Gruyter: Berlin, pp. 113–133.

Beal, Joan 2004b. 'English dialects in the north of England: morphology and syntax', in Edgar W. Schneider, Kate Burridge, Bernd Kortmann, Rajend Mesthrie, Clive Upton (eds) *A Handbook of Varieties of English Volume 2: Morphology and Syntax.* Mouton de Gruyter: Berlin, pp. 114–141.

Beal, Joan 2004c. *English in Modern Times 1700–1945.* London: Arnold.

Bell, Allan 1984. 'Language style as audience design', *Language in Society*, 13(2): 145–204.

Bell, Allan 2001. 'Back in style: Reworking audience design', in Penelope Eckert and John Rickford (eds) *Style and Sociolinguistic Variation.* Cambridge: Cambridge University Press.

Berk, Lynn M. 1999. *English Syntax: From Word to Discourse.* Oxford: Oxford University Press.

Bhatt, Rakesh M. 2004. 'Indian English: syntax', in Edgar W. Schneider, Kate Burridge, Bernd Kortmann, Rajend Mesthrie, Clive Upton (eds) *A Handbook of Varieties of English Volume 2: Morphology and Syntax.* Mouton de Gruyter: Berlin, pp. 1016–1030.

Biber, Douglas, Stig Johansson, Geoffrey Leech, Susan Conrad and Edward Finegan 1999. *Longman Grammar of Spoken and Written English.* Harlow: Longman.

Biber, Douglas, Susan Conrad and Geoffrey Leech 2002. *Longman Student Grammar of Spoken and Written English.* Harlow: Longman.

Bickerton, Derek 1973. 'On the nature of a creole continuum', *Language*, 49: 640–669.

Bloomfield, Leonard 1933. *Language.* New York: Holt, Rinehart and Winston.

Bourdieu, Pierre 1991. *Language and Symbolic Power* (trans by Gino Raymond and Matthew Adamson; edited by John B. Thompson) Cambridge: Polity Press.

Bowerman, Sean 2004. 'White South African English: morphology and syntax', in Edgar

W. Schneider, Kate Burridge, Bernd Kortmann, Rajend Mesthrie, Clive Upton (eds) *A Handbook of Varieties of English Volume 2: Morphology and Syntax.* Mouton de Gruyter: Berlin, pp. 948–961.

Burchfield, Robert (ed.) 1996. *The New Fowler's Modern English Usage.* Oxford: Clarendon Press.

Burridge, Kate and Jean Mulder 1998. *English in Australia and New Zealand.* Oxford: Oxford University Press.

Cameron, Deborah 1995. *Verbal Hygiene.* London: Routledge.

Cameron, Deborah 2001. *Working with Spoken Discourse.* London: Sage.

Cannon, Garland, Tom McArthur and Jean-Marc Gachelin 1992. 'Borrowing', in Tom McArthur (ed.) *The Oxford Companion to the English Language.* Oxford: Oxford University Press, pp. 141–145.

Carter, Ronald 2004. *Language and Creativity: The Art of Common Talk.* London: Routledge.

Chambers, J.K. 1995. *Sociolinguistic Theory.* Oxford: Blackwell.

Chambers, J.K. and Peter Trudgill 1998. *Dialectology.* Cambridge: Cambridge University Press.

Clark, Urszula 2004. 'The English West Midlands: phonology', in Edgar W. Schneider, Kate Burridge, Bernd Kortmann, Rajend Mesthrie, Clive Upton (eds) *A Handbook of Varieties of English Volume 1: Phonology.* Mouton de Gruyter: Berlin, pp. 134–162.

Cruse, Alan 2000. *Meaning in Language.* Oxford: Oxford University Press.

Crystal, David 1992. *An Encyclopedic Dictionary of Language and Languages.* Oxford: Blackwell.

Crystal, David 1997. *The Cambridge Encyclopedia of Language* (2nd edn). Cambridge: Cambridge University Press.

Crystal, David 2003. *The Cambridge Encyclopedia of the English Language* (2nd edn). Cambridge: Cambridge University Press.

Crystal, David 2004. *The Stories of English.* London: Penguin.

Cutts, Martin 1995. *The Plain English Guide.* Oxford: Oxford University Press.

Davies, Diane 2005. *Varieties of Modern English: An Introduction.* Harlow: Longman.

Dixon, John, Berenice Mahoney and Roger Cocks 2002. 'Accents of guilt? Effects of regional accent, "race" and crime type on attributions of guilt', *Journal of Language and Social Psychology*, 21: 162–168.

Edwards, Walter F. 2004. 'African American Vernacular English: phonology', in Edgar W. Schneider, Kate Burridge, Bernd Kortmann, Rajend Mesthrie, Clive Upton (eds) *A Handbook of Varieties of English Volume 1: Phonology.* Mouton de Gruyter: Berlin, pp. 383–392.

Eggins, Suzanne 2004. *An Introduction to Systemic Functional Linguistics.* London: Continuum.

Fairclough, Norman 1995. *Critical Discourse Analysis.* London: Longman.

Fairclough, Norman 1996. 'Border crossings: discourse and social change in contemporary societies', in H. Coleman and L. Cameron (eds) *Change and Language.* Clevedon: Multilingual Matters, pp. 3–17.

Fairclough, Norman 2001. *Language and Power* (2nd edn). London: Longman.

Fennell, Barbara 2001. *A History of English: A Sociolinguistic Approach.* Oxford: Blackwell.

Finegan, Edward 2004. 'American English and its distinctiveness', in Edward Finegan and John R. Rickford (eds) *Language in the USA: Themes for the Twenty-First Century.* Cambridge: Cambridge University Press, pp. 18–38.

Foulkes, Paul and Gerard Docherty 2005. 'Phonological variation in the English of England', in Britain, D. (ed.) *Language in the British Isles* (2nd edn). Cambridge: Cambridge University Press.

Fowler, Roger 1977. *Linguistics and the Novel.* London: Methuen.

Fowler, Roger 1986. *Linguistic Criticism.* Oxford: Oxford University Press.

Giles, Howard and Peter F. Powesland 1975. *Speech Style and Social Evaluation.* London: Academic Press.

Goatly, Andrew 2000. *Critical Reading and Writing.* London: Routlege.

Goodman, Sharon and David Graddol (eds) 1996. *Redesigning English: New Texts, New Identities.* London: Routledge.

Gordon, Elizabeth and Andrea Sudbury

2002. 'The history of southern hemisphere Englishes', in Richard Watts and Peter Trudgill (eds) *Alternative Histories of English*. London: Routledge, pp. 67–86.

Gordon, Matthew J. 2004. 'New York, Philadelphia and other northern cities: phonology', in Edgar W. Schneider, Kate Burridge, Bernd Kortmann, Rajend Mesthrie, Clive Upton (eds) *A Handbook of Varieties of English Volume 1: Phonology.* Mouton de Gruyter: Berlin, pp. 282–299.

Görlach, Manfred 1997. *The Linguistic History of English*. Basingstoke: Macmillan.

Graddol, David, Jenny Cheshire and Joan Swann 1994. *Describing Language* (2nd edn). Buckingham: Open University Press.

Graddol, David, Dick Leith and Joan Swann (eds) 1996. *English: History, Diversity and Change.* London: Routledge.

Gramley, Stephan and Kurt-Michael Pätzold 1992. *A Survey of Modern English*. London: Routledge.

Grice, Herbert P. 1975. 'Logic and conversation', in P. Cole and J. Morgan (eds) *Speech Acts, Syntax and Semantics III*. New York: Academic Press, pp. 41–58.

Gupta, Anthea Fraser 1992. 'The pragmatic particles of Singapore Colloquial English', *Journal of Pragmatics*, 17(3): 39–65.

Gupta, Anthea Fraser. Singapore Colloquial English. At the Language Varieties Website <www.une.edu.au/langnet/singlish.htm>

Halliday, M.A.K. 1993. 'Some grammatical problems in scientific English', in M. Halliday and J. Martin (eds) *Writing Science*. Pittsburg: University of Pittsburg Press, pp. 69–85.

Halliday, M.A.K. and Ruqaiya Hasan 1976. *Cohesion in English*. London: Longman.

Halliday, M.A.K. and Christian M.I.M. Matthiessen 2004. *An Introduction to Functional Grammar*. London.

Haugen, Einar 1972. 'Language, dialect, nation', in Anwar S. Dil (ed.) *The Ecology of Language* Stanford: Stanford University, pp. 237–254.

Hewings, Ann and Martin Hewings. 2005. *Grammar and Context: An Advanced Resource Book*. London and New York: Routledge.

Holmes, Janet 2001. *Introduction to Sociolinguistics* (2nd edn). London: Longman.

Honeybone, Diane 1996. *The English Language: Past, Present and Future: Study Guide 3.* Milton Keynes: The Open University.

Huddleston, Rodney and Geoffrey K. Pullum 2002. *The Cambridge Grammar of the English Language.* Cambridge: Cambridge University Press.

Hughes, Arthur, Peter Trudgill and Dominic Watt 2005. *English Accents and Dialects* (4th edn). London: Arnold.

Jespersen, Otto 1922. *Language: Its Nature, Development and Origin.* London: Allen and Unwin.

Kachru, Braj 1985. 'Standards, codification and sociolinguistic realism: the English language in the outer circle', in Randolph Quirk and H.G. Widdowson (eds) *English in the World: Teaching and Learning of Language and Literature.* Cambridge: Cambridge University Press, pp. 11–16.

Kerswill, Paul and Anne Williams 2000. 'Creating a new town koine: children and language change in Milton Keynes', *Language in Society*, 29: 65–115.

Kortmann, Bernd 2004. 'Synopsis: morphological and syntactic variation in the British Isles', in Edgar W. Schneider, Kate Burridge, Bernd Kortmann, Rajend Mesthrie, Clive Upton (eds) *A Handbook of Varieties of English Volume 2: Morphology and Syntax.* Mouton de Gruyter: Berlin, pp. 1089–1103.

Kortmann, Bernd and Clive Upton 2004. 'Introduction: varieties of English in the British Isles', in Edgar W. Schneider, Kate Burridge, Bernd Kortmann, Rajend Mesthrie, Clive Upton (eds) *A Handbook of Varieties of English Volume 1: Phonology.* Mouton de Gruyter: Berlin, pp. 24–33.

Kuiper, Koenraad, and W. Scott Allan 2004. *An Introduction to English Language: Word, Sound and Sentence* (2nd edn). Basingstoke: Palgrave Macmillan.

Labov, William 1966. *The Social Stratification of English in New York City.* Arlington, VA: The Center for Applied Linguistics.

Labov, William 1972. *Language in the Inner City: Studies in the Black English Vernacular.* Philadelphia: University of Pennsylvania Press.

Labov, William, Sharon Ash and Charles Boberg 2006. *The Atlas of North American English*. Berlin: Mouton de Gruyter.

Ladefoged, Peter 2001. *Vowels and Consonants: An Introduction to the Sounds of Language*. Oxford: Blackwell.

Lakoff, George and Mark Johnson 1980. *Metaphors We Live By*. Chicago: University of Chicago Press.

Lakoff, Robin. 1973. 'Language and woman's place', *Language in Society*, 2: 45–80.

Lanham, Richard A. 1991. *A Handlist of Rhetorical Terms* (2nd edn). Berkeley: University of California Press.

Leech, Geoffrey and Jan Svartvik 2002. *A Communicative Grammar of English* (3rd edn). London: Longman.

Lippi-Green, Rosina 1997. *English with an Accent: Language, Ideology, and Discrimination in the United States*. Routledge: London.

Malcolm, Ian G. 2004. 'Australian creoles and Aboriginal English: morphology and syntax', in Edgar W. Schneider, Kate Burridge, Bernd Kortmann, Rajend Mesthrie, Clive Upton (eds) *A Handbook of Varieties of English Volume 2: Morphology and Syntax*. Mouton de Gruyter: Berlin, pp. 657–681.

Maybin, Janet and Neil Mercer (eds) 1996. *Using English: From Conversation to Canon*. London: Routledge.

Maybin, Janet and Michael Pearce 2006. 'Literature and creativity in English', in Sharon Goodman and Kieran O'Halloran (eds) *The Art of English: Literary Creativity*. London: Palgrave Macmillan, pp. 3–48.

McArthur, Tom (ed.) 1992. *The Oxford Companion to the English Language*. Oxford: Oxford University Press.

McArthur, Tom 2002. *The Oxford Guide to World English*. Oxford: Oxford University Press.

McIntosh, Angus, Michael Samuels and Michael Benskin 1986. *A Linguistic Atlas of Late Mediaeval English*. Aberdeen: Aberdeen University Press.

McMahon, April 2002. *An Introduction to English Phonology*. Edinburgh: Edinburgh University Press.

Mercer, Neil and Joan Swann (eds) 1996.

Learning English: Development and Diversity. London: Routledge.

Milroy, James and Lesley Milroy 1999. *Authority in Language: Investigating Standard English* (3rd edition). London: Routledge.

Milroy, Lesley 1980. *Language and Social Networks*. London: Basil Blackwell.

Milroy, Lesley and Matthew Gordon 2003. *Sociolinguistics: Method and Interpretation*. Oxford: Blackwell.

Orton, Harold, Stewart Sanderson and John Widdowson 1978. *The Linguistic Atlas of England*. London: Croom Helm.

Oxford English Dictionary Online <www.oed.com>

Patrick, Peter L. 2004. 'British Creole: phonology', in Edgar W. Schneider, Kate Burridge, Bernd Kortmann, Rajend Mesthrie, Clive Upton (eds) *A Handbook of Varieties of English Volume 1: Phonology*. Mouton de Gruyter: Berlin, pp. 231–246.

Pawley, Andrew 2004. 'Australian Vernacular English: some grammatical characteristics', in Edgar W. Schneider, Kate Burridge, Bernd Kortmann, Rajend Mesthrie, Clive Upton (eds) *A Handbook of Varieties of English Volume 2: Morphology and Syntax*. Mouton de Gruyter: Berlin, pp. 611–642.

Penhallurick, Robert 2004. 'Welsh English: morphology and syntax', in Edgar W. Schneider, Kate Burridge, Bernd Kortmann, Rajend Mesthrie, Clive Upton (eds) *A Handbook of Varieties of English Volume 2: Morphology and Syntax*. Mouton de Gruyter: Berlin, pp. 102–113.

Poplack, Shana 1980. '"Sometimes I'll start a sentence in Spanish *y termino en español*": Toward a typology of code-switching', *Linguistics*, 18(7/8): 581–618.

Preston, Dennis R. and Nancy Niedzielski 1999. *Folk Linguistics*. Berlin: Mouton de Gruyter.

Rampton, Ben 1995. *Crossing: Language and Ethnicity among Adolescents*. London: Longman.

Rickford, John 1999. *African American English: Features, Evolution, Educational Implications*. Oxford: Blackwell.

Sacks, Harvey 1992. *Lectures on Conversation. Vols 1 and 2*. Gail Jefferson (ed.), Oxford: Blackwell.

Schmied, Josef 2004. 'East African English (Kenya, Uganda, Tanzania): morphology and syntax', in Edgar W. Schneider, Kate Burridge, Bernd Kortmann, Rajend Mesthrie, Clive Upton (eds) *A Handbook of Varieties of English Volume 2: Morphology and Syntax.* Mouton de Gruyter: Berlin, pp. 929–947.

Schneider, Edgar W., Kate Burridge, Bernd Kortmann, Rajend Mesthrie, Clive Upton (eds) 2004. *A Handbook of Varieties of English Volume 1: Phonology.* Mouton de Gruyter: Berlin.

Schneider, Edgar W., Kate Burridge, Bernd Kortmann, Rajend Mesthrie, Clive Upton (eds) 2004. *A Handbook of Varieties of English Volume 2: Morphology and Syntax.* Mouton de Gruyter: Berlin.

Searle, J.R. 1975. 'Indirect speech acts', in P. Cole and J. Morgan (eds) *Syntax and Semantics 3. Speech Acts.* New York: Academic Press, pp. 59–82.

Sebba, Mark 1997. *Contact Languages: Pidgins and Creoles.* London: Macmillan.

Singleton, David 2000. *Language and the Lexicon.* London: Arnold.

Stockwell, Peter 2000. *The Poetics of Science Fiction.* Harlow: Longman.

Stockwell, Peter 2002. *Cognitive Poetics: An Introduction.* London: Routledge.

Stuart-Smith, Jane 2004. 'Scottish English: phonology', in Edgar W. Schneider, Kate Burridge, Bernd Kortmann, Rajend Mesthrie, Clive Upton (eds) *A Handbook of Varieties of English Volume 1: Phonology.* Mouton de Gruyter: Berlin, pp 47–67.

Stubbs, Michael 2001. *Words and Phrases: Corpus Studies in Lexical Semantics.* Oxford: Blackwell.

Talbot, Mary 1998. *Language and Gender: An Introduction.* Cambridge: Polity.

Tannen, Deborah 1990. *You Just Don't Understand.* New York: William Morrow.

Thomas, Alan R. 1994. 'English in Wales', in Robert Burchfield (ed.) *The Cambridge History of the English Language Volume V: English in Britain and Overseas.* Cambridge: Cambridge University Press, pp. 94–147.

Thomas, Linda 1996. 'Variation in English grammar', in David Graddol, Dick Leith and Joan Swann (eds) *The English Language: Past, Present and Future.* London: Routledge, pp. 222–258.

Trudgill, Peter 1999. 'Standard English: what it isn't', in Tony Bex and Richard Watts (eds) *Standard English: The Widening Debate.* London: Routledge, pp. 117–128.

Trudgill, Peter 2001. *Sociolinguistic Variation and Change.* Edinburgh: Edinburgh University Press.

Trudgill, Peter 2004a. 'The dialect of East Anglia: phonology', in Edgar W. Schneider, Kate Burridge, Bernd Kortmann, Rajend Mesthrie, Clive Upton (eds) *A Handbook of Varieties of English Volume 1: Phonology.* Mouton de Gruyter: Berlin, pp. 163–177.

Trudgill, Peter 2004b. 'The dialect of East Anglia: morphology and syntax', in Edgar W. Schneider, Kate Burridge, Bernd Kortmann, Rajend Mesthrie, Clive Upton (eds) *A Handbook of Varieties of English Volume 2: Morphology and Syntax.* Mouton de Gruyter: Berlin, pp. 142–153.

Trudgill, Peter and Jean Hannah 2002. *International English: A Guide to the Varieties of Standard English* (4th edn). London: Arnold.

Ungerer, Friedrich and Hans-Jörg Schmid 1996. *An Introduction to Cognitive Linguistics.* London: Longman.

Upton, Clive 2004a. 'Synopsis: phonological variation in the British Isles', in Edgar W. Schneider, Kate Burridge, Bernd Kortmann, Rajend Mesthrie, Clive Upton (eds) *A Handbook of Varieties of English Volume 1: Phonology.* Mouton de Gruyter: Berlin, pp. 1063–1074.

Upton, Clive 2004b. 'Received Pronunciation', in Edgar W. Schneider, Kate Burridge, Bernd Kortmann, Rajend Mesthrie, Clive Upton (eds) *A Handbook of Varieties of English Volume 1: Phonology.* Mouton de Gruyter: Berlin, pp. 217–230.

Upton, Clive, D. Parry and J.D.A Widdowson 1994. *Survey of English Dialects: The Dictionary and Grammar.* London: Routledge.

Upton, Clive and Carmen Llamas 1999. 'Two language variation surveys large-scale and long-term: a retrospective and a plan', in J.M. Hernandez-Campoy (ed.) *Cuadernos de Filologia Inglesa.* Vol. 8. Universidad de Murcia: 291–304.

Upton, Clive, William A. Kretzschmar, Jr and Rafal Konopka 2001. *Oxford Dictionary of Pronunciation for Current English.* Oxford: Oxford University Press.

Wagner, Susanne 2004. 'English dialects in the Southwest: morphology and syntax', in Edgar W. Schneider, Kate Burridge, Bernd Kortmann, Rajend Mesthrie, Clive Upton (eds) *A Handbook of Varieties of English Volume 2: Morphology and Syntax.* Mouton de Gruyter: Berlin, pp. 154–174.

Wales, Katie 2001. *A Dictionary of Stylistics* (2nd edn). Harlow: Longman.

Wee, Lionel 2004a. 'Singapore English: phonology', in Edgar W. Schneider, Kate Burridge, Bernd Kortmann, Rajend Mesthrie, Clive Upton (eds) *A Handbook of Varieties of English Volume 1: Phonology.* Mouton de Gruyter: Berlin, pp. 1017–1033.

Wee, Lionel 2004b. 'Singapore English: morphology and syntax', in Edgar W. Schneider, Kate Burridge, Bernd Kortmann, Rajend Mesthrie, Clive Upton (eds) *A Handbook of Varieties of English Volume 2: Morphology and Syntax.* Mouton de Gruyter: Berlin, pp. 1058–1072.

Wells, John. C. 1982. *Accents of English 2: The British Isles.* Cambridge: Cambridge University Press.

Wolfram, W. and Schilling-Estes, Natalie 2006. *American English* (2nd edn). Oxford: Blackwell.